HIGH
PROBABILITY
TRADING

HIGH PROBABILITY TRADING

Take the Steps to Become a Successful Trader

MARCEL LINK

McGraw-Hill

New York Chicago San Francisco Lisbon London
Madrid Mexico City Milan New Delhi San Juan
Seoul Singapore Sydney Toronto

Copyright © 2003 by Marcel Link. All rights reserved. Printed in the United States of America. Except as permitted under the United States Copyright Act of 1976, no part of this publication may be reproduced or distributed in any form or by any means, or stored in a data base or retrieval system, without the prior written permission of the publisher.

2 3 4 5 6 7 8 9 0 AGM/AGM 0 9 8 7 6 5 4 3

ISBN 0-07-138156-2

McGraw-Hill books are available at special quantity discounts to use as premiums and sales promotions, or for use in corporate training programs. For more information, please write to the Director of Special Sales, Professional Publishing, McGraw-Hill, Two Penn Plaza, New York, NY 10121-2298. Or contact your local bookstore.

This publication is designed to provide accurate and authoritative information in regard to the subject matter covered. It is sold with the understanding that neither the author nor the publisher is engaged in rendering legal, accounting, or other professional services. If legal advice or other expert assistance is required, the services of a competent professional person should be sought.
> —*From a Declaration of Principles jointly adopted by a Committee of the American Bar Association and a Committee of Publishers*

This book is printed on recycled, acid-free paper containing a minimum of 50% recycled de-inked fiber.

Dedicated to both the readers (and by saying both I do hope there will be more than two of you) who are doing whatever they can to become better traders and to those traders who do nothing to improve, because the latter make making money a little bit easier for you and me.

Thanks for choosing the book. I hope that it helps and that you enjoy it.

CONTENTS

PREFACE   xi

PART I

THE BUILDING BLOCKS

Chapter 1
The Tuition of Trading   2

Chapter 2
Setting Realistic Goals   24

Chapter 3
Leveling the Playing Field   46

PART II

USING THE NEWS

Chapter 4
Trading the News   60

PART III

TECHNICAL ANALYSIS

Chapter 5
Increasing Your Chances with Multiple Time Frames   78

Chapter 6
Trading with the Trend   96

Chapter 7
Using Oscillators   122

Chapter 8
Breakouts and Reversals   149

Chapter 9
Exits and Stops   178

Chapter 10
Making the High Probability Trades   211

PART IV

TRADING WITH A PLAN

Chapter 11
The Trading Plan and Game Plan   230

Chapter 12
System Trading   243

Chapter 13
A Little about Backtesting   267

Chapter 14
Employing a Money Management Plan   286

Chapter 15
Setting Risk Parameters and Making a Money Management Plan   299

PART V

SELF-CONTROL

Chapter 16
Discipline: The Key to Success   322

Chapter 17
The Dangers of Overtrading   336

Chapter 18
The Inner Side of Trading: Keeping a Clear Mind   363

INDEX   385

Trading is easy; anyone with a few bucks can do it. Making money, however, is a whole different ball game. A simple fact of trading is that almost 90 percent of all commodity traders and those who day trade equities lose money. Investing in stocks, by contrast, was always looked at as a safe long-term play, but as I write this, I have to say that may not be the case anymore. So why is there such a high percentage of losing traders? Do they all have something in common that makes them lose continuously? Why do a select few traders repeatedly make money while the masses lose? What are the common traits that winning traders possess that losers don't, and vice versa? Can losing traders become winning traders? What do bad traders do that good traders avoid? More important, what do winning traders do that is different?

With such a high percentage of traders losing, there have to be some things they all do that cause those results. Throughout this book I will try to answer these questions as I detail how successful traders behave differently and can consistently make money by making high probability trades and avoiding common pitfalls. As important as learning how to trade successfully is learning how to avoid losing. People who are not clear on this will have trouble turning the corner and becoming winning traders. I won't just point out what traders' weaknesses are; I will help readers overcome and avoid those common mistakes while showing how a successful trader would react in the same situation. The goal is to teach all traders to have the mindset of a successful trader.

There is no easy recipe for becoming a winning trader, but hard work, experience, capital, and discipline are some of the basic ingredients. Although most people will lose money, by learning to trade with the percentages, I believe the average person can become a successful trader. Most of the best traders started out on a frustrating note but were able to turn it around. Sure, some traders may get lucky at first, but trading is a learning process that takes years to master. Much of that learning consists of being able to tell the difference between high and low probability situations. By doing this one can begin to filter out trades that have a low probability of working while being more aggressive on others.

Many trading books I've read make it seem that trading is a piece of cake and that anyone can do it after reading the book. That's not the case. Reading will help, but experience is a much better teacher. One of the best ways of improving, in my opinion, is by correcting past mistakes. It's easy enough to tell a trader how to trade and to teach him that the trades offering the highest potential reward for the lowest risk offer the highest probability of success. Yet there is nothing a book can teach that a $1000 loss can't amplify. No book can teach you how to handle losses mentally or how emotions affect one's trading. Only having real money on the line will make you feel the pain and exuberance that can cause traders to behave erratically. Paper trading can help with some things, but one needs to risk actual money to learn how to handle emotions and risk. People follow their rules to a T in paper trading, but as soon as real money is on the line, they begin to ignore those rules.

As a trader trades, the first few years will be filled with countless mistakes. These mistakes are important because only when traders realize what they are doing wrong can they start to concentrate on not making those mistakes over and over again. By weeding out the bad trades, a trader becomes an overall better trader. It is important to show why some trades are bad even if they turn out to be winners, simply because they have a high risk/reward ratio. Some trades are not worth the risk and should never be done. To trade successfully one needs to consistently make trades that offer low risk compared to the reward.

I may tend to repeat main points throughout the book; this is not because my editor wanted a bigger book but because these things are important and repetition will make them stick in the reader's mind. After reading *High Probability Trading* one should be able to distinguish between different types of opportunities and take the winning approach. If you are currently trading and have lost money, this book will help you uncover why while leading you to overcome those faults. It will help you learn when to trade and when not to trade. It will help you realize the importance of and how to write a trading, game, and money management plan, without which one should not be trading. A trading plan need not be elaborate, but every trader should have one.

Having traded both stocks and commodities, I will talk about both throughout this book and will use the term *market* to refer to both. This book was originally planned to focus on commodity traders, but I expanded it to benefit equity traders as well. Trading is trading whether one is trading IBM, Yahoo, pork bellies, or S&P 500 futures; it's all basically the same. There are some differences, such as margin, leverage, software, expiring contracts, and limit locks, but for the most part if you can trade one, you can trade the other. The book does have a bias toward the short-term trader, but its overall goal is to help all traders, from beginners to seasoned vets, whether they are short-term day traders or position takers.

WHAT IS HIGH PROBABILITY TRADING?

I define high probability trading as trades with a low risk/reward ratio that are backtested to have a positive expectancy with predetermined money management parameters. The best traders always trade when the odds are in their favor, not just because the market is open. They trade for a reason: *to make money*, not to amuse themselves. For the most part high probability trades are made only in the direction of the major trend. If the market is uptrending, a trader will wait for a dip and test some support level before entering. Dips are just waves in a trend, and though shorting them can be profitable, these are low-percentage trades and should be avoided. High probability traders know how to cut their losses and let their good trades run. You cannot come out ahead of the game if you lose $500 when you lose and make only $200 on the good trades because you are too eager to take a profit. As important as letting profits ride is knowing when to take a profit. Many bad traders let winning trades dwindle into losers because they don't know when to get out of a good trade or have no exit rules. Exiting a trade is even more important than making it, because that's what determines whether you win or lose. If a trader randomly put on trades but knew how to exit them properly, he would probably be a winning trader.

Though going with the trend always offers the best success rate, trying to pick tops or bottoms can have a high degree of success if the right pattern is prevalent and the trader is quick to realize when he is wrong. When trying to pick the end of a trend, traders will be wrong often, and so they must be able to quickly accept the fact that they are wrong. When one is correct in picking a top or bottom, the reward can be substantial, so cumulatively these trades can have a high probability of success. It doesn't matter what one's trading style is: If a trader is disciplined and has a solid trading strategy and money management plan, he can make money.

To be a high probability trader one needs to have a trading plan. This includes trading strategies and, more important, knowing how to manage risk. This book will help a trader develop all the skills and tools needed to make a proper trading plan. As each person has a unique style, there is no perfect trading plan that will work for everyone. Each individual has to make a plan that best suits his trading and psychology. Once a plan is set up, most of the hard work has been done, yet many traders fail to spend the time to develop a plan and instead jump straight into trading.

WHAT MAKES A TRADER GOOD?

In a nutshell, a trader who makes money is one who works as hard during nonmarket hours as he does when the market is open. These traders know in advance what markets they will trade and what their actions will be. They patiently wait for the market to give them an opportunity to enter and are agile in getting out when they are wrong. They look for markets or stocks that are in a trend and wait for a retracement in order to get into the trade. They do not try to outguess the market or think they are better than the market; they take what the market gives them. They have full control of their emotions, are always focused, and do not spread themselves too thin or overtrade.

A Trader Who Has a Good Chance at Success Has the Following Attributes

Is properly capitalized

Treats trading like a business

Has a low tolerance for risk

Trades only when the market provides an opportunity

Can control emotions

Has a trading plan

Has a risk management plan

Is incredibly disciplined

Is focused

Has backtested his trading methodology

A Trader Who Has a Good Chance at Failure Has Any of the Following Attributes

Is undercapitalized

Lacks discipline

Overtrades

Does not understand the markets

Rushes into trades

Chases the market

Is afraid of missing a move

Is stubborn and marries a position or idea

Misinterprets news

Is always looking for home runs

Lets losers get too big

Takes winners prematurely

Takes trading too lightly

Takes large risks

Has little control of his emotions

ABOUT THE BOOK

Throughout this book I'll give many personal examples, as well as examples involving traders I've known who are both good and bad traders. I've known traders who began terribly but were able to turn it around and many who just never learned. I'll use these examples to help get my point across in stressing what to do and what not to do. I protect these peoples' identities to keep from embarrassing some of them. I'm not too proud to say that I was a horrible trader, and I detail all my losing habits as well as those I've seen in others along the way. I always had a great sense of market direction, but there were too many other issues that kept me from succeeding. Once I was able to conquer those weaknesses, and learn to trade with the odds in my favor, my trading turned around. My turn-around came mostly from watching both good and bad traders and starting to emulate the traits of the successful ones while avoiding anything I had in common with the bad ones. Getting better was also a result of analyzing my losing trades and trying to learn a lesson from them. Eventually it gets to be painful to lose; as with a child who must touch a hot oven once, pain can be a good teacher. One thing that helped me was sitting next to a guy who was just awful; he made the same mistakes over and over and over again. I was able to notice a few similarities I had with him and quickly decided that it was time to change them. Watching him trade helped me get a clearer picture of my mistakes.

High Probability Trading will walk the reader through what I believe to be the most important aspects of being a successful trader. The book runs through most aspects of trading, starting with the building blocks every trader needs to succeed and ending with discipline and the emotional factors traders face. In between, there is a thorough discussion on technical and fundamental analysis, on making and using a game plan, a trading plan, and a risk management plan, and on how to write and backtest a system. It will help readers learn to trade with the odds in their favor while avoiding the proven losing situations. I conclude each chapter with a short section called "Becoming a Better Trader," followed by some tips on what to do and what not to do, and some questions traders can ask themselves to make sure they are doing the right thing. This should help identify strengths and weaknesses that could guide one onto the path of becoming a winning trader.

A LITTLE BIT ABOUT ME

I was a living example of what a trader should not do. If there was a way to lose money trading, I think I did it. Trading since 1990, I consistently lost money for 7 years before turning it around. I was persistent and determined enough to know what I wanted and to work hard at getting it. With 14 years in the trading industry as a clerk, floor trader, retail broker, and trader, I have seen or made just about every mistake a trader can make. Having had the luxury of being in constant contact all those years with both successful professional traders and those who didn't have a prayer, I've been able to see the different qualities they possess. I have seen how they can have the same trades on, yet the good traders make money while the poor ones never seem able to. It was through my brokerage customers that I was finally able to see on a regular basis how and why the average trader repeatedly loses money. More important, I was able to see the traits I had in common with bad traders, and I realized I had to change my style if I wanted to succeed. Overtrading, for example, was my biggest albatross until I noticed that every other trader who overtraded lost as well; the more selective traders were the ones who continuously made money. Throughout this book I'll detail the steps I took to evolve into a better trader and show how anyone with determination can do so as well. Learning to change a bad habit is not easy, but it has to be done to become a better trader.

A BRIEF PROFESSIONAL HISTORY

After a short stint as a stockbroker in 1987, I worked as a crude oil options clerk on the floor of the New York Mercantile Exchange. A few years later I scraped together $30,000 and got a seat trading New York Financial Exchange (NYFE) and dollar index futures. Being undercapitalized, I lasted only a few months before I lost half my capital on one mistake. Not having enough money to trade from the pit anymore, I joined forces with another trader, forming a trading partnership. We went to trade out of a brokerage office, with several other experienced former floor traders. It was here that I learned to read charts and began to work on system writing.

From 1995 to 1997 I took a break from trading full-time to go to graduate school. When I finished, I decided to start a discount brokerage firm, Link Futures. Online trading had just started creeping into the futures industry, and relatively few firms had an Internet presence. Link Futures offered deep discount brokerage and had a trading room where traders could trade. Unfortunately, as the online trading craze caught on, larger firms started undercutting each other in price, and once again I was undercapitalized: I did not have the advertising budget to compete and make the business thrive. The bright side was that my trading started to get consistently better as I watched what my clients did wrong.

In March 2000, when I was offered a position trading equities, it didn't take much thought to decide to go for it. My potential as a trader was much larger than it had been with the brokerage firm, and so I made the move to become a proprietary equity trader. Very few people can say they love their jobs, but I can honestly say I do.

A final note: I refer to traders by using male pronouns. I'm not a sexist; I'm just making it easier. Although trading is primarily a male industry, there are female traders who have done quite well. My partner at Link Futures was a woman, and she was a great trader.

Enjoy the book.

PART 1

The Building Blocks

CHAPTER 1

The Tuition of Trading

How To Make Money Performing Vascular Surgery Using Household Tools and Kitchen Utensils. I don't think people would read such a book with the expectation of being able to do open-heart surgery out of their garages in their spare time, yet people go into trading with little or no experience and expect to succeed just after reading a book or two.

Doctors, lawyers, and engineers need to go to school for years before they are expected to be professionals and earn a living. A pro baseball player spends a few years in the minors before getting called up to play with the big boys. Football and basketball players start out by playing college ball for 4 years, and then only the best get drafted. Electricians, plumbers, and welders are apprentices first. These people do not just decide to work in their field and start doing so from day 1; they work up to it.

So why should traders think they are any different or better? After all, they are trying to enter what I believe is the hardest profession of all with hopes of being successful with little or no experience. The same way it takes years to become a surgeon, a trader needs to put in time before expecting to be capable of doing it successfully. Just as in every other profession, a trader needs the proper education. Unfortunately, Harvard doesn't offer any degrees in trading. The only "schooling" traders get in learning their profession is hands-on, and the money they lose can be considered their tuition. It is through these losses that they will, they hope, gain the experience needed to be a great trader.

THE LEARNING YEARS

The first few years of trading should be considered "the learning years." This is not the time to try to make a killing; instead, one should concentrate on preserving capital and educating oneself. This time should be treated as if one were in school to learn. Countless mistakes will be made when one is first starting to trade, simply because one doesn't know any better. It's okay to lose a little, and traders should be prepared for this when they are first beginning to trade. Your capital should not be considered trading capital; instead, think of it as "learning capital." At the beginning you should risk only a small portion of your money, just enough to get your feet wet and start the learning process. Too many traders are gung-ho from the start, concentrating only on making money, not on becoming better traders. Keep in mind that most successful traders began by losing quite a bit of money. Even most of Richard Dennis's turtles lost money their first year before becoming some of the world's most successful traders. Almost all the stories you read in *Market Wizards* are about traders who got blown out once or twice before learning from their mistakes. It doesn't matter whether one is investing in stocks or day trading bonds; it takes a lot of hard work and experience to be able to trade well. While many beginners may give up after a rough start, the ones who accept the learning curve, don't get discouraged, and are properly capitalized have a good chance of making it in the long run.

A Sampling of What Traders Need to Learn How to Do
Enter orders
Read charts
Use technical analysis
Understand how different markets trade
Trade off news
Write systems
Test systems
Become disciplined
Make a money management plan
Manage risk
Learn how to take a loss
Know when to trade and when not to trade

Make a trading plan

Control one's emotions

Equally Important, Traders Need to Learn What Not to Do: A Few of These No-Nos Are

Chasing the markets

Trading while undercapitalized

Overtrading

Letting losses get too large

Marrying a position

Taking winners prematurely

Taking on too much risk

Trading for the excitement

Being stubborn

Trading is an ongoing learning process, not something that can be learned overnight by reading a book or going to a seminar. People can read five books on learning to play tennis and take a few lessons, but until they get out there and practice, practice, practice, they won't be competitive. Trading is not much different; it takes lots of practice to get good. The only difference between tennis and trading is that when you are bad at tennis, you still have fun and maybe lose a few pounds while getting in shape. With trading you may still lose a few pounds, but that's because you may not have money for food.

PAPER TRADING HELPS, BUT IT'S NOT THE REAL THING

No matter what one may have read in a book or how long one has paper traded, as soon as a person starts trading for real, everything changes. Mistakes one never even thought of start popping up left and right, and the best way to avoid making them is to make them, lose money, realize they were mistakes, and consciously be aware of them the next time the same situations arise. Losing real money will make you feel a pain that paper trading can't. Eventually, if you lose enough, you learn not to make the same mistakes over and over. Although paper trading is a good way to start and traders shouldn't risk money until they've done a fair amount of it, it is not the same as putting real money on the line. Losing $1000 on paper is quickly shaken off; when it's real money, it can be emotionally gut-wrenching and depressing, and when it happens on Friday, it ruins the whole weekend. These emotions aren't normally felt in paper trading, where there is no pain or grave sense of having made a mistake. No one gets a margin call when paper trading and has to liquidate positions, and everyone gets the best prices on every trade. With real money at risk, trading becomes a different ball game. Things that would not be done on paper are done when real money is on the line. Risk aversion levels change, profits are taken too quickly, losses are allowed to grow too big, and slippage and commissions become a major factor. These are just a few things that paper trading can't simulate, and though it's important to risk real money, it is wise to start on paper until one gets a feel for the markets. I also recommend voraciously reading everything one can get one's hands on. There is always room for improvement, and after 15 years in the business I'm constantly trying to learn more about trading.

THE TUITION OF TRADING

The Cost of Learning

From everything I've ever heard, read, and seen, a trader needs about 3 to 5 years to get through the learning period. During this time in which he is learning and honing his skills, a trader will be paying his "tuition of trading" the same way lawyers, chefs, and doctors pay $25,000 a year to learn their craft. Since there is no school where he can go, the beneficiaries of his tuition are other, more experienced traders for schooling him and teaching him a few lessons. In time he will get reimbursed by the newer starry-eyed "students" eager to get their education. Overall one should be prepared to spend at least $50,000 in tuition money. With every bad trade, one gains a little knowledge and hopefully does not repeat the same mistake. Trading is without a doubt one of the hardest professions; it requires lots of hands-on experience to be good at it. They say that experience is always the best teacher, so don't get discouraged by losses; look at them as part of the learning process.

Start-Up Capital

Unless you are as "lucky" as Hillary Clinton, who was able to make $1000 grow into $100,000 trading cattle futures in a year, you will need a bit more money than that to get started. In my opinion, to be realistic and have a fighting chance to succeed one should have a minimum of $25,000 to $50,000, a 3-year horizon, and a very understanding spouse. Many people go into trading with a $5000 account and think they are sufficiently funded to start trading. They figure they have enough money to cover the margin requirements or buy the stocks they want, and so that should be enough to start trading. They never consider that they can lose; instead, they expect to start making money from the get-go, but this is rarely the case. Most individuals end up losing money at first; 80 to 90 percent of first-time traders are losers within a year. The more money one has to start with, the more likely it is one will be around at the end of a year. If you try to start trading and have only a few thousand dollars to do it with, I'd recommend saving your money or putting it into mutual funds. There is little room for error with such a small account, and it takes only a few mistakes to be wiped out quickly.

SMALL VERSUS LARGE ACCOUNTS

The average retail account we opened at Link Futures was for about $3000 to $5000. Ironically these small accounts normally took on the most risk and lasted only a few months. The accounts that were for $25,000 and up were more conservative and lasted the longest, not because these people were better traders, but because they could afford to make a few more mistakes.

Working Capital

Trading requires more capital than most traders think is necessary. Not only does one need to be able to get through the beginning stages, one needs to make sure he has enough ongoing capital to succeed once that period is over. There is nothing more frustrating than being short on funds when the right move comes along. This happened to me several times. The great rally I'd be waiting for would finally happen, but I wouldn't have enough money to trade it because I had already blown the little I had. It seems that the best moves always came when I was out of the market. I remember bitching several times from the sidelines how this was the move I had been waiting for and I had to miss it because of a lack of working capital. Now that I'm no longer trading with limited funds, I don't have to worry about this: I know I'll be around for the next move. This doesn't mean I can be less careful; I still need to worry about not losing too much because I don't want to put myself in a hole. But at least I've stopped worrying about blowing out and having to raise capital; now I can focus my attention on trading.

People can't be trading with scared money and must accept the fact that they probably won't make a living from their trading the first few years. They need to be able to finance their trading for several years, not just for the first few trades. If one starts trading with a sum of $25,000 to $50,000 and is conservative, one has a chance of succeeding, maybe not right away but in due time. A trader shouldn't be discouraged when he loses; he needs to accept it as a cost that's part of learning and use every dollar lost to his benefit. Except for an occasional good period, I'd say I lost over $75,000 over a 7-year stretch before I was able to trade consistently well. I was a slow learner.

Enjoying Life

Apart from trading capital, you need to be able to pay bills and enjoy life. It is extremely important to be well financed so that you can take your mind off other things when trading, foolish things such as how I will pay rent, eat, go to a movie, and so on. When one begins to worry about this, trading suffers. One of the worst things someone can do is to hope to live off trading profits. You need as much money in your account as possible; when you start taking some out to pay bills, it has the same effect on your account that losing does. I know a lot of guys who tried trading full-time and had to move back home with their parents or have a spouse support them for a few years. All these people were miserable compared to the trust fund babies who had enough money to support themselves and trade. Not being able to take a vacation or go out on the weekend can take a toll on a person.

You need to be able to enjoy life; if you are trading with money that you planned to use for a nice vacation or new car, you are not properly capitalized. You would not believe the difference it makes when trading is more relaxed because there are no monetary problems to worry about. When I first started trading on the floor, I borrowed money to get my seat. I needed to make money right away to start paying off my debt, and so I was in a bad financial position from the start. I had to work nights and weekends to support myself and was never able to give trading the attention it required. I wasn't able to hang out with friends on the weekends or just have fun, as I always had to work. That was a bit depressing, and it was reflected in my trading.

The Tools

Aside from having enough capital to learn, trade, and live off, if one plans on doing it right, one needs to make sure he has the proper tools to do it with. Just as a professional in every other field needs a bag full of tools, a trader does as well. This includes charts, quotes, trading software, live feeds, and a good computer. They may not be cheap, but they are worth their price to competitive traders. Money should be set aside to ensure that one will have all the tools needed for as long as one needs them. When I first started trading on my own, off the floor, I didn't invest in them as well as I should have. Later on, when I was spending over $1000 a month on various things, it helped my trading immensely. Chap. 3, "Leveling the Playing Field," will discuss some of the tools that can help someone become a better trader.

LEARNING FROM MISTAKES

Everybody makes mistakes and has losing trades. The difference between a successful trader and a losing trader is how those mistakes are dealt with. The good traders take note of what they did wrong and try to learn from their mistakes; bad traders make the same mistakes repeatedly and never learn. After losing money time after time buying a stock after it just ran $2 in 10 minutes, astute traders finally get the idea that it's not a high probability trading strategy to buy stocks as they are running up. The ones who keep chasing trades are similar to a fool repeatedly trying to knock down a door by using his head as a battering ram. They keep doing it because they never know which is the blow that may knock down the door. It doesn't matter to them that the odds of this trade's working are low, they figure they are due for a good trade, and they don't want to miss it when it happens. Every time you think you did something wrong, stop and think about it; ask yourself what it was you did wrong, how you can prevent it in the future, why you made the decision, and what you should have done. You should also do this when you did something right. Little mental drills like these will help you get the most out of trading.

A mistake doesn't mean being wrong on market direction; roughly half the time traders will be wrong. It's how one deals with a losing trade that is the difference between making a mistake and making a good trading decision even though it turns out to be a loser. Once someone knows he is wrong and gets out, this is a good trading decision; holding on while hoping to get bailed out is not. Mistakes can also happen on trades that turn out to be profitable. Chasing a market, whether you make money or not, is a mistake.

Making mistakes and learning from them are part of trading and its learning process. This is why traders who are well capitalized have a better chance of surviving; they have room to make and learn from mistakes without blowing out. A small trader can easily lose all his capital before fully understanding the lesson the market was trying to teach him.

AN EXPENSIVE LESSON

When I took my first big hit, I lost $12,000, which was about half my capital, on an option-related position. I did many things wrong that day that I would never do now. I was greedy, impatient, overtraded, and undercapitalized, and I ignored risk management. Looking back, I can see my mistakes; when I first made them, I didn't think making a mistake was possible. You can read 20 books on trading, but there is nothing like experience to teach you how to handle these situations. Despite having had such a hard beginning, I take all my experience and money lost as part of my learning process and hope that with every mistake and dollar lost I've gained something.

DON'T REINFORCE BAD BEHAVIOR

Aside from learning from mistakes, a trader needs to recognize the things that work so that he can continue doing them. Unfortunately, sometimes one can make bad trading decisions and get bailed out by the market. For example, a trader can hold on to losing trades too long in hopes of a turnaround in the market and then actually get it. If a trader gets rewarded for this once, he may feel he can get paid for it in the future and may end up holding onto losers too long every time. It's not a good trading practice to hold a stock $3 against you and then get out with a 5-cent profit as it turns back in your favor. Not a good balance of risk and reward here, is there? It may look like a winning trade and people are always happier gaining a few cents than losing a few dollars, but even though this is a profitable trade, it's still a bad trade that may reinforce bad behavior. One should have been out of the trade down 80 cents and not have let it get so far against them; one should not be rewarded by it. The best that could happen to someone who does this is to lose 10 points in the trade; at least then that person will learn to use stops.

Every day I review my trades and take note of any bad trades I may have made and file them away in my mental Rolodex in the "do not repeat" folder. Reinforcing negative behavior is as bad for a trader as is not learning from mistakes. I'd rather have a losing trade on which I did the right thing than a winning trade on which I acted imprudently. I feel good when I exit a bad trade right away and then watch the market get worse. I consider that a good trade; losing is part of trading, and losing properly is what makes good traders better.

THE CURSE OF MAKING MONEY FROM THE GET-GO

Most of the best traders started their trading careers on a horrible note, losing for several years before becoming successful. Anybody who walks into trading and expects to make money from day 1 is in for a surprise. Actually, one of the worst things that can happen is that someone starts making money right away. The odds are, it was partially due to luck, and the trader may think he is good yet still not know a thing about the market. He may be tempted to trade more aggressively then he should, and when his luck runs out, his mistakes will be costly compared to what would happen if he made them at the beginning. Look at everybody who made money left and right during the NASDAQ boom of 1999 and early 2000. These people were not traders; they bought something, and it went up. It didn't matter what they bought: It went up, they chased a stock $10 or $20, it didn't matter, it went up. They may have believed they were great traders, but most of them have not fared too well since the bubble burst and many have lost everything.

I suffered from making money too quickly. When I first started trading in the New York Financial Exchange (NYFE) pit, I had had a goal of making $200 a day, but in my second week I had a $1000 day. Then making $200 seemed like peanuts. It was one of those days when luck was on my side and everything I did worked out. That was probably the worst thing that could have happened to me because after that I tried to make $1000 every day. The way I did that was by overtrading and trading more contracts than I should have; unfortunately, when I started making mistakes, they cost more than they should have. I started overtrading on a regular basis, and as a new trader, no matter how much money I had, I should have been trading one contract, learning, and preserving my capital. Instead, I was more concerned about how much money I could make.

PRESERVING PRECIOUS CAPITAL

A fellow trader told me early on as he saw me overtrading to concentrate on *preserving precious capital*. He used to write "PPC" on the top of his trading pads to remind himself to preserve precious capital. He said, "Forget about making money; just try as hard as possible not to lose any. Every dollar you have is precious, and fight as hard as possible to keep it in your pocket and out of someone else's." If you keep making smart trades and preserving your money, you'll be standing long after most other traders, and that gives you a greater chance to win. The key to being a winning trader is to not lose a lot when you lose. If you cut losses, the winning trades will take care of themselves. This reminds me of what my college tennis coach once told me: If you hit the ball over the net four times, you'll win 80 percent of the points. He said, "Don't worry about winning points. Let the other guy lose them; just keep hitting the ball in play and you'll do just that. It's easier to win when you switch your focus from trying to win to trying not to lose; your opponent will take care of that himself. There's no need to go for winners every time; you end up hitting more shots out or wide when you do that. Just hit the ball to the other guy's weak spot and you won't get hurt."

HANDING OUT $20s

When I started on the floor, an experienced trader told me to try to imagine that I was standing in the middle of the pit with a stack of $20 bills that I would have to hand out as I lost them. Instead of losses just being on paper, if I actually had to shell out cash with every tick a position went against me, I'd get out quicker. People don't think of losses as intensively as they do when spending real cash. It would be easier to put a stop to a bad trade if you had to hand out $500 in cash in an hour. When it just comes out of your account, you don't feel it as painfully.

THINK SMALL

One must be careful in the first year or two to understand that this is not the time to make a killing but the time to learn. Trading volume and risk need to be kept minimal. If you are trading stocks, trade just 100 shares; in commodities do just one contract and trade less volatile markets no matter how much money you have. Keep it as simple as possible, trade only a few markets instead of trying to jump into every market or stock. Get to know how certain markets act before you start to spread yourself too thin. Ignore the temptation to trade more, especially when on a winning streak. This is hard for many traders to do because their emotions take over. It means nothing to people to make $150 on a trade when in their heads they are thinking they can make hundreds of thousands per year. They are too eager to get to that stage without learning the basics first. Remember that you will without doubt make mistake after mistake during the first year or two, and so it's best to do it on a small scale. When one gets into trading, it should be not for a year but for a lifetime. If you plan to still be trading in a decade, what does it matter if your first year's profit is small? It's nothing in the greater scheme of things. However, if you try to rush it, trading may not even be a 1-year event, as you won't have any capital down the road to keep going.

BLOWING OUT

I know people don't want to hear this, but most of the best traders have blown out more than once before becoming the best. I always thought, "Yeah, but not me." Well, it happened to me more times than I care to remember. I've known people who have completely blown out $5000, $25,000, $50,000, $100,000, and $5 million accounts and everything in between; no one is immune. There have been several times when I wiped out and was forced to take a break from trading. If you read *Market Wizards*, you'll see that blowing out was a common trait among almost all the traders; it comes with the territory and is part of the training process.

Blowing out can be a valuable learning experience for a committed trader. It is the time to regroup and find out why you lost. The answer will almost always be overtrading or being undercapitalized, but traders need to learn it for themselves. Any other mistakes result in losses which normally can be overcome, but when people start overtrading and taking on too much risk, it doesn't take long to lose everything. A word of warning: Most of the time it comes after a good winning streak. One reason you want to be properly capitalized is that it gives you the ability to endure the losing streaks when they happen. Blowing out doesn't have to happen if a trader starts with enough money and is frugal. If it happens to you or has happened, don't be discouraged, just take it in stride. If you understand why it happened and think you can fix your mistakes, try again. If you can't figure out why, keep searching for the answer before risking more money.

BEING COMMITTED

Blowing out should not discourage someone who is determined to be a trader. If it happens and one is committed, one will come up with more money and start again. Those who survive the early years have a good chance to succeed because they are committed and never quit. Many people end up as losers because they give up after a losing period, but to be a winning trader one must be determined to win and be in it for the long haul. It's more than just hard work; it is the desire to grow and to do what it takes to improve oneself. Being committed isn't just about having the capital to survive; it means looking at one's faults and always working to correct them. Being committed is a lifelong process. As long as one trades, one must keep working at getting better and evaluating failures. It means reading books, going to seminars, and being the best one can be. It's crucial to believe you are the best trader in the world. If you have doubts, you will never be able to succeed, as you will live up to your own low expectations.

KEEPING A JOURNAL

Part of being committed is keeping track of your progress, and a good way to do this is by keeping a trading journal. A journal will help in evaluating performance and in seeing patterns developing in trading that show what one is doing right or wrong. Doing this on a regular basis will help you see what works and what doesn't or what markets one does better or worse in. A trader can gather valuable information on himself by keeping a journal. A trading journal is nothing more than a notebook where you write down all your trades, why you did them, and how they turned out. It need not be elaborate, but it should be kept even by experienced traders. People have selective memories, and the best way to remember the facts of what you've done is to write them down. Though this may be annoying to do for every trade, it will help, especially for those who tend to overtrade, as you'll have less time to trade when you have to write down everything you do. It will also help build the one thing every successful trader needs: *Discipline*.

Institutional traders have desk leaders, managers, and software that monitor their every trade. They are constantly being evaluated, and so they can correct mistakes. I, for example, used to get a weekly printout of my trading performance. It told me how I did by the half hour, how long I held both winning and losing trades, my winning percentage, my average loss and gain, and how I had done on individual stocks. I noticed that I did not trade well in the first half hour of the day, so I cut back dramatically during that period. I held losers too long, I didn't make money trading certain stocks, and I tended to trade a lot, and so these became the areas I concentrated on. To cut my holding time on losers, I started writing down what time I entered each trade on a spreadsheet, and after 45 minutes if I was still holding it and losing money, I'd exit the trade. As for my strengths, they were afternoon trading and trading boring stocks such as Gillette, Coke, Colgate, and Home Depot. I tended to have a much better success ratio on them, and my losses were smaller. If I didn't have this information, I would not have been able to concentrate on my strengths and would still be trading stocks on which I mostly lose.

For the trader who doesn't have the luxury of a manager or program that monitors him, a journal is the best way to go. It allows you to keep tabs on yourself and gives great insight into trading patterns while identifying strengths and weaknesses. Find out what stocks or markets you do better in and which ones get the better of you. Maybe you can never make money on Fridays or buying into a news story. If you know this stuff, little by little you can start weeding out the things that give you the most trouble, leaving you with a higher percentage of trading situations where you succeed.

THINGS TO INCLUDE IN A JOURNAL

What You Bought or Sold

This is pretty basic: Keep track of the stock or commodity and whether you bought or sold it. I use a simple plus or minus sign to indicate this. I like knowing if I'm better on the short side than I am on the long side and which I do more of. Some people have a preference for one side of the market and may be long 90 percent of the time even in a down market. Knowing you do this can help you reevaluate and balance out your trading.

What Time You Did the Trade

Some people trade better during different times of the day. Some are just horrible at lunchtime; some do well in the morning but not as well in the last hour. These are all things that can be monitored in a journal. I know I trade better in the afternoon than I do in the morning. I can trade better in the last half hour than I do in the first half hour; I also tend to trade best between 11 and 2, as I can see a trend or reversal develop. By knowing this, I know when I should trade with more size and conviction and when I should be cutting back. Keeping and reviewing a journal will help identify the time periods when you trade best so that you can take advantage of them.

Why the Trade Was Made

The most important thing one can have in a journal is why a trade was made. If one were to write down the reason why every trade was made, one's trading would improve dramatically. "I was bored" or "I bought IBM because it just rallied $3 in 20 minutes and I didn't want to miss any more of the move" are not good reasons to make a trade. If someone wrote this in his book and then was happy with the decision, he would still have a long way to go. Many trades are made with little thought behind them, but when having to justify every trade, one may avoid the stupid ones. If the entry had said, "I bought IBM because the Dow was strong and had just dipped a little but was holding steady; meanwhile, IBM retraced 75 cents from the high and was sitting at its trendline and looked like it would resume the uptrend," this would be a valid reason to make a trade. By doing this you will force yourself to make better trading decisions as you will weed out the low probability ones. I also like to make note of whether I chased the market or waited for a pullback. By the end of this book you should know what distinguishes a good trade from a bad one.

How Strongly You Felt about the Trade

Rate your trades on any scale you want and see how you do. I used to plan all my trading scenarios for about 10 markets every night. I had buy and sell scenarios on each commodity, and I would rate them from one to five stars, with five stars being the best. After a while I noticed that my five-star trades worked like a charm while my one-star trades were potluck. I didn't get as many five-star trades as one- and two-star trades, but if I had been patient enough to wait only for them, I'd have done much better. By doing this one can see which trading scenarios work best and can concentrate on those scenarios. If you can distinguish between different opportunities, you are on the way to making only high probability trades and ignoring those which are marginal.

Profit Goals

Profit goals are good to have so that you don't end up holding trades past their prime. You should have an idea of how much you think you can make on a trade before you put it on. This helps you manage your positions once you have them. Once you reach the target you wrote down, get out or lighten your position. Don't try to second-guess your earlier decision because the market looks better now. Of course it does; it just rallied to reach the level you had hoped it would reach, and you're emotionally excited as you now have a profit. When you do this, you end up trading with emotions and no longer with a clear head. Once a target has been reached, it is time to take profits and reevaluate, let the market retrace a bit, and then buy it again.

Stops

Just like having a profit goal, writing down a stop level will help you: It will limit your losses and let you know when you should be out of a trade. When this is done with a clear head, the results are better than they are when you are in a bad position and it is hurting you.

How Much You Made or Lost

It is always good to keep track of your average wins and losses to make sure you are managing your risk properly. By writing them down you can notice that maybe you make $300 on winning trades but lose about $900 on the losers. If you see this kind of pattern, you have to cut losers more quickly and let the profits grow. Unless you have a way to figure these numbers out, you can never know if it is a problem or think about improving on the ratio. With an Excel spreadsheet, you can easily find the average per winning or losing trade.

Hold Times

As important as knowing how much your winners and losers are is knowing how long you hold them. Losers need to be gotten out of much more quickly than winners. I used to hold losers forever, either hoping they would turn around or refusing to admit I was wrong. Now I use 45 minutes as a maximum guideline for holding on to a losing trade; after that I get out. Once a trade is not working, one has to admit that and get out of it. Too many people see a profit and get out quickly while doing the opposite with bad trades. Once again, unless you write them down, you will never know how you rank on hold times.

System Traders

If trading off the signals given by a system, one should keep track of any times one overrides the system. This will let a trader see if he is doing better than the system or is better off not tampering with it.

Trading Decisions

You may also want to keep track of whether you made a good trading decision or not. Did you get out of a loser quickly? Did you hold a good trade too long? Did you exit too quickly? Did you follow your rules? Did you wait for a pullback? By repeatedly writing down what you did right and wrong, you will reinforce proper trading behavior in the future. It makes it easier to point out any weaknesses you may have so that you can work to correct them. If you see that you are always writing down "exited winner too soon," you can start working on that problem. If you didn't write it down, you may not know that it is a problem.

REVIEWING THE JOURNAL

If there was ever a profession that required continuous on-the-job training, trading is it. Keeping a journal is like taking class notes; it should be reviewed on a regular basis if it is to help. Just keeping one isn't good enough; one should go over it carefully to see where one's strengths and weaknesses lie. When you start reviewing your trading performance, you can begin to get on the right track. Every day I review my trades on my way home. I try to understand what I did wrong on the bad ones and what I did right on the good ones. I don't consider how much money I made when I decide if a trade is bad or good. Getting out of a losing trade quickly is a good trading decision to me. Not all trades will work, and the more quickly you cut the losers, the better off you'll be. But the trades I concentrate the most on are the ones on which I did something stupid. I kick myself in the head about them because I should know better. A mistake like holding on to a trade after my indicators have turned and giving back a lot of profits is a mistake that I prefer not to make again. As I review my trades, I try to figure out why I did what I did and what I could have done differently so that the next time I'll walk away with a bigger profit. Did the market give me a sign I should have noticed?

Besides looking at my mistakes, I compliment myself when I trade smartly. For example, last Monday I was down $3000 by lunchtime (that wasn't the smart part), but I recognized I was on the wrong side of every trade. I got out of my trades and took a short walk outside to clear my head. When I came back, I was able to see the market more objectively. After that I was able to make back $2500 by getting on the right side of the market. I was tickled pink that I had only lost $500, and I considered the day a success. A day like this helps reinforce the behavior of exiting everything when I'm having a difficult time.

PROFESSIONAL TRADERS

Why does it seem the average trader always loses but the professionals make up the majority of the 10 percent of winning traders? One of the reasons institutional traders succeed better than does the average trader is that they have much more capital behind them. They can and do make the same mistakes but don't have to worry that one mistake will end their careers; with capital and management behind them, they can survive those mistakes. When they start out, they go through a training program, are assistants, work on a desk with proven traders, or are given small accounts where they can't do much damage. When they screw up, it costs the firm virtually nothing compared to the mistakes of larger, more established traders. As they get better, they are given more buying power and freedom. This doesn't happen overnight but may take a few years as they go through their learning years.

TRAINING PROGRAMS

Many professional traders go through extensive training before they are expected to succeed. When I started trading equities, they told me that they expected all new traders to lose for the first 2 years. Those who come in planning to start making money immediately will be disappointed. During those 2 years traders learn how to trade. For the first 3 months they don't even trade but instead just sit in classes all day learning about the different trading opportunities and paper trading. Afterward they are given limited share size and are forced to follow strict rules until they prove themselves. Only then are they given more share size, buying power, and the freedom to trade independently. The firm risks very little on these new traders during this period. Even when one loses $50,000, it means nothing to the firm; they see it as a part of a new trader's tuition.

Major firms such as Goldman Sachs, Bear Stearns, and Merrill Lynch go to the top business schools around the country and offer the top students disgustingly large sums of money to enter training programs to become traders. They don't just hire these people to trade; they hire them to train them to be traders. The reason they take only these elite candidates is that these people are proven learners. The firms figure these people will be easier to teach than someone who was only able to get into a mediocre graduate school with modest grades.

One should start to wonder: If professional trading firms expect their traders to take a few years to develop and are willing to risk a large sum of money in training them, why does the typical average trader think he can open a futures account for $5000 having never traded before and expect to make money immediately? Even those who trade on the floor don't just go out and get a seat; most of them were clerks for years before they ventured into the pit to trade. I spent 3 years on the floor learning everything I could before stepping into the ring to trade. People should be realistic about their progress and plan on having enough capital to get them there. They should not get discouraged if they lose their initial capital; instead, they should see it as a part of the tuition toward their ultimate goal—being a winning trader.

IT TOOK TIME AND MONEY, BUT HE FINALLY GOT IT

Here is an example of someone who went on to become a top trader after paying his dues. It's a guy I know whose brother was a big floor trader. It was his brother who got him started on the floor and fronted him capital to trade with. In the first year he lost well over $100,000, making every mistake possible. He wasn't discouraged and had much more capital to work with as long as his brother was around. The second year started off badly as well, but he was able to turn it around and lose only a little. By the third year he started being a regular money-making machine. He's been trading about 15 years now and consistently makes seven figures a year. His tuition was expensive, but he stuck it out to become a great trader. If he had had to stop after losing $20,000, he never would have had the chance to succeed.

SOME PERSONAL THOUGHTS

Trading is just too hard for a person to expect to make it from the very beginning. I've suffered so much from being undercapitalized that I think I could have turned my trading career around much sooner had I been better capitalized and used the early years to gain experience instead of trying to make a living straight out of the gate. It's just too hard to make it when you put everything on the line with no real source of backup income. I pressed from the beginning and tried way too hard to become rich overnight. I was a bit overconfident when I started and thought I knew better than the people with experience who were kind enough to try to teach me. Many times I ignored them because I thought they were too cautious and weren't making enough money. Yet they were consistent and made money all the time. I had to learn it for myself, and that cost me a lot of money. As I mentioned, I lost over $75,000 before I was able to turn it around. I may have done better if I had had all the money at once, but my money came out in a steady stream over a period of 7 years. I was forced to do odd jobs, working nights and weekends, for years while I struggled as a trader. All the money I made on the side I would dump into the market only to see it quickly dwindle not because I was a bad trader but because I was always undercapitalized, which I guess makes me a bad trader who was trading against the odds. I would trade well for a while and then hit a cocky streak and blow most of it in a week. Then I'd have to drive a cab for the next 24 hours to get enough money to afford the margin on my soybean position. It's impossible to trade well when one is too concerned about making money, covering one's margins, and trying to live off one's trading income.

BECOMING A BETTER TRADER

Becoming a better trader takes time, but one can do it if one is committed, is willing to put in the time, and has enough capital to succeed. Don't come into trading and expect to make money right away with little preparation or capital behind you; it will take time. People need to have enough capital to survive as they learn the ins and outs of trading. A $5000 account will probably not be enough to give a trader a chance to succeed. Traders can try to trade with a small account, but they need to have realistic expectations of how much can be made. They also must be prepared to blow out once or twice on the way to success. Blowing out is not as bad as it makes one feel; it's better to think of it as a rite of passage into trading.

When a trader first starts out, he needs to remember that it's not how much you make but how little you lose that keeps you in the game. Preserving capital should be a bigger priority then making money. Mistakes are important; they happen to everyone, especially when one first starts trading. Don't get discouraged when you do something stupid; learn from it and try not to do it again in the same situation. Keep a journal of your trades and review it constantly to identify strengths and weaknesses. If you make the same mistakes over and over again, it's time to reevaluate whether trading is for you.

Overall I'll stress that you should take it slow and preserve your capital until you've been trading for over 2 years; even after 5 years traders are still in for a surprise or two. By taking it slow you give yourself the chance to be around for the long haul. After you've paid your tuition and dues, you are ready to graduate and make a living from trading.

The Problems Traders Face When Starting Out

1. Ignoring the learning curve
2. Being undercapitalized at the start
3. Lacking working capital
4. Lacking formal training
5. Lacking schooling
6. Lacking supervision
7. Expecting success too soon
8. Expecting large profits from the get-go
9. Blowing out

Things to Help You Survive While Improving Your Trading

1. Take your time.
2. Trade and think small.
3. Pay your tuition of trading.
4. Learn from every mistake.
5. Let experience be your teacher.
6. Make sure you have enough money to last.
7. Preserve precious capital.
8. Paper trade before jumping in.
9. Keep a journal.
10. Review your trades constantly.
11. Be committed.
12. Enjoy yourself.

Helpful Questions to Ask Yourself

Do I have enough capital to trade with?
Why did I do what I did?
What should I have done?
How can I prevent it next time?
Am I rationalizing each trade I make?
Am I taking time to reflect on what I did wrong?
Am I giving myself a little praise when I do something right?

CHAPTER 2

Setting Realistic Goals

I received a letter from a guy who owned a real estate agency. He had just taken a course on how to become a millionaire trading commodities and thought he was ready to give it a try. He sent the same letter to a few other brokers as well, hoping to get the best deal. It went something like this:

> I am looking to start trading commodities in the next few weeks. I have never traded before but just finished reading Ken Roberts's course, and I'm currently paper trading. I plan to open an account with $25,000 and start slowly, looking to make about a thousand dollars a week. After a few months, when I feel more comfortable, I will increase my trading volume so that I can begin to make more. My goal is to be able to a make about $5000 per week within a year so that I can quit real estate and live off my trading. As I do plan on trading a lot and making my own decisions, I am looking for a discount broker with good rates to just enter orders through. Please reply with your best offer as soon as possible as I'm eager to get started.

I responded with my normal sarcasm, writing something very similar to this:

> We would be happy to offer you a rate of $15 a round turn. But before you get started, I'd like to point out that you are not being realistic about your goals. You are planning to make about $200,000 to $250,000 on a $25,000 account; that's a yearly return of 800 to 1000 percent. The best hedge fund managers and professional

traders are ecstatic when they achieve a 35 percent return for the year. You have never traded before, yet you think you can outperform these people by leaps and bounds. Even just making $1000 per week is a 200 percent return and is quite a stretch for a new trader. Yes, it can be done, but you fail to take into account the fact that you will have losing weeks as well. Your goal as a new trader should be to trade lightly and learn. If you were to make $5000 for the year, you'd be doing fine and achieving results better than those of 90 percent of all traders. Also, for a new trader I wouldn't recommend a discount account at the very beginning. You will be making quite a few mistakes along the way and might benefit from the guidance of a broker. We offer broker-assisted accounts for $25 a round turn which are ideal for beginning traders. Once you are more comfortable with your trading, then by all means I recommend the cheapest rates available. Please call me if you'd like to further discuss your trading needs or open an account.

Needless to say, he thought I was a little crass with my reply and didn't open an account with us. He opened an account elsewhere and started trading online. Two months later he called me up to transfer his account to my firm; he had remembered what I wrote and liked my honesty. He had lost about $17,000 and had begun to believe that trading was harder then he thought. He learned the hard way about setting realistic goals. Six months later, after losing a little more, he gave up and went back to real estate full-time. He could have been a good trader, but he never gave himself the proper time to learn to trade. Instead, he tried to make too much too soon and ended up losing most of his money before getting through the learning period. I can't say I was much different when I started. I used to make charts and tables of how with my $5000 I'd make $2000 a month till I had $10,000. Then I'd start making $3000, $4000, $6000 as my account grew, and before long I'd be turning out $25,000 a month on my way to Easy Street. Eventually I found out that the road to Easy Street takes a lot of turns and is filled with detours, roadblocks, and potholes.

SETTING REALISTIC GOALS

Being Realistic in Real Life and in Trading

Being realistic about success is hard for many people. Living in New York City, I see many people with dreams rather than realistic goals. Thousands of people come here every month with the aspirations of breaking into and making it big in the acting, music, modeling, and designing industries; some even come here to make it on Wall Street. They've all heard that the odds of making it are about the same as those of being hit by lighting twice and then being bitten by a shark, but nevertheless they come with high hopes and starry eyes to end up becoming the best darn professional waiters and bartenders they can be. When I was first starting to trade, I worked in a restaurant as a waiter. I was surrounded by wannabe stars, models, actors, dancers, you name it, yet my dreams were even crazier: I was the only aspiring star trader.

When it comes to setting goals, you have to be realistic no matter what the arena is. Whether it's in real life or in trading, you need to think on a realistic level. Many investors and traders think they can quit their jobs and start making a living day trading with a "small" $25,000 account. Some even have the silly notion that they can do it with $5000. They read in a book how a trader or two turned $5000 into $10 million and figure they can do it as well. Yes, it is possible and does happen on occasion, but for the few times it does, there are tens of thousands of traders who are going bust. By setting their sights lower, people may not make the millions they dreamed of but can end up doing just fine anyway.

"Ninety Percent of All Traders Will Lose . . . but Not Me"

I was at a training seminar for brokers once, and the speaker said that one method he had of getting customers was to give free seminars on trading. At those seminars he would tell people that only 10 percent of them would end up making money trading. He told them that 90 percent of his clients end up losing and went through the reasons why. Then he would ask the audience,"Who thinks they will be in the elite 10 percent?" and every time, every hand would go up. These people had just been told the plain truth about trading—that most of them would lose—yet none were realistic about it. Most people imagine or talk about the great possibilities of trading but not the realities. They all imagine that they will be the success stories, and no one expects failure even when told how good the chances of it are. Though it's important to believe you will succeed, you should also understand the possibility of failure if you are not careful.

"I Just Want To Make 10,000 Percent; That's Not Unreasonable, Is It?"

By setting realistic goals not only can one achieve them, one can keep from getting hurt. When goals are ridiculous, one is only setting oneself up to be highly disappointed. A trader who tries to make a living from a $10,000 account has to try much too hard and can achieve that goal only by overtrading. Once someone starts to overtrade, the chances of surviving drop quickly. Not only do such traders have to overtrade and take on too much risk, they have to achieve outrageous returns to get there, which in all honesty is hard to do. Everybody has dreamed of taking his account and turning it into a million dollars in a couple of years, but they say the only surefire way of getting an account to $1 million is to start with a $2 million account. One thing I've noticed over the years is that the traders with the most money are the ones who tend to do the best; it's the old adage that it takes money to make money. Having a bigger account doesn't make someone a better trader; it just gives a trader more room for error, the ability to risk less per trade, and greater staying power. The longer one can stick around, the greater the chance to succeed becomes. One reason I think these traders last longer is that when someone has only a few thousand dollars, it doesn't mean that much if he blows it all. These people will take chances because what does it really matter if they lose it—$2000 won't change their life. Now for someone with a $100,000 account, that's a lot of money to lose, and he is going to try harder to protect it.

It is also a bit more realistic for someone with a $100,000 account to be able to make a modest living trading. If these traders aim to make $1000 per day, they have to try a lot less hard and risk a lot less than does someone who has only $10,000. Even then, they are asking for a 200 percent annual return. When trying to do this with a small account you are asking for a 10,000 percent return. Anyone who could do this would have Morgan Stanley knocking at his door offering an eight-digit salary to come work for them. Don't get me wrong: You can make $1000 in a day with a lot less; I've done it with $2000 accounts. However, make one mistake and you're done. The reason the pros succeed and can make millions is that they are trading with multi-million-dollar accounts and trying to make only a modest 20 to 35 percent per year. They do this by being more selective in their trades, looking to take out steady profits without trying to make a killing on any trades.

Instead of having a dollar goal they concentrate on making good trades, and the money comes as a result.

THE DANGERS OF UNREALISTIC GOALS

One of the biggest downfalls in my early trading career was the day I made over $1000. It happened in my second week, and after that it became my daily goal. When I made over $1000, I had a great day; everything I did worked. Most days, however, don't work out that way, and not every trade will be a winner. Yet I was determined that I would make $1000 a day after that, and so instead of trading the one contract I should have been trading, I started to overtrade 2s and 3s. I started trading other markets and was constantly looking for trades. I always had too much on, and it hurt me. My original goal had been to make $200 a day, which was very reasonable with one contract, and I was doing fine until I set my sights on unreasonable goals.

MAKING REAL GOALS

In making a goal, first and foremost, make it reasonable. Instead of setting goals at extreme levels, make them very modest and obtainable. If you have only $10,000 to trade with and try to make $1000 a day, your goal is possible trading bonds or the E-mini S&P 500, but is it reasonable? It means you have to be margined to the hilt on every trade and consistently capture decent-size moves. Not only that, it comes out to a 50 percent return per week, which is rather ridiculous. Instead of this, a real goal may be to try to be profitable every week, have a 45 percent win/loss ratio, and make an average of 8 points on winning trades while risking only 4 on losing trades. Setting small obtainable goals like this will definitely put you in the right direction.

DON'T FORGET ABOUT THE LOSING DAYS

People may set goals of making, say, $400 or $500 a day in hopes of reaching $100,000 for the year. The $400 may be reasonable and easily achieved, but when trying to figure how much they will make at the year's end, they kind of forget to calculate any losing days. They assume they can consistently make the same amount every day and totally ignore the losing days. The reality is that they will probably have about the same number of losing days or more as winning days, and the losing days can tend to be worse than the good days. I've seen people who were trying to make $400 a day lose $2000 in the blink of an eye on a bad day. The next thing you know, the trader ignores his original goal and tries to make double what he just lost on his bad day to keep on his schedule. This leads to overtrading, and that's never good. *Never try to make back losses.* If you think $400 is a reasonable goal, keep to that; it may take a few days to make back the loss, but the result is better than that from overtrading. If you are going to have goals for winning days, you should also have goals for losing days, and those goals should be less than what you hope to make on a good day. If $400 is your goal on the upside, you should have a goal of not losing more than, say, $300 on a bad day. Once you start taking into account the losing days, making that $100,000 becomes a harder task, and $20,000 may be more realistic for the year. I think all traders should set goals so that they have something to strive for but keep them reasonable and remember they're only a guideline, not something that has to be done every day.

MINIMUM ACCOUNT SIZE

I keep mentioning how people try to trade with too little money. So what is the minimum amount someone should trade with? While it is hard to pinpoint a figure as to a minimum amount, a safe bet would be about $25,000 to $50,000 for futures and $100,000 for equities. When trading with these amounts it's reasonable for a decent trader to expect to make about $5000 to $10,000 per month in a good month while still being somewhat conservative in his trading. These minimum account sizes are sufficient to be able to margin oneself properly and survive the mistakes traders will make. The more you have, of course, the better your chances become. There are times when a trader has to go through a string of losers to get a few good trades, and by being undercapitalized he doesn't give himself the chance to be around when the good trades happen. This is why the smaller the account is, the less likely it is that a trader will make money in the long run. Five thousand dollars is just too small to withstand a losing streak at the start. If you have a small account, that's okay; just set your goals to match your capital and trade according to your means. You can still trade but you will have to trade less often and in markets or stocks that are less volatile and look to make a lot less.

MORE GOALS THAN MEET THE EYE

Goals shouldn't just be set on overall performance. There are several different levels where one can set goals, such as per market, wave, day, year, and length of learning curve.

MARKET GOALS

Average True Range

I'll start on the smallest level—how much the market can move—so that you can estimate what you can make or lose. You need to have realistic ideas on how much each market or stock can give you or cause you to lose on a trade. This applies to both day trading and taking on long-term positions. To do this, one needs to know the Average True Range (ATR) of the market or stock on which one trades. This can be done for any time period bars one looks at.

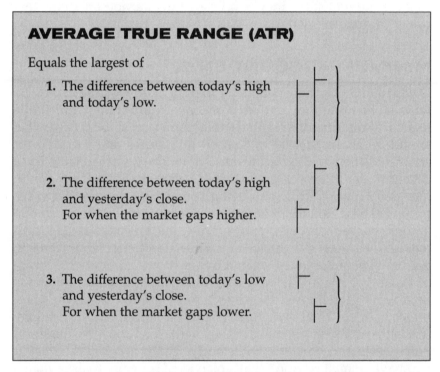

AVERAGE TRUE RANGE (ATR)

Equals the largest of

1. The difference between today's high and today's low.

2. The difference between today's high and yesterday's close.
   For when the market gaps higher.

3. The difference between today's low and yesterday's close.
   For when the market gaps lower.

If one is daytrading a stock with an ATR over the last 10 days of $4 per day and it has already had a $3.75 move for the day, this may be a good time to be realistic about how much higher it can go, and one should start looking for an exit point. This trade is most likely done at this point, and staying in to squeeze out every last penny from the trade is going against the odds. The stock has moved its average range, and unless it's a special day, it most likely will start to fizzle out or hit resistance. The smart traders are either covering or reversing at around this time, and the momentum may soon change. A trader is better off missing the last leg of a move and getting out before the masses do than hoping it keeps going. If he waits too long and decides to exit after it turns, it may be too late and he will be scrambling to get filled as it gets away from him. It's critical to get out when the market lets you; this is especially true when trading with size, as a large order may not get filled very well once the market turns. Sure, there will be days when it will move $5 or more—*So what?* On average it won't go much beyond its $4 average range. The percentage play is looking to get out when the market is within 80 percent of the average daily range. Take a look at Chart 2–1. For

CHART 2–1

Daily Chart of AMAT: Average True Range Indicator Equaling 3.99

months the average range of AMAT has been about $4; there have been relatively very few days when it has moved much more than this. Those who are aware of how much it can move on a daily basis are in a better position to profit from it. If you got out on a day when it continued moving and missed part of the move, it's okay. You made the high probability trade by getting out, and in the long run you will be paid off by making the high probability trades.

If you don't have software that gives you the ATR of a market, you need to figure it out by hand or with Excel. The average range of a market changes over time, and so you must constantly keep abreast of it. Stocks I used to trade, such as Ariba (ARBA), that once had a range of $15 per day now have a 50-cent range; others that had a $4 range may now have a $2 range; soybeans have wider swings in the summer than they do the rest of the year. You have to keep reevaluating the ranges of markets over time so that you're not stuck thinking they are something different from what they are. I like to look at the average of the last 5 and 10 days when determining the average true range of a market. Once you have a rough idea of how much a stock or market can move, you can figure out what is realistic. It is unrealistic to believe a $15 stock with an ATR of $1 will move $5 in a day, but a $70 stock with a $6 ATR could easily do it. If you day trade, you also may want to know the ATR of a 30- or 60-minute period bar so that you don't hold on to short-term trades too long as well.

Stop Looking for the Big One

There will be times where something affects the market or stock and it has an extreme day, trading well beyond its normal range. A news-related move or a breakout of a technical level from which the market explodes can make a market move more than its normal range, but these days are the exceptions, not the norm. Many times I get caught up in the frenzy of the market and forget this. Some days when the Dow Jones is falling hard and has dropped about 200 points, I start thinking that this could be the big one, the day they talk about for years. I start loading up on the short side in hopes of a 500-plus drop in the Dow. I end up losing big on these days because in reality there have been only a handful of really big days over the history of the market. Yet I think or hope it will happen every week. I'm not being realistic about the probability of its happening. Ninety-nine percent of the time the market has reached its saturation point at these levels, and when I start thinking it looks like it can crash, it turns around. The market has reached its normal extreme, and the smart play is to do nothing unless the market strongly tells you to do something. If you get out and the market keeps going, don't get discouraged, because that was where the probabilities were. The ironic thing is that I wrote this section on the bus on my way to work this morning, and at lunchtime the market was down about 200 points. I covered my shorts to practice what I preached, and sure enough, it collapsed, falling close to 400 points for the one of the largest down days ever. Though I wished I had caught the whole move, I did the right thing by covering. I was able to get in later, after the market really showed weakness.

Profit Goal Per Trade

Besides knowing the average range of a market, a trader must remember that the market moves in waves. Whether a stock moves $30 in 2 months or $4 in a day, it very rarely does so in a straight line. It gets there in waves, and though a stock may have an average range of $4, it may have upwaves of a point and downwaves of half a point throughout the day. Though soybeans may have an average range of 12 points a day, you are unlikely to capture it all in one quick move. Instead you can grab 5 points here, 4 there, and 2 a few other times. The best day traders try to hit a lot of singles in their trading and keep booking modest profits. When you swing for the fences, you tend to strike out a lot more; it's better to hit three or four singles in a day than to go for homers. Going for the smaller waves is safer and usually more profitable.

Riding the Waves

There is no simple formula to figure out the lengths of a typical wave, nor is there a hard formula; you just have to know the market you are trading. Different time frames, such as 5 minutes, 60 minutes, daily, and weekly, will have different size waves. They will change on days when there is more or less activity, and not each wave is the same in size. Profits should be taken based on what the market is willing to give, not on what a trader wants to make. When a wave is ending, it's time to get out; holding out for the top dollar may be costly when a market turns, and you may get stuck sitting in a position for hours as you wait for a wave to continue. The best way to get a feel for the lengths of the average wave is a combination of knowing the market, having a working knowledge of Elliott wave analysis, and using trendlines, channels, and oscillators to determine when the market is overbought or oversold. In the technical analysis section of the book I'll dwell on this further.

Chart 2–2 shows a 2-minute chart of AMAT, which has a daily average true range of about 4 points. It opened higher by about 2 points, and after about a half hour (Point A) it stopped going up and began selling off. By 12:30 (Point B) it had dropped $4 off its high, reaching its average daily range. At this point a great short had exhausted its move and turned into a good long for the rest of the day. The smart money knows what the range of the stock is and stops shorting the stock when it nears its ATR. Shortly after Point B it does try to break down again, but it stalls at Point C, and this is when the rally begins.

Let's get back to trading the waves. On the down move from 10 a.m. to 12:30, which was just over $4, AMAT did not move straight down. Instead it stalled at the up arrows. Unfortunately, I put those arrows in after the fact; I'm still working on making them

CHART 2–2

Intraday AMAT: Trading the Range and Catching the Waves

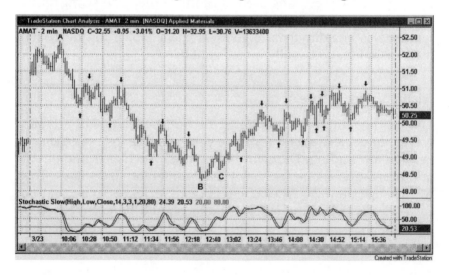

appear on their own beforehand. The downwaves ranged from about one to two dollars, with about a buck and a half being the average. The upwaves were about three-quarters of a dollar. As the market rallied after Point C, it did so in waves similar to the ones on the way down. The reason for these waves is that day traders are taking their profits after getting a quick move. One thing that makes day trading hard is that it takes 30 minutes for a stock to drop a point but only 10 minutes for it to pop up three-quarters of a point. You have to be agile and alert to be a good day trader, but once you get a feel for how big the market's waves are, you can start anticipating them. When trading waves I use stochastics and a stall in momentum to help time my entries and exits. You can see in Chart 2–2 that the up and down arrows are aligned with the turning points in the stochastics indicator below. All the market is, is a function of what all traders are thinking the price should be. If they all expect to take profits after a drop of a point and a half, one must be realistic and might as well take profits also. If one stays in through the waves, one will see a dollar profit become a quarter-dollar profit and may be scared to lose on the trade and take it then, only to reshort it 5 minutes later when the stock continues to go down. If I get a 1.5-point to 1.75-point move, I'll take it and look to short the next bounce. Even if I miss the next move, I still know I traded correctly and I'm okay with it. When the waves are small, I'll sit in the trade until I think the major move is done. Otherwise I get chopped up and pay too much in commissions. By getting in and out of waves, one can keep taking profits and be out of the market when it reverses.

For Longer-Term Traders

The same goes for long-term trades. Markets rarely move straight in one direction without having pullbacks and waves. Like intraday charts, long-term charts have trendlines and oscillators that can help a trader exit a trade before suffering a pullback. When stochastics are high and a stock is near the top of its channel, it's time to look to exit a trade and take what profits one may have. You can begin to look for a new and better entry point into the trade in the next few days if it backs off a bit. Many traders see a stock near the top of a channel and automatically think it will break out. Most times it doesn't, and a trader needs to be able to respond quickly to a market before it pulls back. Once you get the concept in your head that it's okay to miss the beginning and end of a trade and that what is important is capturing the middle part of it, riding the waves becomes easy. Chart 2–1 shows how a stock moves in waves. In the first half of the chart, when AMAT fell from 115 to 40, every time it looked like it would crack down, it had upwaves of 10, 15, or 25 points. People who shorted this at the wrong time were hurting. In the latter part of the chart, when it became range-bound, there were several times when it looked like it would break out, but each time it changed direction and started a new wave. Those who waited for the bounces or pullbacks to enter would have fared better than did those who rushed in.

PERSONAL GOALS

Aside from having goals about how much money you want to make or how much you expect the market to move, you have to have goals that will be everyday steps in helping you improve. In setting goals it is better to keep them simple and easy to obtain so that you don't get discouraged. If you set a goal, you want to be able to achieve it, but don't make it so easy that it is impossible not to achieve; you need to stretch yourself just a bit. Some self-improvement goals are described below.

Work on Your Weaknesses

Everyone has unique weaknesses that keep him from being the best he could be. One of every trader's goals should be to identify those weaknesses and work on them. This is really two goals, not one. The first one is to find your weaknesses, and the second is to fix them. Throughout this book when you find something that pertains to one of your weaknesses, make a note of it and concentrate on changing it.

Learn from Mistakes

Mistakes are part of trading. Don't ignore them but learn from them; they are crucial in your development as a trader. Learning from your mistakes should be high on your list of goals and one of the things you should strive for. You will make mistakes throughout your trading career. If you can keep from making the same mistakes over and over, you will improve dramatically as a trader.

Keep Losses Reasonable

This is a simple goal but one that is hard to do sometimes. Be reasonable about losses in a stock or commodity. If a stock you are day trading has a $3 range, don't lose $2.50 on it every time you trade it. A loss of 50 to 75 cents is more reasonable. If you are trading with $10,000 in your account, don't lose $1000 on any given day or trade. People who lose more than 5 percent at any given time are risking too much and setting themselves up for failure. Try to keep losers to under 2 percent of your equity, the lower the better.

Preserve Precious Capital

One of your goals should be to not lose your money. You want to be around in a few years, so do what you can to make sure you will have money then. The best way to do this is to concentrate on not losing money. Forget about making money; your goal should be not to lose it. If you can achieve this, you will be in a good financial position when you become a good trader.

Stop Chasing the Market

This is one area where beginners get hurt easily. They see a big move in a market, get excited about it, and then buy it as it is still moving up or short it as it is dropping. You have to be realistic about just how much it can move in a straight line. Even when a stock is flying, it will still retrace, and the harder it rallies, the stronger the retracement will be. You need to wait for the market to stop going up and either consolidate or pull in before getting onboard. Otherwise you have a good chance of buying the highs and getting caught in a retracement that may shake you out. Even if you miss a trade completely, it's better to wait for a pullback. If you don't get it, so what? There will be another trade another day. By learning to wait for a pullback, you will improve your chances of success as you cut back on trades that hurt you.

STAYING REALISTIC

Staying Realistic Even When the Market Is Unrealistic

Between 1999 and April 2000 people made a lot of money buying any tech stock they could get their hands on. Those people weren't good traders; they were lucky ones. They could do no wrong in that period and unfortunately got a little too cocky and paid dearly in late 2000 and 2001. They never developed any money management skills or realistic ideas of what a stock should do. A stock should not go from $6 to $150 in 3 months, split, and then do it again. Yet people were beginning to think this was normal. When the market finally got realistic, those people lost much of the money they had put into the market.

Unless one gets an incredible bull run like the NASDAQ of 1999 to April 2000, when stocks went from $15 to $200, a stock typically will go up only 20 to 35 percent a year in a good year. Those folks learned the hard way that trading is not as easy as it looks, and that one should have realistic goals even when the market is not acting realistically. Eventually every trend will end, and traders need to be realistic about it when it happens by covering or even taking the other side. I know too many people still holding Lucent at $2 when they bought it at $60; at some point they needed to realize that this stock was not going higher. It seems that every day someone calls up on CNBC's *Buy, Sell, or Hold* program and says, "I bought Lucent at 60. It's 2 now. What should I do?" Now it's too late to do anything. Action should have been taken months ago, when the stock was overvalued.

Being Realistic about How Long It Takes

As I mentioned in Chap. 1, trading is not easy or something most people can master right away. You shouldn't expect to be a success overnight, and you need to be realistic about how long that will take. I'd say that it takes 2 to 5 years before you have paid all of your tuition and dues as a trader. During the first couple of years the overall goal of a trader should not be to make x amount of dollars; it should be to still have enough capital to be trading with after that time is over with; making money will come on its own. It takes years of fine-tuning one's skills and enough capital to survive to end up on top. When going into trading one should be aware of this. Even if a trader starts off with a bang, he is not necessarily a good trader. He has yet to experience a bad streak, and when he does, he may be overextended and lose his profits quickly. Many people start out thinking they will be able to support themselves right away and end up not having enough money to survive. It took me years to be able to support myself from trading alone. During most of my early career I had to constantly work nights and weekends to support my trading habit. I drove a New York City yellow cab, started a limousine car service company, waited tables, did income taxes at an accounting firm, and played guitar in a few bands. I always thought "Just a few more months and this trading thing will kick in," but those months lingered into years.

Being Realistic about Failure

Finally, you have to be realistic about the possibility of failure. Although everybody goes into trading with aspirations of making money and a positive attitude is essential in doing so, people should be aware that failure is a good possibility. About 90 percent of traders will fail, and the more honest you are about those numbers, the easier it is to avoid falling into that category.

MAKE TRADING YOUR BUSINESS

One way to get more realistic about trading is to consider it a serious full-fledged business. To succeed, one should be no less serious than any other individual who starts and owns a business. When starting a business one should always make sure to have enough capital to see it through properly. No one expects a new venture to turn a profit right away. Without sufficient start-up and working capital any business is likely to fail. Even before the doors open and income starts coming in, there are bills to pay. It takes time to develop a steady cash flow and establish oneself, no matter what the business is. Yet traders expect to make a profit from the get-go. If you are going to run a business, and I don't care what kind it is— a restaurant, retail shop, consulting, garbage disposal, or IBM—you don't want to do it on a shoestring budget. Most businesses that fail do so within the first 2 years, with the overwhelming reason being undercapitalization.

People don't just jump into a business venture without thinking it through carefully; they do a lot of analysis, create a realistic plan, and make sure they are financially equipped to get started. In addition to capitalization, decisions should be made carefully. If someone owned a clothing store, he wouldn't buy a line of jeans simply because they seemed okay at first glance or he was scared to miss the latest fad. A smart businessperson would see if any competitors had them, determine the demand for them, and see if the markup and potential profits were worth the cost of taking on the extra inventory, not to mention determining whether the space in the store could be used for a better purpose. After taking all these things into consideration, he might make a decision about whether to invest in the new line of jeans. It's a well thought out process, not a whim. He wants to avoid any hit-or-miss situations if possible. If he misses the first stage of a fad, he knows he can always buy them later, if the demand is established and the risk of investing in them is reduced.

More so than in any other business, trading involves risk and should be taken with the utmost seriousness. When one is trading, every trade should be made with the thought of running a business. As a businessperson, a trader should have the goal of making the decisions that will lead him to make the most money possible with the least risk. If a trader cannot separate trading as a business from trading for the thrill of the action, he should go to a casino and play craps; the results will be the same. Unfortunately, some people are too caught up in the excitement of trading rather than focusing on working to make themselves better traders. Only when a person starts treating trading like a real business, and not just a means of entertainment, can he begin to be more objective.

MAKING A BUSINESS PLAN

One thing that separates a successful business from one that fails is a solid business plan. A business plan details a company's objectives and goals, and sets out the stages in which it will obtain those goals. If one is trying to raise money, a business plan is essential, but even for those who don't try to get external capital, a business plan is a tremendous asset in getting a business off the ground and running it successfully. Something very few new traders do that could help them immensely is to make a business plan, just as if they were going into any other business. A business plan is not easy and can be time-consuming, so I understand why few traders do it; however, if people took the time to do it, it would help them.

A business plan for a trader is similar to a disclosure document that a Commodity Trading Adviser or Commodity Pool Operator would use to raise money. It has all the same ingredients a business plan would have in any other field. Making one with the idea that you are trying to persuade other people to give you money will help you realize all the costs and factors, big and small, that go into trading. It will let you begin to treat trading with the seriousness it deserves. You will see just how hard it is to achieve unrealistic returns. It will help you figure out exactly how much money one needs and what every possible risk involved is. You should clearly spell out all your trading ideas, your parameters, what the potential is, and any problems that could arise. Doing all this will let you see all the risks involved and what your goals should be instead of setting them too high. You'll be able to see how much capital is available for trading, how much there is to live on, and how much is being saved for emergencies. By doing this a trader can actually see that he may be undercapitalized to trade for a living if he has only $10,000 in the bank. Instead of making a business plan a trader should make a trading plan. I'll discuss how to make one later in the book; for now here is a sampling of what should be in one.

Some Ingredients That Go into a Trading Plan

Trading style, strategy, or system

Time frame you will need to succeed

Costs involved

Money management plan

Potential profits

Risks

External and internal factors that could affect your performance

Why you expect to succeed

TRUE STORY OF A HAPLESS TRADER

One example that sticks in my mind of someone who was not realistic about what he or the market could do is the following. One of my clients had a friend who wanted to try trading. He opened an account with $4000, originally to trade options in grains. After his check cleared, I called him to tell him he was ready to go. He had been watching CNBC at the moment, and they were going on and on about how strong the NASDAQ was (this was just around the NASDAQ peak in March 2000, and it was extremely volatile). It was down a little at the moment, and he started asking me a lot of questions about the NASDAQ E-minis and eventually decided he wanted to buy one. I tried hard to dissuade him. I told him that trading one of the most volatile markets on his first trade wasn't a good idea and that if he was wrong, it could quickly cost him over $1000. He didn't care; he thought that since it had just had a dip, this would be a good place to get it, since the market would continue to rally as it had been doing every day. He placed a stop $1000 away, not thinking it would ever get hit. After about an hour I had to call to tell him he was down $800 and see what he wanted to do. As we were on the phone, it went down even farther and he was convinced that it would bounce, so he canceled his stop and insisted on buying a second contract. After a 2-second rally the market continued to drop. Next time I called him he was down over $2000 and decided it was time to get out of the trade. Then of course the market rallied hard. Now he was frustrated that the market had rallied and he wasn't in it. He told me he would wire more money and bought two contracts instead of one. As soon as he did that, the market went straight down, this time even harder than the first time. As he watched his account get to under $1000, he froze and for the first time asked my advice. My advice was to get out and take the losses, but he was too shell-shocked to do so. Eventually I had to liquidate his positions for him. By the time everything was said and done, he had lost practically all his money, and this was his first day of trading. He had not been realistic about what could happen, and it cost him dearly. He had never done his homework, had no idea of risk or of what the market was capable of doing, and traded well beyond his means. He closed his account the next day and never traded again.

MY PERSONAL EXPERIENCE

My problem was that I always tried to trade like I had a million dollars. I was trying to make the same as the guy next to me; it didn't matter to me that he had a half million in his trading account and I had only $30,000. I risked much more per trade than I should have, as I was willing to lose the same amount as a guy who had 10 times as much money as I had. I ended up losing because my expectations were too high and were impossible to meet. I had to overtrade constantly to try to reach my goals, and it never worked in the long run. Another mistake I made was repeatedly ignoring how much a market could move and thinking it would go forever the stronger it got. I gave back many good trades because I was not realistic about taking profits. It took some time to learn how to be more realistic when it came to taking profits and losses, but after watching good traders repeatedly do it, I was able to get the hang of it. Even though I still believe that I should let profits ride, I do it realistically; in the past I would just let them ride into losers. I've become realistic about how much I can make on the amount I have to trade with. I stopped trying to make more than I should, and even though my best days now are comparatively smaller than they used to be, I have more good days and a lot fewer really bad days. I've learned that trading is about survival, not about how much you make.

BECOMING A BETTER TRADER

Becoming a better trader means having realistic goals, not just about yourself and what you are capable of but about what the market can do. Learn how the markets you trade react and what you can expect to make on them. You will become a better trader by having the proper capital to succeed or the proper expectations with the capital you have. Someone with $5000 needs to have lower goals and expectations than does someone with $50,000. It also means understanding how long it takes to achieve success and the possibility of failure; blowing out is always a possibility, but it is something one can learn from if one is committed to being a trader. It's common to lose money at first; most successful traders began that way. Don't expect to be a star trader overnight; give yourself at least 2 years to learn the markets. Though it is always important to be realistic, to be a better trader you have to believe that you are the best trader on earth and keep envisioning that every day. If you don't, you will never become the best.

Most of all, I think it's critical to be realistic about how much money can be made and how much one needs to start with. The major reason people end up as losers is that they attempt to trade with insufficient capital. The more money one has to start with, the better one's chances of success are. Trying to trade with a $2000 account usually results in disappointment. People end up being losers not because they are bad traders but because they are undercapitalized to get through any rough patches. Even believing that a $10,000 account can generate a living is far-fetched, yet novice traders believe that they can achieve 500 to 10,000 percent returns from the beginning. Top hedge fund managers and professional traders, on the other hand, are glad when they make a 35 percent return for the year. You shouldn't worry so much about how much money you can make; instead, have a goal of not losing all your money. If you set realistic and easy-to-achieve goals, you will find that you will become a better trader.

The Problems Traders Face When Not Being Realistic

1. Not believing they can lose
2. Overtrading
3. Risking too much
4. Shooting for the stars
5. Being disappointed and discouraged
6. Blowing out
7. Expecting a stock to triple every year
8. Having an unpleasant personal life

Things to Help You Become Realistic

1. Keep your goals modest.
2. Remember that not every day will be a winner.
3. Trade with more money.
4. Know the average true range.
5. Know the average length of a wave.
6. Stop looking for the big one.
7. Look for smaller returns.
8. Put in your time and gain experience.
9. Learn from mistakes.
10. Keep losses small.
11. Don't chase a market.
12. Remember to stay realistic even when the market is not.
13. Treat trading like a business.
14. Make a trading plan.

Helpful Questions to Ask Yourself

Are my goals reasonable?
Are my expectations of the trade reasonable?
Am I being realistic?

Have I missed the move?

Am I looking to take out too much on the trade?

Am I risking too much?

Am I making businesslike decisions?

CHAPTER 3

Leveling the Playing Field

I remember my high school history teacher telling us that Napoleon once was asked which side he thought would win the war. He responded, "The French, of course. We have the biggest cannons."

COMPETING WITH THE PROS

Imagine entering your car in the Daytona 500. Sure you may be a good driver and have a brand-spanking-new, top-of-the-line foreign sports car, but in your wildest dreams would you ever believe that you had a chance of winning against professional race car drivers with state-of-the-art racing machines? No matter how good you may be, you will never be able to compete with them until you have the same experience, know-how, and equipment. Not only would your chances of winning be slim, you'd be lucky if you didn't wipe out. Trading should be thought of in the same way. You are not just trying to survive and make money; you are also competing with professionals who most likely are better equipped to succeed than you are. When you are not on the same playing field with them, it's easy to lag behind.

People sometimes don't realize that the market as a whole is composed of the aggregate positions of every trader. From every one-lot trader to every hedge fund manager, together they make up the market's price. The market is trading at its current price and will go where it will go not because of any chart, indicator, or news story but because that's where traders' positions say it should go. When a typical small trader tries to make a buck, he has to keep in mind that he is competing against the world's best traders. These are pros who have the latest and best equipment, information, order flow, experience, capital, and buying power, which help give them an edge. They can be market makers, hedge funds, specialists, traders on institutional desks, powerful individuals, floor traders, or large producers or users of a commodity. They have the ability to move and support markets and/or play games with it. They can give the impression that there is interest in a market or be discreet about their intentions. Their goal is to make money, and as far as they are concerned, you are there to help their cause.

The point of all this is that these people are your competition, and an individual one-lot part-time trader doesn't have the same chance to succeed as a trader at Merrill Lynch with millions in capital does. Professional traders spend thousands of dollars a month to have access to the latest equipment, software, news, information, and straight-to-the-floor service. Meanwhile, some people are trying to compete using the newspaper as their source of quotes and information. Consider that when you are trading a contract of crude oil with $5000 in your account, you are up against floor traders who have a minimum of $50,000 in their accounts, hedge funds with millions in capital, or Exxon. Who do you think is better capitalized and in a better position to succeed? A trader on a professional desk may sit in front of two or four large monitors with real-time quotes—not only the futures prices; he probably has the cash prices as well. He has enough real estate on his screens to keep multiple charts in front of him at all times while still looking at news, quotes, and any proprietary trading systems he may have. Many firms hire quantitative people for the sole purpose of creating and backtesting systems, which can do a remarkable analysis of the market. The average trader, in comparison, may have only a ruler and chart to do his analysis.

LEVELING THE PLAYING FIELD

If one wants to be a serious trader, one should do whatever possible to get on the same playing field as a professional. Since everyone else is trying as hard as possible to win, it's important to get all the edge you can. You won't win a battle with rocks and sticks when fighting against those who have cannons and missiles. Institutions have always had deep budgets, the latest technology, and the ability to have all the real-time news, quotes, and information available. Only recently, with the coming of the age of the Internet, has the average trader been able to have many of the same tools at his disposal. Hey, if professional traders are spending tons of money to get these things, don't you think it may help a little? Now anybody, even with a limited budget, has a chance to come closer to being on the same playing field as institutions spending millions. Through the Internet, individuals can pretty much get (at a relatively low cost) the same tools and information that once were limited to institutional traders. Not everything is free or cheap, but at least it's out there, and there is an abundance of software that can give the non-professional trader a little help. Despite having everything readily available in real time, many novice traders still hope to compete successfully by using free but delayed quotes, charts, and news. An old computer, antiquated software, slow execution, and not having access to the floor can also hurt traders' bottom lines. It wasn't too long ago that as a broker I'd be giving quotes out all day long, and if I wanted someone to see a chart, I'd have to fax it to him. Now that traders can get all that for themselves, they should take advantage of it. If traders want to be on the same playing field, they need to consider paying for the proper tools; though it may cost a little, it can dramatically improve their bottom lines.

THE INTERNET AND ONLINE TRADING

There is little question that with the growth of online trading and deep discount brokerage, trading volume has increased as neophyte traders, believing that they have the same advantage as pros sitting at a trading desk, have stepped up their trading or entered the arena. Just a few years ago having the ability to see real-time charts, quotes, and news was something very few nonprofessional traders had. Now it's available to anyone. Though today's improved technology may not make you trade any better, it does let you trade more accurately and faster so that everybody has the chance to make money as a short-term trader. This doesn't mean that everybody will make money, but people at least have a fighting chance.

DAY TRADING HAS BECOME EASIER

Once day trading was limited to professionals and floor traders, but with the leveling of the playing field from online trading, better technology, real-time charts, lower commissions, improved liquidity, and wider daily ranges in the markets, the average trader now has a fighting chance to compete in the day trading arena. When I first started trading, day trading was for floor traders and a few select professionals; it was just too costly to get the data and charts needed for the average trader to do it properly. Back then when a 6-point move in the S&P 500 was considered a big day and commissions were higher, there was little room for a day trader to make money. Today with 15-, 20-, and 30-point intraday swings common, an Internet connection, and dirt-cheap commissions, there is an opportunity for the average trader to make money day trading and scalping. As more and more people started day trading, the liquidity improved and the spreads narrowed, taking away some of the power that market makers and specialists held while giving more people a chance to succeed.

ONLINE TRADING

When I started Link Futures, I was amazed at how eager people were to trade online. Bypassing a broker and paying less in commissions was a dream come true for many investors. Online trading allowed people to trade hassle-free at less than half the price they used to be able to, creating a tremendous advantage for experienced, active traders. The number of people who just want to trade their own money online without a broker's advice or assistance seems to be growing constantly. Besides the cheaper rates, some people hate having to deal with a live broker, especially the pushy type. Traders like the independence of being able to trade when they want to and not having to worry about what a broker will think. They like the fact that they can take their sweet time in making decisions and can cancel an order 50 times if they want to without feeling like a nuisance.

Trading online has revolutionized the brokerage business and has become a tremendous advantage for the average retail trader. Though it has its benefits, I do not recommend it for traders who are starting out. There is just too much to learn at the beginning, and it is so easy to make mistakes, that a broker will, without a doubt, be helpful. Besides the basic trading errors, such as buying an overbought market, new traders will make mistakes because some don't even know the difference between a limit and a market order, what the symbol of a stock is, or when contracts expire and go into delivery.

The Bonuses of Online Trading

Reduced Commissions

Due to online trading, trading costs have dropped dramatically, resulting in an invaluable tool to the average trader. Commissions haven't just gotten cheaper for discount trading, but full service brokers who have to compete for business have lowered what they charge as well.

Speed

When trading electronic futures contracts and NASDAQ stocks, you get back fills in seconds. In other markets, the time it takes to place and get an order executed has dropped dramatically as well. The overall result is that day trading is easier for the average trader.

Flexibility

Entering, changing, parking, and canceling orders has become easy and convenient to do. There is no need to call a broker every time you want to do something.

No-Pressure Trading

Online trading lets you avoid pushy brokers calling with the recommendation of the day or trying to get you out of good positions so that you generate more in commission revenues.

Information

News, quotes, charts, fundamentals, and research reports are available at no extra cost when you have an online account. With just a click of the mouse, pretty much everything that you could need is there for you.

Monitoring Positions

Being able to see all your positions update live is a nice bonus that wasn't around when I started trading.

The Drawbacks of Online Trading

Beginners Still Need Guidance

Until one gets comfortable with trading, it is best to stick to a traditional broker. It doesn't have to be a full-service broker, but at least you want someone on the other end of a phone looking over your shoulder a little and pointing you in the right direction when you stray or make one of the many common mistakes you are prone to make as a new trader.

Not Knowing How to Place Orders
Until one learns all the different type of orders, the guidance of a broker is invaluable; otherwise it is too easy to make a mistake.

Lack of Risk Controls
A main reason people end up losers is that they don't know how to manage risk. Without any supervision people can trade themselves into a deep hole. A good broker can alert a trader when he is getting into trouble, while an online trading platform cannot.

Makes It Easy to Overtrade
A trader sitting behind his computer with access to real-time quotes, charts, and news can let it go to his head. He may think he is as good as a pro and can easily overtrade and take on too much risk. Don't mistake online trading for an open invitation to trade nonstop. Overtrading is something a trader should make sure he doesn't do.

THE TOOLS

If you require real-time information, the days when only the big players have it are over; now it's available to everyone who has an Internet connection. If you need something, you can pretty much find it on the Web. Though you may still have to pay for most things, there is an abundance of free information. The only difference between what you can get for free and what you pay for usually lies in the flexibility of what can be done and time delay versus real time. If you don't need real-time information, you can get all the news, reports, quotes, and charts you want for free. The things available on the Web these days can be generic, such as simple quotes and charts, or very specific and directed toward people who use Gann, Elliott wave analysis, or neural works.

Quotes and Charts

Quotes and charts are vital to a trader, without them he is trading blindly. Quotes alone will just tell you where the market is at the current moment, but a picture is worth a thousand words, and if you want to see what the market has been doing, you need charts.

There is an abundance of free places to get quotes and charts on the Net, but for quality real-time charts you may have to pay.

I've been using TradeStation as my charting platform for years. It is not the cheapest software available, as it does much more than just give charts and quotes: It also gives me the ability to write and test systems and then keep track of them, alerting me anytime they generate a signal.

PAPER CHARTS

To get a better feel for the market, every trader, whether he has the greatest charting software on his computer or not, should get paper charts and update them by hand. It gives you a unique hands-on feel for the market that a computer cannot. CRB Futures Perspective (www.crbtrader.com) has great daily futures charts that I buy about once a month and update by hand. I also manually update monthly charts to get a big picture of the market. Not too long ago this was the only way for the average trader to get charts, but now anyone with an Internet connection can get free charts at the end of the day. At the very least one should print out these charts, updating and drawing in trend-lines by hand. It's more personal than just looking at charts on your computer and will help keep you in better touch with the markets.

News

News is another important option one should have, not so much to trade off, but because one may want to know why a stock or commodity is doing what it is doing. If something acts differently than it should, I like to know why. Although I'm not one to trade on the basis of news, I like to keep abreast of things and see which stocks are currently in play. I get most of this information from my news wire service, but when I'm trading, I don't look at the news that much, which is why it's good to have the television on as well. I keep CNBC on all day. It keeps me informed on what the market is doing and what it has done but, unfortunately, not on what it will do, and after sitting in a room with 12 guys all day, Maria Bartiromo is easy on the eyes.

System-Writing Software

If you are serious about trading, look into a program that can back-test your ideas. I'm a big fan of TradeStation. Besides being an advance quotes and charting software (all the charts in this book were made with TradeStation), it allows one to create indicators and write and test systems with historical data before risking real money. I find TradeStation to be an invaluable tool in my trading. It allows one to write anything from simple little moving average crossover systems to the most advanced systems and indicators imaginable.

If you want to improve on your trading, this is the program to get. It may be a little more difficult to use and a bit more expensive than some of the other programs, but it is the industry standard for the serious trader and brings you one step closer to leveling the playing field.

TIMES HAVE CHANGED

When I first started using a computer to look at charts, I had a 486 with a 13-inch monitor and a dedicated phone line that I used to get a real-time feed from Future Source. I paid about $1000 a month and thought it was the greatest thing in the world. I then started using TradeStation on that computer, and every time I called up a chart, it would take a few seconds for it to come up, but I still thought I had the greatest setup on earth. Years later I look back and can't believe how antiquated all that was and what a difference trading with better technology makes. The difference a few years made is like night and day. Computers are faster, programs are more sophisticated, everything is readily available, and it's all cheaper. Instead of one slow computer and a tiny monitor, I now have two computers and look at three giant monitors to give me all my charts, news, quotes, and positions. Having multiple screens is important to me because I need to be able to keep charts on several stocks and futures while also looking at a quote board, news headlines, my positions, and any software I have, all at once. Looking back, I can't believe how much easier technology has made trading. If I were using my old computer to do what I do now, I think it would explode.

It Takes More Than Just the Right Tools

Even if a trader has the greatest tools at his disposal, that won't make him a winning trader. It will definitely be an asset, but he still needs to know how to trade, manage risk, and develop discipline. You are trading to make money, so don't skimp on your equipment. Don't worry about paying for a good computer, a live feed, real-time quotes, and good software. It's a cost of doing business and in the long run should pay for itself. I deliberated on buying TradeStation for over a year before spending $3000 for it. As soon as I got it, I began backtesting the systems I had been using and discovered why I had been losing money. Some of my trading ideas just didn't work. I had thought they did, but when I backtested them, they didn't. After evaluating them, I abandoned them to work on better ones. The money I spent on the program was nothing compared to what it saved me as I stopped losing as much.

It's not only the tools. Even when they have the same tools, amateur traders still need to realize that they may not be on the same playing field or have the same edge that a professional does. Professional traders get catered to and pay hardly anything in commissions, while small traders are seen as a nuisance. An institutional trader has an edge because he can call the pit himself, get accurate bids and offers, find out any relevant information, and even stay on the phone all day with a floor clerk; these traders get preference because of their size. Some even have their own personnel on the floor to ensure quick execution and better fills.

PROFESSIONALS VERSUS INDIVIDUALS

One of the things that separate the individual from the professional trader is how much they pay in commissions and the kind of service they get. When an individual trader gets an online account and pays only $12 a round turn in futures or $8 a trade in equities, he may think this is dirt cheap. But if he were to compare it to what professionals pay, he'd see he is at a grave disadvantage. I'm not referring only to traders who pay only clearing costs and don't even pay commissions, such as floor traders and those who trade for brokerage firms. Traders such as hedge funds, CTAs, and big accounts of all types will pay a fraction of the cost a regular retail account pays. This allows them to make a profit with less of a move. People who find that they are constant losers may be so because of what they pay in commissions. Even discount commission rates can be a huge drawdown on a trader's bottom line. If one had the same rates as a pro, getting over the hump could get easier.

Apart from the money they save, the big advantage comes from the service the big traders receive. Large traders are sought after by brokers, who will bend over backward to satisfy them. This means they get preferential treatment and excellent service. They have the ability to bypass a broker and call the floor directly; they can get accurate quotes while being able to work an order based on those quotes. When a regular trader calls his broker to get a quote, the broker usually gives it to him from his screen, but by the time the trader places an order on the floor, that quote may be off a bit. Having the advantage of getting direct to the floor service gives someone an incredible edge over a trader who has to put in a market order without knowing the exact price of the market. It can easily mean two ticks a trade, and that adds up in the long run.

Professional traders also have an advantage in that they have order flow and buying power behind them. When a small trader buys something, it means nothing to the market. When a mutual fund buys a stock, it could move the market. Professional traders can start buying discreetly until they build a position, and only then will they start openly showing their interest to buy and try to drive up the price. They can start showing huge bids and make it known that they are buying in order to get the attention of other traders, who can help lift the price. Large institutions also have the ability to call other large traders when they see action in the market in order to see what's going on or why people are buying. Small traders are always the last to know, as they have to wait to hear or read on the news about why a stock has moved. By the time they find out, the move may already be over.

For all these reasons and more, it is tough for a small independent trader to get ahead, which is why one should try to do everything possible to level the playing field.

BECOMING A BETTER TRADER

Becoming a better trader has become easier in recent years. The average trader now can pretty much have all the same information in front of him that a trader at the biggest firms has. Back in the days when nobody had a personal computer or an Internet connection, day trading was limited to a select few. Even for long-term traders, there was hardly any way to see a daily chart on a stock unless one went to a broker's office, went to the library and looked at Value Line, or made one by hand. Today everyone has that chance. Becoming a better trader includes doing your best in getting as good technology and information as you can. My trading got much better when I invested in the proper tools. I don't think I could ever go back to trading with the antiquated tools and methods I once used. Day traders especially have to take advantage of anything that can help tilt the tables in their favor. Don't be afraid to pay for something that will help you; it's a cost of doing business. And try to pay the lowest commissions you can without sacrificing service. Remember, you are competing against people who pay next to nothing in commissions. The less you pay in commissions, the easier it is mentally to get out of a bad trade, since you don't have to worry about making back the commissions, plus it's more money that stays in your account.

Though online trading may be the cheapest way to go, one should really know how to trade before venturing to trade without supervision. However, once you are comfortable trading, then by all means take advantage of the low cost of trading online.

The last thing to keep in mind is that no matter what you do, you are still competing with the best traders, the ones who have the most money, experience, technology, and access, so do whatever you can to be on the same playing field as they are. Every little step you take will get you just that much closer to succeeding as a trader.

Why Traders May Not Be on the Same Playing Field

1. Lacking the proper technology
2. Lacking experience
3. Lacking real-time information
4. Lacking the proper trading capital
5. Getting slow execution on trades
6. Not having access to the trading floor
7. Paying too much in commissions
8. Lacking order flow and buying power

Things to Help You Level the Playing Field

1. Make sure you have enough capital.
2. Get real-time quotes, charts, and news.
3. Use the Internet to your advantage.
4. Get a quick and reliable Internet connection.
5. Use free information on the Web.
6. Update charts by hand.
7. Take advantage of online trading.
8. Pay lower commissions
9. Use system writing software.
10. Get a fast computer.

Helpful Questions to Ask Yourself

Do I have the tools it takes?
Do I need a faster computer?
Do I need real-time quotes?
Are my trading costs too high?
Should I be trading online?

PART II

Using the News

Trading the News

In February 1999 *Futures* magazine's front-page story was titled "Code Blue for Crude, How Low Can Prices Go?" After crude dropped from $27 to under $10 in less than 2 years, they predicted that the market would stay in its dismal state. They stated that the market was suffering from oversupply, no demand, OPEC's failure to reach a consensus on production cutbacks, and the warm weather due to El Niño. The "experts" did not foresee the market moving much higher any time soon. Well look at Chart 4–1 and see what happened; the article pretty much pinpointed the bottom of the bear market in crude. Immediately afterward, it exploded with an almost $30 up move to its highest levels in 10 years, surpassed only by the price of oil during the time leading up to the Gulf War. The moral here is to be wary of what you read and hear; a major news event or story may just be the signal that the smart money was waiting for to get out and end the move.

THE FUNDAMENTALISTS VERSUS THE TECHNICALISTS

There are basically two schools of traders: the technical analysts who trade off charts and the fundamental analysts who trade off the news and the underlying conditions of the market. There is also a middle ground where traders use both, but those traders are basically technicalists or fundamentalists who use the other source to

CHART 4—1

Monthly Crude: Calling the Bottom

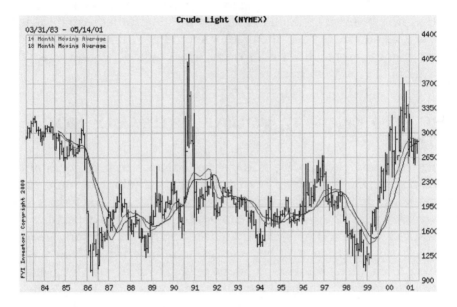

Crude Light (NYMEX)

confirm a belief. A technical trader can use fundamentals when evaluating market conditions or to see if overall market sentiment has shifted. For the most part, I'm a staunch believer in using technical analysis as the main method of trading, but I still think it's important to know why the market is doing what it is doing. A change in underlying conditions can alter a market's direction, and it is important to be aware of it.

Fundamental traders tend to be long-term traders who are looking for major economic shifts in a market. They use fundamentals to determine what the overall direction of the market should be, not to jump into trades. Some are short-term traders who believe that every move in the market is based on the smallest news item relating to it. But most moves in a stock are not a result of earnings expectations, and not every move in the grain market is a direct result of the latest change in the weather forecast. If a person were to base all trading decisions on what he read or heard, odds are, that person would be a losing trader. Learning from experience that the market doesn't always do what it should do, many professionals pay little heed to the actual news when trading. Instead they are more concerned with how the market reacts to the news. Many times when the market doesn't react as it should, they may be more inclined to fade a news story rather than trade in the direction it suggests the market should go. I find that some of the highest probability trades come when fading the news, as I'll explain later in this chapter.

IF YOU KNOW IT, YOU'RE PROBABLY NOT THE FIRST

For the most part, novice traders use the news incorrectly: Many read an article in the *Wall Street Journal* and barrel into a trade, not realizing that the news was discounted in the market days or weeks earlier. They forget that top trading firms have departments whose job it is to know exactly what is going on with any given stock or market before it becomes general knowledge. They have their own meteorologists who have determined the long-term weather report before the average trader gets it on the Internet. They have economists and analysts who are always trying to be one step ahead of everyone else. More important, they can get to the source of the news before anyone else can. Think about it: Most of the time when the public gets information, it has to hear or read a news story somewhere. That means that someone already knows it. For if you see a story on Reuters, the reporter had to type it in first, and so he had to know it before you; that means he got it from someone else who knew it before he did. What makes you think that the chain is that short? The story easily could have found its way to a trading desk at Goldman Sachs by the time it reached the reporter, and by the time he reports it and you hear it, a trader at Goldman could have reacted already.

Once the public gets hold of news, it is probably not fresh anymore, and it may have already been taken advantage of. Many times you will see the market react first and wonder why it did so, only to hear the news a little later; by this time it may be too late to do anything, and the best thing to do is to ignore it completely. Never chase a news-related spike. Let the market settle down first and digest the news. If you miss the trade, there will always be another one. If you happen to be in it already, don't get excited or panic. Again, let the market settle down before doing anything.

Example of How the Public Is the Last to Know

A great example of how the average trader is the last to know something and of how once people do know, it has already been factored
into the price, happened to me recently while I was trading the stock
Rambus (RMBS) (Chart 4–2). Luckily, I was on the right side of this
move. I was short in the stock, and then all of a sudden it dropped
hard, as if it had fallen off a table. The stock market in general had
opened sharply lower that morning because of bad unemployment
numbers (see Chart 4–3) but had been ripping higher all day long
after that. I had mostly long positions, but to balance such positions
I like to find some stocks that are reacting weakly in a strong market.
Rambus was one of those; it was not able to uptrend and stay positive on a day when most stocks were going much higher. There was
obviously something wrong with it. I didn't know what, and I didn't
care. RMBS appeared on my screen as a relatively weak stock.
Looking at a chart, I saw that it was not as strong as everything else,
and so I shorted it at around 1 p.m. It didn't go anywhere, but I
thought that if the market failed, it would probably drop, so it was a
good short to have. Then, all of a sudden, at 2:30 the bottom fell out
of it and I had no idea why; in the next 12 minutes it dropped about
$3. I knew it had to be news-related, because a stock does not fall like

CHART 4–2

1-Minute RMBS: Making a Move before the News Is Out

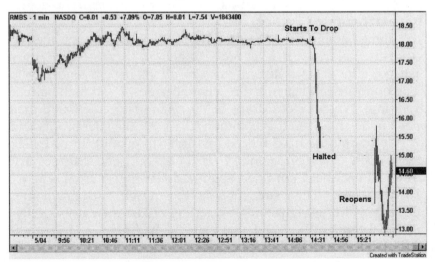

CHART 4-3

5-Minute S&P 500: A Strong Day after Bad News

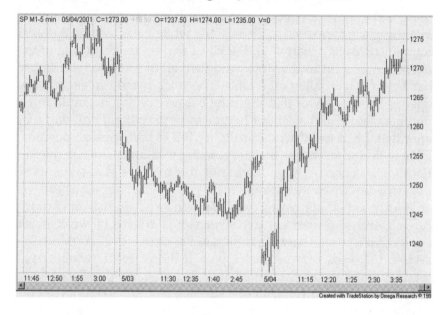

SP M1-5 min 05/04/2001 C=1273.00   O=1237.50 H=1274.00 L=1235.00 V=0

Created with TradeStation by Omega Research ® 199

this otherwise, though I hadn't heard anything. Then NASDAQ halted it because of news pending, and it didn't trade for an hour as the market waited for the news to be announced. Finally, at 3:40, news was released that a judge had thrown out a patent infringement case that Rambus had filed against its competitor Infineon Technologies AG, and it resumed trading.

Immediately after it resumed trading, it was down another buck fifty. I placed a market order to get out because more times than not after a news item is known, things have a tendency to trade opposite to their initial reaction; besides, I had made a nice profit in it. When a stock drops before an announcement and then opens up even lower, it is common to see people take profits and for it to trade back up. I placed my order to get out immediately after it opened, and apparently I wasn't the only one to do so, as it ran up so fast that I got filled about a dollar higher from where I placed my order. Then, sure enough, it went right back down after I got out. I did the right thing by getting out because it was rallying and I thought it would shake off the bad news and go right back up to retrace the drop.

Looking at this example, one can see that some people had to know in advance about the pending news release: They started to unload and/or short the stock way before it was halted and an hour and half before any news came out. By the time the public got the information, it already had dropped $3. So how do some traders have a head up on the news? Why were some people able to react before the trading was halted? The reason could be that institutions have direct access to important personnel and information in the companies they make a market for. If a major court decision is about to come out, they may be on the phone all day with someone at the company. Whether this is the reason or not, what's important is that by the time the general public got hold of it, the big players already had acted on it. It fell 20 percent on the day, but most of that came before the news was made public. Unless one knew beforehand, there was no way to act on it.

BUY THE RUMOR AND SELL THE FACT

The problem with news-related trading is that most people don't know what to do with it. I've seen too many traders hear some news, see a quick burst in price, and jump in, not wanting to miss the boat. The next thing they realize is that they just bought the high of the market as they watch it dip hard. If you've been around trading a little while, you've probably heard the expression "Buy the rumor, sell the fact." The most effective traders respond by watching price action and then fading a news story. They know that the news has already been factored into the current price of the market, and once the market gets what it was expecting, the anticipation is gone. With the anticipation gone, people take their profits and get out, causing the market to reverse. It's before the news comes out that the market makes its move; afterward there is no advantage anymore, and so the smart money gets out.

IF IT SHOULD GO LOWER BUT DOESN'T, IT'S GOING HIGHER

The news doesn't really matter. What is important is the other traders' aggregate position and what they are expecting when the news comes out. As soon as news comes out, the smart traders look to see how the market reacts and what the other traders are doing.

A rule of thumb for when news comes out that should affect a stock or commodity is that if it is bad news and the market shakes it off and rallies, this is a bullish reaction to the news, so buy it. It probably means that the market has already discounted the news. On the flip side, if good news comes out and your stock or commodity fails to rally, the high probability trade is to short it. It's more important to see how the market reacts to the news than to know what the news is. Experienced traders look to see what happens after a news item comes out, and then they react accordingly. They hope to see a market fail to react the way it should have and then fade the news. The more anticipated the news is to be positive or negative, the more likely it is that it will be potentially disastrous to trade on the side of the report. If the market was expecting good news, it may have run up accordingly before getting it so that the market is priced with the news taken into consideration. Many times the reason for the market to end its move when news comes out is that traders were already long in anticipation of news, a rate cut, or a heat wave, and then the event or news does come out as expected. Once it comes out, the market may fail to continue because it may be saturated with longs and there is no one left to buy. As the final suckers rush into the market, the smart money sees it as an opportunity to take profits. When the news does make the market react the way it should, the best thing to do is to wait for it to settle and then get in on the right side. If you jump into it early, there is always a good chance that you may get caught in a retracement or spike.

The same morning that the RMBS situation happened, the monthly unemployment numbers were released, and it was the biggest jump in new claims in a decade. The market reacted to this bad news by opening a lot lower; the Dow was quickly down over 100 points, and the S&Ps about 20 (Chart 4–3). But before long the market wouldn't go much lower, and by 10 a.m. it started to rally. By the end of the day the Dow was up 148, and the S&Ps were up 18. This was a great example of how to trade news. The news was bad and the market couldn't go lower, and so buying was the right play. Looking at the chart, you can see how the S&Ps opened down 17 points and then went down a little more. After the first half hour, however, it could not break lower and began to rally. Whenever news comes out that causes an extreme move in a market's open, if it cannot follow through, the best way to trade that market is to fade the news. As you can see, the market tried to go lower but failed and then broke highs. This meant that the market overreacted to the news but then took it in stride and decided it wasn't important enough to make the market go down. At that point people started covering their shorts and going long. It also was the case in this situation that bad news was good news as people started thinking that the weakening economy would encourage the Federal Reserve to cut interest rates again.

IS IT GOOD NEWS OR BAD NEWS?

What defines good news is often subjective and hard to determine because good economic news can be counterproductive to getting the Fed to cut rates. It seems that the Fed's reaction to every piece of news that comes out is more important than the news. Traders need to be alert to a situation such as the bad unemployment data described above. Yes, it's bad for the economy, but if the economy gets worse, the Fed may cut rates, or at least not raise them, and that will make the market rally. There are also many times when a company announces that it will be laying off people. This sounds like bad news for the company, but many see it as a cost-cutting method and thus a way for the company to improve its bottom line down the road. This type of news can make a stock rally even though one would perceive it as negative news.

THE MARKET WILL DO WHAT IT WANTS TO DO

Many times unexpected news may come out that is the opposite of what the market has been doing. Initially the response is a rapid, hard move the other way, but once traders take a deep breath and reevaluate, the market normally will continue in its set trend. I can't count how many times a downtrending stock reports better than expected earnings, has a quick bounce, and then spirals back downward. The news isn't important here; it is more important to see how the market reacts to it after the initial move. Fundamentals should be believed only as long as the technical signals agree. Too many times a trader will stick with a news story and not let go no matter what the market ends up doing. Opinions mean nothing to the market; the market goes where it wants to, not where you think it should go. If the market shakes off news and continues its trend, a trader should ignore the news and follow the market.

UNEXPECTED VERSUS EXPECTED NEWS EVENTS

Look at how the market reacted to the unexpected rate cut by the Fed on January 3, 2001 (Chart 4–4). After being in a huge downtrend for weeks, the market exploded upon hearing this unexpectedly good news. I happened to have had one of my worst days ever that day, as I had gotten heavily short 30 minutes before the cut and ended up losing $5 to $10 per share on stocks I had just shorted. The unexpected cut drove the market straight up, and the S&Ps rallied some 70 points by the end of the day. Yet the facts were that the economy was weak, and by cutting rates unexpectedly, the Fed acknowledged this. The next few days, as people came to their senses and the initial euphoria of the cut wore off, the market backed off and began to continue the downtrend it had been in. It took a few more days for people to begin expecting the Fed to cut rates again at the next Open Market Committee meeting on January 31, and this caused the market to start drifting up in anticipation. On January 31, the Fed cut

CHART 4–4

Daily S&P 500: Unexpected and Expected Rate Cuts

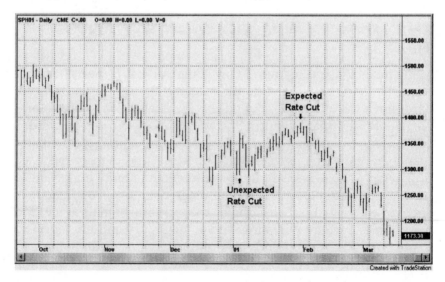

Created with TradeStation

rates again, but this time it was expected and the market didn't react with a pop. Instead, it immediately sold off, marking the top of the upwave that had been created soon after the initial cut. It's funny how the market reacted to the same news on two different occasions. The news was the same—the Fed cut the discount rate by 50 basis points—yet one time the market had an intraday explosion and the second time it failed miserably. Why? Because the second time it was expected that the Fed would make a cut after its meeting, and the market had rallied for weeks on that expectation. As soon as the market got what it wanted, there was nothing more to look forward to. In this case the smart money says thanks and gets out as it "buys the rumor and sells the news."

GETTING THE MOST OUT OF THE FUNDAMENTALS

Get the Whole Picture

If you are going to trade on the basis of news, do it right and get the whole picture, not just a piece of it. If you are buying soybeans because you heard about massive floods that were expected to kill crops and thus lift prices, don't forget that the Midwest is not the only place where beans are planted. How are crops in Argentina doing? What about Europe—can they take up the slack? What is worldwide demand? Are there are stockpiles? Sure, the weather will affect the crops, but don't expect the market to explode just because of that; everything else has to be in sync as well. If you plan to trade effectively using fundamental analysis, you need to look at the overall picture of any news involving the market. A lazy trader may get only a piece of the puzzle.

For example, when trading crude, one may want to know what the current productions levels are, where stockpiles stand and how they compare to previous months, what OPEC is doing (increasing production or cutting back), and the weather. All these things affect the overall picture of the market and can give you a general direction in which the market should be heading. For example, if stockpiles are high, production is expected to stay strong, and the winter is expected to be warm, you can assume that prices will keep going lower, and so you would want to trade the market from the short side.

In trading stocks, besides knowing everything about the company, you need to know what is going on with the market and the economy in general. How is the sector? How are retail sales? How is consumer confidence? Are interest rates going up or down? Has the gross domestic product been in an uptrend? What is the unemployment situation? All these things will help a trader, but one shouldn't dwell on every little news release that comes out. I just like to know these things so that I can have a general idea of what the stock and market should be doing.

Trading Scheduled News Releases

The most important thing a high probability trader wants to do before a scheduled news release is to be flat. The market can go either way when a report comes out, and by having a position you are adding too much risk to your trading. It's not worth trying to guess which way the market will go after a report comes out. When a trader starts doing this, he becomes a gambler, not a trader. This mostly applies to short-term traders, as I don't believe one report will make much difference in the price of a stock in the long term.

The way I like to trade a scheduled report is by looking at how the market reacts just a few minutes before the release of scheduled news. Whichever direction it's moving in is what the consensus is thinking. If the number is in line with expectations, this is the direction the market *should* move, and any surprises may cause it to go the other way. If the market cannot continue in the direction it had been moving and the news was as expected, the best thing to do is to fade it because it just failed to react according to what it should have done.

Many times the initial response after the announcement is a spike upward which quickly retraces, sometimes to keep going lower and sometimes to come back and rally. Part of high probability trading is not taking high-risk trades; jumping onboard too quickly before the direction is determined is dangerous. The best thing to do in these situations is to sit back, wait until the market picks a clear direction and the noise settles, and then jump onboard. I used to try to trade the initial spike, but I ended up getting hurt badly a few times, so now I wait. Once the market has picked its direction, there is still a lot of room to make money. Chart 4–5 shows a great example of how the market faded the news after a Fed cut. At 2:15 (Point A) on March 20, 2001, the Fed announced that it would cut rates again. Though this was good news for the market, it was anticipated that the Fed would do what it did. The initial response in the first 15 minutes was a drop followed by a quick strong move up, but not much higher than where the market had been before the news. Soon afterward, the run-up failed to continue and the market started coming off again. At this point you have to start thinking that there was good news and the market couldn't break higher even though it tried to. This would be the time to start thinking about shorting. Yes, a half hour has gone by, but now you have a clearer picture of what the market is doing. As soon as it breaks the lows it made right after the announcement (Point B), one should begin shorting. At that point the market has digested the news and picked its direction, and so one should forget the news and trade the market.

Don't Marry a Fundamental Opinion

One mistake that traders who focus too much on fundamentals can fall into is to get an opinion in their heads and stick with it even after the market turns. They may believe that the weather this year is the

CHART 4–5

1-Minute S&P 500: Trading the Market, Not the News

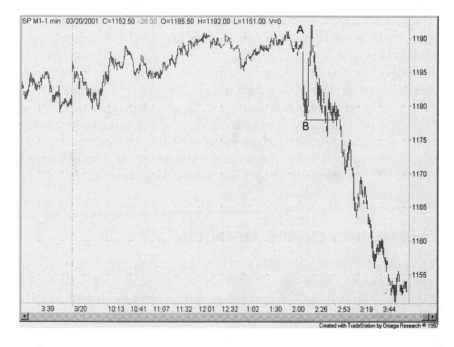

SP M1-1 min 03/20/2001 C=1152.50 -28.00 O=1185.50 H=1192.00 L=1151.00 V=0

Created with TradeStation by Omega Research ® 1997

best it has been in years for harvesting corn. Due to the ideal weather, there should be a banner crop and corn prices should drop. Yet after a few weeks the price fails to drop even though the temperature and rainfall have remained perfect. The stubborn traders will stay with this position and even add to it because they have become set in their opinions. They ignore the fact that the market says, "Hey, look, prices are going up. Why don't you buy it, moron?" They just keep looking at the forecasts and are convinced they are right, yet they ignore the fact that China has not had rain in 6 months and is buying all the grain in sight. When the market fails to do what it is supposed to do, there may be another factor driving it, and a trader can't be stuck with an opinion if he plans to succeed.

I've seen too many traders get hurt as they fight the market when they are clearly wrong, believing the market should go the other way because of some fundamental reason. This happens a lot in the stock market. Someone buys a stock at $188 because the company makes a chip that will revolutionize the world and then holds the stock until it reaches $4 because he still believes they have a great product and are a solid company; at some point one has to realize one is wrong and join the right side of the market.

When the NASDAQ market began to collapse in March 2000, many people refused to acknowledge it because they had the opinion that the economy was booming and that many of the tech and Internet companies they had invested in would keep going up nonstop. They failed to realize that these overvalued stocks would go back to being fairly priced when the economy slowed down. When the market started dropping and was clearly in a major downtrend, people stayed long because they were married to their opinion that their stocks would go higher. The drop in prices kept screaming that the market was no longer a strong market, but many people saw it as an opportunity to buy more at discount prices or hold on to their original positions because the market should have started to return to its strength. They were wrong and paid dearly for not changing their opinions.

CHANGING ONE'S OPINION

It's not easy to change an opinion based on fundamentals, which is why you must always get the whole picture and keep looking at the technicals driving the market. A chart won't lie to you: It tells you the market is going up, down, or sideways. If you are long a stock and the chart is not going higher or is pointing lower, whatever you thought would make it go up is not working anymore. Don't fight it. It doesn't pay; just get out and reevaluate. The method I use to change my opinion of the market when I'm starting to realize that I am wrong is to say to myself, "If I had no position on, which side would I like to be on?" Questioning myself makes it a little clearer that I should not be in that position anymore; the hard part is actually getting out of it.

LEARN TO BE OBJECTIVE

When it comes to being objective about a fundamental idea remember to not think with your position. Two people can hear the same news and look at it completely differently because of their positions. A typical example occurs when an economic number comes out that is good for the economy. Those who are long-biased will think, "Wow, the economy is doing great; this market will keep going up." Those who are short will look at it and think, "Great, the economy is getting too strong; the Fed will not cut interest rates again, so the market should sell off." The market can go either way in these situations. The market will tell you where it should go, and your opinion doesn't mean anything to the market. By focusing on the market and not on the fundamentals, one can be more objective and have a better grasp of what is going on.

BECOMING A BETTER TRADER

Becoming a better trader requires learning what to do with fundamental analysis and knowing how to trade the news. Start by getting a fundamental picture of the market. Whether you trade corn, pork bellies, Japanese yen, JP Morgan, or Microsoft, you should find out what is making it move in the direction it is moving. Look at the whole industry and any world events that may have an impact on your market or stock. If you can determine that corn is going higher because world production has been slow the last 2 years, you have a small advantage over many traders. You know that as long as the fundamentals don't change, you are better off trading the market from the long side.

Another way to improve your trading is to confirm your fundamental opinion by looking at charts. If the corn chart is going up, you know that the fundamentals are working, but if it is flat or going down, you need to question it. Maybe there is something else driving the market, but whatever the case, don't stay married to a trade if it is not confirmed in the charts. As a trader you must be willing to change your opinion often because the market never stays the same. Don't get opinionated in a trade. If it doesn't react the way you thought it would, get out and move on. A lot of traders fail because they hold on much too long if they believe the market has to move with the news.

As for breaking news and reports, don't forget that the market already may have discounted them in its price. Don't be surprised if once the news comes out, the market goes the other way as people "sell the facts." When you are trading on the basis of news, don't trade the news but trade the market's reaction to it. Jumping into a trade on the basis of a news-related event is not a high probability trade; it's more of a gamble than anything else. Instead, try to determine what should happen and then react according to what the market does. If it is good news and the market keeps going up, buy on a dip. If it is good news and the market doesn't go up, I normally would short aggressively. If news is due to come out, set up different scenarios in advance of what should happen; that way you will be prepared to react no matter what happens.

The Problems of Trading the News

1. Trying to predict market's response
2. Marrying a fundamental opinion
3. Losing objectiveness
4. Ignoring the market's trend
5. Getting caught in a spike
6. Never being the first to know
7. Trading discounted news
8. Taking a gamble

How to Increase Your Chances with Fundamental Analysis

1. Get the whole picture.
2. Use fundamentals to determine what is driving the market.
3. Complement it by using technical analysis.
4. Get a long-term idea of where the market is going.
5. If it should go up and doesn't, it's going lower.
6. Don't be afraid to fade the news.
7. Don't jump into a trade as soon as the news comes out.
8. Let the market digest the news.
9. Don't trade your opinion; trade the market.
10. Be able to change your opinion.
11. Buy the rumor, sell the fact.
12. Remember, bad news may be good for the market.
13. Don't gamble: Be flat before a report.

Helpful Questions to Ask Yourself

If I had no position, which side would I like to be on?
Which way should the market respond to this news?
Did I give the market enough time to digest the news?
Am I married to my opinion?

PART III

Technical Analysis

CHAPTER 5

Increasing Your Chances with Multiple Time Frames

The next few chapters aren't meant to be a full-depth, end-all discussion of technical analysis. They just discuss the indicators and patterns that I have found to work best for me in finding high probability trades. There are countless numbers of different indicators and patterns one could use, and since each person has a different trading style, it is best to get a full understanding of technical analysis before deciding what works best for you. Since I concentrate on only a few select areas of technical analysis, I'd recommend getting a good book on the subject and devouring it if you want to know more.

Though fundamental analysis can help one get a good idea of the direction in which the market should be going, it is hard to get an edge over other traders unless one has prior knowledge that something is happening. However, having proficiency in technical analysis can be a great asset to a trader and could supply the edge one needs. A technical analyst believes that a chart already discounts any effect news has on the market, and many traders ignore the news because of this. They know that if anything is important, it will be spelled out in the charts. They don't need the news to tell them that a stock should be going higher; they can see it for themselves. Whatever the news is, knowing how to read a chart will give a trader a clearer picture of what the market is doing. Even those who are sticklers for fundamental analysis can benefit by looking at charts not only to confirm the news but also to time their trades.

Looking at a chart, it is easy to see if prices are going up, down, or nowhere; what is difficult is trying to make heads or tails of indicators, price patterns, and what the market will do in the future. Five different people can look at the same chart and see five different things, making technical analysis a bit hard. Some indicators will tell you what has happened, while others will try to predict what will happen in the future. No matter what you look at, though, they all have one thing in common: They don't know tomorrow's price, and so they can never be 100 percent accurate in predicting the future. This is why different people will see different things when looking at them.

In the next few chapters I will go over a few types of trading strategies (trend following, breakout, reversal, and range-bound) based on technical analysis. Each requires looking at different things and using a different style of trading. In a trend-following situation one uses different indicators (or the same indicators differently) than one does in a range-bound market. Trendlines and moving averages, for example, are excellent trend-following indicators. In a range-bound market one can look more at oscillating indicators, such as stochastics and RSI, which can help pick turning points in the markets.

As you read these chapters, one thing to keep in mind is the importance of using volume when you are looking at what the market is doing. Volume is used to confirm price movement. When price moves with strong volume, the market is more likely to follow through, whether it is a reversal or a matter of following the trend. Volume shows the demand for the stock or commodity and determines the strength of the trend. If price moves up while volume increases, a trend is more likely to stay strong. When volume begins to wane, it could indicate that everybody who wants to be long already is. At that point there is no one left to participate in the buying, and so momentum may soon change.

Even though it is not an exact science, I believe the traders with the best working knowledge of technical analysis have an advantage over other traders. They are able to pick out the better trading opportunities and have a better sense of where to place stops. Many people can misuse technical analysis if they are not careful, and so I'll discuss both the proper and the not so proper way to use the different indicators I look at. For simplicity, I will not always give examples for the long side and the short side of the market. Just assume that for anything that works on the long side, the opposite will work on the short side. If I tend to talk more about going long and uptrends, it is not because I have a bias; it's just easier sometimes to describe things from one side of the market.

LOOKING AT MORE THAN ONE TIME FRAME

Some years back I went to visit a friend who was a seasoned oil trader at his office. He had always been a good trader, making money regularly first on and then off the floor. He primarily traded crude oil, and after crude closed at 3:10, he'd make a trade or two in the S&P futures during their last hour. Despite looking primarily only at one market at a time, he had an arsenal of computer monitors in front of him. He used CGQ charting service, and they provided him with four computer monitors. He had charts of crude oil with different time lengths on them. On one screen he had 2-, 5-, and 10-minute charts; another screen had 30- and 60-minute charts; the third had daily and weekly charts; and he used the last one for news and quotes. Not only that, he updated daily charts by hand and had a monthly chart going back to the contract's inception on his wall. I was quite impressed with his setup. By comparison, I had one monitor that was divided into four 5-minute charts, each looking at a different market. Who do you think had a better view and an advantage in trading crude?

I asked him which time frame he used to trade with, and he told me he used all of them. His trading strategy was to make a trade only when he got confirmation in all the different time frames. First of all, he would trade primarily in the direction of the overall trend, and he used the daily and weekly charts to get that trend. These two time frames gave him a clear picture of the overall direction and where the major support and resistance levels in the market were. Then he would narrow down his point of view by looking at the 30- and 60-minute charts. These were the time frames he used to decide what he wanted to do. He liked to see them trending or reversing and thought they gave a clearer picture of the market for the next several hours to a couple of days. Once he had determined what he wanted to do, he would monitor the 2- and 5-minute bar charts closely to time his entry. He would wait until they showed a stable place to enter where if he was wrong, the market wouldn't have room to hurt him much.

He explained that unless he thought the trade was a good trade on every chart, he wouldn't take it, and on the rare occasions when he did, it would be with a light number of contracts because the probability wasn't very good. When everything matched up, though, the probability of a trade working greatly improved. Watching his setup and the way he traded opened up my eyes to a higher level of trading, that of using multiple time frames.

SHORT-TERM VERSUS LONG-TERM PERSPECTIVES

When it comes to which time frames traders prefer to look at, traders are usually divided between long-term and short-term prospectives. A long-term trader may focus on daily, weekly, and monthly charts, while a shorter-term day trader may look at 1- and 5-minute bar charts. There is also an in-between ground where swing traders may hold positions for 2 or 3 days and mostly use 30- and 60-minute charts for their analyses. All these people can do quite well sticking to the time frames that work best for them, yet they should not narrow their views to just one time frame. Since each time frame has a different perspective on the market and traders can make money at each level, why not use them all to benefit your trading no matter what time frame you prefer?

Each trader has to pick the time horizon that best fits his style of trading. Traders prefer different time perspectives for many reasons. Some feel they can control risk better by getting in and out of trades quickly and focus on a shorter time frame. Some like to be in position longer term and are not concerned about the intraday ups and downs of the market. Some have only enough money to day trade commodities, not enough to cover a position overnight. Some don't feel comfortable taking a position overnight and so they exit their trades before the close. Others believe that momentum can carry a trade for a few days. Even among day traders, some will hold for just a few minutes, looking for a quick scalp, while others will hold for several hours. Some hate paying commissions and therefore hate to day trade nonstop; instead, they prefer to make one or two good trades and hold them for hours. Whatever the case, every trader has a different time horizon in which he feels comfortable trading.

Though the shorter time frames can get a trader in and out of the market quicker while identifying small market patterns, unfortunately, the overall picture can be missed if one is too narrowminded. Short-term traders may spend too much time looking at 1- and 5-minute charts, though moves in these time frames can be erratic and unpredictable. By looking at 60-minute charts, a short-term trader may be able to catch stronger, more stable moves and see things that are not apparent on a 5-minute chart. One can gain a lot by looking at daily and weekly charts because the patterns there are even more significant and can indicate where the real momentum of the market is. A trend on a 5-minute chart does not hold as much weight as one on a weekly chart does.

A CHART IS A CHART

One thing I want to stress is that a chart of the market is the same whether it's a 1-minute chart or a weekly chart. For the most part, if one didn't know what the numbers on the chart were, it would be hard to tell what time frame one was looking at. All charts pretty much have the same patterns and formations no matter what you are looking at, so once you get comfortable looking at a chart in one time frame, you should have no problem looking at any other chart. Take a look at Charts 5–1 through 5–4. Despite that they have different time lengths, there is nothing that really distinguishes one from the other.

MULTIPLE TIME FRAMES: WIDENING PERSPECTIVES

My trading improved dramatically when I began to expand my view of the market by looking at multiple time frames to make trading decisions. When I first started, I was a very short-term trader and looked only at 5-minute charts. I used daily charts to get ideas from, but when it came to entering trades, it was always just the 5-minute time frame I looked at. I never looked at anything else because I rationalized that since I was looking for quick short moves, I did not have to bother with 10-, 30-, or 60-minute charts. The daily charts gave me the big picture, and I thought weekly charts were overkill for my purposes. I found 1-minute charts to be too hard to read, as they were choppy and didn't have enough data in them to give me a clear picture, so I preferred to stay within the 5-minute time frame.

Eventually I realized that doing this was equivalent to playing golf with only a wood and a putter. In order to succeed one needs to have a club for every distance and situation. Traders also should have a wider tool selection than just the basics at their disposal. I've known too many people who were comfortable on just one or two time levels and never considered looking at anything else. By expanding their point of view they would be able to see the market much more clearly. Not only would they see it better, they would be to able start timing their entry and exit points better.

By looking at the higher time frames one can see what the direction of the major trend is and where the support and resistance levels are. By knowing the major trend, one should have an idea of what direction to be taking trades in. If a trend on the daily and weekly chart is up, long trades are the higher probability trades. Once that criterion is established, shorter time frames should be used to find and time trades in that direction. The 60-minute time frame is extremely important because I think it defines the intermediate (2 to 5 days) move. By trading in its direction, I believe you will get the most momentum out of a trade, as long as there is no support or resistance level or it is not in overbought or oversold territory. (As I go through the technical analysis section of the book, I will expand on the concept of using different indicators and systems and combining them with multiple time frames.) Then, when you are ready to make a trade, you want to use the smaller time frames. It is much easier to wait for an opportune moment to enter a trade and control risk by using the 1-, 5-, and 10-minute charts. If you know you want to go long, why not look at the waves on the shorter charts to make sure that you are not buying into a run-up or that you waited until the market finished retracing? In either case you will lose much less if you are wrong while increasing the chances of the trade working. This multiple time frame process applies to all traders, from scalpers to those who hold for weeks. By getting a full all-around picture one can find, time, and monitor trades better.

GETTING THE BIG PICTURE

Sometimes if you are looking at a 5-minute chart, a down move may look great and you will be tempted to short it at every opportunity. When you begin to expand your outlook, however, and look at the 60-minute or daily charts, you may see something completely different. What you thought might be a good short trade may just be a little dip in a strong market that you would not have noticed unless you looked at the longer time frames.

Chart 5–1, a 5-minute chart of Intel, shows a good example of this. Between 11/08/01 and 11/12/01 Intel had a decent sell-off that started with a failed rally on the morning of 11/8. On the next day it came off a little, but not much. But on 11/12 it opened lower and then sold off after a failed quick rally, making for what seemed like a good shorting opportunity, especially around Point C. But if one had shorted it on the morning of 11/12, one would not have made a high probability trade, though one could never tell by looking at the 5-minute chart. Had a trader taken the time to look at daily (Chart 5–2) and 60-minute (Chart 5–3) charts, he would have seen that shorting was not a wise decision. These are the time frames that tell what the real trend is and in what direction traders should be looking to get involved. The daily chart shows that Intel was clearly uptrending and that the last few days had been nothing more than a normal dip. If you looked at the stochastic indicator at Point C on the 60-minute chart, it looked like it was becoming oversold. At this point you would not have wanted to buy yet, because short-term momentum was still down, but you should at

CHART 5–1

5-Minute Intel: The Little Picture

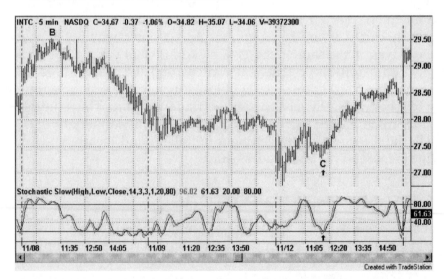

Created with TradeStation

CHART 5-2

Daily Intel: The Big Picture

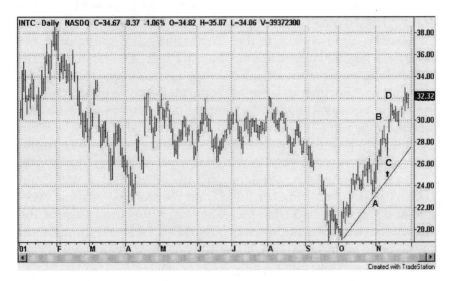

CHART 5-3

60-Minute Intel: The Monitoring Time Frame

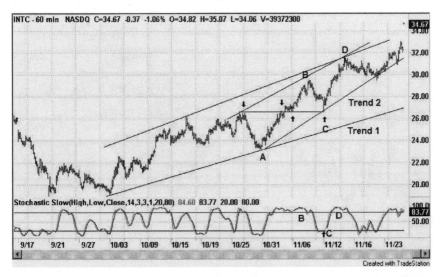

least have known that you didn't want to be short because the longer-term momentum was strong. You can also notice by looking at Chart 5–3 that at the current price the market had seen both support and resistance several times over the last few weeks, and so there was a good chance of the drop stalling and going back up. When you get the larger picture, you can easily see that going short had a low probability of succeeding because the market was uptrending. Shorting an uptrend is normally not a good trade. In these situations waiting until a long signal is given will result in a higher probability trade. Once you can see that the stock is not moving any lower and you can use 10- and 30-minute charts to confirm that, you can start looking for a place to buy. Going back to the 5-minute chart, I'd look to buy at around Point C on 11/12/01. The reasoning for this is that the stochastics were oversold and the stock had tried breaking lower but couldn't, plus the market had support, as shown on Chart 5–3. The next thing I'd do would be to go to Chart 5–4, a 1-minute chart, to really look for an entry point. I would enter a long trade when it either hit the trendline or broke the congestion area in the gray circle. Both happened within minutes, and so depending on how bad the slippage was, is

CHART 5–4

1-Minute Intel: Timing the Trade

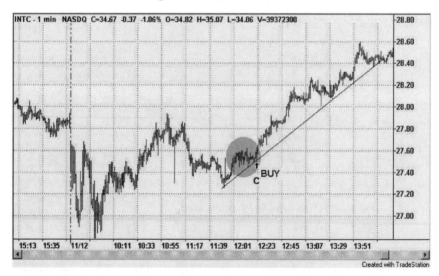

INTC - 1 min   NASDQ C=34.67 -0.37 -1.06% O=34.82 H=35.07 L=34.06 V=39372300

Created with TradeStation

where you would have gotten filled. Once you are in the trade you can get out with a quick profit almost immediately if that is your style. If you are comfortable with holding trades longer, you could revert back to the 60-minute time frame and maybe hold until Point D, where it hits the channel line.

WHEN TRADING A STOCK, LOOK AT THE GENERAL BIG PICTURE OF THE MARKET

Another way to get the big picture when trading stocks is to use a mix of the overall market, the sector, and the stock. One can use daily and 60-minute S&P 500 charts to get the overall direction of the market and then do the same for the sector to decide which direction to trade in. After making this assessment, one can use a 5-minute chart of individual stocks to time trades. By keeping track of the sector and S&P futures instead of each individual stock, you will get a good idea of what the market is doing and the stocks should follow. This is a good strategy for those who like to trade different stocks in the same sectors. It's still important to know that the direction of a stock follows the market; otherwise, you may be trading against the trend of the stock, which is not a great idea.

MONITORING THE TRADE: LOCATING SUPPORT, RESISTANCE, AND STOPS

After a trade is made, no matter how long a trader intends to hold the position, he needs to monitor it. This is best done on levels higher than those in which he normally trades. The reason for this is that one can see moves much more clearly when one has a longer perspective. Support and resistance levels become much more apparent as one gets farther from the current time period. The smaller the time frame is, the harder it is to judge where a good exit point is. A person who is concentrating only on a short time frame will miss things that are obvious to those who are looking more carefully. Since I like looking at 5-minute charts to enter trades, I prefer 60-minute charts to monitor my trades because this is the next major higher time frame. A scalper may prefer 10- or 30-minute charts if he is holding for only a few ticks. A longer-term trader may have to use a weekly chart to see where the levels are in his trades.

Look at Chart 5–3 again and you can see that below Point A would be a great place to put a stop if you had gotten long at Point C. You also could have placed a stop below the trendlines, Trend 1 or Trend 2. You may want to add to the long if Point B gets broken and then use Point C for a good stop. These are areas that are not really apparent if you see them on a 5-minute chart; though they can be seen on the daily charts, the picture is a bit clearer on the 60-minute chart. The 60-minute chart also makes it easier to see when the market may be stalling. You can see that at Points B and D the market is moving too far away from its trendline and has become overextended as it nears the top of the channel. The stochastics indicator also can alert you that it is in overbought territory and is beginning to turn at Points B and D. This makes it a good time to exit the trade because there is a chance the trend may be stalling, especially at Point D, where two channel tops coincide. If you are looking too far up in time frames, it will take too long to notice that the tide may be changing and profits may slip away before you get a good exit sign.

As far as stops go, once nearby support or resistance levels have been broken and you are still in the trade, look at the next higher major time frame to get a more significant support or resistance level. The farther out you go, the better the stop will be but the more it will cost you if it is hit.

TRADING AROUND THE TIME FRAME THAT BEST SUITS ONE'S STYLE

Since few traders have the same style and will hold trades for different lengths of time, there is no perfect set of time frames that works for everyone. As a rule of thumb, I'd say that the monitoring time frame should be about 5 to 12 times higher than the one you are most comfortable looking at. When I'm day trading, I tend to look mostly at 5-minute charts, in which case I'll use 60 minutes as my basis to make and monitor trades. I consider 60 minutes to represent the intermediate term and to be the middle ground between long- and short-term trading. I'll look even higher to make sure it's in the right overall direction and then go down to the shorter periods to time entries. After a trade is made, I'll use the 60-minute time frame to monitor the trade and to get stop and target levels, but I still look at the 5-minute time frame to get price action and enter and exit the trade. If I'm looking to hold trades for a longer period of time, I use the 60-minute frame as my main time frame and the daily as my monitoring frame. Even if I hold something for days, I'll still look at the 5-minute bar chart when it comes time to make or exit the trade itself.

For an active day trader who is scalping and making quick trades that last only a few minutes, the best trades are still those which are in the direction of the 60-minute and daily time frames. A scalper will want to use a smaller set of time frames in general but should know what the major trends are. Instead of using daily and 60-minute charts for support and resistance and to place stops, he can use a 10-minute time frame to monitor trades. The 10-minute time frame can become the critical time frame to trade around, and the 1-, 2-, or 3-minute frames can be used to time trades. I don't enjoy trading in this short a term, but many people have found it quite profitable to do so.

THE BENEFITS OF INCREASING TIME HORIZONS

By increasing your time horizon you can add a few advantages to your trading. Besides getting a clearer picture of the market, you can learn to hold on to winners longer and reduce the number of trades made.

Holding On to Winners Longer

Everybody has heard that the key to making money is to cut losers and hold winners, yet many people have a tendency to get out of good trades too quickly. They get too excited about a profit, don't want to lose anything, or are not looking at the market from the right perspective. By looking at longer time frames one will uncover aspects of the market that are not apparent in another time frame. A trader may see that a market has more room to move and that getting out too soon may mean missing a nice opportunity. If a trader keeps looking at very small time frames, he will be shaken out of the market too often when in reality he shouldn't be. The best way to prevent this is by increasing the time frame used and thus letting good trades grow.

Higher Time Frames Will Help You Stop Overtrading

Some people believe that by using shorter time frames they are reducing risk because they can exit bad positions more quickly. While this may be true, they not only exit winners much too soon, they pile up commissions in the process. If one is looking at 1- and 5-minute charts to make trades, one obviously will get more signals to trade with. Every little blip on the chart may make a trader get in and out of trades, because on a small time frame these little moves may seem important, although in reality they are not. If you take a simple moving average crossover system and use it on a 5-minute chart, you may get five signals a day. If you use it on a 60-minute chart, you may get only three signals a week, and if you look at a daily chart, you may get a signal every other week. When I started basing and monitoring trades on 60-minute charts, the number of trades I made dropped dramatically simply because I got fewer trading signals. Instead of trading 20 times a day, I started holding good trades for a few days. I stopped getting whipsawed and reduced my total commission and slippage costs by hundreds of dollars every day, so making a net profit became much easier.

CONFIRM TRADES BY USING THE SAME INDICATOR OR SYSTEM ON DIFFERENT TIME FRAMES

Something that a trader can do to increase the probability of a trade working is to have a system that generates signals and then use it on more than one time frame. Once he gets a buy signal in the longer time frame (60-minute, daily, or weekly), a trader can use that as a condition to enter orders in a shorter time frame if he gets a signal generated from the same system. If one were looking at a simple moving average crossover system as in Charts 5–5 and 5–6, one would get a buy signal on the 60-minute chart when the moving averages crossed to the upside (Point A) on 11/02/01. This would give the trader the go-ahead to start making short-term trades in the long direction only. Once he applies the moving averages crossover system to the 5-minute chart, Chart 5–6, the trader can buy every time he gets a long signal. When the averages cross back down on the 5-minute chart, he can use the crossover as an exit point (x), not a place to go short. Once he is out, he can just wait for the next

CHART 5−5

60-Minute Microsoft: The Go-Ahead Signal

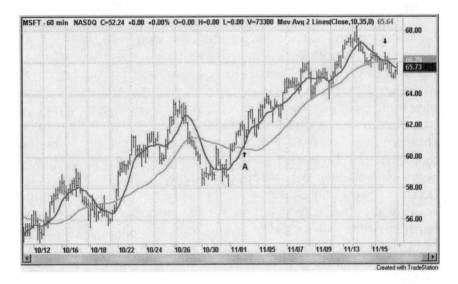

CHART 5−6

5-Minute Microsoft: Trading in the Right Direction

upward crossing on the 5-minute chart to buy again. In this situation one would only be buying for about 2 weeks; short trades wouldn't be taken until the moving averages on Chart 5–5 turned lower.

Trading in this style makes for high probability trading because once you already have a buy condition in the higher time frame and get confirmation in a shorter time frame, momentum is working in your favor. Signals from a longer-term chart are much more significant than are those on shorter-term charts, as they provide momentum for the shorter time frames. The shorter-term signals that are in the direction of the longer-term signals tend to be stronger than are the countersignals. When you trade with the momentum of the market, as opposed to fighting it, you become a better trader. When you get opposite signals, it is a no-trade situation as in effect they cancel each other out. Instead you would just wait for the market to give you a better opportunity. There is no harm in sitting out for a day or two until something good comes along. Remember that about half the time you would be losing anyway, so why not try to cut out as many weak trading situations as possible?

You don't have to use the same system either. You can have one system that alerts you that it is okay to trade in one direction and then use a completely different system in a shorter time frame but take trades only in the direction of the longer-term system.

SCALING INTO TRADES IN DIFFERENT TIME FRAMES

If you trade multiple contracts, one thing you can do is put on a portion of your normal position when you get a signal in a shorter time frame. If it is working and you get a signal in the next time frame, add to it; if you later get another signal in an even higher time frame, add to it again. By doing this you can build into a position and get onboard early to catch a larger part of the move. If the trade doesn't work, you lose only a portion of what you normally would risk, and when the time comes when everything is working in sync, you will have a larger position working for you. This works great for breakout systems. Since the market will start to break out from the smallest time frame first and work up to the longer ones, it may take a few days to see a breakout on a longer-term chart. You can catch a piece of the move early by taking a small trade when you first see it on a

5-minute chart and add as it becomes more apparent. If you are wrong, you won't lose that much.

LEARN HOW A MARKET BEHAVES IN DIFFERENT TIME FRAMES

One thing a trader should do is get to know the behavior and characteristics of a stock or market he trades, in its different time frames. I know there are some stocks that tend to run for 3 to 5 days, closing on their highs when they do. After a run-up they come off for 1 or 2 days before continuing back on their trends. Intraday, they have moves that last about 45 minutes with counterwaves lasting 15 minutes. When one is looking at 60-minute charts, they tend to follow through the next day. Some markets have a tendency to gap overnight more than others do. Some stocks will have huge spreads for no reason when the specialist feels like it, while others are tight all day. Every stock is different, but as a trader gets to know his markets better, he will see patterns over and over in each time frame that will help him to time trades.

I know there are some markets that may have great long-term charts but are too erratic and thinly traded for a trader to try to look at them in a very short time frame. Some markets can't be traded with a 5-minute chart, while some make for great trading. Cocoa, for instance, is a market I find too difficult to day trade because it is thin and the moves can appear to have no rhyme or reason at times. That hasn't stopped me from trading cocoa; I just do it on a longer time frame and give myself more leeway in terms of how much I will risk on it. In other markets, such as bonds and the S&Ps, I'll feel comfortable trading for very short term moves. They have incredible volume and are so active that one can get in and out without worrying that there will be nobody on the other side of the trade. It takes a while to get to know a market's behavior, but make it one of your goals to learn how they act and you will trade them better.

BECOMING A BETTER TRADER

Becoming a better trader means being able to look at the market from many viewpoints. Focusing on one time frame will narrow your view and opinion of the market. Therefore, it is important to get a bigger picture of the market. A successful trader is one who knows what the market is doing not just at the current moment but in all its time frames. This gives him a better picture of what the major trend is and where there is possible support and resistance and a place to put stops. When you get signals in multiple time frames, using the higher ones to get the green light to take a trade and the smaller ones to time a trade, you will increase your chances of success.

A short-term trader shouldn't make all his decisions by using 1- and 5-minute charts, and a position trader needs to look at more than just daily charts. Whether a day trader or position trader, one should always be looking at many different time frames to time, plot, and monitor trades. After a trade is put on, look at the higher time level to monitor it for support and resistance levels and to see where to place stops. Look for reversals or moves too far from the trendline and/or moving average. Use the higher level to help hold winning trades longer and cut down on overtrading.

I find it best to use at least four time frames for day trading: the daily or weekly to get an overall picture of the trend, the 60-minute to keep track of the market, and then the 1- and 5-minute for entry and exit timing. No matter what technical indicators or systems one uses, trades should look compelling in every time frame. If you have a trade that is working on a small time frame and you get a signal on a longer time frame as well, this is a good place to add the trade. Overall, the more of the market you can see, the better you will be at trading it, as you will get a clearer picture.

The Disadvantages of Not Using Multiple Time Frames

1. Seeing just a piece of the puzzle
2. Having no real idea where significant market levels are
3. Getting trapped in a pullback
4. Not knowing when the market is overextended
5. Trading against momentum
6. Having poor timing when entering trades
7. Overtrading
8. Not holding long enough
9. Getting shaken out too soon

High Probability Trading with Multiple Time Frames

1. Gain a better perspective on where the current market is.
2. Get more in tune with the market.
3. Get the overall picture of the market.
4. See the trend more clearly.
5. Time your trades more effectively.
6. Monitor trades with a higher time frame.
7. Look to see if the market is overextended.
8. Find better support and resistance levels.
9. Avoid overbought and oversold areas.
10. See profit levels more easily.
11. Cut back on trading by using higher time frames.
12. Hold on to winners longer.
13. Add to good trades at each time frame.
14. Trade only when all time frames are in sync.
15. Use the same system in different time frames to confirm trades.

Helpful Questions to Ask Yourself

Do I have a clear picture of the market in all its time frames?
Am I trading in the direction of the major trend?
Is the monitoring time frame overextended, overbought, or oversold?
How much room does it have to go?
Am I timing my entries?

CHAPTER 6

Trading with the Trend

More money probably is lost in trading by people fighting the trend and trying to pick tops and bottoms than for any other reason. Traders need to remember the old adage "The trend is your friend" and try to trade with it. Trades that have the highest probability of working are usually in the direction of the trend; fighting the trend means fighting the market's momentum. A trend is in place for a reason: The market participants as a whole believe that the market should be headed in that direction. When this is the case, it is wise to be on the side of the momentum, not against it. Unfortunately, people's psychology leads many to try to catch tops and bottoms throughout a trend, as they believe the market has already moved too much.

WHAT IS A TREND?

The basic definition of a trend is that in an uptrending market (downtrends are just the opposite) the market will move in a series of upwaves that make higher highs, with any downwaves considered countermoves and not dropping below previous lows. The upwaves will be longer than the countermoves and will move with more momentum. A characteristic of a trending market is that the closes are near the high of the bars in an uptrend and are near the low of the bars in a downtrend. The stronger the trend is, the closer to the extremes the closes will be.

Chart 6–1 shows a typical trending market. Here the S&P 500 index has been in a major downtrend for more than a year. You can see that the upwaves (countermoves) are much smaller than the drops and that the market has consistently made lower lows, while none of the major upwaves were able to break higher than a previous upwave.

THE TREND

Trend following is one of the most widely used aspects of technical analysis, as trading with the trend has always been thought of as the best way to make money trading. Unfortunately, markets don't always trend, and so when there is a clear trend, one should take advantage of it. Trading with the trend can lead to very profitable trading, because that is the path of least resistance. The first thing a trader needs to do is figure out what the trend is. Without knowing that one should never make a trade. Once a trend has been identified, always assume that the best trades are made in the direction of the prevailing trend until proved otherwise. To determine what the long-term trend is, use daily, weekly, and monthly charts. The longer a trend has been established, the better it is. For instance, in Chart 6–1 the uptrend that has been prevailing for the last 3 months of the chart

CHART 6–1

Daily S&P 500: A Trending Market

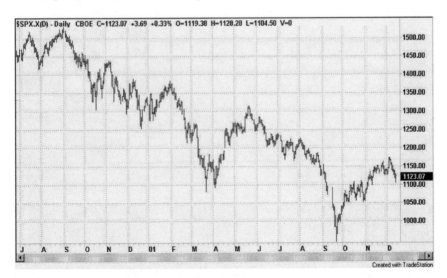

$SPX.X(D) - Daily   CBOE C=1123.07 +3.69 +0.33% O=1119.38 H=1128.28 L=1104.50 V=0

1500.00
1450.00
1400.00
1350.00
1300.00
1250.00
1200.00
1150.00
1123.07
1100.00
1050.00
1000.00

J   A   S   O   N   D   01   F   M   A   M   J   J   A   S   O   N   D

Created with TradeStation

is not nearly as strong as the major downtrend of the last 15 months. It will take more work for the market to break the longer major downtrend than it will for it to fall back into the downtrend. The uptrend for now is just a countertrend. Another thing to remember is that the shorter the time frame chart one looks at, the less meaningful a trend will be. A trend in a 5-minute chart can break and reverse much more quickly and easily than can one in a daily chart.

TRENDLINES

Although one can pretty much see a trend on a chart without the aid of a moving average or trendline, drawing a trendline helps give a better picture. A trendline is simply a line drawn on a chart that shows the direction of the market. The most accepted way to draw one is to connect the lows in an uptrend, as in Chart 6–2, or the highs in a downtrend. The longer the trendline is and the more times it touches the chart without being penetrated, the stronger and more reliable it is the next time the market tests it. Though you need only two points to make a trendline, if you have three or more it is much more significant. A trendline that is too steep is not very reliable and is easy to break; a trendline with a slope of 20 degrees will hold much better than will one with a slope of 60 degrees. The trendline in Chart 6–2 is moderately sloped and is one I would feel

CHART 6–2

60-Minute KLAC: Trendline Drawn at Market Lows

Created with TradeStation

comfortable trading from. The market touched this trendline four times in 4 months, and so I would consider it significant and continue to only buy until it gets broken. When a market is in a clear trend, it is not worth going against it; instead, one should wait for a retracement to get in on the right side.

A trendline acts as the equilibrium between buyers and sellers as they struggle with the balance between supply and demand in the market. The market goes up because there are more buyers than sellers and goes down because there are more sellers than buyers. In an uptrend (Chart 6–2) the trendline is the point where the buyers take over and the sellers back off. As the market gets farther away from the trendline, the buyers will begin to lighten up and some sellers may appear. This will cause the market to retreat back to the trendline where the buyers are eagerly waiting to get back in again, and the process starts again.

CHANNELS

After you have drawn in a trendline, the next thing to do is to look for a channel. Basically, a channel is formed by drawing a new line that is parallel to the trendline but connects to the highs in an uptrend. This new line will then form the top of the channel. Chart 6–3 is the same 60-minute chart shown in Chart 6–2 with the top channel line added to it.

CHART 6–3

60-Minute KLAC: Adding a Channel

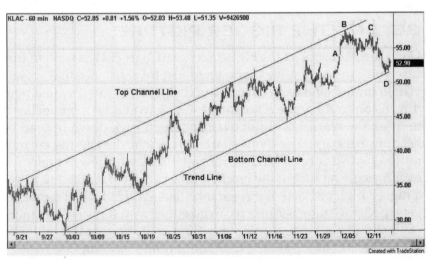

Created with TradeStation

In this uptrending channel, every time the market makes new highs, it stops at the resistance line created by the top of the channel and then begins to retrace back to the trendline. Channels can be used to know when the market is overextended and so that one can exit before a pullback or wait for the market to back off before getting in. If the market is near the top of the channel, one should never buy because the downside risk is greatest and the odds of its breaking out of the channel are low. If there is a clear break of the channel and it can be confirmed in a higher time frame that there is room for the market to keep going, one can consider getting in, as I'll discuss further in Chap. 8 on breakouts. Just be careful when chasing breakouts because the market tends to have many false intraday breakouts.

One thing that a channel can help identify is when a trend may be losing steam. If in Chart 6–4 the market fails to reach the upper line on an upwave, as at Point C, it may be a warning sign that the trend is weakening or will soon end. This does not mean you should go short, because unless proven otherwise, trading with the trend is the way to go. However, at the least you should be alert that the trend could be ending so that you can prepare to go short if the trend is broken. The highest probability trade will still be to wait for the market to pull back to the trendline before getting into a trade. This is a great trade because if it breaks the trendline, you will know immediately you are wrong, and so the risk is small. If the trendline holds, you can catch a good move as long as you can hold a winning trade.

GETTING THE BIGGER PICTURE

Don't forget to look at the bigger picture (Chart 6–4) as well. In this case you can see that the market had just hit resistance that wasn't visible on the 60-minute chart. The daily charts add a whole new dimension to the trade. Looking at it, one would be more inclined to think the market will roll over and head back down instead of heading back up. The daily chart shows that despite the current rally, KLAC has been kind of range-bound, with lower highs for over a year, and that in the recent 3-month run-up it failed to make a higher high or break the resistance line. At this level the market gets harder to trade because it can go either way. But since the most recent trend has been up and it is sitting on its up trendline at Point D, one should take the long trade until it fails at Point D.

CHART 6−4

Daily KLAC: The Bigger Picture

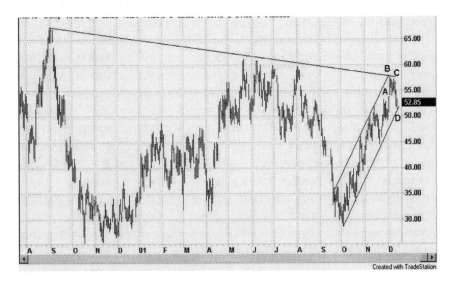

Created with TradeStation

BREAKING THE TRENDLINE

Though a clear break of a trendline is at the very least the time to exit a trade, it is not always a signal to reverse or enter a trade in the direction of the break. Sometimes when a trendline gets broken, it merely starts a newer, less steep trend or goes sideways for a while but not lower. At other times it is merely a quick move through the trendline, but comes right back after a bar or two. As the market approaches a trendline, your first thought should be that it will respect it, but always have a backup plan in case it doesn't. Whether it's a real or a false break, one should be prepared and have a scenario for either case before it happens.

DON'T CHASE THE MARKET

The Countermoves: Pullbacks and Bounces

Although the best trading opportunities are when one is trading in the direction of a major trend, don't jump into a trade just because you've determined what that direction is. You have to remember that the market will never go in one direction nonstop. Regardless of the time frames one is looking at, it will almost always have pullbacks or bounces that are against the trend. These events usually are associated with profit taking and overextensions of the market. They are a normal part of a trending market, and one should be aware of and be prepared for them. In each of the charts discussed above, every time the market got too far from the trendline, it would make its way back to the trendline. Sometimes the countermoves are strong and fast, and a trader who gets in too far away from the trendline may get caught in a big move against him yet still be right in the long term. This is why timing an entry is crucial. If you just jump into trades because the market is trending, you will be guilty of chasing the market. If your entry is poor, the safety net of the trendline can get too far away to get you out with a small loss. Just beyond the trendline is normally an ideal spot to place stops. The farther your entry point from it is, the more it will cost you if the market retraces back to and/or breaks the trendline.

RUSHING INTO TRADES

I know a guy who loses money month after month, and the reason is that he always rushes into trades without studying them carefully or waiting for any sort of retracement. He sees a stock break high on the day and puts an order in to buy, gets filled, and then for the next hour complains that he bought the high of the move. He always seems to buy a stock after it has had a $1.50 run-up in 10 minutes. He is scared to miss a big move, and so he rushes in and then wonders why he can't make money. The worst part is that he tends to exit these trades at the bottom of their retracement because he can't take the pain anymore and then watches them go to new highs, where he buys it again.

Time Frames

What is chasing to one person may not be to another, as everything is relevant to the time frame in which one normally trades. People who use different time frames will have different reasons for getting into trades. If you are a day trader and focus on 5-minute charts, you will be getting in at different places throughout the day because there is good support on a 5-minute chart, whereas a longer-term trader may be waiting for a major pullback to get in. A day trader still needs to know what the recent trend of the stock is and should then trade primarily from that direction.

For example, by looking at Chart 6–3 you know that you should be trading from the long side. Then, by looking at Chart 6–5, a 5-minute chart, you can make shorter individual trades that would not be considered chasing the market. If you looked at Chart 6–3 at around Point A, you might think that it was too late to get into the trade and that the chance of making money was over. But if you look at 12/04/01 and 12/05/01 on Chart 6–5, which corresponds to Point A on Chart 6–3, there are several places one could get in for short-term trades that look like safe trades. However, once you get to Point B, which corresponds to both the top of the channel on the 60-minute chart and the resistance line on the daily chart, you no longer want to be buying, because the odds now indicate that it may retrace a bit. This is a typical example of how using multiple time frames can help. Basically, you want to find the support and resistance levels in the longer time frame, and then isolate entry points in the shorter one.

DON'T FIGHT THE MARKET

Many traders get destroyed by fighting the trend, insisting that the market is due to reverse itself. They may try to catch short-term countermoves in hopes of making a few quick points, or they are

CHART 6–5

5-Minute KLAC: Timing Trades

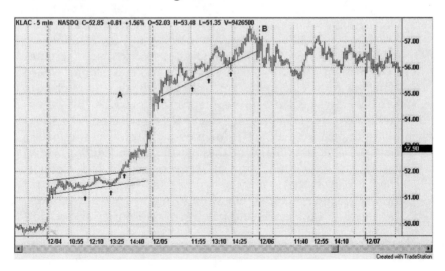

Created with TradeStation

always looking to catch tops and bottoms in hopes of capturing the big moves. All these traders end up trading against the longer-term trend and against the odds.

Some of my worst days were when I'd come in thinking I would only be shorting for the day because the market had been weak. On days like this I start out with a short and make money, and then the market looks like it will bounce for a little while. I start thinking, "I'll make a quick long trade for a few ticks and get right out." Then I end up buying and it doesn't work, and so I'm sitting long in a market that I wanted to be shorting. I don't get out as I'm waiting for the next "bounce" so that I can exit with a small loss. Meanwhile, I'm thinking, "Since I expect that bounce, let me double up," which eventually ends up costing me even more. I have learned that trading the countermoves is just not worth it: The risk/reward ratio is pitiful in these trades, and I'm better off sticking to the direction of the market. When you are wrong and are going against the trend, it can hurt because the trend can return with force. Someone who is going to countertrade has to be as nimble as a rabbit and be willing to take a small loss often. I find it better to sit out and wait for the countermove to finish than to try to make a few ticks on it.

NEVER TOO HIGH OR TOO LOW

I remember trading in the summer of 1998. That summer saw the lowest commodity prices in decades. I was buying 30-year lows in hogs and grains, thinking they could not go any lower, only to watch them go to 40-year lows. I was trying to pick a bottom in crude oil at $17, $16, $15, $14, $13, and $12 a barrel before giving up. The drop in price in stocks in 2000 is another example: When stocks went from $200 to $100, people thought they were cheap. When they dropped to $50, people bought more. At $20, they thought, "Wow, what a bargain." At $5 they gave it one last shot, thinking the market had gone down enough and was way overdone. One year later many of these stocks were trading below $5 per share with little hope of recovering. The big lesson I learned here was that a market is never too cheap or too dear. Trends will go on as long as they want to, not to a price one thinks is too cheap. A trader needs to pay attention to price action, not opinions.

TREND-FOLLOWING INDICATORS

Since the market trends only for a limited period of time, traders need to be able to tell when it does trend so that they can take advantage of trading with the trend. There are several trend-following indicators that can help a trader identify trends and their strength, so that he can determine which side of the market he should be on. Throughout the rest of this chapter I will describe what I believe to be the most important of these indicators and strategies.

KISS

I'm a big fan of KISS, not the band, —okay, maybe one or two of their songs— but the expression "Keep it simple, stupid." I think that by overcomplicating indicators and systems one can create more trouble than it's worth. Some of the best systems are the simplest, and some of the best traders use the smallest indicators with great success.

The indicators that I tend to use more than others in my trading are trendlines and channels, stochastics, moving averages, MACD, RSI, ADX, volume, volatility, and Elliott wave analysis. Though others may work well for different traders, these are the ones I prefer to use, and they are by no means the end-all of what a trader should use. Many different indicators tell you the same thing in a different way, and since I like to keep things simple, I stick to just a few.

MOVING AVERAGES

What They Do

Besides trendlines and channels, there are other indicators that can determine trends and their strength. Moving averages are probably one of the most common and easy-to-use indicators. Though you can use one, two, or three averages and simple or exponential moving averages, they basically tell you the same thing: what the market has been doing. If they are going up, the market has risen, and if they are going down, the market has fallen. It's that plain and simple. Moving averages, like any other indicator, do not have a crystal ball that will predict where prices will go; they are a lagging indicator. This lag may cause a trader to miss the beginning of a move, as the market will have already made its move when a signal is finally given. It will also identify a top or bottom after the fact. But it does indicate the direction of the trend and therefore gives you the direction from which you can make higher probability trades because prices usually tend to stay in the direction of the major trend. As long as the market stays above the moving average in an uptrend, the trend should be considered intact.

Moving averages work by replacing old prices with new prices. If the new bar is higher than the one it replaces, the moving average will go up; as long as this continues to happen, you will see a trend. When prices begin to stall or change direction, you will soon see it in the moving averages, as at Point X in Chart 6–6 of the daily S&P 500 chart, where prices stopped going down and the 10-period moving average turned upward soon afterward. It took the longer 35-period average a couple of more weeks to turn, but it did.

EXPONENTIAL MOVING AVERAGES

Though a simple moving average is more common, many people like to use an exponential one because it gives more weight to the latest price action. I have never found there to be much difference in using them compared to using regular moving averages. They do hug the data a little closer, allowing for earlier signals, but some of these tend to be false signals. Try them both and use the one you like better.

CHART 6–6

Daily SPX: Multiple Moving Averages

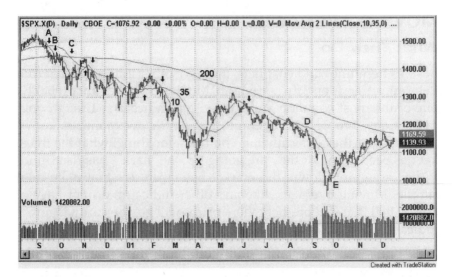

Created with TradeStation

Choosing Moving Average Periods

Different period moving averages will hug prices in different ways, and depending on what a trader wants, he will choose the moving average periods he prefers to look at. Smaller period moving averages will lead to a tighter followed trend but can whipsaw a trader around A longer one will give you fewer trades but will keep you in the market longer after the trend has changed. A longer period also will get you into a trade a bit later after a move starts. In general, though, the longer the average is, the better it defines a trend once it is established.

Although some moving averages work better with different stocks and commodities as well as in different time frames, I use the same one for all the markets I look at. If a trading strategy works, it should work across the board and not be optimized for each market. I like using 10- and 35-period averages on intraday charts and add the 200-period one on daily charts. They work for me but may not work for traders who hold for different lengths of time. A scalper or a more aggressive trader may want to use a shorter period average, such as a 3-, 5-, or 10-period average. By using shorter ones, a trader will trade more often, with smaller profits and losses and more commissions. I find it best to stay with slightly longer averages and trade less. The longer the average is, the less likely one is to get chopped up, as it holds a trend better.

Chart 6–6 shows how 10-, 35-, and 200-day averages show different things in the market. The 200-day average is almost like a trendline, indicating the major trend of the market and acting as resistance when the market gets close to it. The 200-period average is commonly used to determine the trend of the market; a break above it would mean that the trend of the market might have changed. I use it as a way to monitor the market's long-term direction. The 10- and 35-day averages are indicators of shorter-term trends, with the 10-day average riding the market much more closely and giving signals the most quickly, but the market can whipsaw around it during a choppy period. The 35-day average is smoother and acts more as a trendline for the medium term. When choosing the periods you like best, experiment with many different lengths until you find the ones that work best for you.

Multiple Moving Averages

Though some people may use only one moving average and take signals when the market is above or below it, most of the time traders will look at two or three moving averages at once. It is common to use the point where moving averages cross as the entry point in a system. Having more than one average not only alerts you to entry and exit points when they cross but can confirm the validity of a trend, as a market that rides above more than one moving average is stronger. If a trend is a strong one, prices will stay outside the band formed by the moving averages, as in the period between Point D and Point E on Chart 6–6. During this time the market fell hard and stayed below both the 10- and 35-period averages. Once the market trades back within the band (Point E), a trader has to be careful of the averages crossing the other way.

When looking at two moving averages such as the 10- and 35-period ones, you could take trades every time one line crossed another, as indicated by the arrows on Chart 6–6. If you are using three averages as in this chart, you could take a small position at Point A, when the 10-day average crosses the 35-day average, and then add to it when the market and the 10-day average cross the 200-day (Point B) and add some more when the 35-day average crosses below the 200-day average (Point C). This helps you build into a good position on the right side of the market. On any up arrows you can either lighten up or get out of the whole position. I wouldn't recommend going long because the main trend is down. Lightening up at the up arrows ensures that you are partially in the trade the whole way down and that you book some profits. If you do get out of your position, you can always get back in at the next crossover.

Typical Moving Average System

A simple moving average crossover system a day trader can use involves looking at three moving averages on a 5-minute chart, say, 10, 35, and 50, as in Chart 6–7. The largest one is a monitoring average, and one also can use a 60-minute or daily chart for this. I've indicated the entry and exit points that the following type of system would generate with arrows and x's. This is just an idea for a simple system and not one that I would recommend using on its own.

Long Scenario

Buy when the close is above the 50-period average and the 10-period average is above both the 35- and the 50-period averages. If the close is above the 50-period average but the 10-period average is below the 35-period average exit longs but do not go short.

Short Scenario

Sell when the close is below the 50-period average and the 10-period average is below both the 35- and the 50-period averages. If the close is below the 50-period average but the 10-period average is above the 35-period average, exit shorts but do not go long.

Many people just use two averages, but having a third will cut down on trades and force one to trade in the direction of the longer trend. The longer average helps you avoid some of the choppiness that you would experience in flat markets. This type of system works great in trending markets but not as well in sideways, choppy markets. In choppy markets, trend-following systems just do not work well, so anything you can do to avoid them will help.

CHART 6-7

5-Minute KLAC: Moving Average Crossover System

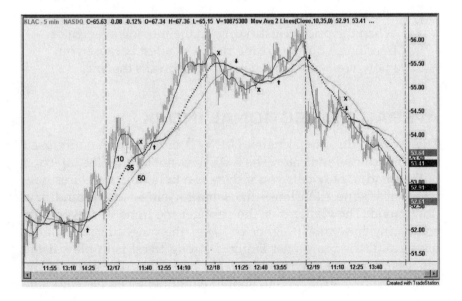

Created with TradeStation

Basic High Probability Rules for Using Moving Averages and Trendlines

- Assume that the main trendline or moving average will hold and not be broken. If it is strong, it should act as support and resistance when the market approaches it.
- The stronger the trend is, the more likely it is that price may not touch the line as people anticipating this may get involved more quickly in fear of missing the next wave.
- Trade only in the direction of the trend and the moving averages. When there is a crossover between two averages, trade only in the direction of the crossover.
- When the market is overextended and it's time to get out, it's best to not reverse the position but to merely exit and wait until the trendline and/or moving average is retested or broken.
- When the bands from both moving averages begin to narrow and converge, get ready for something to happen. This doesn't always imply that the trend will change or that one should cover, but there is a good chance of that happening, so be prepared to make a move.
- When the market is trending and you are looking for a place to get in, wait for it to retrace to one of the moving averages or trendlines.
- When the price is just riding on the moving average or trendline, your downside risk is smallest because you know you will be out as soon as it breaks the line.

AVERAGE DIRECTIONAL INDEX

The average directional index (ADX) is another commonly used trend-measuring indicator. The ADX does not tell you the direction of the trend; it only tells you if there is a trend and measures how strong it is. The ADX looks the same for either an uptrend or a downtrend. The higher it is, the stronger the trend is. It works by comparing how much higher or lower the ranges of subsequent days are. If the ranges get larger, a strong trend is in play; if the ranges are smaller, the trend is weak. When the ADX is rising, the trend is getting stronger and should continue; when the ADX line starts to weaken, it may indicate that the trend is ending. On its own, the ADX lags price action and is not a great indicator, and so one should not use it to trigger trades. Instead, it should be used as a way to get confirmation of whether the market is trending or choppy and how strong it is.

How to Use the ADX

The way to use the ADX indicator is to first determine the direction of the trend by looking at the chart, trendlines, or moving averages and then use the ADX to determine the strength of the trend. I find it more helpful on daily charts to get trading ideas than to use it on intraday charts, which can be choppy. Both the level and the direction the ADX is moving are important. The 30 level on the ADX is considered to be a strong indication of how well a trend is doing. When it is above 30 (Chart 6–8), you can consider the trend strong. If it is below a 20 level (Periods A and B in Chart 6–9), the momentum could be considered weak; during these periods the market was rather choppy and directionless. The level between 20 and 30 is considered neutral. The higher the level, the stronger the trend; even if it starts to point down but is above 30, it is still a momentum situation. When it is rising, one should trade only in the direction of the trend. Though it is always best to wait for a pullback, the higher the ADX is, the less likely it is that a full pullback will occur. By knowing what type of market environment you are in, you can use systems that trade one way when the ADX is below 20 and another way when it is above 30.

Finding a Trending Market

One thing that comes with experience is the ability to figure out which market environments lend themselves best to trading. A choppy, flat market is hard to trade and can lead to overtrading, while a trending market can be easier to trade. If a market is in a strong trend, you don't need to get in and out as often. Instead, you can hold a position until the trend ends, making for a nice potential win and saving on many transaction costs. Reasonable stop-loss points are easier to determine in a trending market, and so you avoid getting stopped when you shouldn't. If a trade is missed and the market is trending, you can avoid chasing it by waiting for the market to come back to the trendline before entering. By learning to use the ADX properly, you can help find a stock or commodity that is trending well. Since it is easier to make money when one is trading in a trend, if you can find the markets that are in good trends, your odds of making money increase. Chart 6–8 shows a daily chart of cotton, which has been in a strong downtrend for a year. Though this is obvious to even the most naive trader, the ADX helps confirm it. When the trend first developed from December to April, the ADX steadily rose and stayed above 30 the whole time, indicating a strong trend. From July to September, the downtrend eased a bit and the market went sideways; during that period the ADX dropped and leveled in the low 20s until it started to rise again, indicating that the downtrend was getting strong again. Once the ADX rose above 30, one should have been looking for places to get short.

When the ADX is below 20, you can consider the market to be choppy and range-bound, and a trending system will not work well, resulting in whipsaws. Look at the daily chart of KLAC, (Chart 6–9). During Periods A and B the market was sideways and choppy; at both of those times the ADX was below 20, which would help you see that there was no trend. If you want to trade

CHART 6–8

Daily Cotton: Confirming a Strong Trend

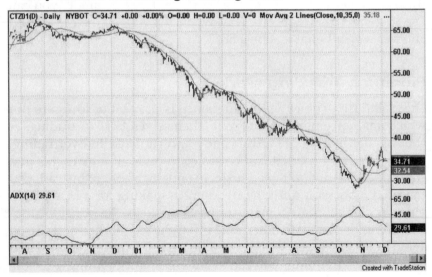

during these times, you may want to consider using oscillating indicators (Chap. 7), which work better in sideways markets. When the stock was trending as at areas C and D, the ADX was rising sharply during the downtrend and holding steady near 30 in the uptrend. Both are signs that a strong trend was in play. At Point E the ADX is strong but is beginning to peak; this may imply that the downtrend is losing strength. A declining ADX indicates that the trend is weakening and that a patient trader will be rewarded by not rushing into a trade. At this time you can either wait for a more opportune time to get in or look for a change in market direction. You also can look at the ADX line for tops, as at Point E. When the ADX peaks and is above 30, you can look for a possible retracement in the market.

Using the ADX to Take Profits

A good method for using the ADX is to judge when to take profits. If you are trading on the basis of a trend and have a low and/or declining ADX, profits should be taken more quickly because they may not last too long. Any time the ADX is below 20, one should

CHART 6-9

Daily KLAC: Using the ADX

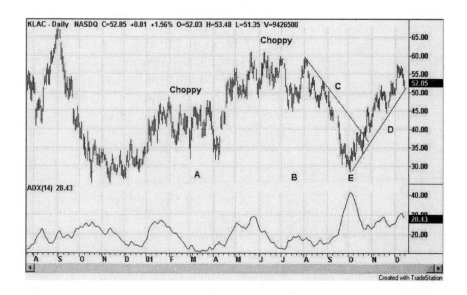

Created with TradeStation

take profits sooner. A low reading is an indication of a weak trend, and so you may not want to hold anything for the long term. If, however, the ADX is above 30 and rising, you may consider holding a position longer than normal instead of being tempted to take a quick profit. Since you always want to let profits ride in a strong trend, by looking at ADX you can get a heads-up to determine when the market is stronger. The stronger it is, the more you have to fight the temptation to get out. You also can use the ADX to see when it is peaking. If the ADX looks like it is strong but peaking, you may want to take off some of the position while holding the rest to see if the trend keeps going. If it dips below the 30 level, the market may become trendless and choppy, and you can start looking to get out instead of looking for the trend to continue.

RETRACEMENTS

Sometimes the markets will have a nice run for a few days in a row with each bar making higher highs and higher lows, and it looks like it can last forever. Don't be fooled. This pattern rarely lasts more than a few days as the market typically congests or retraces after a strong move. Many times after a big daily move that is larger than normal you will see the market pull back a little for the next day or two before continuing the move. This occurs mainly because many traders want to lock in profits or are waiting for a confirmation of the move before they get aggressive. This retracement or congestion is a place to get into the market; when it is running up is the time to wait. It doesn't matter if you are looking at 5-minute or weekly charts; markets almost always retrace after an extended run. Smart traders know that the best trading opportunities usually come after a retracement to a support area and are made in the direction of the original trend. Although many people try to trade the retracement itself, that is a low probability trade since it goes against the overall force of the market.

Even in the strongest moves there will be retracements. Look at the 5-minute chart of EBAY (Chart 6–10). Even though the stock had a nice $6 drop from Point A to Point D in 3 days, it wasn't all straight down. At one point (between Points A and C) it had a sharp bounce of almost $3, and there were a few other times when it jumped a dollar or so. After its 3-day drop to Point D, EBAY had a modest rally the next day as the sharp sell-off needed to take a breather. Yes, there was money to be made by buying the bounces, but the ensuing sell-offs were quite strong. If one was not nimble and did not have impeccable timing, one could easily have gotten hurt by trying to catch the bounces.

Measuring Retracements

So how far should the market retrace? The normal levels that traders look for are a third, a half, and two-thirds of the previous move. These numbers are very close to the ever so popular Fibonacci levels of 38.2 percent, 50 percent, and 61.8 percent. After an extended move, look for the market to test these levels on a pullback. Trends normally will resume if the market retraces to the 38.2 percent or one-third level and doesn't break through. These are levels everybody looks at, and probably the reason they work so well is that this is a self-fulfilling prophecy. As the market reaches these levels, traders are conditioned to get back in or the ones who are countertrading and riding the pullback know it's a good place to get out because a stall is very likely. The market is drawn to these levels like a magnet, so make sure not to place stops here; instead, place them a little farther away, such as at 35 to 40 percent,

CHART 6-10

5-Minute EBAY: Retracement Levels

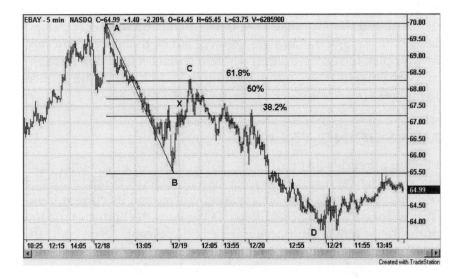

Created with TradeStation

because at that point the market probably is headed toward the 50 percent level. The levels at 61.8 percent or two-thirds are considered the breaking point of a trend. If these levels break, the major trend is over and then a new one is beginning. In Chart 6–10 you can see that after the first run-down from Point A to Point B, the market retraced up to the 38.2 percent level (Point X), where it stalled for a little while. Once it broke through there, it stopped dead in its tracks at the 61.8 percent level (Point C). If you study charts, you will see these retracement levels hold time after time, so get into the habit of knowing where they are.

Entering the Market on a Retracement

If you are using retracements as a place to short the market after a bounce, as a good trader should, you won't be the only one. You need to keep in mind that there may be stop and limit orders galore at and around these levels. Sometimes it may be best to try to get in a bit before these numbers are reached, as the market may move too fast for you to get in afterward. It is better to get in too early sometimes and risk a small pullback if you have a solid area of support to back you up than to chase it if you missed it.

For example, if you wanted to short EBAY at Point C and missed it, you may have to chase it down a dollar before getting filled. The better trade is to get in while the market is rallying and is near but hasn't hit the 61.8 percent retracement area yet. If you go short and then it rallies past the 67 percent to about 70 percent level you may get out and the loss will not be that much. You can't always pick the exact location where the market will stop retracing and continue its trend, but by waiting for some significant retracement you are taking much of the risk out of the trade.

MEASURING TRENDS

Finding a trend is just part of the work. Once you have one, figuring out how far it can go is even harder. Fibonacci ratios are also useful in predicting how far a market will extend its current trend. This is done by taking the difference between the high and the low of the major move; multiplying it by 1.382 percent, 1.5 percent, and 1.618 percent; and adding it to the low in an up move or subtracting it from the high in a down move. This is done during a retracement because then you can see what the high and the low of the previous move were. In the EBAY example, EBAY dropped $4.50 from Point A to Point B. If you multiplied that by 1.382 percent, 1.50 percent, and 1.618 percent and then subtracted those totals from the high of 70, you would get targets of 63.78, 63.25, and 62.72, respectively, for the next downwave. It stopped going down at 63.75 (Point D), right at the 1.382 percent level. Coincidence or what?

How to Tell When the Trend Is Ending

It is important to be able to tell when a trend is ending or is over; otherwise a trader may stay in a trade way past the time to get out. Besides the obvious situation of breaking a trendline, one needs to study a chart of the market. A market is considered to be in an uptrend as long as it stays above its previous low. Chart 6–11, a daily chart of sugar, shows that it stayed in an uptrend until Point C, where for the first time it made a lower low than the previous downwave, which was made at Point A. As a final confirmation, when it tried to rally afterward and failed at Point D to make a higher high than before (Point B), the trend was over.

One also can look at the strength of waves. The waves in the direction of the trend should be longer and stronger than those of

CHART 6 – 11

Daily Sugar: The End of the Trend

Created with TradeStation

the countertrend. Once the waves of the prevailing trend start to get smaller and the counterwaves start getting stronger, it may be a sign that the trend is ending. This is what happened in the sugar market, as the downwave between Point B and Point C was much larger than the next upwave between Point C and Point D.

Another indication that a trend is ending happens when a market has been trending and all of a sudden there is frenzied buying or selling into the direction of the trend on strong volume. These moves are normally the result of panic by the side that is wrong, or euphoria about getting into the trend, or adding to positions. You can see in Chart 6–11 how the volume picked up just as the market spiked at Point B. When this happens, it means everyone is rushing to get in and soon there may be no one left to buy, and so the market could easily sell off if there are no more buyers. Once the last buyer has finish buying, the move is over.

The other thing I look for to see if a trend is ending is how the moving averages react. In this case the 35-period average did not go any higher while the market kept moving up at Point B. This by itself could have been a sign that the trend was ending, but I look for a bubble in the moving averages. When the faster-moving average starts to get too far away from the slower-moving average, you will see a bubble, as at Point B. When this happens, the market will tend to snap back so that the distance between the averages falls back to a more modest level; sometimes that snap can cause the market to reverse directions, as it did here.

Admitting the Trend Has Ended

Figuring out when a trend has ended is only part of the problem traders face; admitting it has and doing something about it is another part. Too many people stay in a position long after it has changed directions for several reasons. My favorite is that I say "I'll get out on the next move." I know that I had a dollar per share profit on it a few minutes ago, and I don't want to take 60 cents now. I'm hoping it goes back up again so that I can get the dollar. I wait and eventually lose the 60 cents as well. Another reason is that people end up marrying a position, and even though they know they may be wrong, it is hard getting out of something you have convinced yourself will work. Whatever the situation, if you can tell the trend is over, get out. If it means not getting out at the top or even losing money, get out anyway and do so as soon as possible; being stubborn or hoping it will continue will only hurt you.

BECOMING A BETTER TRADER

Becoming a better trader means first and foremost trading with the overall trend of the market. This alone will increase your chances of success dramatically. Trading with the trend can make the difference between being a winning and losing trader. The moves in the direction of the trend tend to be stronger and last longer than the countermoves, and so it makes sense to trade mostly in the direction of the trend. A successful trader will trade primarily in the direction of the major trend, waiting for retracements to get in. You can find the major trend by using moving averages, trendlines, and channels on the longer-period time frames and then time the trade with the shorter time frames. Experiment with different-length moving averages until you find the ones that fit you best. The longer averages are more reliable, while the shorter ones give quicker signals but can cause a trader to get whipsawed.

Once you determine the trend, you need to know where in a trend the market is. This will prevent you from either chasing the market or getting involved prematurely before a retracement is over. Using different time frames will help you determine the overall picture so that you can see overextensions and places where a pullback may hit support. Never rush into a trade just because you know the trend; waiting for some sort of retracement will increase your chances. Look for retracements of 38.2 percent, 50 percent, and 61.8 percent or wait for the market to go back to its trendline or moving average before getting in. You can't always find the exact place where a market will stop retracing and resume the trend, but by waiting for some sort of retracement, you take some of the risk out of the trade. Use the ADX to figure out how strong a trend is and to help you decide how aggressive to be in taking profits. Also be alert for signs that a trend may be ending. Once you think it is over, *get out*. Forget about trying to catch that last little leg up; just get out before you give back a lot of the profit. Overall, by keeping in mind that the trend is your friend, you will be a better trader.

The Dangers of Not Using the Trend Properly

1. Making low probability trades
2. Being on the wrong side of the market's momentum
3. Chasing the market
4. Not knowing when the market is overextended
5. Looking for small profits against the trend
6. Forgetting that a moving average is a lagging indicator
7. Admitting that the trend has ended
8. Being misled by every break of a trendline
9. Concentrating on short-term trends, which are less meaningful and more easily broken
10. Waiting for retracements in strong trends that never occur
11. Getting caught in a retracement
12. Placing stops on the wrong side of retracement levels and areas
13. Forgetting that there is no such thing as too high or too low
14. Holding trades too long

High Probability Trading with the Trend

1. Know what the trend is.
2. The best trades are made in the direction of the trend.
3. Use multiple time frames to get the overall picture of the market.
4. Assume that the main trendline or moving average will hold.
5. The smaller the slope of the trendline is, the more reliable it is.
6. The longer the moving average is, the better it defines the trend.
7. Wait for the pullback.
8. Don't chase the market.
9. Don't fight the market.
10. Even in the strongest trends there should be some retracement.

11. The closer the market is to the trendline, the better the risk/reward ratio is.
12. Keep it simple.
13. Look for the end of a trend when the last wave doesn't reach the channel line or the previous move.
14. Use ADX to determine the strength of the trend.
15. Hold trades longer in a strong trend.
16. When getting out in anticipation of a retracement, do not reverse a position.
17. Wait for confirmation of a trendline breaking before reversing position.
18. Watch for bubbles between moving averages.
19. Know where the Fibonacci retracement levels are.
20. Place stops outside retracement levels.
21. Estimate how much the market can move.

Helpful Questions to Ask Yourself

Am I trading in the direction of the major trend?
If I get in here, will I be chasing?
Does the market look like it may stall?
How much has the market retraced?
How much will I risk if I get in here?
Where is the support area?
Is the monitoring time frame overextended?
How much room does it have to go?
Do I have a clear picture of the market in all its time frames?

CHAPTER 7

Using Oscillators

A funny thing about trading is that what one person sees as a strongly trending market another person sees as an overbought market that is ready to reverse. This is actually a good thing because as long as people have different perspectives on the market, there will be someone to buy when you want to sell. Knowing when the market is about to turn and when it will be sticking to its trend is a hard thing, but by knowing how to use momentum oscillators such as stochastics and the relative strength index (RSI) properly, one can gain an edge.

OSCILLATORS

I find oscillators to be an important part of my trading, but many people use oscillators without knowing how to use them correctly; others don't even look at them. When used properly, they can be an invaluable tool for a trader. As a piece of the trading puzzle oscillators can inform a trader a lot about market activity, including trend direction, the strength of a move, and potential reversals. Oscillators are helpful in timing entry and exit points and can show traders when they have overstayed their welcome. By using them correctly, one's chances of trading successfully will increase. Oscillators work great at picking tops and bottoms in choppy markets, and when combined with trend-following strategies in strong markets, they can help you time your entry into and exit out of the market. This will help a trader catch strong trades near the beginning of a move and get out of them before the tide turns. As you will see, there are many different ways to use oscillators, and each person has to find the method that best fits his style.

There are several different oscillators one can use, such as stochastics, the relative strength index (RSI), momentum, moving average convergence-divergence (MACD), and price oscillator, and they each have different features; however, they pretty much all look and work the same way. Chart 7–1 shows several different oscillators, and you can see that they all seem to move together. At Points A, B, C, and D they are all bottoming, and at Points E, F, and G they are peaking. Oscillators are indicators that, unlike the market, have a range in which they travel. As opposed to trends, trendlines, and moving averages, which travel with the market, when an oscillator hits the top of its range, it has nowhere else to go. A stock

CHART 7–1

60-Minute KLAC: Looking at Oscillators

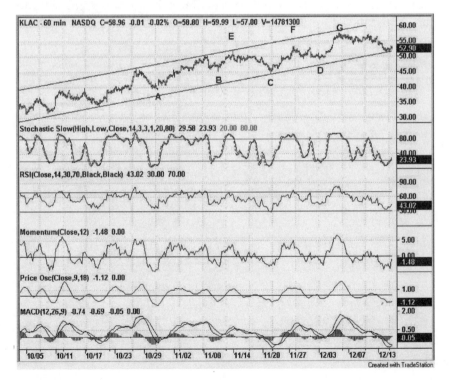

Created with TradeStation

can keep going higher forever, but an oscillator stops at its boundary. Once an oscillator hits its limits, it can either stay at the top or start coming off, but it can't go higher. In Chart 7–1 you can see how the indicators go back and forth between either the 0 to 100 range or around the zero line regardless of what the stock does.

WHAT THEY DO

Oscillators basically reflect the speed at which prices change. An oscillator works by comparing closing prices for any given time frame, using previous closing prices to determine whether the market is gaining or losing momentum. As a market gets stronger, prices tend to close near the top of the bar. When prices make successively higher and larger closes, an oscillator will rise. When prices stop going up as fast, stop making larger highs, and stop closing near the top of their range, an oscillator will begin to stall and show signs of the market being overbought. The market may still be going higher, but when the strength of the moves has slowed or remains constant, an oscillator begins to stabilize and fall. You can see how at Point A on Chart 7–2, the market was still

CHART 7–2

Daily EBAY: How Oscillators Aren't So Clear

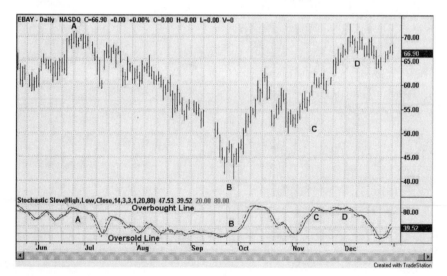

Created with TradeStation

strong but the highs stopped getting higher. This caused the stochastics to start turning down, which preceded the market getting
weaker. The market doesn't always come off when the oscillator
hits an extreme; instead, the oscillator can stay near its extreme
when the market is in an extended trend, as it was in the downtrend from August to October before Point B or between Point C
and Point D. During periods like these one needs to stick with the
trend and use the oscillator as a way to confirm a strong trend in
the market. This is easier said than done, because it is hard to figure out when the market will trend or reverse.

OSCILLATOR BASICS

Before getting into some of the individual oscillators, I want to
point out some of the basics for reading and using them. First of all,
an oscillator normally sits at the bottom of a chart and either ranges
between 0 and 100, or oscillates around a zero line. If it ranges
between 0 and 100, there will be an upper line and a lower line
which represent the overbought and oversold zones (Chart 7–2).
These lines usually are placed at 70 to 80 on the overbought side
and at 20 to 30 on the oversold side. Once the indicator has reached
these areas, it increases the odds that there will be a stall in the
trend or reversal. If it reaches these levels and turns, it is reflecting
price action and can confirm a directional change in the market,
whether a reversal or a slight pullback. When the indicator is in the
overbought-oversold area, a trader should start thinking about taking profits or scaling out of a piece of the position if he is already
in the market. If he is looking to get into the market, he should use
the overbought area as a place to wait for a retracement if he wants
to get long or as a place to get ready to make a trade from the short
side. Oscillators that revolve around a zero line may not have predetermined upper and lower limits; one has to look at a chart to
determine where they may be. With these indicators the zero line
plays an important role in determining when momentum changes
direction. Although different markets have different sets of parameters that work best and although each market may change over
time, I like to keep things simple and use the basic parameters for
all my markets and time frames. I normally use the canned lookback periods because this is what everyone else is looking at and I

don't want to be late to the party or get caught anticipating a move that doesn't happen. For example, when using stochastics, I normally stick with the 14, 3, 3 parameters that most software packages use. I don't need to get fancy and try to find the best parameter for every market. I'm happy with what everybody else is looking at. Besides, it is the concept of the oscillator that is important to me, not the actual parameter that works best. The next few sections describe some of my favorite oscillators.

SELF-FULFILLING PROPHECY

In my opinion the reason oscillators can work so accurately is that they represent a self-fulfilling prophecy. If traders everywhere are looking at the same indicator and it falls to an oversold level, people will start covering their shorts in anticipation of a bounce. As they do that, the market begins to rally just a bit, turning the oscillators up. Now more people see this "signal," and so they begin buying and the market starts to rally accordingly. If the signal is real, the market will continue to rally; if it is false, the market will go back to its prevailing direction.

Stochastics

My favorite indicator has to be stochastics. I have stochastics on every chart I use whether it's a 1-minute or a weekly chart. I use it because I like to see the momentum of the market, whether it is in overbought or oversold areas or still has room to move. I've been looking at it from my first days of trading, even before I really knew what it did or how it worked.

When I was first on the floor back in the late 1980s, there were a few computers scattered around the pits that all the traders shared. I went to look up a chart of crude on a CQG terminal and noticed that someone had left the stochastics indicator on. I liked the way it looked, and so I kept it on. At first I didn't really know how to use it correctly; I just liked the way it always seemed to turn at market tops and bottoms. But as I learned to use it, it grew to become an important part of my trading. When I ignore or misuse it, I find I get hurt by either chasing the market or getting out too quickly or at the worst possible time.

Although this is probably one of the most widely used indicators, most people who use it don't know what it does, how it is derived, or how to use it properly. They use it because it is so popular and seems to work great in predicting market tops and bottoms. Though there are both fast and slow stochastic indicators, the slow one is the one most generally used and the one I'll mention.

The slow stochastic indicator consists of two lines: the %D line and the %K line (dotted in my charts). The %K line measures where in relation to the last five periods the current close is; what you see plotted as %K is a three-period moving average of %K. The %D line is a three-period average of the smoothed %K line. Though there are two lines in the stochastics, the %D line is more important as it is smoother and more stable than the %K line.

SLOW STOCHASTICS FORMULA

$\%K = 100 \times (C - L(5)) / R(5)$

Then take the average of %K for last three periods to get a slowed version %K.

%D = 3-day moving average of %K

C = last close
L(5) = low of last five periods
R(5) = range of last five periods

The stochastic normally is plotted underneath a chart with values ranging from 0 to 100. Overbought and oversold areas typically range between 20 and 30 for oversold and 70 to 80 for overbought; 20 and 80 seem to be the standards. I typically use 25 and 75 as my overbought and oversold lines because that way it will include more signals.

The stochastic oscillator measures a market's most recent close relative to its price range over a specific period of time. The theory is that in an upward-trending market prices tend to close near their highs, and during a downward-trending market prices tend to close near their lows. As the market gains upward momentum, the closes will be at the top of the range and the indicator will be getting stronger. As the trend peaks, the indicator should be at its highest levels. Once an uptrend begins to slow, prices will tend to close farther away from the high of the bar, and this will cause the indicator to turn. Even if the trend is still up and the market is making higher highs, it can be losing momentum if the closes are not near the highs of the period anymore. This will be seen in the stochastic indicator as it stops going up and begins to turn down.

The gray ovals in Chart 7–3 show a typical example of this. During the wave up, the market was strong and the closes were near the top of each 5-minute bar. As the market went up and the closes were strong, the stochastic indicator got stronger until it reached the overbought level. Eventually the market stopped making higher highs but stayed near the highs, going sideways. At that point the indicator began losing strength because the closes were not as strong anymore, and it turned lower soon to be followed by the market.

Though one can use stochastics in different ways, many people have only a limited understanding of how to use them. The only way most novice traders end up using them is to buy when the stochastic indicator reaches oversold levels and turns up or to sell when it reaches overbought levels and goes down. Though this works in choppy markets, it may not work well when one is trading against a strongly trending market; it also is not how the sto-

CHART 7–3

5-Minute S&P 500: Stochastic Ideas

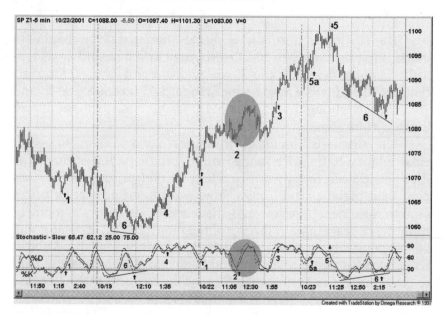

chastic indicator was intended to be used. Using stochastics to pick overbought or oversold areas is just one aspect of using them. Since there are many subjective ways in which stochastics can be used, it can become confusing to use them if you are purely a mechanical system trader, but more on that later.

Some Proper Trading Strategies for Using Stochastics

Look at Chart 7–3 for the following examples and take note that when I mention buying, you can assume the opposite for going short. For now I am ignoring multiple time frames and the long-term trend, but they are still important and I will get back to them.

1. Buy When Both Lines Are above the Oversold Level and Rising

This is one of the most basic trades when one is using stochastics. When both lines are moving in a clear direction, are rising toward the overbought area, and are above the oversold level as in the two examples labeled 1, you can catch waves in the market by getting onboard. The lower the indicator is when you get in, the more potential the market has to keep moving. If the lines start rising below the oversold area, be sure to wait for the lines to cross above it before taking the trade. In a choppy market these trades can be very profitable from both sides of the market; in a trending market it is best to take them on the side of the trend and use a crossover in the opposite direction as a signal to exit or stop yourself.

2. Buy When the Fast Line (%K) Crosses Over the Slow Line (%D)

This is a typical and very common crossover signal. When the fast line (%K) crosses over the slow line (%D), it suggests a buy, but be wary of false signals with crossovers. The cross of %K over %D could be above or below the oversold line, with the ones that happen below having the most potential. Be sure to wait for the line to cross above the oversold area before getting involved, as this is more of a confirmation.

The signal is stronger when the crossover comes after %D bottoms and not before it. Most of the time %K will turn sooner than will %D, but when it turns after %D, it is a stronger sign of a change in direction. Example 2 shows a typical crossover of the two lines.

In a strong trend like the one in this example, the lines may not always reach the oversold area. Regardless where it takes place, this is normally a sign of a move in the direction of the change.

3. Be Long When Both Lines Are above the Overbought Area but Not Yet Turning Lower,

Example 3 demonstrates how a trend can continue even after the market reaches overbought territory. The fact that the market is overbought does not mean the trend will stop dead in its tracks; there may still be plenty of room for the trade to continue. This is what makes oscillators tricky: Sometimes the overbought area can mean the market will turn, and other times it means the market is strong. As long as the indicator stays above the overbought line, one should be long, especially in a strong trend. As an exit or stop, one can get out when both lines dip below the overbought territory.

4. Buy When the Indicator Is Strong and Retests Its Extreme

A strong trading opportunity comes when the indicator moves into overbought territory, prices pull back a bit, and then the indicator retests its extreme, as in Example 4. Though similar to Example 3, this is a better trade, as the market tried to pull back but couldn't. The indicator staying by its high indicates that a strong trend is under way. Sometimes the stochastic can sit in overbought territory indefinitely as the market keeps going. Many traders either miss the move or get hurt trying to fade it. Again, as long as the indicator stays above the overbought line, one should be long, especially in a strong trend.

5. Look for a Failed Move in the Stochastics

I'll use a short for this example. Many times after they've been in overbought territory and topped, the stochastic lines will start to drop, but the drop appears to fail as they turn back up again. If on this upturn the lines can't completely cross over and start going back up, one could go short. In Example 5 you can see that the market tried to rally back up, but the %K was not able to turn back up above the %D line; this failed attempt to reverse is a great place to short the market. Even though it is against the current trend, the failed move in the indicator and the small risk to the highs if you are wrong can make it a rewarding trade with low risk.

The failed move doesn't have to happen after a peak in over-bought territory or a bottom in oversold territory. It can happen any time both lines change direction, and then the faster %K line turns back but stalls at the %D line without crossing it. When this happens, it provides strong confirmation that the initial move was good. In Example 5a you can see how after both lines turned upward, the %K line made a small move down, hit the %D line, and then turned back up. At this point it indicated that the market was still strong. For an exit one could use a clear reversal in the stochastics.

6. Look for a Divergence between Price Action and the Indicator

Probably the most effective and least used method of using sto-chastics is looking for a divergence between price action and the indicator. I'll discuss divergence in more detail later in this chapter, but for now, if you see the market making lower lows while the sto-chastic indicator makes higher lows, you have divergence. When this happens, the indicator usually is telling you that the market has lost momentum and may change direction soon. The two examples labeled 6 show places where the market went lower than it had done on its last wave down, but the stochastics made higher lows as they were starting to uptrend. In the first incident it marked the beginning of a 3-day up move, and the second time it marked the lows of the day.

RELATIVE STRENGTH INDEX (RSI)

Like stochastics, the relative strength index (RSI) is a momentum indicator that measures the price of a stock or future relative to itself over a fixed period of time, normally 14 bars, again on a scale of 0 to 100. It shows the ratio between the periods that closed up and those which closed down over the lookback period. Though 14 is the most common lookback period, you can use different lengths, causing signals to vary. The shorter it is, the more volatile the indicator will be and therefore will produce more signals; a larger lookback period gives fewer but more reliable signals. Like stochastics, the RSI is used to see when a market is overbought, is oversold, or has the momentum to keep going. When a market picks up steam and the RSI gets closer to a top or bottom, there is always a good chance that the market can retrace a little of its move. But be alert, because it may show an overbought signal just as the market is about to break to make newer and newer highs.

Some Proper Trading Strategies When Using the RSI

1. Buy When the RSI Comes Out of Oversold Territory

Most people use the RSI to signal overbought or oversold areas when it goes above the 70 to 80 area or below the 20 to 30 area. Traditionally, buy signals are triggered at 30 (the oversold line) and sell signals are triggered at 70 (the overbought line). I like to wait to see it start to turn up above the oversold line before buying, as a break above 30 is more of a bullish signal than is being in oversold territory. I've included a more range-bound section of the S&Ps for some of the RSI examples as a way to see oscillators in action in different market environments. The four examples labeled 1 in Chart 7–4 show the typical signal of shorting when the market comes out of overbought territory or buying when it oversold. Again, some

CHART 7–4

5-Minute S&P 500: RSI Ideas

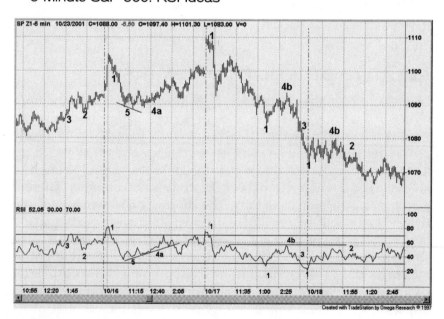

Created with TradeStation by Omega Research © 1997

people like to take the signal when it looks like the indicator peaks, but it is better to wait until it comes out of the extreme territories.

2. Buy When the RSI Stalls at the 50 Line

During strong markets the RSI may not dip down to the 30 line, and so a dip to or slightly below 50 may be considered a buying opportunity. In cases like this the 50 line can be used as a support or resistance line. A retracement will often end when the RSI hits 50. There are a couple of places on this chart (the examples labeled 2) where the market had been in a bit of trend, tried to retrace, but stopped at the 50 line. One needs to be aware that the market won't always reach oversold or overbought areas. If it stops at around the halfway point, that may be a good place to enter.

3. Buy When the RSI Is above the 50 Line

Instead of the RSI being used to show overbought-oversold areas, it can be used to follow the trend. If the RSI is greater than 50, then the trend's momentum is up and one can consider only buying. In general when the market crosses above the 50 line, a buying scenario is in place; when it goes below that line, you can think about selling. The first Example 3 shows how buying the market when the RSI breaks above 50 can put you on the right side of a strong trade. The second Example 3 shows how shorting when it drops below the 50 level makes for a decent trade.

4. Look for Technical Analysis Patterns in the RSI

When using the RSI, one can look at the indicator the same way one would on a chart. One can draw trendlines and support and resistance levels in the same manner as one does on a price chart. The lines tend to be as reliable on an RSI chart as they are on a price chart. I've included a few examples of how one can draw trendlines on the indicator to get the direction in which to trade. In Example 4a, once a trendline has been formed on the RSI, you can buy as long as the trendline holds. Once it gets broken, you can either short or get out of a long. You also can use it to see when the indicator has moved too far away from its trendline as a place to look for a retracement. You can also look for patterns in the indicator, as in Example 4b, where the indicator formed first a double top and then a triple top. This was a level where it could not break through. Both times it reached this level and failed to break through, the market came off fairly hard. As with divergences, looking for patterns in the indicator can lead to some very good trades and help you exit the market.

5. Look for a Divergence between Price Action and the Indicator

Look for divergence between price action and the RSI. This is done the same way one would with the stochastics. Example 5 shows some divergence between the indicator and the market that preceded the market changing directions, following the lead of the RSI, which wasn't able to make a lower low as the futures did.

RSI FORMULA

RSI = 100 − (100/1 + RS)
RS = Average of x periods up closes / average of x period down-closes
x is the lookback period, which is normally 14.
The shorter the period, the more volatile RSI will be.
The average can be exponentially smoothed or regular.

MOVING AVERAGE CONVERGENCE-DIVERGENCE (MACD)

MACD is another oscillator that I use. It is based on exponentially weighted moving averages, thus giving more weight to the most recent data. It is plotted in a chart with a zero line at the midpoint of its range. Unlike the previously described oscillators, which have overbought and oversold areas, the zero line (equilibrium line) is the important line with this type of oscillator. What one looks for in the MACD is the relationship between the two moving averages: the MACD line (dotted on Chart 7–5) and the signal line, which is a nine-period average of the faster MACD line. As the two lines come close together, they are converging, and when they are moving farther apart, they are diverging—hence the name of the indicator. As the move in the market gains strength, the difference between the two lines will grow. When that strength fades, the lines will come closer together until they potentially cross. The difference between the moving averages is plotted as a histogram. This histogram acts as the oscillator and measures the divergence

CHART 7-5

60-Minute S&P 500: MACD Ideas

or convergence of the shorter and longer moving averages. As the two moving averages move away from each other because prices are rising, the MACD histogram will move up and away from the zero level. If the moving averages cross, the histogram will be at the zero level. If the lines are falling, it will be below zero.

Like other oscillators, the MACD can be used to find when the market may be overbought or oversold, especially if the market is in a trading range. Since there are no overbought or oversold areas, one must visually see when the indicator is near the top or bottom of the range to find when the move may be overdone. As with other indicators, not all signals will work out this well, but when carefully used, MACD can be a valuable asset in your arsenal of tools.

Some Proper Trading Strategies When Using MACD

1. Buy When the MACD Line Is above the Signal Line

In general, you should be long only when the MACD line (dotted) is above the signal line and short only when it is below that line.

This can either be seen in the averages or the histogram; if the histogram is above the zero line, it is a bullish sign as it is the equivalent of the MACD line being above the signal line. Example 1 shows how as long as the MACD line is above the signal line, one can do well being long. Taking trades against this direction is not recommended.

2. Buy When the Crossover Is below the Zero Line

Stronger buy signals occur when the MACD line is well below the zero line and turns up to cross above the signal line. The first Example 2 shows a good signal that could have been taken as soon as the lines crossed after being oversold. One also could have taken a short trade at the second Example 2, where the lines cross well into overbought territory.

3. Buy When the Moving Averages Cross above the Zero Line

When the moving averages cross above the zero line, a confirmation of a buy signal is given. At this point a trader may want to add to any position he may have or enter the market if he is not already in it. When the MACD line crosses above the zero line, it means that the shorter exponential moving average (EMA) that makes up the formula is crossing above the longer EMA. This is the same as a bullish moving average crossover signal, as was discussed in Chap. 6. Example 3 shows that when the averages crossed over the zero line, the market really began to move.

4. Look for a Divergence between Price Action and the Indicator

Even better signals occur when the MACD indicator or MACD histogram shows divergence against prices. Example 4 shows that when the market made a new high but the indicator didn't, the move soon ended and the market had a pretty hard sell-off afterward.

5. Look for Technical Analysis Patterns in the Histogram

You can use the pattern of the histogram to trigger signals as well. When the histogram is below the zero line, begins forming a bottom, and starts moving higher, as in both Examples 5, you can try to catch a turn early. When you are looking at a histogram and the bars are getting shorter, the momentum may be losing strength. This may happen before the lines cross or hit zero, giving you a crossover signal. Be careful because as with all oscillators, trying to anticipate a move can lead to getting whipsawed. I use these peaks and valleys in the histogram as a method of determining that a wave may be over and to start looking to either get out or reverse my position.

MACD FORMULA

Fast MACD Line (dotted line) = (short EMA − long EMA)
Signal line = 9-period average of fast MACD line
MACD histogram = fast line - signal line

TYPICAL DEFAULTS
Short EMA = 12-period EMA
Long EMA = 26-period EMA
MACD MA = 9
EMA = exponential moving average

USING OSCILLATORS TO TIME TRADES

One of the most helpful uses of oscillators is for timing entries into and exits out of the market better. A trader who uses oscillators can avoid chasing the market, wait for more opportune entries levels, and avoid getting out at the worst possible moment. If one can improve in these areas, one's trading will get much better. Normally, as a market trends and moves along its way, it does so in waves. As the market runs up and the indicators get high, traders will begin to feel uneasy buying at overbought levels, and this is where the market can stall or turn around. Being aware of where an oscillator is can warn you of a possible overbought condition. When the oscillator is near the high of its range, I would never consider it a good time to buy because the market has already had a move up and the odds of a pullback are stronger. It doesn't have to pull back as the trend may continue, but the odds are strong that it will. However, many traders jump into a trade at these levels without looking at any oscillators or realizing that the market may be overdone. They are afraid of missing a move, prices look strong, and everybody is talking about how much he is making, so they think it will keep going and they end up buying market highs. This is a time when traders should be thinking about exiting positions, not entering them. If the market is overbought and keeps moving higher and you miss a trade because you are waiting for a pullback, that's okay. By waiting for the oscillator to back off or give you a signal, you will be making a higher probability trade than you would by buying an overbought market, even when it keeps going higher. It takes patience to wait for the market to dip, but this patience is what makes traders good.

Let's say you want to buy KLAC and are looking at a 5-minute chart (Chart 7–6). It has just made a move up and catches your attention, and so you look at the chart and see it is at Point A. An astute trader will not buy it here; if he looks at the stochastics, he can see that it is overbought and may come off a little before continuing to go up. Even if it doesn't come off, buying an overbought market is not a great idea. Instead of chasing the stock, he starts watching, waiting to get in when the stochastics have reached oversold conditions. He patiently waits, avoiding temptation along the way, until it reaches Point B. At this level his odds of making money on the trade

CHART 7—6

5-Minute KLAC: Timing Trades

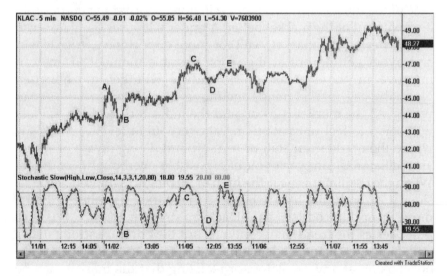

skyrocket compared to what they would be if he chased it at Point A. After getting in, he decides to hold until a good exit comes along, but unfortunately, he was in the bathroom at the peak at Point C. When he came back, it had started to sell off and was nearing the oversold area at Point D. This is the area where many people throw in the towel because they are seeing their profits slip away, or worse, are losing money because they actually bought at Point C. A good trader, however, sees that the indicator is oversold and will wait to see if it turns up before getting out. In this case the market rallies out of oversold territory until it hits the overbought area at Point E and struggles to stay strong. The trader then calls it quits, getting a much better price while having avoided getting shaken out at a worse level. This doesn't always work, but at least one should give the market some time to see if it bounces at the oversold area, especially when the longer-term trend is up. If it doesn't seem to bounce, a good trader will get out; those who hold on too long here never have a fighting chance to succeed.

MISUSING OSCILLATORS

Many inexperienced traders misuse oscillators because they think of them as just an indicator to catch turns in the market. What most traders don't realize, however, is that oscillators weren't created to catch market turns but to be a way to see conformation in a trending market and a tool to assist traders in exiting a trade before the market turns. Yet many people associate them only with capturing market turns. The most common mistake is that people think that when the indicator is overbought, the market will go down. But as I've mentioned, in a strong market it can stay overbought for quite a while and generate many false signals. Readings above the overbought line only mean that price is closing near its high and the market is strong, not that it is about to sell off. There is a good chance that it will, but that is not something it must do. Buying or selling in anticipation of what an indicator says is not a great practice, as very often the market will keep going in an overbought or oversold environment for quite a while. It is better to wait for price action to confirm the move than to jump in anticipation of it. If the indicator stays in the overbought or oversold area for quite a while, one must ignore it and go back to basic trend-following strategies, as they will work best.

IT'S EASY TO LOSE MONEY BY MISUSING OSCILLATORS

As a testament to this, I can only say that I tried using stochastics for years to try to pick tops and bottoms and that judging from my inability to make money, they don't really work when used for that purpose alone. Too many times I tried to pick changes in the market's direction at oversold levels only to watch the market continue to tank. I wouldn't get out because the market was still oversold and was "due" for a bounce. Eventually I found that oscillators work best when combined with other indicators or patterns. It wasn't until I started using oscillators more wisely that I began getting better results from them.

TRADING WITH OSCILLATORS

One of the bonuses of momentum oscillators is that they can locate reversal points much sooner than trend-following indicators can. In a choppy market, trend-following indicators will result in whipsaw trading, but with oscillators one can pick off short-term tops and bottoms. During choppy markets, buying oversold and selling overbought situations can work like a charm; the hard part is knowing when the market is trending or range-bound. Markets trend only about 20 percent of the time, but when they do trend, they can be strong and using oscillators can be costly. Since using oscillators to pick tops and bottoms works best in nontrending markets, one can consider using the average directional index (ADX) to determine when to use oscillators more freely. A simple rule of thumb is that when the ADX is below 20, you can consider the market choppy and range-bound. A trending system may not work in this environment, and so one may want to use a system that is based on oscillators instead, as it may work better.

I have had little luck writing a system that works by using only typical stochastic signals; therefore, I use stochastics as a secondary signal or as an alert that tells me it's okay to trade in one direction or tells me that this is a good place to exit or take some of my position off. This may make mechanical system trading a little discretionary, but sometimes you need to adapt to different market environments and be able to include different market patterns and money management in your trading. A big part of using oscillators correctly is locating patterns in them, such as double tops, trends, and divergence. These patterns can be some of the best ways to use oscillators but are hard to program into a system.

DIVERGENCES

Instead of trying to outguess the market by picking tops and bottoms, using oscillators to look for divergences can make for some of the highest probability trades. Besides the ones I've previously described, several types of divergences can be found in the markets. By being aware of them and knowing how to trade with them on your side, you can get a lot more bang out of oscillators. Looking for divergences is one of the best overall ways to trade when one is using oscillators. But finding them means you always have to be on the alert. Divergences are not easily programmed into computerized trading systems, and so a trader who uses them has to take discretion on his trades. Here are a few divergences one can look for.

1. The most common form of divergence occurs when a market moves one way and the indicator moves the other way. This is typically a sign that the market may have run out of steam, as the last move was not as strong as the prior one and the momentum may have left the market. When the divergences are near market tops, these can be exceptionally good trades. A good example is when the indicator is in oversold territory, turns higher and then turns back down, but fails to break the previous low while the market makes a lower low. At this point there is a good chance that the move will run out of momentum. The RSI in both examples labeled 1 in Chart 7–7 shows this pattern perfectly. The signals here marked the temporary end of a several-day sell-off.

2. A second type of divergence occurs when the market is trending down and then stays pretty flat for a while but the oscillator moves up toward the overbought level. This is a sign that the market has no momentum in the oscillator's direction and can continue its trend with force on the next wave. You can see this in Example 2, where the stock barely moved higher as the stochastics moved to overbought territory. What makes this a high probability trade is that the market did not react as it was expected to, moving up as the stochastic got stronger. As soon as it reaches an overbought condition, new shorts will be looking to jump in, existing shorts may add to their positions, and any longs may give up hope, causing a nice move in the stock. Though in this situation it took

CHART 7−7

Divergences in BGEN

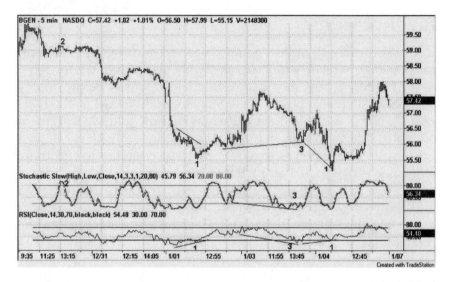

time to work, this would have been a great short, as the market never moved higher after this.

3. Normally one looks to see when the market breaks lower and the indicator doesn't, but when the opposite happens, it is a good signal as well. An example is when the market is headed lower but doesn't make a lower low and the indicator does, as in Example 3. Here both the RSI and the stochastics moved lower but the stock could not break downward. In this situation you could start looking for a change in direction, as sellers could not take the market lower when the indicator suggested it should have gone lower. This was a short-lived bounce and would not have worked well for a trader who tries to catch major reversals, but the loss, if any, was relatively small, and it gives you a good idea of what pattern to look for. It also alerts you to a place to take a profit. You don't always have to try to catch bottoms, but if you have a short position and see this pattern, you may want to at least take a profit.

4. There are times when the market is sloping upward and an oscillator is sloping downward. This divergence should be taken as a warning that something is wrong. More often than not this indicates that price is about to change direction. A good example of this can be found in the two Examples 6 on Chart 7–3. In both cases the market bottomed after this pattern.

DIVERGENCE BETWEEN STOCKS AND THE MARKET

Another form of divergence that I see and use all the time is when comparing individual stocks to the market in general. Say the market is having a strong day, I'm long a bunch of stocks, and I have a nice profit. The S&Ps then make higher highs, and as they keep going up, I notice that my P&L is not getting any better. This means that my stocks stopped moving with the market. When this happens, it implies that the market may soon turn or that a different group is leading the market now; in either case I will get out of my trades. The other way to use this type of scenario is to look for stocks that just won't go up with the market and short them; this acts as a good hedge to any longs you may have.

TRADING WITH THE TREND

One of the best ways to use stochastics is in cahoots with trend-following indicators. You should always be looking to get in the market, in the direction of the main trend. First you need to establish what the trend is. Next, if you know you have a market that is uptrending and you want to take mainly long trades, the best thing to do is to look for dips in the oscillator to the oversold levels to buy. In Chart 7–8, featuring KLAC, you can see great places to enter the market at Points A, B, C, and D. The market has been in a decent uptrend during this period, but at all those points it has just sold off a bit, coming to the trendline or stalling after a drop. In each case the indicator goes into oversold territory, representing a good place to get in. As the oscillator comes out of oversold levels and heads up toward the overbought level, one can use Points Ax, Bx, and Cx as exit points for the first three trades. Ax is a really good exit signal because of the divergence between the price and indicator: As the market kept going higher, the indicator started backing off a little, indicating that the trend might have been losing steam. The other two points could be used to get out of the market when the stochastics crossed below the overbought area. You would want to exit at these times in fear of a market pullback. If it stayed in overbought levels, one should hold, as the trend may be strong. I don't recommend going short at any of these signals because they are against the trend and therefore are not high probability trades. You can see that the market doesn't give you much

60-Minute KLAC: Going with the Trend

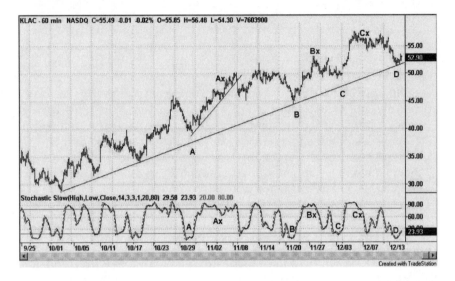

time to take a profit when you are right and can explode in your face when you are wrong. Remember, you don't have to take every trade; just take the high probability ones, in the direction of the trend.

MULTIPLE TIME FRAMES

The way I have found stochastics (like any other oscillator) to work best is to use them in multiple time frames to time trades that are with the major trend. First I'll look for the major trend by using a daily chart, the same way I did in the previous chapters. Once I have that, I'll use the 60-minute time frame to get a better picture of how much room there is left or when there may be a pullback or overextension of a wave. After knowing what direction to trade in, I'll look at the shorter time frames to find trades. If I were using the same KLAC chart, I would use the stochastics not only to get into trades but also as a way to let me know it was okay to trade in one direction or another, in shorter time frames. If the 60-minute sto-chastic for example, is rising, I trade only from the long side in the 5-minute time frame. Whether you plan to hold a trade for a few days or prefer trading in and out of the market, the shorter time frame will help. Using Chart 7–9, the 5-minute time frame, which corresponds to the area between Point A and Point Ax on Chart 7–8, you can time one trade after the signal at Point A on the 60-minute chart. On the 5-minute chart you can see that if one had taken Signal A when it was given on the 60-minute chart, one would have had to sit through a $2 pullback. Waiting for the 5-minute stochastic to reach the oversold area and turn up gets you into the market at a much better level. Though it didn't work immediately, it was a much better entry point, and the risk was lower. Once in, a trader can revert back to the 60-minute chart, holding until Point Ax, or a more antsy trader can make several trades during that time period by using the 5-minute chart. I've indicated some possible entries and exits with up and down arrows; remember, trades should be taken only from the long side, as long as the higher time frame is bullish. The two Point Ds, indicate that there was some divergence between the market and the indicator, and so buys at these points are extra good trades.

Since I'm on the topic of multiple time frames, I'll reiterate that one doesn't have to use the same indicators on the different time frames. Some people may like to use volume, trendlines, ADX, and RSI on the daily time frame, then MACD and moving

CHART 7–9

5-Minute KLAC: Timing Your Trades a Little More

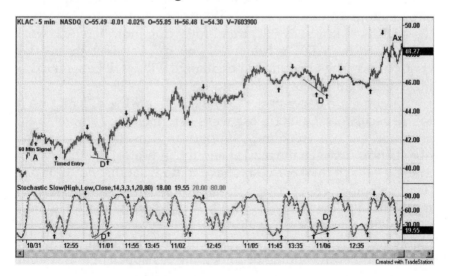

Created with TradeStation

averages on the 60-minute time frame, and stochastics on a 5-minute chart. It can be mixed up any way that gives a trader a good feel for the market.

BECOMING A BETTER TRADER

Becoming a better trader means not just using oscillators but using them to their fullest potential. Oscillators should not be used to pick tops and bottoms, instead, they should be used to trade in the direction of the major trend. When the market is in an uptrend, use the oscillators to wait for a pullback in the market; when the retracement is oversold, look to get in. One becomes a better trader when knowing where a market is with regard to being overbought or oversold. A smart trader will not rush into a trade when he knows the market is overbought; instead, he will wait for a better entry point. Similarly, he will not be scared out of a position when the market drops and reaches oversold levels. This is actually the level at which to get into a trade, not out of it as many traders do. One of the most helpful uses of oscillators is to aid you in getting in and out of positions at better levels. If you wait a little longer, there is a good chance you can get out at a better level.

Even when the market is trending strongly and the oscillator stays overbought, it is better to wait for the first pullback to get in than to chase a strong market. Of course, when there is a strong trend, one should revert back to basic trend-following indicators, as oscillators won't work as well. What is helpful is knowing where the ADX is. If it is above 30, trend-following indicators will work best. When the ADX is below 20, you can consider the market choppy and range-bound, and oscillators will work better at picking overbought and oversold conditions.

Becoming a better trader also means knowing different ways to use oscillators. One of those ways is to look for patterns in the indicator, such as trendlines, support and resistance levels, and divergences between the market and the indicator. Another way is to realize that a market doesn't have to do what the indicator predicts it should. The fact that the indicator is overbought doesn't mean that the market will sell off. It can keep going for quite a while, with you patiently waiting for it to reverse. Remember, the market does what it wants to do and not what it should do, so don't be stubborn waiting for something to happen or anticipating a move that never comes. If the market is strong, it will keep moving up despite the overbought reading. One also can improve by combining indicators in different time frames to get different perspectives and an overall better picture of the market. Overall, by using oscillators correctly one should be able to time trades a little better.

Problems of Not Using or Misusing Oscillators

1. Getting poor entry and exit levels
2. Getting whipsawed by buying overbought markets and selling oversold markets
3. Holding losers too long because you think market is "overdone"
4. Getting many false signals with oscillators in a strong trend
5. Chasing the market
6. Getting out at the worst moment
7. Not knowing when the market is overextended
8. Believing the market must follow the indicator
9. Trading against the trend, looking for reversals
10. Missing market reversals

High Probability Trading with Oscillators

1. Trade in the direction of the major trend, buying when retracements are oversold.
2. Exit trades as the oscillator is peaking.
3. Stop chasing the market by not getting involved if oscillators are at an extreme.
4. Wait for pullbacks to time trades better.
5. Use the oscillator to find better entry points.
6. Be wary of buying when the market is overbought and selling when it is oversold.
7. Use longer time frames to find out how much room is left in a major trend.
8. Look for divergences between the price and the indicator.
9. Look for technical patterns in the oscillators.

10. Look at the ADX to see when the market is in a strong trend or not.
11. When an oscillator stays near the extremes for extended periods, it is a sign that there is a strong trend.
12. Combine indicators to get confirmation.
13. If an oscillator is rising above the zero line, you should only be buying.
14. Hold on just a little longer when you can't take the pain anymore and the market is overdone.

Helpful Questions to Ask Yourself

Is the market overbought?

Am I chasing the market?

Did I wait for a pullback?

Should I bail out or wait to see what happens, since the market is reaching an oversold level?

Am I using the indicator properly?

Am I trading with the major trend?

CHAPTER 8

Breakouts and Reversals

No big move starts without some sort of breakout or reversal.

BREAKOUTS: TRADING ON THE SIDE OF THE MOMENTUM

Some of the oldest, simplest, and most successful trading systems are breakout systems. Many traders like to enter the market on a breakout of a support or resistance level, a break of the highest high in the last *x* number of bars, or when a trendline is broken. The reason breakout strategies work well is that they get a trader in on the side of the momentum of the market. A breakout can occur when a market is trending upward and breaks a previous high to continue in the direction of the trend, the market can break a trendline to start a new trend, or the market can break out of a congestion area. Either way, if it is a true breakout, it can lead to an extended powerful move that a trader can take advantage of if he knows what to look for. An added advantage to trading with a breakout is that if it leads to a big move, one avoids being on the wrong side of the move.

Chart 8–1 shows a few typical types of breakouts. The first, at Point A, occurs when the market is breaking a low it had made previously. In this case it was a low it had made twice in a short period of time. This breakout was in the direction of the trend, and when it did break the level, the market continued steadily on its way down. At Point B, though, it broke Trendline 1 to the upside, and this was the first sign that the market was changing directions. At Point C it broke Trendline 2 to continue moving up and provided confirmation that trend might be changing toward the upside. Finally, the next breakout (Point D) was like the first one, where the market broke a previous high and exploded into the trend. As you can see in the chart, the big moves in the market were preceded by a breakout, whether it was a continuation of the trend or a reversal.

WHAT MAKES A MARKET BREAK?

The market can break out for several reasons. Some breakouts result from a news item, such as a weather report, a miners' strike, or unexpected earnings. At other times a breakout is due to a technical level being violated. Markets are drawn to significant levels that can include previous highs or lows, clearly identified trendlines, channels, moving averages, round numbers, and previous congestion. By knowing where these levels are, a trader can have a good idea of when the market is approaching a level it can break out of.

CHART 8-1

5-Minute MSFT: Some Breakouts

Created with TradeStation

A breakout can be caused by pent-up energy in the market as it keeps testing the same level over and over. Markets may break out because when there is a set barrier that the market has tested several times, it draws a lot of attention to itself. Every time the market approaches that level or line, people are ready to act on it whether it breaks or not. Eventually, if it breaks, it will hit some stops and gain momentum, causing a continued move. There are other times when a market is stuck in flat trading range for a while and eventually picks a side and keeps going. The longer it tests an area, the bigger the ensuing breakout probably will be. Sometimes a breakout results when the market has exhausted its move, and a retracement gains momentum. If enough traders liquidate and switch positions, this can cause the market to break its previous trend and start a new one. I'll discuss the patterns that can lead to the market breaking out in more detail throughout this chapter.

TYPES OF BREAKOUTS

Breaking Previous Highs or Lows

Probably the most common type of breakout strategy is to buy when the market breaks a previous high or short when it breaks a previous low. For example, in Chart 8–1, when the market broke below the previous lows of Point A, one could have taken a short. Another popular strategy is to get in when the high or low of a set period, say, 20 bars, is broken. Thus, at Points B and C, when the market broke a 20-period high, one could have gotten long. By trading like this, you are getting in on the side of the market on which the momentum is trending. With this type of breakout you can either trade with an established trend or catch a reversal in the market.

Breaking Trendlines

The next type of breakout occurs when the market breaks through a trendline or moving average instead of a horizontal support and resistance level such as a previous high or a triple top. Trendline breakouts such as the ones at Point B and Point C on Chart 8–1 are important to be aware of because they can signal the end of a trend and the start of a new one. At the very least, if a trendline is broken, a trader should start liquidating his positions if he is on the wrong side of the break.

Trendline breakouts are easy to see as long as you draw the trendlines in; the hard part is for traders to convince themselves that they need to exit a position if they are on the wrong side of it.

RANGE-BOUND BREAKOUT PATTERNS

Sometimes the market may not be trending but going sideways, staying in range-bound areas such as channels, triangles, flags, and rectangles. These are places where the market has met some congestion between support and resistance while trying to pick a direction. These areas of congestion develop while the bears and bulls wrestle with each other as they try to decide what the overall direction of the market should be. During this time the market bounces in a small area. While the market is range-bound you can use the top of the range to sell and the bottom to buy, but beware because eventually it will break one way or the other. The market can break either in the direction of the longer-term trend or as a reversal. The longer it stays in a channel or range, the bigger the move tends to be when it finally breaks out of the range, as it will have gathered more attention. A rule of thumb for when a market breaks out of a congestion area is that the move will be about the same length as the congestion area is wide. If you look at Chart 8–2 and measure the distance between Point Y and Point A (the move), it is the same as the width between Point X and Y (the congestion). This doesn't always work, but you'd be amazed how often it does, and it is a good way to look for a place where the market can stall.

Rectangles

Rectangles are sideways patterns with clear support and resistance levels that the market keeps hitting, as you can see in the rectangle on Chart 8–2. During this period KLAC stayed in a $3 range for 2 weeks. In a rectangle the market goes to its previous high and low and cannot go farther. As the market hits the bottom of the pattern, buying comes in as traders think this is the cheap range of the market. Shorts take profits because they see a support level. At the top, the opposite happens. Eventually, though, the market will break one way or the other. When that happens and you want to measure a potential move, you should do so from the point where the break occurs (Point C). As in the previous example, the market once again stalled after it had traveled the distance of the width of the congestion.

CHART 8–2

60–Minute KLAC: Breakout Patterns

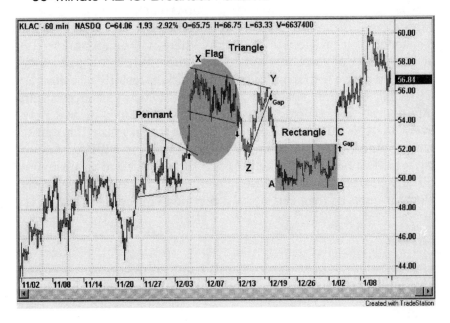

KLAC - 60 min NASDQ C=64.06 -1.93 -2.92% O=65.75 H=66.75 L=63.33 V=6637400

Created with TradeStation

Triangles, Flags, and Pennants

Triangles, unlike rectangles, are congestion areas that don't reach the previous high or low on subsequent waves. They come in different forms, such as wedges, flags, and pennants. They can be ascending or descending with a flat bottom or top or can have both the top and bottom trending until they narrow to meet at a point before breaking out in a direction. Though they can look different, they are basically the same: a congestion pattern looking for a direction in which to break. The main difference between a flag and a pennant is that a flag forms a channel and moves against the trend, while a pennant has more of a triangular pattern and is not necessarily against the trend. In Chart 8–2 you can see a pennant, a flag, and a triangle; the flag is in the shaded oval and is part of the larger triangle (XYZ).

Gaps

Sometimes when a market breaks, it does so with a gap, as a few of the breaks did in Chart 8–2. Gaps are an indication that there are many more people on one side of the market than the other. If they can keep the momentum, the market will have a sustained break-out. Although many gaps eventually get filled in, breakaway gaps can be the beginning of a major move in the market. Some gaps are caused because as the market approaches a level of support or resistance or a previous high or low, there will be an abnormally large number of stops just outside that area. When those stops get hit, it can cause a sharp move in the market, resulting in the gap. Other gaps can be caused by a news event such as a crop report, interest rate cut, or earnings warning. Many times after a news event there is such a rush to get in that it can make the market jump. Some gaps result from overnight activity in a different country which causes the market to open the next day at a substantial difference from where it closed. Whatever the cause is, be on the alert for gaps, as they can signal a big move in the market.

News

Though all breakouts can be seen through technical analysis, breakouts can be caused by the market's fundamentals. News can cause the market to break in two ways. The first occurs when there is some unexpected news, such as a sudden strike in a copper mine, a company declaring bankruptcy, or a cutback in the production of oil by OPEC. These events can make a market move regardless of the direction in which it was traveling before. If the move is strong enough, the market can have a substantial break in the direction of the trend or as a market reversal. The second situation occurs when the market makes its move in anticipation of news such as a rate cut. Once the news becomes public, you are likely to see the market reverse and break the other way as people cover their positions into the news as they "sell the fact." Trading in anticipation of news is always dangerous because the market can have a major move after the news is released. Trying to guess which way a report will affect the market is not trading but gambling. One is better off waiting for the inevitable pullback instead of trying to guess which way the market will go.

HOW NOT TO TRADE BREAKOUTS
Jumping the Gun

As I mentioned earlier, breakouts can happen in the direction of the trend or occur as a reversal. Trying to guess if, when, and which way the market will break is not an easy job. One thing traders do that hurts them is to anticipate breakouts that never amount to anything. Instead of waiting for the market to break, they rush in to buy when it is at the top of its resistance level, hoping for the breakout. Chart 8–3, a 5-minute S&P 500 chart, shows how it is easy to do this. After a range is set by Points 1 through 4, one can be strongly tempted to buy at Point 5 as the market nears the top of the range. When a trader realizes at Point 6 that this is not working, he may go short and maybe even add to his position at Point 7. Markets can stay range-bound for extended periods of time, and a trader who is trying to outguess the market by entering every tempting breakout he sees can get hurt. Instead of jumping the gun, a trader should wait to see a market make its move before doing anything.

Chasing Breakouts

Another mistake traders make is to chase breakouts. They get alerted to a market breaking and get too caught up in the excitement of the market to trade it properly. Unless they catch the actual breakout,

CHART 8–3

5-Minute S&P: Waiting for the Breakout

Created with TradeStation by Omega Research © 1997

they can get too deeply into the move, which increases the odds of the market going against them. Point 8 in Chart 8–3 is an example of this. If someone puts a market order to get in once the market actually breaks the highs of the day, he is likely to get filled at around Point 9. At this point the market has just had a 10-point move, going from lows to highs, and so there is a strong chance that it will retrace a bit. To have the patience to wait 20 minutes, an hour, or even 3 days until the market provides a better entry opportunity is too difficult for many traders. They feel that if they don't act immediately, they could miss a great trade. It's not always easy for a trader to walk away from a tempting trade, but this is the difference between a high probability trader and a low probability trader. There will be many, many trading opportunities, and if one is missed, *so what?* A trader shouldn't let it get to him. You will be better off missing a few good trades while weeding out the mediocre ones as you wait for the trades that have a higher probability with a better risk/reward ratio. By waiting for the market to test the old resistance line at Point 10 one can make a higher probability trade than by chasing it after a 10-point move.

When a trader misses a good entry point and then chases the market, the stops become much bigger, increasing the risk/reward ratio. People can get shaken out of good positions if they get in too late, because as the market drifts back toward the support area, the pain can become too much, causing them to sell at a loss. Chasing the market also results in higher slippage costs. If you are trying to buy and the market is rallying, the offers will be moving away, and so your entry level will be worse than you had hoped for. When you wait for the market to pull in, it is easy to get filled on limit orders and you can buy on the bid, getting a better price.

HIGH PROBABILITY TRADING OF BREAKOUTS

To increase the probability of a breakout trade working, one can do a few things. By looking at different time frames to see the market more clearly, adding indicators such as the ADX or stochastics to time trades better, using volume to see if a move is substantiated, or adding filters to keep from rushing into a trade, one can improve the odds of capturing a breakout. The next few sections will explain how to make the most of breakout situations.

Range-Bound Breakouts

In looking at Chart 8–3, you see a range-bound 5-minute S&P chart, but you really learn nothing about the market by looking at it. The first thing you should do is look at a longer time frame. When you look at the 60-minute chart (Chart 8–4), you can see that at Point 1 (the area corresponding to Chart 8–3) the market had been in an uptrend and recently retraced a little; you also can see that the stochastics were above 50 and rising. These two things should tell you that when the market broke out of its little range, the odds were stronger that it would break to the upside. Breakouts or break highs or lows in markets that are already in a strong trend make for great places to trade and will produce the highest probability results. By trading on the side of the major trend you can avoid the lower probability trades.

When you add stochastics and the ADX to the 5-minute chart, as I did in Chart 8–5, you can see that when the market looked like it might have broken out at Point 5, 6, or 8, the stochastics were telling you to wait because the move may have been overextended. The ADX was weak throughout this period, which implies that

CHART 8–4

60-Minute S&P: The Bigger Picture

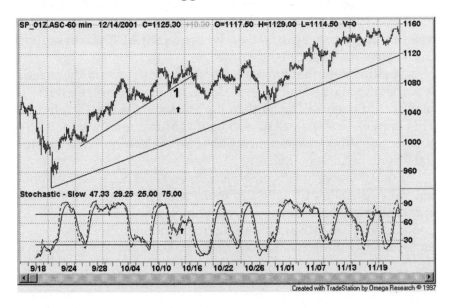

Created with TradeStation by Omega Research © 1997

CHART 8−5

5-Minute S&P: Timing the Trade

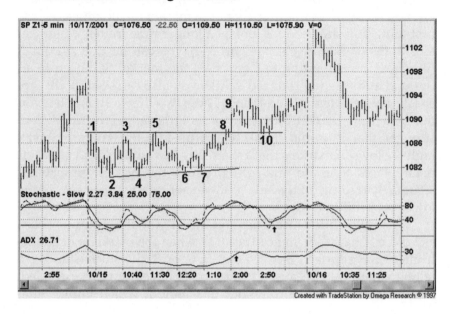

SP Z1-5 min 10/17/2001 C=1076.50 -22.50 O=1109.50 H=1110.50 L=1075.90 V=0

Stochastic - Slow 2.27 3.84 25.00 75.00

ADX 26.71

Created with TradeStation by Omega Research © 1997

there was no trend in the market and one should not have looked for or chased a breakout in the direction of the main trend. If the ADX is strong (above 30), a breakout of a range or a previous high has a good chance of success if it is on the side of the major trend. You can see that once the market did break, the ADX was at around the 30 area, making for better odds.

Another sign that the market would break toward the upside was that the market had opened down for the day and each low it made could not break lower than the low set in the first 30 minutes. This implies that the negative pressure of the open was not very convincing. When the traders couldn't take it lower, a break toward the upside became more likely.

Point 7 is a very tempting place to go short because the previous rally after Point 6 failed to make a higher high and the stochastics turned back down as well. Shorting at Point 7 would be a good trade because the risk is small (to the previous little wave up), and if the trendline was broken at Point 7, the market could have really taken off. The only problem is that everything else was telling you to wait for a bullish breakout. When the market failed to make a lower low at Point 7 and held support, this, in my opinion, was the ideal place to go long. At this point you also have a weak ADX, telling you the market is range-bound, the stochastics are coming out of oversold territory, the market is at the intraday trendline, and the major trend is up; you can't ask for much more than that. Odds are, though, if I had gotten long, I would have bailed out when it hit the resistance line just before Point 8, thinking it would stop because it was overbought. Even if it goes through, it is a smart trade to get out at that level; at the very least one should take a piece of one's position off.

Once it does break the resistance, a trader has to fight the temptation to get in imprudently. Markets have a habit of breaking a level only to retest it. Here the stochastic is in overbought territory after having had a decent run, and one is better off waiting until the market retraces, hits support, or becomes oversold, as it did at Point 10, before getting in. At this level you know that if it doesn't work right away and dips below the top channel line, you can get out with a small loss. If you bought at Point 8, the ideal stop would be larger, near the lows of the day, which gives the trade a higher risk/reward ratio, which is something you want to avoid.

A quick reminder: When using the ADX, if it is low, there is a good chance that the market will not break out in the direction of the major trend, but it could more easily break through a trendline. When the ADX is strong, look for breakouts that go with the major trend and expect trendlines to hold.

Trendline Breakouts

Another type of breakout occurs when the market breaks through a trendline or moving average to, one hopes, start a new trend. Though you normally would want to trade with the trend, no matter how strong the trend is, eventually it will be broken. You shouldn't anticipate a breakout every time the market approaches the trendline, but you should be prepared to act if it does. The longer the time frame one is looking at, the more significant a breakout will be, but it looks and works the same on every level. Also, when a market approaches a trendline, the steeper it is, the more likely it is that it will get broken.

Chart 8–6, a daily chart of cotton, demonstrates several times how the market broke through trendlines to start a new trend. By

CHART 8-6

Daily Cotton: Trendline Breakouts

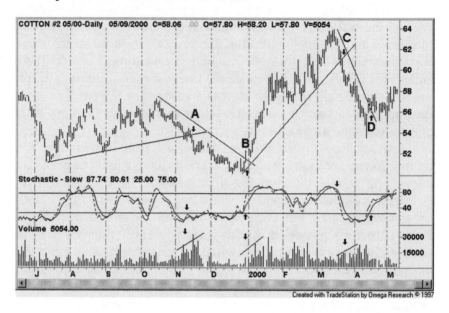

Created with TradeStation by Omega Research ® 1997

including the stochastics indicator in the chart, one can determine whether the breakout has more potential. I like to look at stochastics when getting into a breakout because I want to make sure the market may still have room to move when I get in. When the stochastic is just starting to turn in the direction of the breakout, there will be a better chance that the trade will work than there is if one gets long when the market is overbought. The break at Point B is extra good because the market had stopped downtrending and went sideways in a little range before breaking both the trendline and the top of the range simultaneously while gathering volume and still being oversold.

USING VOLUME TO CONFIRM BREAKOUTS

Volume is another good tool you can use to see what may happen at trendlines or tops and bottoms. If the market is approaching a trendline and the volume is dismal, it most likely will stall as there is little interest in pushing it through. However, if the volume is picking up, the odds are better that it will break through with momentum. Volume gets strong as the market breaks out of its range, because a solid breakthrough involves new traders entering the market, scared traders covering positions, and even more traders reversing positions. When a combination of these things happens, the momentum can drive the market straight through a barrier and keep it from looking back. When the volume is weak, it means that not everybody is getting involved and then it's a fight to see who will win. It could go either way at this point, and that increases the chance that a breakout will be a false one. This uncertainty and lack of conviction make a low-volume breakout a low probability trading situation.

Unless there is an increase in volume, one should not get involved heavily in a breakout right away. Instead, it is best to wait to see what happens. Hopefully, the market will retest the level it broke from and find support. At this point you can look to get involved if it seems that it cannot go lower and place a stop under that support level. When the volume is strong, the initial move can be stronger and the chances of it retesting the breakout level are diminished, and so one has to act faster.

If you look at Chart 8–6 again, you will see that there was an increase in volume preceded by a lull every time the market broke out. These two signs can help you identify when a breakout has a better chance of working. The lull in volume beforehand indicates that traders are losing interest in the trend. When the volume picks up, it is due to people switching positions and getting in on the other side. When shorts turn into longs, the volume doubles and it helps the market push through a trendline. Many traders ignore volume, but by paying attention to it you can scope out better trading opportunities.

BREAK OF A COUNTERTREND

Some of the best breakout trades come after a market that has been trending in one direction has a retracement. When that retracement's trendline gets broken, it is a great signal because it leads you back in the direction of the major trend. Look at Chart 8–7, a daily chart of Cisco during the heyday of the NASDAQ bull market in 1999. The stock had been in a nice uptrend for a year when it experienced a few pullbacks; Trendline A and later Trendline B are

CHART 8-7

Daily Cisco: Breaking Countertrends

CSCO - Daily NASDQ C=19.05 +0.00 +0.00% O=0.00 H=0.00 L=0.00 V=0

Created with TradeStation

examples of those retracements. When you see countertrends like
these, you can trade the break of them aggressively. The reason
these are great probability trades is (1) you are getting in after a
retracement, (2) you are trading in the direction of the major trend,
and (3) with the major trendline being so close, it acts as both support and a great place to put a stop-loss order without risking too
much. The rewards in these cases can be explosive, as was the case
when the market broke Trendline B, and the risks are minimal, so
take these trades any chance you get.

BREAK HIGH BREAKOUTS

Another type of high probability breakout in the direction of the
major trend is to buy when the market breaks a previous high in an
uptrend or go short when it breaks a previous low in a downtrend.
When a market is uptrending, every time the highs start getting
higher, the uptrend is confirmed. Therefore, by getting in when a
previous high gets broken, you are trading in the direction of the
trend. If you were looking at Chart 8–7, you could have entered
into the market in a hundred different places as it kept breaking

higher all the time. A strategy of buying every time the market breaks, say, a 10-day high, when the market is in an uptrend will keep you on the right side of the market. If it's a strong trend, you need only get in once and hold; if it is not, you need to know when to take a loss and keep trying until you catch a good move. If you trade these types of breakouts, one stop you could use would be to get out if the market broke a 3-day low or something to that effect. This kind of breakout strategy may be wrong quite often, but the results can be great when it does work.

REVERSALS

Everybody has hopes of catching a market reversal at the bottom and then riding it for all it's worth. Whether it's trying to pick the intraday low or a major 3-month market swing, getting in at the bottom and catching the whole move is a trader's dream. Unfortunately, that is easier said than done. Trend traders normally get in after the turn, and wave traders get out too soon if they do happen to catch the bottom. Trying to catch reversals by nature means going against the trend, but there are times when this is a high probability trade. A dedicated trader who has patience can be very successful at catching tops and bottoms.

Trying to pick tops or bottoms can be frustrating, and losses can amass rapidly as a trader may be wrong quite frequently when he is going against the trend. A trader trading against the trend must respect stops and be quick to accept losses. Many times he will have to try three or four times before hitting one. During this time a lot of people give up out of frustration or lack of capital, and as luck will have it, the next time is the one that would have worked like a charm. This is why a trader who trades for reversals must have deeper pockets and be consistent. You can't give up because it didn't work a few times. Later in the book I'll discuss the importance of having and backtesting a system so that you know how many consecutive times it has been wrong in the past and how big of a drawdown it can produce. This may help you decide whether this trading style is for you.

WHY MARKETS REVERSE

When a trendline gets broken, it is the simplest form of a market reversal. A trendline acts as a point of equilibrium between the bears and the bulls, and so when the market breaks it, there is a chance that the direction will change as the other group takes control. Besides the typical break of a trendline, there are a few other conditions you can look at that will tip you off that the market may be reversing. A market also may reverse directions because it has just finished one of its typical wavelengths, it has reached overbought or oversold levels, or, if it is range-bound, it might have moved beyond its normal range. Apart from these conditions, the following are a few situations and patterns that you should learn to recognize, as they can alert you that a market may be reversing.

Reversal Days

Very often when the market changes direction, it does that with a reversal day pattern. A reversal day or bar is one where in a downtrend the market makes a lower low than the previous day's low and then goes higher than the previous day's close. These days are normally high-volume days that can cause the market to change direction, at least temporarily. A key reversal day is one where after making a lower low, the market makes a higher high than it did the previous day. You can also have a 2-day reversal, where on the first day the market drops lower and closes off its low but is not positive for the day and then on the next day the market goes straight up from there, breaking the close from 2 days before.

In Chart 8–8 I've included a few reversal day patterns. You will notice that when the signal was combined with an overbought or oversold reading in the stochastics, the trade worked quite well. Not every trade works great, but those which do can more than make up for the ones that don't. The key with this type of trading strategy is to be able to hold a winning trade for a while because you may be getting in at the beginning of a new trend; on the other hand, you need to be able to get out right away when you are wrong. A typical stop when using reversal day bars is to use the low of the day (in an upward reversal) for an exit.

MY FIRST TRADING SYSTEM

My earliest and favorite day trading system was based on reversal days. I would keep track of every commodity that made a higher high or a lower low compared with the day before. When I found

CHART 8-8

Daily S&P 500 Index: Reversal Days

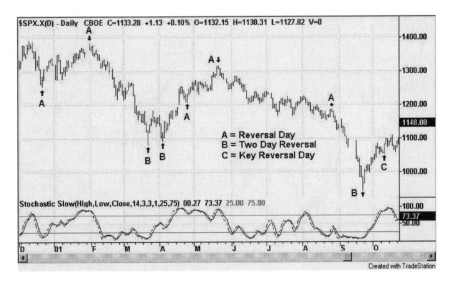

one, I would place a stop to get me in, just at the other side of unchanged, so that if it went through it, I'd be in the market without even thinking about it. If the market finished the day moving strongly in my direction, I would hold on to see if it followed through the next day. Sometimes these day trades last for several days as the market keeps going. The signals with the highest probability of working are in the direction of the major trend and come during a retracement as they bring you back into the trend. I still incorporate this strategy into my trading today.

Reversal Patterns

Reversal patterns can take the form of V-shaped or saucer-shaped (rounded) tops or bottoms or can come in the form of double or triple tops or bottoms. Double or triple tops are significant reversal patterns that are made when the market reaches the previous high but fails to make a new high. This is a sign that the trend is losing strength. Double tops often take the shape of an M, and double bottoms the shape of a W. In Chart 8–9, an intraday chart of Intel, you can see both a double top and bottom and the M and W formations they form.

CHART 8-9

10-Minute Intel: Reversal Patterns

INTC - 10 min   NASDQ C=33.68 +0.48 +1.45% O=32.87 H=34.16 L=32.75 V=35833700

Double Top
M Formation

Double Bottom
W Formation

B

A

V Bottom

4/23   4/24   4/25   4/26   4/27   4/30   5/01   5/02   5/03

32.00
31.00
30.00
29.00
28.00

Created with TradeStation

When you see a market that reaches its previous level and can't go further, there is a good chance it will be reversing direction soon. The way to trade these patterns is to identify the double top or bottom and then look to see if it breaks the trend it had been in. If the market is reaching its previous low and fails to break lower, one can take a small long position as soon as the market fails to make a lower low, knowing that there is a clearly defined risk level (the previous low) where one can place a stop. After this level, if the market starts to bounce as it did at the double bottom in Chart 8–9, one could add to the position after either Trendline A or Resistance Line B gets broken. Keep in mind that just because you see a double bottom it doesn't mean the market will reverse; it could easily go right through that level at any time. However, being able to identify one can help you catch a good trading opportunity in the market.

V-shaped reversals are another pattern to look for, but they can happen quickly and unexpectedly and so are hard to anticipate. They usually occur when the market is moving strongly in one direction and you don't expect a turn at all. In cases like the one in Chart 8–9, you may be more tempted to short than to buy at

CHART 8-10

10-Minute Intel: Rounded Top

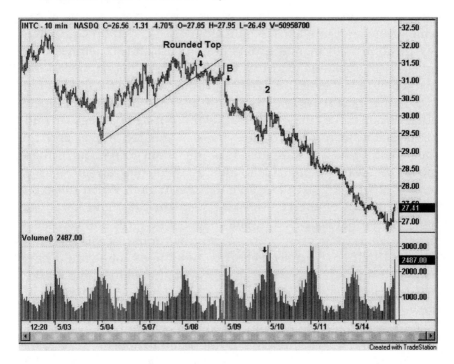

the V bottom because the trend is definitely down. But when you see a break of a trendline coming after a strong move, you should no longer be thinking about shorting. Instead, a high probability strategy is to look for a place to buy with a stop at the low. You also may want to check other time frames to get a better feel for whether the market should be bought.

Saucer, or rounded, reversals are a little easier to spot as they take more time to develop, giving you more of a warning as the market slowly stops going in the direction in which it had been going. In Chart 8–10 you can see that it took the market 2 days to stall at the top of the range. After it made a high, it started coming off slightly, but it stayed somewhat strong, although it could not break higher. When it broke the trendline at Point A, one could have taken this as a good place to short or waited until Point B, where the market clearly broke lower, indicating that the up move was over.

The "Can't Take the Pain Anymore" Reversal

I can't count the number of times I've gotten shaken out of a position at the worst possible time because I was on the wrong side of a move and couldn't take the pain anymore. I ended up liquidating my position with market orders at any cost and sometimes even reversed the position. Most of the time when this happened, the market ended its surge and went the other way the second I got in. This is the most frustrating thing a trader can do, and it happens often. What makes these reversals stand out against regular pullbacks is the increased volume, the exaggerated move, and the speed with which it happens. It is important to recognize these moves because by being able to identify them, one can save a lot of money or find a great place to enter the market. When these big moves run out of energy, they can snap back fast and hard. The new energy that is caused by the snap can be great and can cause the market to switch directions. A typical example of this is seen in Chart 8–10. If one had been short before Point 1, one would have had to sit through a pretty steep rally just afterward as the market spiked up at the close and opened much higher the next day on above average volume. Many people would panic or not be able to take the pain and exit at Point 2, only to watch the market come right back and then some. What is important to note here is that the volume was stronger than normal on the open, but the market couldn't go higher afterward, indicating the spike may have ended. The trade one can make in these situations is to wait for these big moves against the trend and then fade them as they start to die down. After one of these extended moves the market can come in hard, so try to take advantage of them. Looking at a longer time frame is helpful in these situations because it can help you determine just how much more room a market has to go.

WALKING AWAY

When I can't take the pain anymore, I look to see if the stochastics are at an extreme level. If they are, I'll walk away for 10 minutes; if the market doesn't improve when I get back I'll get out no matter what. I try not to reverse my position because that is chasing the market and constitutes a low probability trade. Instead I'll take a little break and wait for the next move. The important thing here is that when one of these moves occurs and the volume is strong, there is a good chance that the trend will end.

Key Number Reversals

When a stock, commodity, or index hits or nears a nice round number such as 10,000 on the Dow, 2000 on NASDAQ, $20 in crude, or a significant technical level such as a previous high and can't break through it, look for a reversal. As the market approaches these numbers, people get in just to push it there, but as soon as it gets there, interest dies down because the chase is over. This is a psychological barrier that is self-imposed. When a market starts dropping and approaches a round number, buyers wait to see what it does. There will be an abundance of limit orders at the number that will start getting hit, causing a slight bounce. People on the sidelines then may rush in, causing the market to bounce even higher; then the shorts start to cover and the down move is temporarily over, causing a reversal. When you do see the market headed for a key number, you should assume it will bounce off that number. However, be prepared for a breakout just in case.

MEASURING THE MOVE

When a market breaks out of a trading range, a trader should try to estimate the potential move so that he can measure the risk if the trade goes sour. Without a good mix between the two, no trade should be taken. It doesn't make sense to take a trade with a 20-cent potential profit but with a chance of losing a dollar. Aside from the traditional Fibonacci retracement levels described in Chap. 6, there are a few other ways to measure a potential move. One way, as I mentioned earlier, is to take the width of the sideways congestion to measure the move after a breakout. Markets tend to move in uniform ranges, and so you can use the size of the previous wave or range as a guide for the next one. If the market had been consolidating sideways for about 5 inches on your chart, look for a 5-inch move when it breaks out of the range. If the last wave was 3 points, you can use that as a goal for the next move. Also, if a market has been trading in a channel, the width of the channel can be used to estimate a move.

On Chart 8–11 (the same 5-minute S&Ps chart from earlier), when the market broke out of its sideways range, the move it made up almost equaled exactly the distance of the width of its sideways range. These two rectangles are practically the same. If the market does break and travels the expected distance of the previous range, look for a place to get out instead of getting greedy, hoping for

CHART 8-11

5-Minute S&P 500: Measuring the Move

more. Otherwise you may end up watching the market slip away, as ended up happening here.

WHEN TO GET IN

One question that hits a trader when a breakout first occurs is whether to get in immediately or wait until the close of the day or period. Both strategies have merits and drawbacks. Waiting for an end-of-period confirmation will help one avoid many false signals, but on a big day one could miss a large chunk of a move by waiting. However, if one takes the intrabar trade, there is a better chance that the market will pull back. Traders have different preferences concerning when to take a signal. The way I prefer to trade is to use the initial breakout as an alert to get involved and then use my indicators and different time frames to time a trade. If I miss an entry, as does happen on a good strong move, I wait until the end of the day to take the trade in hopes of seeing it follow through the next day. The important thing not to do when you miss an entry is to chase it. If you miss it, just wait for the next one.

Using Stops to Get into the Market

One way to enter the market when a breakout is anticipated is with a buy or sell stop. For example, if you are looking at Chart 8–11 and you see the sideways range (the first shaded rectangle) that could result in a breakout, you can place a buy stop just outside that area so that if it gets broken, you'll be in the market. This method is good because it gets you in quickly without hesitating or missing the trade. You won't be late to the party, watching it from the sidelines, and it keeps you from chasing it. As soon as the break occurs, you are in, and yours will be one of the initial orders that cause the market to break with a burst. Another place to use an entry stop on Chart 8–11 would be when you see the triangle forming at the beginning of the chart. Though it's hard to guess which side it will break out on, a triangle does have to break at some point. Putting stops on both sides of it is not a bad idea because then when you get in on the break on one side, you'll have a protective stop on the other side. You can see in this chart that without a stop to get in, one would have missed the major part of this move completely. Using stops to enter the market is great for traders who are too busy to watch the market and those who can never pull the trigger. By placing a stop you know you will be in if the market breaks, no matter what. Unfortunately, by doing this you cannot be careful about false breaks.

Adding Filters before Getting In

To avoid getting caught in a false move, some people like to add a filter or buffer to their systems. Filters aren't necessarily a tool for trading breakouts, but they can be helpful. Some traders like to see a set percentage move outside the breakout level before they get involved; others like to see three closes outside the range. Many times the market pops its head above a trendline only to come right back. By knowing that you will take a trade only if it breaks the trendline by more than 3 percent, 3 points, or three closes, you avoid those times when the market fails to follow through. While filters can help, there is a trade-off, as they can lead to missing a good part of a move if the initial break was explosive. Chart 8–11 provides an example of how adding a filter works. At Point A, the market dipped below the trendline it had formed in the afternoon but quickly came back up. Using a 3-point buffer, for example, would have kept one from shorting this false break. Filters can be whatever a trader wants them to be. When you are writing and testing a trading strategy, try out different ideas until you find one that works well for you. One thing to keep in mind when you are using filters is that the more volatile the market is, the larger the buffer zone should be, because in a volatile market a move can be greater and still be false.

THE IMPORTANCE OF DISTINGUISHING BETWEEN HIGH PROBABILITY AND LOW PROBABILITY BREAKOUTS

Trading breakouts requires a patient and dedicated trader. Many breakouts will lead to false signals, and though overall they may have a low percentage of success, when they do work, they can be very rewarding. This is why a trader can be wrong five times out of six and still do quite well trading breakouts. By being more selective and having the patience to wait for a solid entry point, a trader can improve his chances significantly. Using volume, oscillators, and longer time frames and waiting for a pullback are all ways to improve the chances of a breakout working. Figuring out the difference between which breakouts will have a better chance of working out and which trades won't work as well can make an average trader good and a good trader great. When a breakout is unexpected, it tends to act the best. When the support has been very strong and everyone is expecting it to bounce, the surprise of seeing it breaking through makes people liquidate and switch positions, adding fuel to the fire. But when the breakout seems like it was a sure thing, much of the move may have taken place already as traders were anticipating it, and then there is no one left to push the market.

TYPICAL BREAKOUT SYSTEMS

A typical breakout system experienced traders use is to buy at the breakout of the highest high of the last x periods (I'll use 10) or to short the lowest low. For an exit you can get out on a pullback that breaks a three-period low; this could be with a loss if it happens right away or with a profit if it happens after you've been in for a move. This trade gets you into the momentum of the market and then gets you out when that momentum is lost.

The Signals

Entry signal: Buy on the opening of the next bar if the current bar closes higher than the highest high of the previous 10 bars.

Exit signal: Exit if the current bar closes below the lowest low of the last three bars.

Another simple system is to buy when a downward sloping trendline plus a small buffer zone gets broken. This uses a filter that eliminates the random noise that could cause the market to break a barrier without much significance behind it. Instead of buying when a down trendline gets violated, buy when it gets violated by 10 ticks or whatever you like. For an exit you also can use a filter that stops you out if the market dips back below the trendline for 2 consecutive days. This keeps you in if the market retests the trendline and dips below it for just a bar. Apart from helping weed out false trades, a filter will help cut down on the total number of trades a trader makes, which in the long run can be critical in a trader's career.

The Signals

Entry signal: Buy if the current bar's close is higher than the trendline plus 10 ticks.

Exit signal: Exit if both the current bar and the previous bar close below the trendline.

30-Minute Breakout System

One of the oldest day trading systems around is based on the assumption that when the market is trending up, the lows are made at the opening and the highs are made toward the end of the day. The 30-minute breakout system does nothing until the market has been open for 30 minutes. After the first 30 minutes the market will have established an opening range (the high and low of the day so far). A trader must wait for this first half hour of trading to determine this range and then take trades on the side of whichever way the market breaks out of that range. Thus, using a 30-minute chart, if the market breaks out toward the high end of the opening bar, one will buy, and then one will place a stop below the low end of the range. This puts the trader on the right side of the market and keeps him from trying to find tops and bottoms. This works even better when one is trading in the direction of the major trend. If the market was in an uptrend, you would want to buy only if the market broke the high end and would ignore the trade if it was toward the downside. You can get involved with a stop or wait for the first close of a 30-minute bar outside the range. There are many variations on this system. Instead of 30 minutes, it could be 45 or 60 minutes, and some people wait for the second half hour to finish before actually placing a trade. This means that even if a buy signal is given after 35 minutes, one waits to see if it is still a valid signal after 60 minutes is up. If it is still above the high of the first 30 minutes, it is a buy. You can also use a buffer of a few ticks above the high to confirm that it is not a false signal.

The Signals

Entry signal: Buy on the close if the time is greater than the open plus 30 minutes and the current bar closes higher than the highest high of the day.

Exit signal: Exit if the current close is the lowest low of the day.

BECOMING A BETTER TRADER

Becoming a better trader means being able to recognize and act when the market is breaking out of a range, pattern, or trend. This goes for when you are previously in a trade and it starts turning, and to get in a new trade when the market does break through. A good trader is always ready to act when the market approaches a level from which it could break. It may or may not break, but by being alert when it is near a potential break level, one can react quickly if it does. To become a better trader one needs to incorporate a few tools to learn when a breakout has a good chance of working. These tools include using trendlines, breakout patterns, oscillators, reversal patterns, and volume. Looking at higher time frames is also helpful in determining the validity of a break. A good trader should be able to distinguish which patterns can lead to a breakout or reversal and how much potential the market has to move afterward. Knowing how much a market can move is important as a smart trader only takes trades that have a larger potential reward than risk; it also keeps you from being too greedy. Breakout trades are not meant to be quick in-and-out trades. Some of the best moves will happen after a break, and so you can do quite well by capturing one or two good breakouts and staying in them as a trend develops.

As with all other trading situations, the trades with the highest probabilities are the ones that are made in the direction of the major trend, and so when those trades come along, one should be more aggressive. Finally and most important, I believe that one should never chase a trade. If you chase, the risk can become too much to handle, so wait for the pullback. It could take a long time to get it, but one gets rewarded for patience in trading.

Breakouts Pitfalls

1. Ignoring risk/reward ratios
2. Not having a real idea of where significant market levels are
3. Trading against the major trend of the market
4. Not getting out when one is on the wrong side of a breakout
5. Anticipating breakouts before they happen
6. Holding on too long when a breakout fails
7. Not measuring the potential move
8. Ignoring volume
9. Getting in too late after missing the move
10. Forgetting that stops can be a bit too far away if the entry point was poor
11. Not having the patience to wait for a pullback
12. Getting trapped in a pullback
13. Chasing, in which case a trader stands a good chance of watching the position quickly go against him
14. Not waiting for good entry points makes it easy to overtrade

High Probability Breakout Trading

1. You need patience to trade breakouts.
2. Wait for good entry points and pullbacks.
3. Trade on the side of the momentum of the market.
4. Hold out for the big move if a new trend begins.
5. Breaks of countertrends in a strongly trending market are good signals to take.
6. Use stops to get in.

7. Be prepared to do something when the market approaches a potential breakout area.

8. The best breakouts are those which move and work right away.

9. If it does not work, get out.

10. Use the size of the previous wave, range, or congestion to measure the next move.

11. Look for breakouts after a consolidation period with high volume.

12. Keep track of volume.

13. Look for the side of the market where there is more price action.

14. Look for a break in the direction where volume seems heavier.

15. Use filters to weed out false breaks.

16. If a stop area is too far away, the risk may not be worth the reward.

17. When a breakout is unexpected, it tends to act the best.

18. Breakouts in the direction of the major trend work best.

19. The steeper a trendline is, the more likely it is that it will get broken.

20. Use other indicators to help determine the chance of a breakout working.

21. Use higher time frames to get a better picture of the market.

22. Scale into positions until the market finds some support.

23. Take some profits early on a breakout in case there is a pullback.

24. Pay attention to the reversal patterns that could precede a breakout.

Helpful Questions to Ask Yourself

Am I getting in too late?
Did I get in before the market broke?
Should I wait for a retracement?

Did I use volume or any other indicator to see if the break-out was a high probability one?

Am I trading more aggressively when the break is in the direction of the major trend?

How much room does it have to go?

Exits and Stops

M any traders expend too much effort finding entry signals and patterns and not nearly as much time as they should exiting a position. They get in expecting the trade to work with little planning, if any, on how to exit the trade on either the winning side or the losing side. Once in the trade, they have no idea what to do except sit back and count their winnings or watch dumbfounded as the market goes against them.

Anyone can enter a trade, but one of the keys to success is knowing when and how to exit it. I would venture to say that most trades are profitable at some point, even those made randomly; by having a good exit strategy one can learn to capture more profits and lose less. With the exit being so important, I'm amazed it is not stressed in books as much as a setup of a trade is. Without protective exit strategies it is impossible to be a successful trader. I will do my best to explain how to let profits ride and where to place stops so that losers can get nipped in the bud before they amount to anything damaging.

CUTTING LOSSES AND LETTING PROFITS RIDE

Probably the most quoted golden rule of trading that anybody who has ever traded has heard is "Cut your losses and let your profits ride." Surprisingly, many traders do the opposite. They have a winner and quickly get out, and when they have a loser, they hold on to it, praying for a reversal as they watch it get worse and worse. Until a trader can learn to get out of a losing trade, place a stop properly, hold on to a good position, and know when to take a profit, he will find it hard to be successful. Getting into a position is only one piece of the trading equation. Knowing when to get out on both the losing and winning sides is another and probably even more important part of trading. Most losing traders lose because their winners are too small compared with their losers. A lack of really good profitable trades can hurt a trader as much as all his losing trades will. It is expected that more than half a trader's trades will be losers—that's part of trading—so in order to compensate, the winners have to be bigger than the losers. I can't tell you how many people I've seen repeatedly take small profits of just a few ticks and then let a loser grow astronomically. This is not a strategy that will get you far.

GETTING OUT TOO SOON

There is no feeling worse than missing a great trade because you erred on the side of safety and exited prematurely. When you get out of a trade with a 30-cent gain and then watch it move another buck fifty in 20 minutes, it can be heart-wrenching. Some traders are so concerned about taking profits and having a high winning percentage that they take many small winners because they are scared to lose. Taking too many small profits without letting good trades develop is a bad practice that may keep you from becoming a big trader, as you never allow a potentially powerful trade to get going. Sure, you will have more winning trades and a higher win/loss percentage, but this may come at the expense of total profits in the long run. There are traders who do quite well by repeatedly taking small profits, but what is key for them is that they take even smaller losses.

IT'S All RELATIVE

There are many traders who make a living by capturing small moves over and over and this is a great way to trade, but they also are able to take even smaller losses. If you are a trader who is capable of losing only a few ticks before getting out, you can make money trading for small gains and not trying to capture the big trades. The size of your winners should be relative to that of your losers. If you have small losers, your winners can be modest; if you have medium-size losers, you must have large winners; if you have large losers, you need jumbo winners; and if you have jumbo losers, you will need to learn the phrase "Would you like to jumbo size that?"

LETTING PROFITS RIDE

I guess I can start with letting profits ride because I'm sure you as a trader would rather hear about that than about losses. Nobody can ever accuse me of getting out of winning trades too soon; I always hold on if something is working. My problem has always been holding losers longer than I should, not letting profits ride. Here's a little story about holding a trade that is working. To get the gist of the conversation you will need to throw in a few dozen colorful adjectives that my editor thought I shouldn't use.

About a year and a half ago I was short SUNW when it was still trading near $100. It opened at its high of the day and started to sell off, so I shorted it, as did most of the other guys in the room. After about 2 hours I mentioned how good of a short it was and said that I had 5 points in the trade. This was a mistake, because soon afterward, everyone in my room was telling me how I should cover since I had a good profit in it. The stock kept making lows with barely a bounce, and I told them that when it stopped going down and gave me a reason to, I'd cover. They all had gotten out 4 points before, and for the next 4 hours their afternoon was spent trying to manage my position. When I had $7 in it, they said, "Wow, take your profit." When I had $8, they said it again. I finally got annoyed at them and gave them a piece of my mind. I asked them (begin using adjectives freely), "When should I have gotten out, at $2, $3, $5, $7, or $8? What makes any of those numbers a good amount of profit to take? You were telling me to get out with $5. If I had mentioned it when I had $4, you would have said the same thing. How do you know the opportune time to get out? I see how all of you are out of it and nobody wants to short it now because you're afraid to short into such a big down move, so you have nothing better to do than watch my position; just leave me alone." I held the stock until just before the close and made over $10 per share in it, having my best day ever trading stocks up to that point.

I learned two lessons that day. One, never let other people's opinion affect your trading; two, don't get out if a trade is working, no matter how much you have in it. That stock went straight down the whole day, and there was never a reason to exit. Moves like this don't happen often, but when they do, they should be taken advantage of. When a trade is going your way, you want to hold it as long as you can without giving back profits. It takes only 1 or 2 good trades to make up for 10 small losing trades, and so if you are in a good trend, stay with it. Have a trailing stop or retracement level you are willing to let a profit retreat to, and if it doesn't hit it and you see no other reason to exit, hold on for the ride.

A lot of traders I know find it hard to hold onto a trade that is working well. They get out too soon because they've been conditioned that way, but there are times when the right thing to do is hold. One way to hold on longer is to have a plan in advance that keeps you in the market until a certain target or condition is met, unless of course you get stopped out. By having a target or condition you will avoid the temptation of getting out with a quick profit. As I'll explain later, you should have a trailing stop to protect your profits, but unless the reasons for being in the trade have changed, let your profits ride. There will be times when you feel that it is time to exit a trade with a winner, such as after a big buying climax, where the market makes a big move on increased volatility. This is normally the time to get out with a winner instead of giving it the opportunity to come back. After a big move the odds are strong that the market will retrace a bit, and so it is smart to take some profits. You can always get back in when the market stabilizes. But if the market is going your way steadily, there may be no reason to get out except that you are too fidgety to hold a winning trade.

EXIT STRATEGIES

Exiting in Stages

The problem many traders face is that they don't know what to do when they have a gain in a position. When some people are getting out, others are adding, and still others are taking some of the trade off but keeping a piece of it. Someone once posed this question to me: "You have 1000 shares in a stock and it takes off, making a nice run, and then begins to consolidate. What do you do? Add to it, get out, or take half off the board?" All three of these choices are good ones, yet they are all different, and so it is a hard question to answer.

The first instinct of many traders is "Hey, I just had a good run in the stock. Let me ring the cash register, take my profits off the table, and go play golf." Other people may think just the opposite, and they add to the position, thinking, "This stock is strong and has just consolidated without coming off, so it may be poised for another good run. Why look for something else when I already have a good stock? Let me make my capital work by adding to my winners." The right choice depends on the market, your target goals, and your risk levels. I think the best choice is to take profits on a portion of the position and hold the rest in case the market continues its move. By doing this, at the worst you should make some money. If the market starts to go back up, you can always take advantage of the strong move by adding to the position you have left. But while the market consolidates and runs a risk of coming off, you are at least cutting your exposure and booking some profits.

As part of a good exit strategy one should learn how to scale out of a trade in stages. Trades don't need to be exited all at once; instead, one may do better by scaling out of them. But few people will think this out beforehand; they just get in and out of a trade all at once, with little thought. One of the things I recommend to traders who have enough capital is to trade in multiples of three contracts or 300 shares. I sometimes like to exit one-third of my position with a small profit on the first wave; the next one I'll cover where I would have covered if I had been trading only one contract, and for the final third I'll hold, trying to capture the big move. You have to be strict with the exits on the losing side as well. If it doesn't work immediately, you want to exit a third of your position quickly; with the other two-thirds you may use your normal stop area or exit when you know the trade is hopeless. By learning to scale out of winners you will allow yourself to get out with a little profit and give yourself a chance to catch a big move.

Getting Out When It's Time

Everyone has experienced a trade that started off great only to turn out to be a loser or a trade that went from a small loser to a really bad loser. Many times you know you should be getting out, but for some reason or another you miss the chance and get stuck in the position. *Failing to exit a trade when it is time to do so more often than not will be costly.* Once an exit is missed, a trader has two choices: wait for the next opportunity to get out or get out no matter what the price is. Waiting for the next chance or hoping to get bailed out is how a trader can get into trouble. Once you know you are wrong, you should exit the trade without looking back.

WHEN YOU WANT TO GET OUT, GET OUT

One bad thing traders fall into the habit of doing (and I do this a lot) is to try to get the very last tick on every trade. You are short and see that the stock just made a low of 24.10. As you are putting in your order to buy it, it jumps 10 cents. Now you don't want to get out at this price; you want the low because you are a greedy bastard. You put a bid in at 24.11 so that you can get out near the lows, but the market never goes back down. You are "stuck" as it keeps bouncing 20, 30, 50 cents off the low; before you know it, your profit has disappeared and you are at breakeven. You could have gotten out with a 60-cent profit if you had gotten out of the market when you first wanted to, but no, you wanted more. Next thing you know, you are facing a loss while still hoping for new lows.

Traders aren't perfect and so you will never know where the bottom is. When it is time to get out, do so; you don't need to try to squeeze every last penny out of a trade. At least exit part of the position at the market and maybe wait for the market to come back for the remainder. This applies to both winners and losers and to getting into a trade as well. Don't miss a move because you are too cheap to pay up for it. If you want something, pay the offer, and if you don't and miss it, don't moan about it.

Exiting When the Reasons Why You Entered Have Changed

Once the reasons you got into a trade have changed, you should get out of the trade. For example, if you bought a stock because it was strong relative to the market and it no longer seems strong, exit the trade. If you get into a trade because of a support level or some indicator and it fails to do what it should do, don't wait to get stopped out; as soon as you know you are wrong, get out. If the indicator doesn't turn as you hoped it would, hoping even harder is still not going to make it turn. Accept the fact that you were wrong and exit the trade. It doesn't matter if you are up or down; once the reason you made the trade is no longer there, you should be thinking about getting out. An example would be when you buy because the market is near a trendline and you think it will continue to trend. If it breaks the line, you were wrong, so don't hesitate to get out.

LOSSES ARE MORE IMPORTANT THAN WINNERS

Just as every real estate investor knows that the three most important things are location, location, location, a trader should know that cutting losses, cutting losses, and cutting losses are the three keys to successful trading. Even more important than how much you make on a trade is how little you lose on the losses. When you are considering exit conditions, the first thing you want to know is where you will be getting out with a loss that will not do much damage. Only after you know what your worst-case scenario risk is should you start thinking about how much you can make. *Losing positions must be gotten out of as soon as they merit it.* Staying in a bad position because one doesn't want to take a loss is not how a trader makes money. Learning how to lose correctly is one of the most important things a trader can do. Though holding on to a good trade that is working is critical, unless you know how to exit bad positions, you won't get very far as a trader. If a trader is properly capitalized, no single trade will kill him. Sticking to a stop is important because a small loss means nothing, but a large one can be devastating.

One thing you should try to get into your head is that a loss is different from losing. Every trader will have lots of losses; they are part of trading. Losing, in contrast, is the result of letting little losses become large losses. Many people think that by taking a loss they are losing, and this is just not the case. The more quickly they understand that losses are normal and are expected half the time, the sooner they will be able to exit bad trades immediately. A winning trader is one who knows how to lose. The good trades will come no matter how bad a trader you are. If you can learn to minimize the losing trades, you'll have a chance of success. This means holding a winning trade for as long as it is working. There is also a fine line between cutting losses short and taking losers too quickly without giving trades a chance to work. You need to let trades develop, but you also need to be quick to get out when you know you are wrong. A good exit strategy will be a mixture of letting trades work to their best potential and not letting any trades hurt you.

THE GOAL OF THE STOP

Stops should be an important tool in a trader's arsenal of weapons, but many traders don't know how to use or place stops. They may place stops randomly, not basing them on what the market suggests a good place may be. Instead they have a dollar amount they are willing to lose and use that for a stop. In placing stops, it is critical to place them where the market suggests is a good place to put them, instead of basing them on how much a trader can afford to lose. Otherwise, stops can become too close and trades that could have been good may be stopped out as losers because they were never allowed to work. Even worse is the situation where stops are too far away and a trader loses more than he has to.

Although stops can be used to enter trades, for the purpose of this chapter stop orders are orders that are placed at a point that will limit and control losses while letting you know you were wrong. The first and most important goal of a stop is to control losses. This is what keeps a trader in the game for the long run, giving him a chance to succeed. Without stops a trader can let bad trades get really bad and could lose track of his game plan. To be a successful trader one needs to know how to preserve capital. This is done with good money management skills, risk control, and knowing where to place stops.

Having a predetermined stop point will let you relax a little. You don't have to keep questioning the market or your decisions. You know exactly when you will be out, and you should know this before you even make the trade. Once you have a stop, it's like having insurance; it lets you sleep nights because you already know the most you can lose. Knowing where you will get out before a trade is made is important so that you can manage risk and determine if the risk/reward ratio makes the trade worthwhile. Not having a predetermined stop, even a mental one, can lead to trouble. This leads into a good point. Stops can be placed physically into the market or can be kept mentally. Most traders are not disciplined enough to keep mental stops, and so until they develop that discipline, they should place stops into the market.

LOSING TRACK OF REALITY

I've been in trades that start out being small losers, and I don't get out because I expect a bounce. The market then drops a little more, and I add to my position because now I *know* a bounce will come. It doesn't, and the market keeps getting worse. What should have been a $2000 loss is now $5000 and then I can't get out because I can't fathom losing that much on a trade. I hold on, praying for a bounce that never comes, and I end up losing $8000 for the day, 4 times my acceptable loss. If I had had a stop in the market, I would not have lost track of reality and would have lost only $2000, as I should have, and would have been able to move on to the next trade. Instead I have a day that throws off my confidence and affects my trading for days to come.

STOPS ARE NOT FAIL-SAFE

Though stops are important and should be used, they aren't always the safety net one would think they are. For one thing, they can make someone lackadaisical about the market, causing that person not to pay attention to a position after getting into it. Also, when the market is moving fast or gapping, one can get filled at a price that was not where one had hoped it would be. You may have planned to lose only $1500, but you may lose $2500 if the market is moving or gapping.

Feeling Too Safe

There will be times when a trader is in a position that is bad or wrong but he is not down much. He may have a stop 10 ticks away and it is only 3 ticks against him. He may no longer think it is a great trade, but since it hasn't been stopped out yet, in his mind it is still a good trade and is worth holding on to. He had put the stop where he thought was a good place to get out, and until the market reaches that level, he believes he is on the right side of the market. This is bad thinking. When you are in a trade and it is not working the way it should, or you start feeling uncomfortable with it, get out and forget about what you thought was a good level before. Don't think you are safe because the market hasn't stopped out the trade yet. You never need to wait to get stopped out. If the trade feels wrong, just exit it even if it's barely against you or slightly in your favor. This can save you a lot of money in the long run. Say you got into the market because of a breakout and it fails to follow through as planned; instead it just lingers. There is no need to wait until the market hits your stop level to get out. If it isn't working as it should, odds are that eventually it will hit your stop so why not take the small loss now and try again later?

GETTING LAZY

I like to use time stops, where if a trade is not working after 45 minutes, I get out. Unfortunately, I sometimes get into the habit of ignoring small losses if I've had the trade on for only 20 or 30 minutes. I figure I'm not down too much and they still have time to work, so I hold, watching them get worse, until I finally exit them 20 minutes later. This is something I have to be more diligent about not doing, but it is easy to get complacent when you have stops in the market that you think are good.

Slippage

Slippage is another problem one encounters with stops. It is not uncommon to have a stop at one price but get filled at a substantially different price, especially if the market is moving against you fast. There are times when a news event such as a presidential race miscount, an interest rate cut, or an earnings warning can cause the market to gap. A break of a resistance level can do this as well. Stops in these incidents get violated and filled farther away than expected as the market moves right through them. Sometimes a market opens up the next day 3 points from where it closed and above where a stop may have been placed; in this case stops are automatically elected as the market opens regardless of the level of a stop. There is nothing one can do about this except curse out loud and move on to the next trade. When I got caught on the short side of the surprise rate cut on January 3, 2001, there was nothing I could do to get out of my trades with a small loss. Though I didn't have physical stops in the market, I knew that I wanted to get out if the market broke the high made at Point B on Chart 9-1, a 1-minute chart of QLogic (QLGC). I had just gotten short at Point A, thinking the market had failed to make a new high. I also shorted a handful or two of other stocks at the same time. When the rate cut happened at Point C, there was nothing I could do to get out without some major damage. I placed a market order to get out and ended up getting filled at about Point D, $12 from where it broke the high at Point B. I lost about $5 to $7 per stock from where I had wanted to get out on the others as well. Even if I had had stops in the market, I don't think I would have done better than losing about $3 to $5 per stock, which is still quite a lot of slippage.

MISUSING STOPS

Stops That Are Too Close

Other than not using stops, the thing traders do wrong most often is placing them in the wrong spots. One of the most frustrating things for a trader is to have a position on, have the market go against it until it gets stopped out, and then have it immediately reverse and go the way you wanted it to. A good stop is a combination of a spot that will protect you against a large loss, not letting you get hurt, and a spot that will will keep you in a position, letting it breathe a little so that it has time to develop if you are right. Some traders end up having stops that are too tight and don't give their trades the room they need to develop. This is influenced by the fear of losing too much money on any trade, taking the saying "Cut your losses" too seriously, or not having a clue where to place

CHART 9-1

1-Minute QLGC: Blowing through Stops

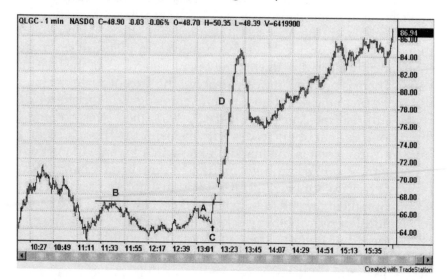

Created with TradeStation

a stop technically. Hence, poor traders place their stops within the market's regular movements or inside a trendline and then get frustrated when they are stopped out near the low of the move. They may have been correct in their assessment of the market, but if they entered at a bad level or the market was volatile, they would get stopped out, not having given themselves enough room to take advantage of the pursuing move. After they were stopped out and the market started going the way they thought it would, they might get right back in, usually at the same place where they entered before.

Stops that are too tight are a surefire method of losing money. Yes, losses will be small, but by placing stops within the regular trading range of the market, these stops will be hit a lot. If you have stops that are too close, the percentage of winning trades will decrease, and many trades that could have been good winning trades will end up being small losers because they were never allowed to develop fully.

I had one client trading the E-mini S&P 500 who refused to lose more than 2 or 3 points on any trade. That's $100 to $150, practically nothing when one is trading the E-mini, which easily moves 20 points a day, or $1000. It can move 3 points in any given 10-minute period. A stop of 2 or 3 points is within the normal standard deviation of the market's typical 10-minute move and most likely will be hit. Unless the entry levels are impeccable, it is hard to give a trade room to work with stops this close. The result was that he would make about 10 trades a day and get stopped out on about 80 percent of his trades, which was great for me as a broker but not too good for him. What was remarkable was that he was almost always correct in picking market direction. If he had placed his stops better, he would have been a successful trader. He went through his first $5000 in about 6 weeks and constantly added more money after that to meet margin requirements. He never learned from his mistakes, making them over and over. He was too afraid to lose big on any one trade, and so he dwindled his account to nothing with a barrage of small trades. If he could have mentally afforded to lose only $100 per trade, he should have been day trading a market such as corn, which has a daily trading range of $200 to $300. For the E-mini S&P these stops were much too tight, and they never gave the trades enough room to develop.

Stops That Are Too Far

The flip side of having stops that are too close is having stops
that are placed farther than they have to be. If someone is using
a set dollar stop, he can end up putting the stop way beyond a
safe place. What happens then is that the market goes to where a
proper stop should have been and then keeps on going, eventually reaching the stop. Having stops that are too far is senseless.
A trader may end up losing $500 when he should have lost only
$300. If one consistently places stops that are too far away, one's
account may get wiped out much faster than would someone's
who is more prudent about where he places his stops. There are
times, however, when a proper stop has to be placed too far away
from the market, such as after there has been a substantial move
and the market has moved too far away from a support level.
The only technically correct place to put a stop may cost you
more than you want to lose, and in that case a trade should not
be taken as the reward is not worth the risk. In these cases it is
better to wait for a safer opportunity to come along than to risk
too much.

The More Volatile the Market, the Wider the Stop

Always keep in mind that the more volatile the market is, the farther away a stop must be for it to be effective. If you cannot handle
large losses, markets or stocks with wide swings should not be part
of your game plan. I usually have a stop of 50 cents to $1 in most
stocks. However, if you are trading a volatile stock such as Yahoo
was when it had a $15 daily range, you could be down a buck fifty
as soon as your order is filled. With these crazy stocks I had to be
willing to risk $3 to $5 or I'd be stopped out way too often, only to
watch them shoot up $8 an hour later. This doesn't apply only to
different stocks or markets but to the same ones at different times.
In mid-2002 Yahoo was a $12 stock with barely a $1 daily range,
and so a 50-cent stop was more adequate than a $5 stop. Soybeans
have more volatile swings in the summer than they do in the winter, and one must be willing to risk more to trade them at certain
times. If you don't feel comfortable risking too much, the more
volatile markets are not for you, and you should stick to markets
you can stomach.

Placing Stops

As I'll describe soon, stops should be placed outside technical barriers and/or the normal trading range of the market unless you enjoy getting stopped out. Stops should not be based on how much you can afford to lose; instead, they should be placed where the market tells you a good spot is. To avoid getting stopped out needlessly, never place a stop where you think the market should go; instead, place it a safe distance away from where your gut tells you. Never place it at or within a whole number, trendline, moving average, high or low of the day or week, or any significant support or resistance level showing on either the time frame you are looking at or a higher one. Markets are drawn to round numbers and trendlines because that is where everybody is thinking they will go, and so it is best to place a stop outside these levels—and not just outside of them but with some breathing space as well. If you place them too close, there is a chance that the market will hit them on a quick burst when it reaches that level and takes out other stops. Proper stop placement is not easy. The rest of this chapter will describe the different type of stops one can use and how and where one should place them as well as where not to place them.

TYPES OF STOPS

The Money Management Stop

This is the kind of stop where you get into a trade and place a stop that allows you to lose only a fixed dollar amount. Money management stops should be used to keep a trader from hurting himself, but in my opinion, these are the most commonly misused stops there are and should not be used the way people use them. Most people who use these stops get into a trade and then place a stop that will prevent them from losing more than $500 or whatever amount they feel comfortable with. The goal of these stops is to prevent a trader from losing more than he can afford to lose on any given trade. The problem is that they are placed with no regard to what the market is doing. Risk is as much a function of the market as it is of what a trader can afford to lose. There are times when a $500 stop in a market is way too much, and other times in the same market it is not enough to let a trade breathe. In Chart 9–2, a 60-minute soybean chart, if you had shorted at Point A, hoping the market would break lower, and you could afford only a $500 stop,

you would have been stopped out at Stop Xa. Xa is just a randomly placed stop as far as the market is concerned and is not a good
place to have a stop. If you had waited for a bounce and gotten
short at Point B instead of Point A, you could have placed a stop at
Stop Xb, which is also a $500 stop but one that is properly placed
above the previous high of Point X. Stop Xb is a technically correct
stop that keeps you in the market, letting you capitalize on the
trade, while Stop Xa is randomly placed in the middle of the wave.

    Money management stops also can be a problem when one is
trading different markets. Some markets are more volatile than
others, and what may be a good dollar amount stop in one may not
be so good in another. A $500 stop in corn, for instance, is a safe
stop that most likely wouldn't get hit in a day; a $500 stop in the
S&Ps can get hit in about 5 minutes. One must know the markets
or stocks to be able to determine how much each one can hurt him.
Using an arbitrary dollar amount to risk is a lazy man's stop, and
everyone knows the lazy way is never the best way to do anything.
Finding a good stop area takes work and is based on technical
analysis, not on how much a trader can afford to lose. You need to
know what you can afford to risk in order to know if you should

CHART 9—2

60-Minute Soybeans: Stops Should Be Based on the Market

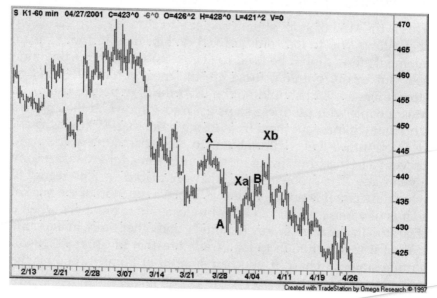

Created with TradeStation by Omega Research ℗ 1997

make a trade and how many contracts you may trade, but this dollar amount should not be your stop.

Using Money Management Stops to Figure Out Position Sizing

The proper way to use a money management stop is in conjunction with a technically placed stop and the size of your position. By this I mean that first one should know how much one feels comfortable risking and is willing to lose on any single trade. A trade should never be made without knowing how much is at risk and how much one can afford to lose per trade. If a trader has a $100,000 account, he may feel comfortable risking $2000 on any specific trade. This doesn't have to be exact to the penny but a rough idea so that risk can be established. This is usually a percentage of total capital, which I'll discuss in more detail in the money management chapters of this book. Look at the charts to find out just how much a trade can lose at worst; the market tells you this, not your wallet. After locating a good area to place a stop, figure out how much per contract it would cost if you got stopped out. Let's say the risk was $500, as in Stop Xb in Chart 9–2. Then divide the $2000 by $500 and you know you can trade up to four contracts on this trade. You need not trade four contracts but if you felt it was a high probability trade, you could. Normally I would take a position one-third or one-half the size of the maximum number of contracts and then add to it later if the trade started to work. If your timing was impeccable and you got into the market with a very small risk, you could consider adding even more contracts at the beginning. However, if the market said that the risk was $2500 per contract to make this trade, the trade just wouldn't be made, since it is outside your risk level of $2000. Zero is also an allowable number of contracts to trade when the risk is too great.

Percentage Move Stops

As with a money management stop, a percentage move stop will tell you how much it is okay to risk on a trade but should be used only if it is technically feasible. With a percentage move stop one can use the market itself as a way to figure out the most one is willing to risk per contract or share. Ways to figure out how much to risk in a market can be based on a percentage of true range, a standard deviation move of the market, or a percentage of the exchange margin requirement. One must know the characteristics of the markets or stocks traded to be able to determine how much each can hurt. I find no more than 30 percent of the daily average true range to be a good amount to risk on any given trade. Always use a higher time frame in figuring out the percentage you are willing to risk. If you are holding trades for the long term, you should get the true range of a weekly or monthly chart to figure out how much is an acceptable loss. When trading commodities, you can use 25 to 33 percent of the margin requirement as a good day trading limit to lose. For longer-term trades, don't risk more than the margin requirement.

When I'm day trading, I try not to allow myself to lose more than 25 to 30 percent of the average true range of a stock on any given trade. If a stock has a true range of $2 per day and I'm down more than 85 cents in it, I've done something wrong. It usually means that my timing was bad or that I'm just dead wrong, and so I will limit my loss by not letting myself lose more than 30 percent of the average range. If a proper stop is farther than this amount, I will skip the trade. Say that the amount I'm willing to risk per market is $300 per contract in soybeans, $100 in corn, $2000 in the S&P 500, $1.00 in IBM, and 40 cents in DELL. I would only take trades that have a per-contract technical risk less than these amounts. Otherwise the trade is riskier than normal and should be avoided.

Time Stops

Stops do not always have to be set by the market or be based on how much money you can afford to lose; they can also be time stops in which you give the market a limited amount of time in which to work out. If it doesn't, you get out. As I mentioned earlier, I like to use time stops. The reason I do this is that I sometimes have a habit of holding on to losers or trades that are not working for too long. Time stops depend on the time frame one uses. For the quick scalper, it can be 10 minutes; for the intermediate day trader, it can be 45 minutes; if you like the 60-minute time frame, you can use an end-of-day stop; and for a position trader, a 5-day stop may work. I use these times to get me out of trades that aren't working. If a trade is working well and my time has elapsed, I'll hold. These time periods are the ones I have chosen as a way to keep myself in check, but each trader may use something he feels more comfortable with. Once you have a stop-loss time limit you like and are in a position that is not working, get out after that allotted time.

I recently started using these stops as a way to get out of dead positions. If I'm day trading and have a position that is not working after 45 minutes, I get out of it because I figure that if it hasn't done anything yet, my money and energy are better spent elsewhere. This applies to trades that are negative or positive by a little. If a trade was good, it should have started working immediately (the best trades usually do). After about 30 minutes, if it isn't making me money, I should know I'm wrong. I'll give it a few more minutes and by 45 minutes, I'll start getting out if I haven't been stopped out already. I like to think I would have gotten out of the trade earlier because it wasn't working, but that isn't always the case. The main reason to use time stops is that many times you'll be in a trade that is not losing much; maybe it's down 10 cents a share and is not hurting you, and so you ignore it. As time goes on, though, it becomes 20, 40, or 60 cents, and before you know it you've held a bad trade for 2 hours and are down almost a dollar in it, and now you don't want to get out. Things that start off badly seem to get worse as time goes on, and so it's better to get out sooner.

A trader should have an expectation of what he wants the market to do and a time frame for it to do it in. If the market doesn't, he should consider exiting the trade — win, lose, or draw. It's okay to lose or make a little when the market doesn't follow through the way one had hoped. There is no need to wait to get stopped out. As a trader you'd rather be trading markets that are reacting than ones that are going against you or barely moving. You are better off looking for new opportunities than baby-sitting something that isn't working.

Technical Stops

Here is the proper way to place a stop: Let the market tell you where it should go. Stops that are based on what the market suggests is a good place to let you know you are wrong are the best stops. The market doesn't care how much a trader can afford to lose; it's going to do what it wants to do. Traders who put in arbitrary dollar amount stops because that's all they want to or can afford to risk are not placing stops properly and are at risk of being stopped out because the stops are within the normal trading range of the market. If you place a stop inside a technical barrier or within the normal trading range of the time frame you are looking at, you might as well kiss the money good-bye, as the odds get higher that you will get stopped out. Always give yourself a little leeway when you are placing a stop. Don't just put it outside the trendline; instead, use a buffer zone or give it a standard deviation move, as I'll explain later. These are many ways to use technical analysis to place stops. They can be placed outside trendlines, moving averages, channels, support and resistance lines, the low of X bars ago, below a Fibonacci retracement level, or at previous market lows or highs. These are areas the market is likely to come to, and if they are broken, that may indicate a change in the direction of the market.

The advantage of using the market to determine risk is that the risk becomes clearer and can be kept small. If it appears that the risk on a trade is too large, the trade is not a high probability one and should be avoided. Don't worry about missing trades. The worst thing that can happen is that you won't make any money. Not making money beats losing money every time, and there will be countless more chances to trade.

Revisiting some of the charts I've used in other chapters, you can see the right and wrong places for stops. Chart 9–3 includes a couple of trades one can make. The first one (Point A) is a breakout of a previous high. If a trader made this trade and could afford to lose only a dollar per share, he would have to place a stop at N (which stands for "no"). This stop is very likely to get hit as it is above the channel and trendline and in the middle of nowhere. It doesn't get hit, but nevertheless it is a poorly placed stop. The better stops are at Level 1, under the channel line, which coincides with the previous low of the market. If the market breaks that level, the next stop will be at Level 2, which is a better place to have a stop as it is below a major trendline. Finally, one definitely would want to be out if it broke at Level 3, a recent major low. Overall, I don't think this is a great trade as the stop levels are quite a distance away. However, at Point B there is a great trading opportunity as one could get in and risk to the channel line at Level 4, which is pennies away. Levels 5 and 6 are similar to Levels 2 and 3. The reason for showing multiple stop areas is that if a trader were trading multiple contracts, he could exit a piece at the first stop and then exit the rest if the others got hit. The stops at Levels 3 and 6 are just too far away at about $7 per share, and so they would be out of the question. The stops at Levels 2 and 5 are more modest but still a little too far away for the day trader and should be used only by a long-term trader. The stop at Level 1 is still a bit too far away, and so that trade could be ignored in this time frame, but since the stop at Level 4 is a technically good stop and is close to the market, it is a great place to take a trade. Tight stops are okay to have when they are technically correct. There is one other possibility a trader could consider. Since the trade at Level A is a breakout, it could be taken, and one can use a move below the break line as a stop. Trades like these get stopped out often, but the losses are small and the gains can be large, and so they are worth a shot.

FINE-TUNING EXITS WITH DIFFERENT TIME FRAMES

When trading, one definitely should look at the larger time frames to get a better idea of where to put proper stops. You want to do this because it is easier to see significant technical barriers when you are looking at higher time frames. But one also can use the smaller time frames to time trades and get out with profits or smaller losses. Chart 9–4 is a 10-minute version of Chart 9–3 with the same stop levels. Before you initially make a trade, use the higher time frame to find

C H A R T   9 — 3

60-Minute Intel: Technical Stops

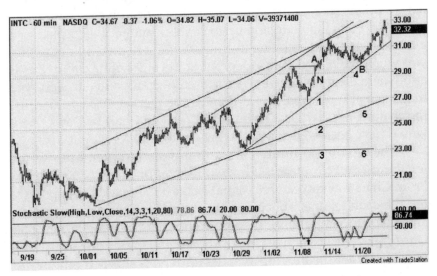

INTC - 60 min NASDQ C=34.67 -0.37 -1.06% O=34.82 H=35.07 L=34.06 V=39371400

Stochastic Slow(High,Low,Close,14,3,3,1,20,80) 78.86 86.74 20.00 80.00

Created with TradeStation

CHART 9-4

10-Minute Intel: Fine-Tuning the Exit

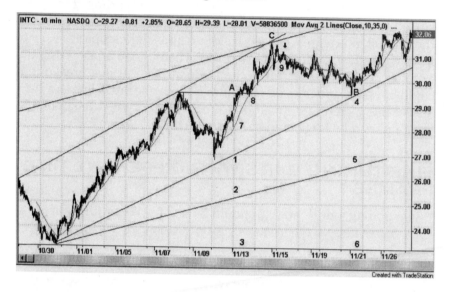

the stop levels. Once you have good stop locations, look at the smaller time frame to trade around those stops. Say you took the trade at the breakout of Point A and placed a stop at Level 1 that was based on the 60-minute chart. If this is a short-term trade, there is no need to risk down to the stop at Level 1; instead, you could place it under the moving average at Level 7. Level 1 then becomes a worst-case scenario stop. As soon as the trade started to work, you could use Chart 9–4 to start moving your stop up to Levels 8 and 9, always placing it a little bit under the moving average as it got higher. By doing this, you would have gotten stopped out at Level 9 with a profit; this is also where the moving averages crossed over. If you were alert, you may have also realized that at Point C the market was approaching the channel lines, which can be seen clearly in Chart 9–3, and that it would have been a great place to get out to wait for a pullback.

The next opportunity comes to a patient trader who waited for the market to retest the breakout level of Point A, at Point B. From Chart 9–3 you can see that at Point B the market is approaching the channel line. This trade should be a no-brainer here. It has an ideal setup: a pullback in an uptrend that is testing a trendline. Once the trade starts working, a short-term trader can use a trailing stop under the moving average until he is stopped out.

Stops Based on Indicators

A stop can be based on an indicator and not on the market itself. For instance, a stop can be to exit the trade if the RSI dips below 50 or if the stochastics don't do what they should. For example, in Chart 9–5 you may want to try shorting at Point 1 because the stochastics appeared to be turning and the market was at the top of its range. For a stop you can tell yourself, "I will get out if the indicator breaks higher than its previous peak." The stochastics did just that 45 minutes later at Point 2, and so a disciplined trader would get out. This type of stop is a bit harder to manage as you always have to watch the market, but this is a perfectly good way to place a stop. Almost any indicator can be used as a stop if you want it to.

Trailing Stops

What happens after you make a trade and the market moves in the direction you were hoping it would, leaving you with a nice paper profit in the trade? The stop you originally had now may

CHART 9–5

5-Minute S&P: Indicator-Based Stop

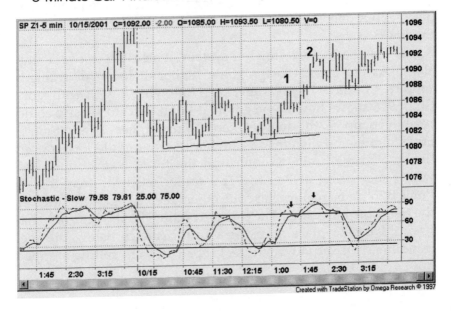

SP Z1-5 min 10/15/2001 C=1092.00 -2.00 O=1085.00 H=1093.50 L=1080.50 V=0

Stochastic - Slow 79.58 79.61 25.00 75.00

Created with TradeStation by Omega Research © 1997

be too far away, and you don't want to risk giving back those profits or what you originally were willing to lose. If you were willing to lose $500 on the trade and now have a $500 profit, you'd lose $1000 if it got stopped out at your original level. Even though the trade hasn't been closed out yet, this paper profit is your money, so hold on to as much of it as possible. Why would you want to give back $1000 from any given point if you normally don't risk more than $500 on any trade? It doesn't matter that you are already in the market; holding on to profits is as important as cutting losses.

To protect your profits you want to use a trailing stop that follows the market. Many traders make the mistake of putting on a trade and placing a stop and then feeling safe because the stop is in, becoming complacent and lazy in managing the position. I wish I could get back a portion of the money I have given away by not moving my stops with the market. I've watched many good trades give back way too much before getting out because I never moved my original stop. Stops should not be onetime decisions; as the market moves, they need to be reevaluated. The best way to manage a position is to keep looking at the market as if you had just put the trade on. As the market moves, it will consistently give you new technical barriers to which stops can be moved so that you can keep cutting your risk. If the stops start getting too far away and there is no great place to put one, the best thing to do is to start lightening up on the position.

If using a trend-following system, it's easy to move a stop along. As the market keeps going higher or lower or riding a solid trend or moving average, keep following it with your stop. Chart 9–6 shows how if one got in at Point A, a stop easily could be moved up as the market kept going higher. Every time it broke higher and then made a higher low, one could have raised the stop to the previous low until the trade was stopped out with a nice profit at Point X. If a trader used the trendline at Point B to time an entry, he could then keep raising the stops as the trendline moves up. The lower trendline is a buffer zone that I would use to place stops at a safe distance below the real trendline. This second trendline keeps you from getting stopped out by false breaks.

CHART 9—7

60-Minute S&P: Trailing Stops

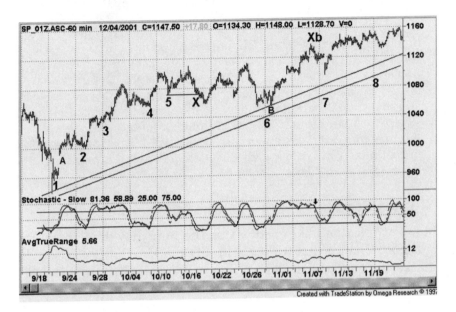

Taking a Winner

The tough part comes when the market has made a good move and is now too far away from a good stop. If there is no visible place to place a proper stop without giving back too much, you need to start thinking about scaling out or exiting with a winner. If this is not a place where you would think about initiating a new trade because it would be too risky, it's okay to get out. Point Xb on Chart 9–6 is a good example of this. Here the market is overextended and the stochastics are starting to drop below the overbought area. Why not get out with a good profit and look to get back in later? At least take part of your profits if you have them; there is no need to risk giving back the whole amount if it does turn. The disadvantage is that there will be times when you exit a trade prematurely by getting out while it is still working. If this is the case, you shouldn't be afraid to get back in the trade at the next pullback even if you get in at a worse spot. At this point, it's a whole new trade and you need to let go of the past. So what if you gave up some profits? You made the smart choice by cutting risk, and now you are in a fresh position with less risk.

THE "CANCEL IF CLOSE" STOP

Some people are good at moving stops; unfortunately, they move them the wrong way. A surefire way of adding to a trader's woes is to keep moving stops farther away as the market gets closer to hitting them. Brokers call these CIC orders (cancel if close). Traders will come up with a hundred reasons why the market will start working as it approaches their stop. They may think that the market has stabilized, the market has gone down far enough, or the RSI is oversold and so it should start bouncing soon. They then move or cancel the stop so that they can stay in the trade for the bounce. Once in a while this may turn out great, but overall, if the stop was placed properly, just let it be. You made it with a sound mind, and it is probably in the place it should be, so don't play with it.

Mental Stops

Many people don't like to enter stops because they think that there is a good chance that if they're in the market, the floor brokers, market makers, or specialists will take them out. Instead, they prefer to hold their stops themselves, placing them as market orders once a stop would have been elected. The problem with mental stops is that too many times they never make it into the market; they end up getting ignored as a trader comes up with 74 reasons why the market will turn around. When it doesn't, a small loss turns into a big one as a trader just sits and watches, hoping the market will come back to where he would have liked to have been stopped out originally so that he can take a modest loss. If you are going to use mental stops instead of placing them for real, you must be disciplined and stick to them. I'm one of those people who hate placing relatively close stops in the market. I've had too many experiences where my close stops got hit as the market made a quick move and then came right back. What I do now most of the time is write down where I should be out of a trade, and if it hits that point, I'll wait a few more minutes to see if it is a real move and then enter a market order to get out. This stop works like an alert to start getting ready to exit the market. I prefer this method, but beginning traders should stick with real stops until they are quite disciplined. I'll place real stops with a buffer when I go to lunch or can't watch the market, but overall I prefer the freedom of a mental stop.

Disaster Stops

If you don't have real stops entered in the market because you think they may get hit by the random noise of the market, you can use what I call disaster stops. These are stops that are rather far away and will get hit only if something major happens, such as an unexpected rate cut. These faraway stops very rarely get hit in normal circumstances, but they can give you a little peace of mind and will keep a trader who doesn't like to enter stops from getting killed if something happens.

WHY STOPS GET HIT

All traders have felt that they were victims of being stopped out for no good reason. You have a stop in the market, it gets hit, and then the market comes back. You feel that "they" are out to get you, but how do "they" always seem to know where you have your stop? The main reason stops get hit so often is that the masses tend to place them all in the same place, and the floor brokers and pros know where that is. Besides having the unfair advantage of brokers on the floor actually telling each other where they have stops, they also know that traders are very predictable. People tend to place stops too close to technical barriers that are a stone's throw from being elected; it doesn't take much to get the market close to them and then push it a little more to reach those stops. After a quick burst as they get elected, the momentum dies out, the market snaps back, and the floor traders start liquidating, having gotten into the market at the highs.

Never place stops near technical levels such as trendlines, moving averages, previous highs and lows, congestion areas, and round numbers such as 10,000 in the Dow. These are too obvious and are very likely to get hit. When a market has made a triple top, you can be sure that there are loads of stops just above that area, which traders may try to trigger. At least the pros know that that's where there is easy money to be made. If the market is just drifting around by these levels, it doesn't take much for a couple of locals to lift it a few points to hit those stops. Since these moves are not based on proper fundamentals, the market tends to come right back to where it was before the push. Remember, don't place stops at very obvious levels; think twice about where you are placing them and use a little bit of a buffer to give you some breathing room.

THE STOP AND REVERSE

Some systems don't call for actual stops to get you out of a position; instead, the stops are used to get in the market in the other direction. These systems are either long or short all the time. The stops merely act like signals in the opposite direction. If one is long two contracts and the trade was not working, one will get a sell signal to short four contracts. An example of this is a simple moving average crossover system. If the short average is above the long average, one would be long; when the averages switch, one goes short. I've used this kind of system a lot because of the "Hey, if I don't want to be long, I should be short" theory. But now I've learned that there are times when the market is not worth trading in either direction and one should be out of it, especially when one of the alternatives is trading against the trend.

STOPS AND VOLATILITY

There are times when you are in a trade and the market will start to move much faster than it had been moving and the intraday swings will get wider. This is a sign that the volatility has increased, and so does the risk involved in holding the positions. As the volatility increases, stops have to be placed wider or they are likely to be hit. When this happens, it is not a bad idea to close out all or part of your position. Even if you end up being light on a great trade, you made the right choice. Cutting risk is one the goals of trading, and by avoiding volatile market environments you can accomplish this. Besides looking at a chart and seeing more violent price swings or larger average true ranges, one can use a standard deviation move to figure out how the volatility of a market is changing. Knowing what the standard deviation of the market is will help you place stops outside the normal trading range of the market.

Calculating the Standard Deviation of a Market

1. Come up with a lookback period for the number of bars you want to get the standard deviation of; 10, 14, and 20 are good ones to use. For the following example I'll use 10 bars as my lookback period with last 10 closes being

   60, 58, 54, 55, 58, 61, 63, 59, 57, 59

2. Sum all closes:

   $60 + 58 + 54 + 55 + 58 + 61 + 63 + 59 + 57 + 59 = 584$

3. Calculate the average:

   $584/10 = 58.4$

4. Subtract the average from each data value:

   $60 - 58.4 = 1.6, 58 - 58.4 = -.4, 54 - 58.4 = -4.4$, and so on

5. Square the results obtained in step 4:

   1.6 squared $= 2.56, - 0.4$ squared $= 0.16$, and so on

6. Sum the results obtained in step 5:

   Sum of all the squares $= 64.4$

7. Calculate the variance by dividing the sum obtained in step 6 by the number of data points:

   $64.4/10 = 6.44$

8. Calculate the standard deviation by taking the square root of the variance:

   Standard deviation = square root of $6.44 = 2.537716$

The standard deviation measures how far each observation lies from the mean. In this case a 1 standard deviation move from the current price is 2.54, which means the market will be expected to move within this amount 68.26 percent of the time. If you use a 2 standard deviation move (5.08), there is a 95 percent chance that the price will be within that range. This implies that 95 percent of the time the market will not move 5.08 from the previous close and 68.26 of the time it will not move more than 2.54 from its previous close.

USING STANDARD DEVIATIONS

Standard deviations can be used to help ensure that that you will not get stopped out on random moves of the market. By placing stops at least 1 standard deviation from the current price you are ensuring that you are not being stopped out by random noise. By placing stops at least 2 standard deviations away you can be sure any stop that is hit is real. When this is done in a monitoring time frame, one can safely place stops outside the normal move of the market. This may be too much risk for some people to handle, but it is ideally where stops ought to be. I wrote an indicator that I use on TradeStation that lets me see where 1 and 2 standard deviations are from the current price. Though similar to Bollinger bands, my indicator shows where 1 and 2 standard deviations are from the high and low of each bar and not from a 20-period moving average. I use a 10-period lookback to calculate the standard deviation. Chart 9–7 shows what it looks like. Band 1 is a 1 standard deviation move from the low of a bar, Band 2 is a 2 standard deviation move, Band 3 is a 1 standard deviation move from the high of a bar, and Band 4 is a 2 standard deviation move. The way I use this is as follows: If I bought at the close of Bar A thinking that the market could propel upward after a reversal day, I then draw a horizontal line from where the 2 standard deviation line is (Point Xa) and use that as my stop. In this case the market broke through it a few bars later, and so I would exit the position at the point where it closed below my line for the first time. If the market goes my way as it would if I had bought at Bar B, again I'll draw a horizontal line and keep raising it as the standard deviation band moves up, using it as a trailing stop. When the indicator stops going up temporarily, I will use the highest peak as my stop. This way my stop is always 2 standard deviations from the highest low. I will stay in until the market closes below the highest point the indicator reached. In this case it would be at Point Xb with a decent gain. Standard deviation stops similar to this trading strategy can be written into computerized trading systems. I'll give more examples of this in Chap. 12 on system writing.

TradeStation's Easy Language Code For Standard Deviation Lines

```
Inputs:   Price(Close), Length(10), StdDev1(1),
          StdDev2(2), Displace(0);
Variables: SD(0), LowerBand1(0), LowerBand2(0),
UpperBand1(0), UpperBand2(0);
```

CHART 9–7

60-Minute KLAC: Standard Deviations

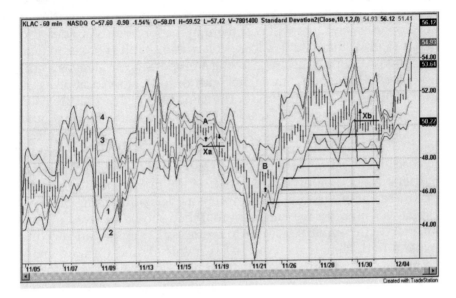

```
SD = StandardDev(Price, Length, 1) ;
UpperBand1 = High + StdDev1 * SD ;
UpperBand2 = High + StdDev2 * SD ;
LowerBand1 = Low + StdDev1 * -SD ;
LowerBand2 = Low + StdDev2 * -SD ;

If Displace >= 0 or CurrentBar >
     AbsValue(Displace) then begin
Plot1[Displace](UpperBand1, "LowerBand1") ;
Plot2[Displace](UpperBand2, "LowerBand2") ;
Plot3[Displace](LowerBand1, "UpperBand1") ;
Plot4[Displace](LowerBand2, "UpperBand2") ;
End;
```

BECOMING A BETTER TRADER

Becoming a better trader means knowing how to get out of the market with a winning or losing trade. You should have an exit plan before you enter a trade; if you don't, you are not thinking trades through. You need to be able to have a target for winning trades and a limit for losing trades. A winning trader is one who knows how to lose; it is also someone who knows how important it is to let winning trades grow as much as possible without getting greedy. Traders who take profits too soon are not allowing their trades to develop fully, and that will cost them in the long run. A trader also needs to learn that taking a loss is okay and that it is better to take a small loss than a large one. Having a proper stop strategy is a critical part of trading. Coming up with a good stop location is as important as putting on a trade. The same techniques that are used to make a trade should be used to get out of a trade. Stops should never be based on how much a trader can afford to lose; these stops tend to be randomly placed as far as the market is concerned. Instead, stops should be placed a safe distance outside technical barriers. A good stop will be based on the market, not on what a person can afford to lose. Though stops assist in preserving precious capital, as a money management tool they should be used in conjunction with technical analysis to figure out (1) if you can afford to make a trade versus the risk that is involved, and (2) how many contracts you can put on safely given how far away a good stop is.

By knowing where to place stops one can prevent oneself from risking more than one needs to or from being stopped out because the stop is too close to the market. Stops that are too close will get hit needlessly if they are within the normal move of the market. To assure that you don't get stopped out by the random noise of the market, it is best to place stops at least a 1 standard deviation move from the current price, but 2 standard deviations is more appropriate. Another option is to use a buffer zone that falls outside the technical barrier at which you are looking to place a stop. One thing that will make you a better trader is having two different stop levels. The first one alerts you that you are wrong, such as a trendline, a moving average, or another technical level. At this point you begin timing your exit if the market doesn't get better. If there is no improvement and your second area (outside a buffer zone) gets hit, you get out of the market. This will keep you in a position longer and therefore give your trade a chance to work. Stops can be mental or can be placed in the market. If they are mental, you must have the discipline to get out when the market hits that level. You also can use stops that get you out of the market if a trade is not working after a set period of time; again, you need discipline to carry this through, but it is a good way to weed out the stuff that doesn't work. Overall, I'd have to stress that when you make a trade, you have to give the exit the same attention you gave the entry.

Mistakes Associated with Exits and Stops

1. Not having an exit strategy
2. Not having a risk management plan
3. Not having any idea where one will exit a bad trade
4. Letting bad trades get ugly
5. Not concentrating on the exit as much as on the entry
6. Never knowing when to get out
7. Taking profits too quickly
8. Getting greedy
9. Using arbitrary stops based on dollar amounts
10. Using the same dollar stop for every market and situation
11. Not looking at a chart to place a stop
12. Placing stops that are too close
13. Placing stops that are too far
14. Not using a buffer zone
15. Letting a stop lead you to get lazy
16. Not moving stops as the market moves in your favor
17. Canceling stops as the market gets closer
18. Not sticking to mental stops
19. Ignoring stops

Getting the Most Out of Your Exit Strategy

1. Let profits ride.
2. Cut losses short.
3. Learn to scale out of trades.
4. Have a reason for getting out.
5. Get out when the reasons for getting in have changed.
6. It's okay to take a loss.
7. Know where you will get out before the trade is made.
8. Ensure that you don't get wiped out.
9. Stops should be based on the market.

10. Keep stops outside technical barriers.
11. Use a buffer zone.
12. Make sure stops are far enough away to give the trade room to work.
13. Use trailing stops to protect profits.
14. Know in advance how much you can lose on a trade.
15. Never risk more than you are willing to lose on a trade.
16. Use multiple stops to scale out of a trade.
17. Use a higher time frame to find a good place for a stop.
18. If you do not have discipline, enter stops directly into the market.
19. Use time stops to get you out of stuff that is not working.
20. Avoid trading markets you can't afford.
21. Stops 2 standard deviations from the market will not get elected due to random noise of the market.
22. Stick to your stops.

Helpful Questions to Ask Yourself

Do I have a stop?
Is there a good reason I want to get out at that level?
How much can I lose on this trade?
Is the risk/reward ratio worth the trade?
Is the stop too close or too far?
Am I trading the right number of shares relative to risk?
Do I have the discipline to stick to a mental stop?
Did I ignore my stop?
Is this stop too obvious?

Making the High Probability Trades

SOPHIE THE CAT

About 3 years ago I was walking home one day when a cute little malnourished cat started following me step for step. When I stopped, she would stop, and when I turned the corner, she turned with me, never more than 3 feet behind. As luck had it, I lived two blocks away from a vet, and so we walked over there to see if anyone had lost her. Nobody had, so I told the vet to check her and I'd take her until I found her owner. I knew she had to have been a house cat because she was so docile and easy to pick up. We left the vet; she followed me home, ate, and took a nap; and then we went to search for her home. We had no luck finding her owner, but I soon got used to walking with a cat in tow. I tried using a leash, but it didn't look very masculine, so I gave up on that idea. Since she enjoyed going out so much, I started taking her to the park across from my apartment every night. One day in the park she saw a bunch of pigeons and crept up close to them, crouched real low, watched them for a few minutes, and then walked back to me. A few days later though, she saw a small sparrow sitting atop some bushes. She crept up to the area and again crouched real low, trying to hide behind the blades of grass. This time she waited without moving, intensely looking at the sparrow for about 15 minutes. Eventually the sparrow flew down off the bush and toward the grass, and Sophie wiggled her behind, leapt about 6 feet, grabbed the sparrow in midair, and pinned it to the ground. I was able to stop her from doing any harm to the sparrow; it flew away a little stunned but unharmed.

The point of this story is that one should trade the way Sophie captured the sparrow. She knew that the pigeons were too big for her and might be a little risky to tackle; maybe she might have gotten one, but there were too many, they were too large to be a sure thing, and there was a good possibility of her getting hurt. Besides, she had just had a good meal at home, and so it wasn't worth the risk. But the sparrow didn't pose much of a risk because it was alone and quite small. Sophie knew she had only one chance at it before it would fly away, and it was too high up in the bushes. Therefore, she waited patiently for the sparrow to make its move, giving her a higher probability of catching it. This wait paid off for her as her timing was perfect. If a trader would have this kind of patience to wait for the market to present itself with low-risk, higher probability opportunities, he would also fare much better.

BECOME A HIGH PROBABILITY TRADER

One of the things that will make a trader better than the rest is being able to distinguish between high probability and low probability trades. Traders will improve their chances of success as soon as they can do this. When I tell people I trade for a living, many are convinced that there is no difference between trading and gambling. Sure, some traders have the same luck as gamblers, but there is a difference; trading is not gambling. A professional trader can make money consistently if he follows a trading plan with strict money management principles and a sound trading strategy. Part of that trading plan is to consistently make only trades that have a high probability of working out and a low risk/reward ratio. Unless one can do this, then yes trading is no more than gambling.

A high probability trade is one that is carefully made with a defined exit strategy and predetermined stop levels. It is a trade that historically has a high degree of working and in which the potential risk is low compared to how much can be made. You also must have a good reason for making a trade, one that you would not be ashamed to explain to someone. Some people make irrational trades with little thought behind them; whether they work or not, these trades are not high probability ones. As you trade more and more, you will know if a trade has a great setup or is being made haphazardly; the goal is to cut out the haphazard trades.

High probability trading is made up of many things, and one of the most important is to make sure the trade is worth the risk. Making high probability trades doesn't mean you will not make losing trades, but at least you will make trades that shouldn't cost you much when they are wrong and have the potential for a nice profit when they are correct. The other important aspect of making high probability trades is using all your knowledge and tools and having the patience to wait for the market to present good trading opportunities. The important thing is to not take unwarranted risk. I've found that a trader does better by trading less, only taking trades that have a great setup, even if it means missing some opportunities. By trading less you can weed out many trades that aren't worth the risk or historically haven't worked out.

HAVING A PLAN

Much of the rest of this book will deal with having and making a trading plan and a game plan. A trading plan consists of a mixture of money management and the proven strategy behind one's trades. This plan helps a trader make smart trades and keeps him from making those which are not so carefully thought out. A game plan meanwhile is the strategy a trader uses everyday to carry out his trading plan. A game plan ensures that each trade has a reason behind it and is not made merely on a whim. Unfortunately, many people trade without the aid of a good trading plan and game plan. A good trading plan should permit you to make only high probability trades. Once you have a plan, the hard part is to follow it. One way to follow a plan is to use purely mechanical systems as the basis for your decision making. Whether you design them yourself or purchase them, these systems should include all the aspects of making high probability trades, including exits, and should be backtested to ensure that they will work. I'll discuss system making, trading, and backtesting in Chap. 12 and 13.

A Few of the Ingredients in Making High Probability Trades
Using different time frames to confirm and time trades
Trading in the direction of the major trend
Waiting for pullbacks

Having a predetermined exit strategy

Planning trades before the market opens

Using a combination of trend-following and oscillating indicators

Having a reason for every trade

Knowing the risks involved

Staying focused

Having discipline

TYPICAL HIGH PROBABILITY TRADING SCENARIO

The following is a perfect example of a high probability trading situation. The different indicators I chose on each time frame were random, but I'm sure they would have worked the same no matter where I used them. Start by looking at Chart 10-1, a daily chart of crude. The shaded area is where the smaller time frames will focus. The daily chart gives you a clear picture of the major trend, which

CHART 10-1

Daily Crude Oil: Getting the Big Picture

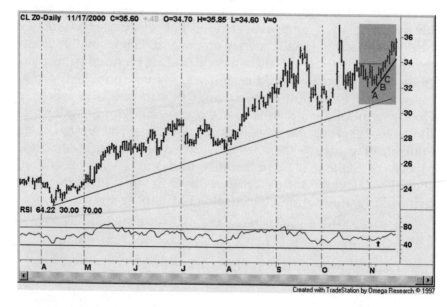

Created with TradeStation by Omega Research © 1997

is quite bullish. The reading in the RSI above the 50 line but below the overbought area shows that the market is strong and still has room to go up. The market has been in a strong uptrend for months and is making what looks like another upwave after breaking a monthlong congestion area from $32 to $34.

Now take a look at a 60-minute chart (Chart 10–2). This will help you find a good place to get involved. In this chart you can see the congestion area a lot better than you can in the daily chart. What you can't see here, though, is that the market has been in a strong uptrend. Say you were a patient trader and had been waiting for a pullback in crude so that you could get in on the long side. Between November 1 and November 3 you got a little pullback to the bottom of the congestion area, and with it you got divergence between the stochastics and the market at Point D1. You also can see that at Point A the market was testing a previous low it had made a few days earlier and that the stochastics were oversold and had recently turned up; you also know the market is in a roaring uptrend. Now you are thinking that this may not be a bad place to buy since the risk would be to get out if the market broke the previous low just a few ticks away.

CHART 10–2

60-Minute Crude Oil: Getting a Better Picture

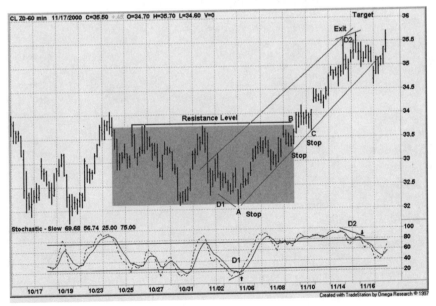

The next step is to look at an even smaller time frame (Chart 10-3) to time a trade. Just before Point A you can see that the market gapped lower that morning, went down for about 30 minutes, and then started to rally (you could use the 30-minute breakout system from Chap. 8 to get you into this trade). As the market rallied, the MACD lines crossed over to the upside and started uptrending, indicating a buying opportunity. Once the market started breaking the highs of the day, this became a great trade to make, first as a day trade and then to hold for the longer term. In this time frame you can easily see where the previous low was and how little you would have to risk before knowing you were wrong. As far as potential profit, it is fair to say that the market could rally to the top of the congestion area at 33.80. The risk versus reward in this trade is 30 cents versus $1.50. Even if you are dead wrong, this trade has a great potential payoff-to-risk ratio and should not be missed. As a longer-term trade you can use the congestion area in Chart 10–2 to estimate how much the market could move. This would give you a target of about 36, making for an even lower risk/reward potential.

CHART 10–3

10-Minute Crude Oil: Timing the Trade

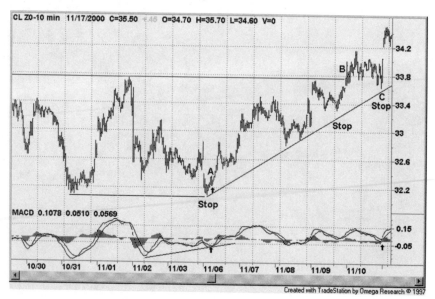

Created with TradeStation by Omega Research © 1997

There are several other possible places one could make trades. Two that I would consider high probability ones are at Point B, when the market breaks out of the congestion area, and at Point C, after the market pulls back from the breakout and retests the trendline. The one at Point C is a better trade because you've waited for a pullback and it is at a trendline, and so the risk is much lower. Here a little patience pays off; even though the trade at Point B ends up being profitable, one gets a better price by waiting.

As far as an exit for any of these trades, since the market was in such a strong trend, as can be seen in the longer-term charts, one would want to hold on as long as possible, using a trailing stop along the way. The first clear exit sign I see is on Chart 10–2 at Point D2. Here the market is reaching the top of the channel, and the stochastics are showing divergence with the market and starting to come out of overbought territory. This is also close enough to the $36 target gotten by measuring the congestion, and so one should have been starting to think about exiting at around that time anyway.

HAVING A REASON FOR EVERY TRADE

Part of making high probability trades is having a good reason for every trade you make as opposed to making rushed, randomly tossed out trades. This is why planning trades in advance can help improve one's trading performance. Sometimes a trader puts on a trade after spending little time looking thoroughly at the risks and rewards involved. He gets impatient, doesn't wait for pullbacks, chases the market, or has too much going on to think properly. Since there are many reasons for making stupid trades and every trade one makes should have a good reason behind it, you may want to take a second before pulling the trigger. Ask yourself, "Why am I making this trade?" If you truly have a good reason after asking yourself that, then make it, but if the reason is not worthy of a trade, lay off it.

Here are some answers to the question "Why do I want to buy now?"

Good Responses

The stock is stronger than the market, and the sector is doing well.

The trend is up, and the market just pulled back to the moving average.

There was bad news on the stock, and it is not going down.

There was a moving average crossover.

I got a signal from my system.

The market broke through a major level and still has plenty of room to go.

There was a reversal day yesterday, and today it looks like it will continue.

The market has dropped its average daily range and now looks to be reversing.

Stochastics are coming out of oversold territory.

The market has just retraced to the bottom of its range, and the MACD is oversold.

Bad Responses

I want to make money.

I've lost a #!$%load of money, and I need a highflier to make it all back with.

I'm bored.

The market is open.

I already bought the stock, and it's cheaper now.

My broker recommended it.

News is about to come out.

It's down a lot already and just has to bounce.

It does nothing but go up.

I don't want to miss the move.

I have extra margin available.

I'm looking for a short-term counterrally.

Maria Bartiromo said it was strong.

DON'T OVERDO IT

Sometimes a trader knows exactly what he should be doing but still loses money because he is not focused on the market as he should be. Some traders look at too many markets and/or have too many positions on, and so they spread themselves too thin. Instead of looking at every market, traders should take the time to become experts on the ones they trade best. Remember that the best traders tend to trade only one market or sector and are experts in it.

Individual trades will suffer when one is looking at too many markets, as one cannot as easily concentrate on waiting for the higher probability trades. If one focuses on a few select markets, stocks, or sectors, it's easier to time entry and exit points, and risk can be controlled better. I know that unless the markets are having a runaway bullish or bearish day where I can put on as many trades as possible and sit back and watch, my best trading comes when I have only two or three positions, as I can concentrate better on them. It's hard to say you made all high probability trades when you have 15 positions on. Unless you use a purely mechanical system on a basket of stocks or commodities, you will never be able to concentrate properly on that many positions, especially when it's time to exit.

HAVING THE PATIENCE TO WAIT FOR THE BETTER TRADING OPPORTUNITIES

I keep repeating how important patience and waiting for the market are. I can't stress this point enough. Like a smart gambler who will only play out poker hands that have a high probability of winning, a trader must wait for the high probability situations. You don't have to make every trade you see or be in a rush to make those you do make. As a trader you have the luxury of doing nothing; it's okay to watch a market, like a cat waiting for a sparrow to land, before trading it. Wait until you get a good confirmation that the trade may work before rushing into it. There is no need to trade on dull, rangeless, volumeless days; you are at a disadvantage on those days. If I had been able to walk away and go home on those days, I would have done much better over the years. Not trading is always a viable option; after all, some of the best trading decisions you'll make involve the trades you are smart enough not to make. I've been a little of an overtrader, and it has hurt me. If I had been a more patient trader and had made only the best-looking trades, I certainly could have turned the corner much sooner.

Over the years I've realized that it's okay to miss a move. There was a time when I would try to catch every blip in the market, but I'm learning to restrain myself and wait for a better opportunity to get in. Not only does there have to be a good reason to make a trade, the timing has to be as good as possible. Rushing into a trade usually means that your timing will be off. A trader is better off missing a few good trades while weeding out the bad and mediocre ones as he waits for the trades that have a higher probability of working with a lower risk/reward ratio. Some moves are prebroadcast and easy to predict. It is worth waiting around for these moves instead of trading on every whim. A trader who is scared of missing a move will keep finding himself always in the market, and many of his trades will be mediocre at best. Once a trader learns to wait for the high probability trades, his chances will improve dramatically.

SOME EARLY ADVICE I GOT

One of the first pieces of advice I got when I started trading on the floor was that you have to make only one good trade a day to make a living. If you can sit back and wait for that perfect setup and make 6 to 10 ticks on it, that's all you need. Every day you'll get one or two situations that look and feel great. Just be patient and wait for them; there is no need to try to beat the market all day long.

RISK VERSUS REWARD

A big part of high probability trading is making trades that have a good mix of risk and reward. To do this, you need to determine how much can be lost on the trade, understand the worst-case scenario, and have some sort of profit target in advance. Of course, the higher the reward/risk ratio is, the better the trade is, but an acceptable ratio will differ from trader to trader and will depend on hold times. On day trades I like to find trades with a minimum of a 2:1 or 3:1 potential payoff, the higher the better. On long-term trades I look for at least a 5:1 reward/risk ratio. Timing trades will help you cut down on the risk portion of the equation.

Once you have a minimum ratio you are comfortable trading with, look at a chart to decide if you will make a trade. Start by looking at the risk; this is where your stop level should be. Next, try to figure out how much can be made if everything works out. This is not always easy to see, but it can be done by using Fibonacci ratios, measuring previous congestions and waves, looking at how much room an oscillator has to move before reaching an extreme reading, and using higher time frames to find resistance levels. If you were looking at a trade that had a $200 risk, would you take it if the potential reward was $100? I hope not. But what if it was $400, $500, or $1000? Yes, you should. Even if you are wrong, it is worth the risk.

Some trades, such as the 30-minute breakout system, have a historically good chance of working. When that is the case you can give yourself a little more leeway on how much you will risk because they will work more often. However, when you are trying to catch quick reversals or are making other risky trades, the amount you are willing to risk must be much less because the odds are high that you will get stopped out.

WHY PROFESSIONAL POKER PLAYERS WIN

A top poker player makes money consistently because he knows the odds of getting any hand. He will only make bets that have a better payoff ratio than the odds involved. Say he needs a 6 to pull out an inside straight and the odds of getting it are 11 to 1. Someone bet $10, and now it's his turn to bet. He will make the bet only if there is more than $110 in the pot. It makes no sense to chase this card if he can make only $50. That's a 5:1 payoff and is not worth the 11:1 chance of not pulling the card. But if the pot has $400, then assuming he thinks his straight will beat all the other hands, he will make the bet every time, as it has a 40:1 payoff. Even if he doesn't get his 6, he still has made the smart bet.

POSITION SIZE

Knowing how to use position size correctly is another thing that will help a trader immensely. Some people think this is one of the most critical aspects of trading. By knowing when to trade more heavily or lightly, a trader can take advantage of good situations when they arise. Those who always put on the same number of contracts aren't distinguishing between different types of market scenarios or determining how risky a trade is. I know there are some trades that I do to test the waters, and I'll trade more lightly, for example, in the morning. During the first half hour the market can move randomly until it picks a direction. I always have trouble making money in the first hour of trading. If I want to trade in the morning, I do so with less volume. The same holds true for choppy markets. They are harder to trade, and so I trade them with less conviction. When the market is trending, however, and just retraced to the trendline and there is a clear stop not too far away, I consider this a high probability opportunity and trade it with more size. I'm not afraid to risk more here because the payoff can be worth it. Most good traders trade with light volume a good percentage of the time. They prefer to wait until the right opportunity presents itself to load up and make money. You need only 2 or 3 good days a month to get rewarded in this business. There is no need to try and make a killing every trade or every day.

LEARNING HOW A MARKET BEHAVES

Get to know the behavior of a stock, sector, or market and you can improve your odds of making money in that market. I've noticed that most markets behave uniquely compared with other markets. This may be due to the psychology of the traders in them. Different markets have different batches of traders behind them, and so they behave slightly differently. One market may have a habit of trending, while another has a habit of staying range-bound. When one sits down at a poker game, one wants to pay attention to how the other players play and what their "tell" (something that gives them away) is. As you learn the behavior of markets better, you'll notice that they repeat similar patterns and have set things they do in both the short and the long time frames on which an alert trader can capitalize. For instance, I used to trade the stock IDTI, and every day it seemed to open down a few dollars, only to run up about $6 after it opened. This worked only when the stock was in an uptrend and not too far overextended beyond the trend. I got used to this behavior and capitalized on it. It didn't work on other stocks, and it lasted for only a few months before it collapsed, but it was rather predictable for a time. By concentrating on a few markets and taking mental notes you will begin to see patterns in the market that you should be able to capitalize on.

MY MORNING DRILLERS TRADE

I've noticed a trend in oil drillers. Every day for the last 3 months they seem to rally at about 10 a.m. for about 45 to 90 minutes. The market shows its hand by first going down and then stalling on a 1-minute chart. As soon as that happens, you have to act quickly because it seems that everybody is looking at the same thing and is rushing to get long. This has become my trade de jour lately, and I'll do it until it stops working. Since this trade has been working so often and has become a high probability trade, I do it with decent size. On this trade I use a stop of the low of the day or a time stop of 45 minutes if it is not working.

LOW PROBABILITY TRADING

One way to increase your chances of making money is to know how to recognize low probability scenarios and then avoid them like a hotel I saw in Paris while I was backpacking through Europe after college. The hotel had a sign on its front door that read, "This hotel has lice." Though the rooms were *really* cheap, it wasn't worth the risk to stay there. Anybody who stayed there was taking an unnecessary risk. Those who were patient enough to walk a little farther would have been rewarded by staying at a hotel nearby that featured only roaches; sure it cost a little more, but it had a lower risk/reward ratio.

An example of low probability trading is trying to pick the tops and bottoms in strongly trending markets. Picking the bottom is known as trying to catch a falling knife. When a market is dropping straight down and you keep trying to pick a bottom, you can get hurt. February 4, 2002, was one of those days when I left my brain at home and traded poorly. I ended positive for the day but I could have had a great day; instead, I barely broke even. The market opened weak after being in a little downtrend after it had peaked a few weeks earlier. Chart 10–4 shows the daily S&P 500 Index, which is clearly coming off. Chart 10–5 shows a daily chart of QLGC, a typical stock I trade. Here too you can see that it was starting to come off again after having just formed a double top.

So what did I do? I bought it and a few of its friends every chance I could because I thought they were due for a bounce. Chart 10–6 is the 5-minute chart, and the up arrows show where I tried to buy. Except for the fourth time, when I made on average about 20 cents per share, I lost on average 50 cents per share every time I tried buying. Playing for these bounces when everything is pointing down in the long run is a waste of money. The only thing it does for sure is add commission costs to my P&L statement. I managed to make money on that day because I had a lot of stocks short

CHART 10—4

Daily S&P: Looking at a Weak Market

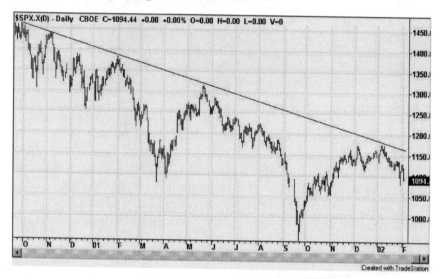

CHART 10—5

Daily QLGC: Looking at a Weak Stock

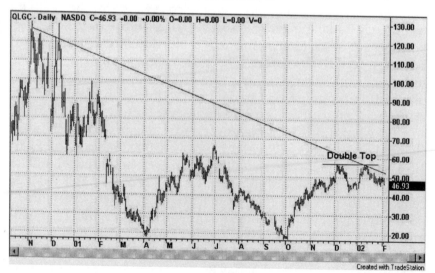

CHART 10-6

5-Minute QLGC: Catching a Falling Knife

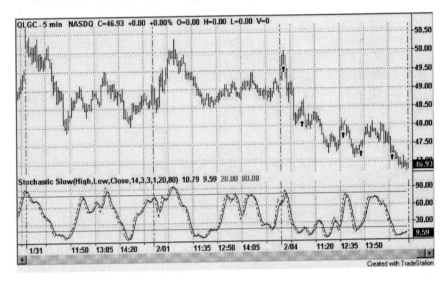

during the day and had more share size on the shorts than on the longs. This was a day that I hope will teach me not to trade low probability situations. I bought near the lows in the market four times, trying to catch a bottom; even if I truly believed that the market would bounce, the smart play was to do nothing.

Other situations to avoid include buying after a market has made a substantial move and is in overbought territory and buying when the market is at the top of a channel or a resistance level. Buying after it has broken below an upward-sloping trendline is also a poor trade, as this may indicate that the trend has ended. Not having exit strategies and ignoring stops is another technique that will help you lose money. Distinguishing between high probability and low probability trades is something that a trader will learn as he trades more and more. Eventually, knowing which trades are worth taking and which are not becomes second nature to the best traders.

BECOMING A BETTER TRADER

Becoming a better trader means being able to distinguish between high probability and low probability situations the same way my cat was able to do. Once you can do this, you can start trading like a pro. In my opinion the best way to do this is by always being aware of what the market is doing in its different time frames so that you are not caught on the wrong side of the major moves. By using a combination of time frames and different technical analysis techniques one can isolate trades that have a better potential to work no matter what time frame is preferred.

Having a reason for making every trade and planning trades thoroughly will help you identify which trades may not be worth the risk they represent. However, unless you take the time to plan out trades, you never know how much is at risk or could be made. Without these two factors it is hard to distinguish between a good trade and a bad trade. Not all trades work out, but if you can eliminate as many poor-percentage and high-risk trades from your repertoire as possible, you will see dramatic improvements in your overall results. Trading less and taking only the best-percentage trades are such an important part of being a great trader that this should be repeated over and over. Ask yourself before each trade, "Why am I making this trade?" If you can't justify the answer, skip the trade. Two of the most crucial things you need to develop a high probability mentality are having the discipline to make and wait for the right trades and having the money management skills to act accordingly when the better trading opportunities come along.

How To Become a Low Probability Trader in 14 Easy Steps

1. Not timing your trades
2. Trading choppy markets
3. Trading the opening of the market
4. Trading against the trend
5. Not looking at charts
6. Trading the news regardless of what the market does
7. Always risking the same amount
8. Always trying to catch the falling knife
9. Overtrading
10. Failing to distinguish between high probability and low probability trades
11. Trading randomly
12. Not bothering with exit strategies

13. Ignoring money management when considering a trade
14. Chasing markets into overbought territory

Becoming a High Probability Trader

1. Use multiple time frames.
2. Trade with the trend.
3. Wait for pullbacks.
4. Think like Sophie the cat.
5. Be patient and wait for the best opportunities.
6. Know the odds.
7. Understand that it's okay to miss trades.
8. Use mechanical systems.
9. Trade only when the risk/reward ratio merits a trade.
10. Learn to adjust risk per trade.
11. Trade more heavily when the odds are in your favor.
12. Do not gamble.
13. Trade only when everything seems right.
14. Have a reason for every trade.
15. Have a plan.
16. Plan your trades before the market opens.
17. Have the discipline to follow your plan.
18. Stay focused.
19. Learn how a market behaves.
20. Think your trades through.

Helpful Questions to Ask Yourself

Did I have a good reason for that trade?
Did I think it through properly?
Do I know how much is at risk?
Am I trading the right number of shares?
Did I wait for a golden opportunity?
Am I trading with the major trend?

Trading with a Plan

CHAPTER 11

The Trading Plan and Game Plan

If you wake up in the morning, grab some coffee, and wait for the market to open to start figuring out what to do, you won't get very far. A good trader will have done his homework and will be prepared for what the market has to offer before it opens. His trades won't be made randomly; instead, they will be part of a trading strategy and will abide to some risk parameters. He will be ready because he will have made a trading plan that includes these things. He also will have made a game plan for the day so that no matter what the market throws at him, he will know how to react.

WHAT IS A TRADING PLAN?

A trading plan is a guideline that a trader uses to concentrate on consistently making good trading decisions. It consists of two parts: First, it's a trading system or trading methodology that generates buy and sell signals; second, it contains money management parameters. Within those categories there are entering a trade, exiting a trade, stop placement, position sizing, and general risk levels. It also includes what markets will be traded and takes into account a trader's emotional makeup and trading style. It also should include a frequently forgotten part of trading: how a trader will review his performance. You can't improve unless you learn from mistakes, and so reviewing is important. Individually, these are all important aspects of trading, but when one combines them all successfully, one is ready to be a winner.

A trading plan is something that needs to be custom-built, as each trader has a different trading and risk style. If a trading plan doesn't fit one's trading style and thoughts, it will be hard follow it. A good plan will help a trader focus on his strengths while letting him avoid conditions that are unfavorable. A trading plan won't change much from day to day, as it consists of a trader's systems and money management plans. What will change, however, is a trader's game plan, which he should make every day so that he can be prepared to take advantage of the market. This may include moving stops, knowing what to do after an unemployment number is released, and waiting for a market to reach a trendline before getting in.

A trading plan is a trader's business plan. Just as almost every successful business has a business plan, a trader should have a trading plan. The best way to picture what goes into a trading plan is to think of it as if you were trying to persuade someone to give you money to trade with. When a commodity trading adviser (CTA) makes a disclosure document, he is in effect making an elaborate trading plan, as everything that should be in a trading plan is in the disclosure document.

MAKING A TRADING PLAN

Making a trading plan can be time-consuming and difficult. Since some people need immediate gratification, they would rather trade than write a trading plan, and so they ignore it. This is a mistake because without one they have no guidance. Having a plan on paper will help you establish and keep to concrete rules while helping you avoid emotional decisions made when the market is heated up or you are losing.

A trading plan doesn't have to be written on paper, but it does help to write one out and periodically review it. If you don't have one written out, I strongly recommend doing so. Even a simple plan is better than no plan. At the very least you should know how much to risk per trade and what market scenarios to trade. A trading plan could be as simple as the following:

> Buy one contract whenever the market gaps lower at the open and is in the top half of its range after 30 minutes; exit if the market breaks the low of the day, or at the close.

Though simple, this is a trading plan: It includes a trading strategy, a money management parameter, and position size. A trader can follow this every day and not have to think very hard about what he is doing. But for a more elaborate and professional-looking trading plan you should go back to the idea of trying to persuade someone to give you money. People who would give you money to trade with want to have a concrete idea of the following things:

- How you will trade
- What type of system you will use
- Which markets you will trade
- How much you will risk
- How much you can lose
- What you can reasonably expect to make
- How much the trading costs are
- The possibility of unexpected variables
- How you will prevent yourself from losing all the money
- How much you will risk at once
- How many markets you will trade
- What your hold time will be

Just think how much better your trading would be if you knew all this in advance. If one follows a plan, trading decisions are made during nonmarket hours, clearing the market hours to time entry and exit points and adjust risk. Taking the time to make a good trading plan will make trading easier.

WHY HAVE A PLAN?

The two main reasons for having a trading plan and a game plan are to ensure that you make high probability trades all the time and to make sure that you know what you are risking before making a trade. The trading plan will include trading strategies that you should have tested to ensure that they are high probability ones with a positive expectancy. Without a plan, one could go long one day and short the next, yet the market may be doing the same thing. By having a plan that generates trading ideas you will have a real reason to be in a trade and will reduce the possibility of making emotional and spur-of-the-moment decisions. Emotional trading decisions are rarely any good. By making your trading decisions during nonmarket hours and not during the ups and downs of the trading day, you will increase your chances of success. Without the help of a trading plan, it's too easy to get sloppy, chase the market, and not have any idea when to get out. A plan also will keep you from overtrading. By not sticking to a plan, it becomes easy to fall into the trap of overtrading or making bad trading decisions when one is losing in hopes of recouping losses. A trading plan will keep you focused throughout the day, as you will never have to go searching for ideas. Finally, with a plan you will know how much to risk and when you should take a loss. You'll know your maximum loss in advance, and so it shouldn't affect your trading if the worst case happens.

TRADING PLAN INGREDIENTS

Trading Methodology or System

The first thing you may want to include is a trading system you will use to trade with. A trading system stripped to its bare essentials is a set of rules and conditions that will get you in and out of the market. The next two chapters discuss how to make and backtest a system. A trader need not have just one system; he can have different trading systems for different markets or conditions. Systems do not have to be mechanical, but they should lay the groundwork for when you should be long or short. Pick the trading style and indicators that best suit you and start tossing out ideas until you find something that works.

Test your systems against historical data. If they didn't work in the past, odds are they won't work tomorrow. Or you can learn the hard way: by losing money in the market. More important than getting you into a trade, a system will have rules for getting you out of the market. Don't ignore the exit; it really is the difference between a winning trade and a losing trade. A good system will have options for getting you out of winning, losing, and breakeven trades. Before entering the trade make sure you know where or why you would get out. The nice thing about having a predetermined set of exit rules is that once in a trade, a trader can relax a bit; he doesn't need to micromanage and worry about every tick in the market. By having a system you will know how and what you will trade every day, and nothing should come as a surprise; if a certain condition is met, you know you will be in the market. Unless these conditions or criteria are in the market you shouldn't do anything.

Again, this doesn't have to be a formal, computerized, mechanical system; it can be any trading idea that you use, but it should be the same all the time. It could be as simple as the following:

> Buy whenever the market gaps lower at the open and is in the top half of its range after 30 minutes, exit on a stop if the market breaks the low of the day, exit with a profit if the market has traveled 80 percent of its average true range, or exit at the close of the day.

You can have a dozen systems like this that you use. The important thing is that they are in your trading plan and work.

Money Management

Though having some sort of trading system is important, the foundation of all trading plans should be a money management plan, as I'll discuss in Chaps. 16 and 17. Without one, regardless of how good a market technician one is, the odds of becoming a losing trader are high. A trader needs to know how to use his capital, how much he can risk, how many contracts or shares to trade, when to increase position size, and which stocks or markets he can afford to trade. A money management plan also will tell you how many markets you can trade at once and how much you should risk in each one.

When making a money management plan, take your time and concentrate on detail. Be specific about what percentage of capital to allocate and how many contracts to trade in each market or market group. Knowing how to use the proper position size is a large part of money management and is important in determining how well you will do. If you trade more than you can afford to lose, you can easily get into trouble, and so that is something you need to watch.

Having a money management plan is something that should be done before starting to trade. Unless the risks are understood beforehand, one is looking for trouble. Many traders lose because they don't have enough money to trade the way they want to and end up overexposing themselves without realizing that they are doing it. By making a money management plan you will know how much you can afford to risk at any given time and how much you can afford to lose. You also should be able to prevent yourself from losing all your money if you calculate the risks beforehand.

What Markets Will Be Traded

Some traders may have a good trading strategy but don't know which markets or stocks to trade. Markets move differently from each other: Some trend more often, while others are choppy. Some are more volatile and have wider ranges, making them more suitable but dangerous for day traders. Some markets are too illiquid and should be avoided. Part of your trading plan will be to pick a core of stocks or commodities you want to trade. For some it's as easy as trading just crude oil; for others it may be trading only semiconductor stocks, while for still others it may be trading every stock that has more than a $2 average true range and over a million shares a day traded. Whatever you plan on trading, know it in advance so that during market hours you can focus on those markets and not have to worry about finding markets. You should also make sure your system backtested well on these markets. I trade a few sectors, and then within those sectors I look at about 5 to 10 stocks. I pretty much trade the same stocks every day. The only exception is that I will look at a stock that is in the news to see if it is worth trading. As far as futures go, these days I look only at bonds, crude, and the stock indices.

Hold Times

As part of your trading plan you will determine what your main trading time frame and average hold time will be. The main time frame will be the one you feel most comfortable trading from. Hold times normally depend on the time frame in which you are trading. If you are Warren Buffett, you may want to hold a good position for 20 years; if you are a scalper, you may hold good winners for 6 to 10 ticks. Everything in between can fit someone's trading style. If you feel comfortable with 60-minute charts, you may have a hold time of 3 to 5 days and may want to limit losses to 1 day. If you use a 5-minute time frame, you can have hold times of 45 to 90 minutes while exiting losers after 30 minutes. These times aren't written in stone; they are just guidelines for what works best with your trading style. Trades should be gotten out of when they merit it, but at least you'll have a reference point. I know that my typical good day trades last about 90 minutes to 2 hours, and for my longer-term trades I'll hold for about 3 to 5 days. I may hold trades longer or shorter, but this is about the average.

The Risk Factors

As with everything in life, you should always be prepared for the worst that can happen. As part of a trading plan try to think of everything that could go wrong with your trading whether you can control it or not. At least by knowing the risk factors involved you can be prepared to do something about them. If you haven't thought them through, you will not know what to do if they arrive. You can have everything planned nice and perfect, and then a terrorist attack changes the market's dynamics. There is little you can do about it; just know that anything can happen in trading.

Some Unexpected Things That Can Happen

You can lose your money if you trade; don't even think about trading if you aren't prepared to lose.

You have a system that works great in trending markets, but then you can't find a trending market.

The Fed unexpectedly cuts interest rates.

The market gaps below your stop.

The markets experience extreme volatility, and the risks triple.

The market locks limit, and you can't exit for 3 days, costing you $3000 more per contract than expected.

Your commission costs become astronomical.

Your computer system crashes right after you put on 20 long positions, and then the market crashes.

A rat bites through a cable on the exchange, shutting down trading.

A stock gets halted for 2 days when you have a position in it.

The seventh largest company in America goes bankrupt.

You become emotionally upset about personal issues and lose focus on trading.

By the way every one of these things has happened to me over the years.

Costs

When you make a trading plan, you have to consider the cost of trading. In Chap. 13 on backtesting systems, I'll discuss just how much of an effect trading costs can have on a trader's bottom line. For now you should know that costs should not be ignored. As part of your plan, make sure you can reduce costs as much as possible. The most commonly thought of cost is commissions, but don't forget slippage and all the little trading fees that can add up. One also should take into consideration how much money will be spent on other trading-related expenses, such as live quotes and software. How do you plan to pay for these things? Through your trading account, or will you have money set aside for this?

Reviewing the Trades and Your Performance

Have a place in your plan for how and when you will review your trades and performance. It doesn't need to be a written journal (though this is recommended), but you should have a method of monitoring positions as well as going over trades to figure out what you did right or wrong. Start with open positions, keeping the focus on whether a trade is still within the parameters in which it originally was made. If it is not or if the reasons the trade was made have changed, you may have to watch the position more closely or get out. How often you will review trades depends on the time frame in which you trade. A long-term trader may need to look only once a day, while a scalper has to do it nonstop.

Some Things That Should Be Reviewed All the Time

Has it reached the target area?
Is it close to the target area and thus should be watched more closely?
Should you add to it or cut back?
Is it not working as planned?
Is your money better spent elsewhere?
Should a trade be closed now or held longer?
Is it approaching a stop level?
Did you ignore stop levels?
Has volatility changed?

After you have reviewed the open trades, go over your losers. I like to review losing trades that I exited correctly with a small loss. To me these are the most important trades of all, and this is a behavior I want to reinforce. I am more proud of getting out of something with a small loss that could have turned out to be worse than I am about having a winning trade. I consider these to be good trades because I did the right thing. I'll remember what I saw to make me get out quickly, and if I see that setup again, I hope to act correctly again. Having had a propensity for letting losers get too big, I like to see that I'm improving in this area. If I let a trade get really bad, I try to see why I did it so that I don't do it again. The next trades I'll review are the ones that I let get away or just acted stupidly on regardless of whether I made money. I'll try not to repeat the same mistake in the future (easier written than done). The last thing I review is my winning trades and again try to learn from them. This doesn't take long to do—just a few minutes after the close—and it is worth much more than the effort one puts into it. Those who never review their trades never learn what they do right and wrong. Don't just review the trades but constantly check the plan for validity. You may be losing money, and the reason may be that your plan is faulty.

THE GAME PLAN

After coming up with a trading plan, a trader should devise a game plan to use on a daily basis. The game plan includes the day-to-day decisions one makes when trading and is what a trader uses to execute the trading plan. The difference between a game plan and a trading plan is that a trading plan may be to buy two contracts when a market is within half a point of a trendline and risk half a point on the other side of it if it breaks through. The game plan will be to identify which markets meet the criteria each day and then how you would time entry into the trades.

Trading decisions are best done during nonmarket hours, and this gives the trader something to work with when the market opens. I go home every night and review the market. I make a list of which stocks I want to buy and which ones I want to short. I look for areas such as support and breakout levels where I want to be involved, and I also know where I'd be out. The next day, when I'm trading, I already have a list of what I want to trade and at what levels; this is my game plan for the day. My trading plan still tells me how much I can risk and what technical indicators I will use to confirm these trades, but on a day-to-day basis I use a game plan. I reevaluate the game plan at lunchtime and make adjustments to it if the market has changed. I try to identify new opportunities to trade in the afternoon and reevaluate my risk levels and stops on open positions.

Lately, part of my game plan has been to buy oil driller stocks at 10 a.m. and then technology stocks at lunchtime, holding them for about 90 minutes each. If it's not working after 30 minutes, I get out. It has been a steady pattern that occurs more days than not, and until it stops working I'll keep it in my game plan.

A game plan helps you stay focused. Without a game plan one can be compelled to trade on whims, out of boredom, because of a news event, to recoup losses, or because some other trader liked a trade. These types of trades are the result of not having or not following a game plan. With a game plan one will have different strategies for different scenarios and will know how to react regardless of what the market does. If something happens, one will be prepared for it, making only anticipated trades instead of trades made for the excitement. Of course there are times when I'll look at the market in hindsight and wish I had been in the move I just missed. But unless the trade is part of my plan, I try to restrain myself and wait for what I find to be better trading opportunities. So what if you miss a few trades? There will be many more trading opportunities, and so it's okay to miss some.

DISCIPLINE

Though not part of the trading plan, discipline is the glue that makes it all come together; a trader needs discipline to stick to his plan. Once you start deviating from a plan, it's easy to start losing and making emotional trading decisions. You start trading markets you shouldn't, you overtrade, and you risk too much, hold too long, and overall make low probability trades.

It is easy to lose discipline on a winning or a losing streak. You should never allow losses to change your trading plan. If you've had a few losses, continue following your plan. Don't change your trading style and become more aggressive or stubborn. A loss is a cost of doing business; ignore it and move on to the next opportunity. The worst thing one can do is to start trading more heavily to make back losses. If you are losing continuously, stop trading until you've examined your trading plan, as it may be the cause. However, don't lose discipline and ignore your trading plan after a winning streak. Many traders get too cocky after a good streak and, thinking they are invincible, make careless trades with too much size. If you have been trading well, it might be the plan that got you there; don't ignore it.

BECOMING A BETTER TRADER

Becoming a better trader involves making a trading plan and having a game plan to trade with. You shouldn't trade without some sort of overall plan that encompasses both risk and strategy. Besides the trading plan, have a game plan for each day that will help you focus on high probability trades. Don't leave home without it, or your trading may be a bit random. A trader should know what he will do every day before the market opens. Whether it goes up or down, he should know what he wants to do. By having a plan that includes a backtested trading system, you will be able to make the same trades over and over without thinking very hard about what to do. If your strategy worked when backtested, there is a good chance it will work in the future. By following the same strategy in the future you can make money consistently.

Becoming a better trader involves having a solid money management plan and risk parameters that will tell you how much to risk. Unless you know what you can afford to risk, it is easy to go bust with only a few bad trades. You need to know how much you can risk, how many contracts or shares to trade, when to increase position size, and what you can afford to trade. This is not something that should be done during market hours. It should be done well in advance, preferably before your next trade if you haven't made a plan already. Don't just think about it; sit down and write it out on paper. Having the discipline to write and follow a trading plan will without a doubt help you. A perfect trading plan is one that you can give to someone and that person will understand exactly how you want to trade.

The other thing I want to mention is that to become a better trader you need to review your trading results on a regular basis. As part of your trading plan you should make a habit of reviewing your trades and trading plan. Review and monitor first your open trades and then your closed trades. Learning from the past is the best way to improve, so don't forget to do it. You should not ignore the plan itself: Keep reviewing it every now and then for weak-

nesses or ways to improve it. A trading plan is a valuable asset to a
trader, so make sure you have one.

Problems Caused by Not Having a Trading/Game Plan

1. Trading off the cuff
2. Straying from good trading strategies
3. Never knowing how much to risk
4. Not knowing which markets to trade
5. Not knowing how many contracts to trade
6. Overtrading
7. Blowing out
8. Being unprepared for what the market has to offer
9. Not knowing where you will exit a trade
10. Not having anything to rate your performance with

Using a Trading and a Game Plan to Your Advantage

1. A trading plan should be treated like a business plan.
2. Together they tie all aspects of trading together.
3. They should fit a trader's style of trading.
4. They keep you focused on proven trading strategies.
5. They let you be prepared.
6. They give you a reason for every trade.
7. They help you keep to a money management plan.
8. They let you relax a little.
9. You'll know the most you can lose.
10. A game plan lets you make well thought out trades.
11. You have pre-established exit points.
12. You will learn to review your trading.
13. They help you avoid emotional decisions.
14. They let you know what markets to trade.
15. You should be disciplined about following them.

Helpful Questions to Ask Yourself

Do I have a trading plan?
Do I have a game plan?

Do I have a trading strategy?
Do I have a money management plan?
Do I stray from my plans too easily?
Am I disciplined?
Do I review my trades?
When was the last time I evaluated my trading plan?

System Trading

As part of a trading plan, a trader should come up with a trading methodology that can be incorporated into a few simple rules for buying and selling. This is the start of trading with a system. Having some sort of system is crucial to a trader; without one, no matter how simple, trading can be random, haphazard, and dangerous. A system doesn't have to be elaborate, etched in stone, or purely computerized; it can be discretionary as well as purely mechanical, but it must give you a guideline to trade with. Systems can be made or bought, but either way they must fit one's trading style. There is no single system that will fulfill every trader's needs. What works for one trader may not work for another, as each trader has a different approach he feels comfortable with. Overall, the point of having a system is to help a trader repeatedly make trades that have been backtested to have a high probability of success.

WHAT IS A SYSTEM?

Simply put, a system is a set of rules a trader uses to make buy and sell decisions. It can be as plain as buy when one moving average crosses the other and sell when they cross the other way, or it can be more complicated and have 10 conditions that must be met before a trade is made. A good system not only will include entry signals but also will account for exits and stops. Just knowing when to get in is only half a system, not a full one. Though some people think a system has to be programmed into trading software such as TradeStation, which then spits out when to buy and sell, it doesn't have to be. A system can be any set of rules, patterns, or conditions a trader uses repeatedly when he sees the market setting up one way or another. I've used systems in which the signals were completely generated by looking at printed daily charts. I would write down where my entry and exit points would be and then wait for the market to approach those levels. Systems can be seen visually on a chart, as in the case of buying a stock that stops going down as the rest of the market keeps dropping. This is hard to program, but it is an entry signal in a system, as it is a clear condition that one can always follow. Systems can also be based on fundamental analysis, such as buying crude when stockpiles are lower than they were the week before and selling when they are higher. Many times I don't use a formal system to trade with: I know what patterns to look for, and if I see them, I'll make a trade. Since I look at different time frames all the time, it is hard to program one system that will read all the time frames. Instead, I use a series of systems and have to look visually for confirmation. I use some discretion, especially when it comes to getting out of a trade. If I see something I like or don't like in one of the different time frames, I'll get out. This is still considered trading with a system because I always use the same guidelines for making my trading decisions.

Traders who use purely mechanical signals, whether they are generated by a computer or not, are known as *systematic traders;* they get a signal and take it without any thought process, never deviating from the system. Other traders who use system-generated signals may do so on more selective processes, taking some trades and not others, depending on market conditions or as they wait for confirmation from another indicator so that they can time their trades better. These traders are known as *discretionary traders.* Both discretionary and systematic styles have their pros and cons, as I'll discuss later in this chapter.

WHY TRADERS SHOULD USE SYSTEMS

I would venture to say that most professional traders use systems for a good part of their decision-making process. Whether it is computer-generated or just a set of rules and conditions they follow, having a system keeps them on track. Some use a fully systematic approach, taking every trade that the computer spits out, while others are more discretionary, using the systems as a guide but using discretion on the final decisions, especially when it comes to deciding how many contracts to trade. The important thing, though, is that they all have a set of rules that they know will produce high probability trades. Even top traders who never write down their rules still repeatedly look for certain setups in the market before they make or exit a trade.

What these professionals know is that a system is there to help them find trades that have a high probability of being successful. They know that by trading with a proven set of rules that have had a positive expectancy of winning, they can increase their chances of making money. Sure, there will be many times when the system is dead wrong (that's okay; if you are right 50 percent of the time, you're doing great), but in the long run if you repeatedly make the same high-percentage trades over and over again, the winning trades should outperform the losing ones. When one trades without a system, then luck becomes a big part of the equation; a proven system reduces the effect luck has on a trader's P&L. The more you can reduce the effect of luck, the better a trader you will be.

Some traders get into trouble because they make trades without any type of system or plan. They have no rhyme or reason to their trades. Each trade they make can have an independent thought process compared with the previous ones: One day they buy a breakout, but the next day, with the same scenario, they may short as the market breaks highs because they don't think it will follow through. To be an effective trader one should have a consistent plan that is followed day in and day out. By having a system, one will have precise rules to follow and will know at all times on what side of the market to be on, if any. There is a much smaller chance of making careless mistakes when one is following a system. There is little guessing as to what to do when you follow a system; the only question is how strictly will you follow the rules of the system. When you do not have a system, you never quite know what to do. Many times I look at the market and think, "We've been in a bull market, and I should be long. No, wait, it's been coming off a little and actually looks better short. Oh, but I don't know, it's already gone down too much, so I should buy." This type of trading can be reckless. With a system you won't have to make decisions like these; the system will tell you what to do.

The other important thing a system does is tell you when to get out of a trade. Some people have great entry skills, but once in a trade, they have no idea when to get out. They let losses grow too much, take profits prematurely, and give back a large portion of the profits, or, worse, let winners turn into losers. They never think about the exit when they put on a trade, and so they don't know when it is time to get out. A good system will take care of that for a trader; if he can follow his system, he will know when to get out.

BUYING OR WRITING A SYSTEM

Writing a system is easy and can be done in a few minutes; writing a good winning system, however, can take weeks or months to develop, adjust, rewrite, backtest, and repeat the whole process until it's just right. If you are using trading software, just learning how to program a system is hard enough; when you add all the time and hard work that go into developing a system, you can see why some people abandon formal system writing. They may start doing it but then give up quickly and either trade with a half-baked system or go back to not using any system. But if you want to get ahead, you should have a solid trading system or strategy to follow.

Buying Systems

If writing a system is too much work or you don't know how to get started, the easiest way to get a system is to use someone else's. You can buy an advertised system that you see in the back of a trading magazine or on a Web site, but I'd be skeptical of any advertised system. I would never sell a great system; instead, I would keep quiet about it, trade with it, and reap the rewards. If I have something good, I don't want other people competing with me in entering orders. When you buy a system, it is unlikely that seller is using it as well; usually it is an older system that he doesn't use anymore.

Another problem I have with buying advertised systems is that many times the hypothetical results they tout are misleading. They say the system would have turned $10,000 into $132,000 in 3 years. Then in tiny print you see that slippage and commissions have not been included and that all profits have been reinvested. However, nobody in reality compounds his winners on every trade; it is bad money management, as one or two losses will wipe out all the profits. Ignoring commissions and slippage will give you results that vary immensely from real results. When everything is considered properly, that $132,000 may only be a $7000 profit in 3 years. Also, keep in mind that they will report results that have been optimized and tested over the data on which the system works the best. You probably could test the system on another set of data and have losing results. The last problem with buying a system is that a trader may not use it correctly if it differs from his trading ideas. Everybody has a unique trading style, and to feel comfortable one should trade with the rules that suit him best.

Don't let this discourage you. I know people who have bought systems that they were able to follow and make money with. There are some good ones out there that have proved to be consistent, and if a trader is disciplined enough to follow a proven system, he should be able to make money with it. One type of system one could buy is a black box system; this generates signals without the trader knowing how the system is made or what generates the signals. I personally can't trade like this; I always want to analyze anything I use first to make sure it fits my trading methodology. But it does work for some people.

Making Your Own System

If a trader wants to start using mechanical systems and does not know where to start, buying one may be a good option. This is also a good way to get started writing a system: Take someone else's and go through it, analyzing it step by step to see what makes it tick. Look for ways to improve on it or make it fit your style better or just steal some ideas from it. I've included some simple Easy Language code throughout this chapter from systems I've written in TradeStation, as well as a full working system. You can use some of those ideas as a basis to start making your own system. You also can find free systems on the Web and in trading magazines. A system you make yourself will be easier to trade with than will using someone else's. Even if you start out with someone else's system, play around with it until you make it your own.

For the most part, this chapter and the next one will discuss how to make and what to look for in computerized trading systems, but this material applies to manual systems as well. If you don't have software that lets you write and backtest systems, you have to do it by hand, but it should still be done. None of my early systems used a computer; everything was done by hand, and it worked just as well. A computer lets you do more and do it more quickly. I used to spend months testing systems by hand to make sure they worked even though I was told beforehand that they would; you should never take anything for granted. Ever since I started using TradeStation to write and test systems, I have been able to do things in a fraction of the time, especially backtesting. What used to take weeks now takes minutes, freeing up tons of time. When I didn't know what to do with all that free time, I decided to write this book.

MY FIRST SYSTEMS

I was lucky enough to use systems from the beginning when I started to trade. Though they were quite simple, I did backtest them by hand, and they worked. My first system was using a point and figure chart I kept while in the pit. In the ring you don't have the luxury of having a computer, and so floor traders keep track of the market by hand with a point and figure chart, filling in the chart as the market moves a set amount. I had learned to make one as a clerk, and then an experienced trader showed me what patterns to look for and how to trade using the chart. Basically it was a simple breakout system that involved taking trades in the direction of the trend. I would measure exits by the width of the previous congestion or exit on a signal in the other direction.

Later, when I started looking at more markets, I would keep my commodity perspective (daily paper charts) with me all the time, updating the markets I traded throughout the day. I kept track of about 10 markets and used a reversal day system that I still incorporate into my trading. That system was simple: If today's low is lower than yesterday's low, then buy on a stop if the market goes positive by a small filter that varies by market. For an exit I used the low of the day as a stop or a signal in the opposite direction.

WHAT YOU SHOULD WANT IN A SYSTEM

In making or choosing a system, there are a few things to look for. You want to make sure it is suitable for your style of trading, and you want something that is simple rather than complicated, that is easy to understand, and that works. The more complicated a system is, the more likely it is that it has been customized to the data. You also want a system that will work over different time frames and markets as opposed to one that works only on a specific market and time frame. A good trading strategy should work no matter what; if it doesn't work across the board, something may be wrong with it. As far as results go, I'll cover that in the next chapter, but you want a system that has a positive expectancy, is consistent, and has relatively small drawdowns compared to profits.

Simplicity

Systems should be kept as simple as possible. Overdoing things doesn't make a system better; on the contrary, it can take away from a good system. Trying to make a system too complicated with too many indicators and variables is a common mistake with some traders; some of the best systems are the simplest. As a rule of thumb, a system should fit on the back of an envelope and be easily explained so that someone can understand what every indicator does and every rule does. Otherwise it's too complicated. Always remember the old adage "Keep it simple, stupid" and you'll be okay.

There are hundreds of combinations of indicators and ideas a trader can look at and use, but for the most part traders rely on just a handful of their favorite ones. I never overdo it with indicators and ideas. I look for indicators that work in most markets and market environments and try not to get too fancy. Money management is more important to a trader's success than are all the indicators in the world; find a few that you like best and keep it simple. If you have a system with 42 variables in it, it gets a little ridiculous. The more indicators and parameters you have, the more likely it is that something will go wrong, and when it does, you won't be able to figure out what it is. As people put more and more rules into a system, it becomes curve-fitted to the data and too difficult to analyze when one is trying to improve on it, as there are too many parameters to look at. People sometimes get carried away writing filters to make their systems catch more trades or avoid others. This is something that should be avoided. Filters should be kept simple, as the more you have, the less likely it is that the system will work as well in the future. If you have a simple system that worked in the past, it is likely that it will work in the future and in different markets better than a complicated curve-fitted system would.

It Should Fit Your Trading Style

One of the most important things about a system is that it has to fit a trader's style and beliefs about the market. One person may have a great system that works like a charm for him, but if another trader uses it, he may lose money with it. This is the case because the other trader may not believe in the signals it gives if they differ from his trading style. Some people, for example, will buy as a market breaks out of a range, but a trader who likes to look at stochastics may second-guess this and not buy because the market looks overbought. Some may like to hold trades for only a few minutes, while others hold for a few hours; this is a personal choice, and it is hard for people to switch holding times once they have set beliefs. I know I am not a quick scalper no matter how hard I tried to be one in the past; if I have a trade that's working, I like to hold on to it. I allow for this in my systems, and make systems that hold on to winning trades longer. A trader with no tolerance for loss may be more comfortable using stochastics in his systems, while a trader who is looking to hold for the long term may have a moving average-based system that keeps him in a trade longer. Some traders just can't short; they feel comfortable only buying. If that is the case, they can make a system that will only go long, ignoring all sell signals.

Rule number one of any system is to make sure you are comfortable using it and believe in the signals it generates. To do this you need to know what kind of trader you are and what makes you tick; you need to analyze your personality and figure out how you want to trade. Are you a person who is in it for the excitement or to make money? Would you be happy trading once a week if you knew you'd make money or do you need to trade 50 times a day? Do you like to trade reversals, trends, or breakouts, or do you have another preference? Do you have a full-time job so that you can't watch the market all day? If so, you may need a system where orders can be placed before the open or at night instead of one that makes trades in the middle of the day, which a full-time trader may use. No matter what type of trader you are, you will work better when you are comfortable with a system that complements your beliefs.

KNOWING WHAT TYPE OF TRADER YOU ARE

As you try to figure out what kind of trader you are and what types of systems you will need, ask yourself the following questions:

How often do you need to trade?

What time frame do you like best?

Are you more comfortable trading with the trend?

Do you like trading breakouts?

Are you a contrarian trader, always looking for reversals?

What indicators or pattern do you like to use?

Are you an aggressive trader, or a risk-averse trader?

Can you trade a boring market or stock or do you need fast movers?

Can you hold positions overnight?

Do you need to get out by the close in order to be able to sleep at night?

Are you too high-strung, or are you laid back?

Do you worry about every tick?

Can you let a trade breathe to maturity?

Do you want lots of small wins or are you looking for big moves?

How big of a position can you handle?

Are you looking to make a living or to have some fun and make a few bucks on the side?

How much are you comfortable losing per trade?

Do you know how to lose?

How often do you need to be right?

What percent of your equity can you handle as a drawdown?

How much can you afford to lose per trade?

Once you can answer these questions honestly, you can start to come up with trading ideas and systems that will suit you and that you'll most likely be able to follow.

THE DIFFERENT TYPES OF TRADING STYLES AND SYSTEMS

There are many different trading approaches that work. Finding the one that a trader feels the most comfortable with is what's important. The next few sections give examples of some different types of systems you could use and can get you started on the path to writing a system or two. I've included the Easy Language code for TradeStation users.

Breakout Systems

The oldest, simplest, and most effective systems are breakout systems. The reason these systems work well is that they will get you into a trade at the start or during the continuation of a major trend. Every trend or major move starts with a breakout of the previous high or low, and if you want to get in on it, a breakout system is for you. A trader using these systems must be willing to be wrong quite often, as they will produce many false signals that can cause one to buy many highs and sell many lows. The key to making money with these systems is that one or two breakouts will be quite substantial and can more than make up for the false signals. Breakout systems are best suited for a patient trader who can wait for a retracement and then hold on to winning trades as long as possible. If you get out too soon, you could end up missing great trades and come out a loser in the long run. Many people like to use stop orders when getting into the market on a breakout. I don't think it is always a good idea to do this because sometimes it's best to wait for the pullback if the market is already overbought. What I do is have a system that alerts me when the market has met the breakout criteria and then I use a different system on a smaller time frame that waits for a pullback so that I can get a higher probability trading opportunity.

The easiest type of breakout system to program is the kind that gives signals when the price exceeds the highest high or lowest low of the last x periods. I will cover exits and stops later in the chapter; for now I'll just worry about the entry signals.

TradeStation users would write the long entry signal as follows:

```
Input: Length(10);
If Close > Highest(High,Length)[1] Then Buy On
    Close;
```

This buys when the close is higher than the highest high of the last 10 (Length) bars beginning one bar ago ([1]).

The Input: Length(10); allows you to easily change the lookback period of the highest high when you are using the charting software without having to go back and change the code. All the inputs for a system go at the top of the system. The [1] ensures that you start counting from one bar ago so that you don't include the current bar in your signal. Since you don't know what the high of the current bar is until the bar is closed, you shouldn't include it in your signal.

If you wanted to get the buy signal before the close of the bar, you could write the signal as follows:

```
If High > Highest(High,Length)[1] Then Buy;
```

One way to avoid receiving false signals and getting whip-sawed is to add a filter to the system that gives you a buffer zone before getting a signal. You can do this in several ways. One way is by adding a few points to the breakout as in the following example, which buys when the close is higher than the highest high of the last 10 bars plus 5 points. This prevents you from getting in if the breakout was just a quick peek through the previous high:

```
If Close > Highest(High,10)[1] + 5 points Then Buy
    On Close;
```

You can also add a buffer that's based on the volatility of the market. Volatility changes with the market, and so as the market gets more volatile, a breakout has to be more significant to be taken. This is done by adding a standard deviation measure to the system, which ensures the market has moved enough outside the breakout level and that this has not happened by chance. If you want to consider the volatility of the market as a buffer, you can add a standard deviation move from the highest high. You can either write it directly into the line of code or make it a separate variable, as I did in the following case:

```
Buffer = StdDev(Close,10)[1]
If Close > Highest(High,10)[1] + Buffer Then Buy
    On Close;
```

Another buffer in a breakout system may be to buy when the market closes above a 35-period moving average for 2 days in a row. This ensures that the break of the moving average wasn't a 1-day fluke. You can add as many periods as you like to this kind of buffer:

```
If Close > Average(Close,35) And Close[1] >
    Average(Close,35)[1] Then Buy;
```

You also may want to throw in a condition that takes a trade only if volume is getting strong. When a system has more than one requirement to get into a trade, you will need to set up conditions and then tie them together to get a signal. In this case something like the following would work:

```
Inputs: Length(10),LengthV(5);
Condition1 = High>Highest(High,Length)[1];
Condition2 = Volume>(Average(Volume,LengthV)*1.25);
If Condition1 and Condition2 Then Buy On Close;
```

The first condition is the break of the highest high of the last 10 bars, as in the first example I gave. The second condition requires a filter that the volume of the current bar is 25 percent greater than the average volume over the last 5 days. This will give you signals only on trades that break out of a range on better than average volume, which is something you want to see, as it may indicate the break may follow through.

Some breakout systems require patterns that are hard to program, such as channels, trendlines, and double bottoms. With those systems, you will have to look visually at a chart to get signals, but if you come up with a set of rules for a trade, it is still a system even if you can't program it.

Trend-Following Systems

For those who want to trade with an established trend, moving averages and trendlines will be the core of their systems. Since trendlines are hard to program, one is better off relying on moving averages in programming trend-following systems. Those who use patterns, such as channels and trendlines as a trading guide most likely will have to make visual systems or draw their trendlines on a chart so that the software can compute signals.

As with breakout systems, those who can hold on the longest will fare the best with these types of systems. In a choppy market you should expect to be wrong a lot. One way to avoid getting whipsawed is to use longer period averages; the downside is that when a trend does start to develop, you will get a signal later than you would if you had a shorter average. This trade-off is something a trader must determine. There is a little time lag between the time a moving average system shows you that a trend has started and the time it actually started. Moving averages are lagging indicators, and so any system that uses them will get you into the market only after a move has been established, but if a strong trend develops, these systems can catch a good portion of the move.

The most basic moving average system would be a two-average/crossover one, buying when the shorter average crosses over the longer one:

```
Input: Length1(10),Length2(35);
If Average(Close,Length1) Crosses Over
   Average(Close,Length2) Then Buy On Close;
```

This will give a buy signal when a 10-period average crosses above a 35-period average. Though the signal is given at the close of the bar, one would place the order at the beginning of the next bar. This is the case because you never know for sure until the actual close if a signal will be given. Sometimes it looks like it may, but in the last few minutes the market moves drastically the other way. You could rewrite this so that you are buying on the open using the information from one bar ago, which would read as follows:

```
Input: Length1(10),Length2(35);
If Average(Close,Length1)[1] Crosses Over
   Average(Close,Length2)[1] Then Buy On Open;
```

One condition in a system could be to take trades only in the direction of the 50- or 200-day moving average; this will always put you on the side of the major trend. You can find the direction of the average by having a condition that let's you see if the moving average is higher now than it was 10 days ago or whatever lookback period you like. If it's higher, it's moving up:

```
Input: BarsBack(10)
Condition1 = Average(Close,50) >
   Average(Close,50)[BarsBack];
```

Another condition could be that you want the current bar to be as close as possible to the moving average before buying; otherwise you may buy an overextended market that could eventually pull back in toward the average. I would do this by adding a condition that says that the price must be within one average true range (ATR) of the moving average. You could use more or less than one ATR, or you can use standard deviation, or points. The following condition ensures that the current close is less than one ATR from the 35-period moving average:

```
Input: Length2(35), ATRlen(10);
Condition2 = (Close - (Average(Close,Length2))
    < AvgTrueRange(ATRlen(10));
```

There are many more things one can do with moving averages. These are just a few examples; the rest is up to the trader's imagination.

Oscillator-Based Systems

No matter how many times you tell people that trading with the trend is the way to go, some will insist on looking for bottoms and tops. Systems based on oscillators are good for these counter traders, who are always looking for reversals, bottoms, and tops. When a market is stuck in a range between support and resistance levels, an oscillating system that buys at oversold levels and sells at overbought levels works better than does anything else, especially in the short term. Oscillator-based systems also can satisfy the needs of a person who always needs to be in the market. There are many ways to write signals based on oscillators, but trying to come up with a computerized signal for the best use of an oscillator—divergence between the market and the oscillator—is not easily done. Divergence is something that has to be seen visually on a chart, but there are many ways a trader can use oscillators in computerized systems. Here are a few signals and conditions that could be used in oscillator-based systems.

The most typical signal using the stochastic lines is to buy when the SlowK crosses over the SlowD. This is written as follows:

```
Input: Length(14);
If SlowK(Length) Crosses Above SlowD(Length) Then
    Buy On Close;
```

One also could add a condition that the stochastics has to cross above the oversold area (BuyZone) while the SlowK line is above the SlowD line. Since the SlowD line will be below the SlowK line, you only need to ensure that the SlowD indicator has crossed a certain level to get a signal:

```
Inputs: Length(14), BuyZone(30);
If SlowK(Length) > SlowD(Length) and SlowD(Length)
    Crosses Above BuyZone Then Buy On Close;
```

Using the RSI, one could use a similar crossover rule:

```
Input: RSILen(10),BuyZone(30),
If RSI(Close,RSILen)Crosses Over BuyZone Then Buy
    On Close;
```

You also could change the area where a signal would be given to any number. If you want to buy only if the indicator goes above 50, change the BuyZone parameter from 30 to 50.

If you want to avoid buying when a market already has made a move and is in overbought territory, you can add a condition to your stochastic system that will take trades only if the indicator is below the overbought area. This will keep you from buying potentially overbought markets. This condition could be used in any type of system to potentially keep you from chasing a market:

```
Input: SellZone(70);
Condition1 = SlowD(Length) < SellZone;
```

The last example I'll give is one that can be used in a strong market. This one is used to buy when the oscillators are in overbought areas, as the market could stay up there for quite a while. This is the opposite of selling when the market is overbought, but in different market conditions one strategy works better than another. You may want to combine one of your entry rules with a rule that takes the average directional index (ADX) into account. The following will buy when the ADX is strong indicating a strong trend and confirmed by a strong reading in the stochastics:

```
If ADX(10) > 30 And SlowD(14) > 85 Then Buy On
    Close;
```

I'll get to exits soon, but with the above example you may want to have a rule that exits the trade if the stochastics drops below 70, which may indicate that the strong trend is dying down. Again, these are just a few ideas one can use with oscillators. Go through Chap. 7 again to get more ideas and then use the ones you like best in writing a system.

ADAPTING TO MARKET CONDITIONS

Traders need to be flexible to adapt to different market conditions. In a choppy market one set of rules may work better than it will in a strongly trending market. If I see that the market is choppy, I stay out or use a system that is based on stochastics instead of moving

averages. I especially avoid anything that has to do with breakouts.
I won't buy highs but instead look for the market to reverse at the
extremes. In contrast, when the market is strong, I use trending indicators and rely on oscillators to confirm the trend or to wait for a
pullback. I avoid trying to pick tops in a strong market but may use
oscillators to buy when they indicate that the market is oversold.

One thing that can help in deciding what type of system to use
is to employ the ADX to help determine whether the market is
trending or trendless. A trader can have one set of rules if the ADX
is below 20 and another if it is above 30.

This could be done as follows:

```
If ADX(Length) > 30 Then
Trending Market System
Else;
If ADX(Length) < 20 Then
Choppy Market System
Else;
Middle Ground System
```

STOPS AND EXITS

A system is not complete until it has stop and exit parameters in it.
It is important to work as hard on the exit side as you do on the entry
side. A system with just entry signals is like skiing downhill for the
first time: You can get started and on your way easily enough, but
you may have to hit a tree to stop, which is not lots of fun, trust me.
Money is made on the exits, not on the entries, so spend as much
time working on the getting out part of your trades as on the getting
in part. Though I do have rules built into my systems to get out of
the market, I very often end up setting my exit parameters visually,
using different time frames to do so. Sometimes I get out of positions
before I get an exit signal because a position just stopped performing
the way it should. There is no need to wait to get stopped out or to
give back profits. When a trade stops working, I get out. If it returns
to the right path later, I'll get back in, but for the time being there is
no need to risk a pullback.

The simplest way to make sure you account for stops and
exits is to have a stop and reverse system, which means the system
is always in the market. These systems will have you either long
or short and use a signal in the opposite direction as an exit/stop.

The problem with this is that on short-term systems there will be many times when you are trading against the major trend of the market. Though I used to use stop and reverse systems frequently, now I prefer to sit out when I get a signal that goes against the main trend.

Stops

I have a standard stop I use in all my systems. It's my canned stop that I will use if I have not gotten out of the market beforehand. The stop I use gets me out of the market if it has moved 2 standard deviations against the spot where I got in:

```
Exitlong From Entry("Buy1") at$ Close -
    2*Stddev(Close,10)[1] Stop;
```

at$ Close refers back to the close of the original entry bar. To use this type of stop, you have to have named the entry signal. The following example names the entry signal "Buy1":

```
If SlowK(Length) Crosses Above SlowD(Length) Then
    Buy ("Buy1") On Close;
```

Other stops could be to get out when the market has dropped below a moving average by some buffer zone:

```
If Close < (Average(Close,Length1)-Buffer) Then
    Exitlong ("Stop1");
```

or if the market has just broken lower than the 5-day low:

```
If Close < Lowest(Low,5)[1] Then
    Exitlong("Stop2");
```

Exits

Besides a signal in the opposite direction, some popular exits are to get out after x number of bars:

```
If BarsSinceEntry = 10 Then Exitlong;
```

or if the stochastics is in overbought territory:

```
If SlowD(Length) > 85 Then Exitlong At Close;
```

or if the market has moved too far from its trendline or moving average:

```
Input: SD(5), Length(35), Period(10);
If (High - Average(Close,Length)) >
   StdDev(Close,Period)*SD Then Exitlong At Close;
```

This exit will get you out when the price moves more than 5 standard deviations from the moving average. You would want to do this because when a market moves too far from its support level, eventually it will tend to snap back. These are just a few examples. You have to test different ideas to see what works best for you. You also may have more than one set of exit rules and stops; if any one of your conditions is met, you can get out.

MULTIPLE SYSTEMS

You don't have to use only one system. Some people trade many systems on the same stock or commodity at the same time. They may trade five systems and take every signal they get so that at times, if all their systems are indicating that they should get in on the same side, they may have five contracts on. If they are getting mixed signals, they may have no positions on, as the signals will cancel each other out. It's a good idea to have several systems because some will work best in choppy markets while others will work best in trending markets. By having one for each type of market environment you may always be involved no matter what the market is doing. When a bunch of systems start working in sync, the odds of a trade working are probably better. When this happens and you take all the signals, you will be trading with more share size, and so you can capitalize nicely on it.

SYSTEMATIC VERSUS DISCRETIONARY

There is a debate about whether system traders should be purely systematic or have discretion in regard to what they trade. Purely systematic traders rely on backtested systems and rules to generate every trade they make. They like having clear-cut signals and will not second-guess the system. They ignore all emotions and thoughts about the market and are disciplined about making a trade as soon as the system alerts them to. Discretionary traders may take some trades and not others; they may use the signals as an alert and then use discretion to time trades, especially if the market has had a run-up. Some people may use discretion when they are trading patterns that can't be programmed, and some may not use a concrete system at all. Regardless, good traders who are 100 percent discretionary, still have solid buy and sell rules they adhere to every time.

One problem with using a system and not taking every trade is that the one trade you decide to skip could be the one that would have made up for the last five losses. People who do this end up blaming good systems for their losses, even though the system actually ended up performing well. It was the trader, not the system, who was responsible for the loss by deciding not to take every signal. Though it's okay to use discretion in trading, a systematic trader shouldn't get into the habit of overriding the system whenever the mood hits. If you are using a good system that has been backtested and you want to be a system trader, you have to take every signal regardless of what you think about each trade, because you never know which will be the one that works like a charm. However, as I mentioned before, it is impossible to program some proven patterns and methodologies into a system. A good trader can see patterns in the market that a system cannot capture. It's hard to program things such as what wave in an Elliott wave pattern is the market in or if the market has retraced 38.2 percent yet. Head and shoulder, cup and handle, saucers, and flags are some patterns that are close to impossible to program in TradeStation. Some of these patterns make for great low-risk trades, and I am always on the alert for these kinds of trades. Sometimes you'll know about an upcoming report that you'd rather be on the sidelines for instead of taking undue risk. Hunches are also impossible to program. There are many times when I'm in a trade and don't feel right about it, and so I get out even though it hasn't hit my stop or target area. One time you may want to override a signal is when there is news that makes the market jump and leaves a big gap. A system may generate a signal, but do you really want to take it if the gap is large? The difference between where the signal was generated and the current price could be several hundred dollars per contract or share. When this happens, it may be best to do nothing and wait to see if the market gives you a better opportunity to get in. You still want to trade in the direction of the signal, but there is no need to rush in.

Overall, it's hard to say whether one should use a fully systematic approach or not. People can make money both ways and lose both ways. The only thing I know is that if you have something that works, don't second-guess it.

COMMON MISTAKES

Finding or making the right system is not easy, and people make many mistakes along the way. Aside from using a system that doesn't suit a trader's style, there are several mistakes traders make when they are using a system to trade with. Though I'll discuss them in more detail in the following chapter on backtesting a system, some of these mistakes include not having enough money to trade a system, giving up on a system too soon, trading a system that does not have a positive expectancy, trading a system that has been curve-fitted, and trading a system that has not been backtested properly or with enough data. If a system is not properly backtested to have a positive expectancy, don't use it; it can cause a lot of unnecessary losses. It's amazing how many people trade a system without ever backtesting it first. Even when a new system has been backtested properly, don't risk a lot of capital on it until you have tested it with real money for a while. Start small or in a market that has low volatility until you are sure the system will perform well in real time before risking your normal amount.

Not Having Goals for the System

Some people keep working on a system forever, but they are never happy with it; they keep changing it or adding to it, trying to make it perfect. They spend too much time writing it and never get around to trading the system. You can avoid doing this by having a goal for the system. Know what you want before you start. If you have well-defined goals for your trading, finding or making a system will be easier. If you are looking for a system with a 55 percent win/loss ratio and with winning trades being twice as profitable as losing trades, with a drawdown of no more the $3000 and 5 percent per month profit, when you get close, be happy with it. Don't try to keep stretching it or you will never get to trade it.

A SAMPLE SYSTEM

Here is a simple system for TradeStation that works. It is based on the signals I explained earlier. Everything inside brackets {} does not get read by the system; it is there to make it easier to understand. This sample system should give you a good idea of what goes into writing a system and what it should look like.

This system buys when the market breaks above the highest bar of the last 10 periods, with a filter of a 0.5 standard deviation move of the last 10 bars. The sell signal is just the opposite. The entry is simple enough, but I made the exit more interesting by using the ADX to give me different exit conditions. If it is strong and the market is trending, the system will stay in until two moving averages cross; if the ADX is weak, the system takes profits after 10 bars; and if it is in between, it will exit if the stochastics reach overbought territory. Finally, the system exits on a stop if the price is more than 2 standard deviations from the entry price.

```
Input: Length(10), BSE(10), LengthADX(10),
    SD(.5)Length1(10),Length2(35);
        {*******ENTRY SIGNALS*******}

If Close > Highest(High,Length)[1] +
    StdDev(Close,10)[1]* SD Then Buy("Buy1") On
    Close;
If Close < Lowest(Low,Length)[1] —
    StdDev(Close,10)[1]* SD Then Sell("Sell1")On
    Close;
        {********** STOPS **********}

ExitLong("Stop1") From Entry("Buy1") at$ Close -
    2*StdDev(Close,10) Stop;
ExitShort("Stop2") From Entry("Sell1") at$ Close +
    2*StdDev(Close,10) Stop;
        {********** EXITS **********}

If ADX(LengthADX)> 30 Then
If Average(Close,Length1) Crosses Below
    Average(Close,Length2) Then ExitLong ("ExitL1");
If Average(Close,Length1) Crosses Above
    Average(Close,Length2) Then ExitShort ("ExitS1");
        Else
            If ADX(LengthADX) < 20 Then
                If BarsSinceEntry=BSE Then
                    ExitLong("ExitL2");
                If BarsSinceEntry=BSE then
                    ExitShort("ExitL2");
```

```
Else
    If SlowD(14)> 85 Then
        ExitLong("ExitL3");
    If SlowD(14)< 15 Then
        ExitShort("ExitL3");
```

BECOMING A BETTER TRADER

Becoming a better trader means using some sort of system in your trading. Whether it's computerized or done visually on a chart, is simplistic or elaborate, a trader should have a solid set of rules that have been proven to work. Unless a trader can start making the same smart trades over and over, he not only will probably lose, he will not know the specific reason he is doing so. With a system, if you are not making money, it is because the system is no good or the trader can't follow it. If the trader can't follow it, he should get one that fits him better. If the system is not good, he should be able to see that and abandon it or fix it. By backtesting a system before using it, a trader can reduce the chances that he is trading with a bad system. The problem when you don't have a system is that you may have no idea why you are losing, as your trades may be made randomly.

Even when you are trading with a solid computerized system, you can still use discretion on some trading ideas, as you won't be able to program every good strategy. There will be times when things don't feel right and you want to get out before a signal is given; as long as you are not cutting winners short on a repetitive basis, this is fine. Overall, though, if your system works, you should try to take all the signals it generates as you never know which will be the good ones.

One thing that is important about systems is that no system is just a signal to get into the market; it should always provide you with exits and stops as well. Even if you use visual stops and not programmed ones and do so all the time, they become part of your system. Either way, it's important to incorporate them into your trading. What's good about having the exits already established is that you don't have to think as hard or worry about getting out too soon or too late; you let the system take care of that.

Making and backtesting systems is not easy work, but those who want to get ahead will take the time to do it, as it is crucial for making consistent high probability trades. System writing can be quite time-consuming, but a successful trader will put the work into doing what it takes to come out ahead.

Why People Lose Money with Systems

1. Abandoning a system too soon
2. Ignoring commissions and slippage
3. Lacking the discipline to follow the rules
4. Second-guessing the signals
5. Relying on misleading hypothetical results
6. Using a system that doesn't fit your style
7. Using a system you can't afford to trade with
8. Using a system that hasn't been backtested properly
9. Adding too many variables and conditions
10. Curve-fitting systems
11. Not keeping things simple
12. Trading with a losing system

High Probability System Trading

1. Use only systems that have a positive expectancy of winning.
2. Learn to backtest a system properly.
3. Use systems that adapt to different markets.
4. Have solid rules to trade by.
5. Work as hard on the exit as on the entry.
6. Include stops in your system.
7. Use a system that has consistency of returns.
8. Keep things simple.
9. Use a system in a higher time frame to alert you of trades and to monitor stops.
10. Use a system in a smaller time frame to time entry and exit into the market.
11. Use systems with a small relative drawdown.
12. Know the most you can lose.
13. Look for signals in different systems to confirm a trade.
14. Use discretion when it is needed.
15. If you are going to be a true systematic trader, take every trade.

Helpful Questions to Ask Yourself

Do I really have a system?
What is my system?
Is it too elaborate?
Does it have stops and exits?
Has it been backtested properly?
Do I believe in it?
Do I second-guess it too often?

CHAPTER 13

A Little about Backtesting

You wrote a system that you think is okay, and now you are ready to go. Not so fast. Having a system means nothing unless you "know" it works. There are several ways to figure out whether a trading strategy works. The first is not much fun when it doesn't work: using real money to test it. The second way is to paper trade with the system for a few months before risking money with it. The most effective way, though, is to backtest it on historical data. That means taking your system and checking to see how it would have done if you had used it on past markets. Not too long ago, this meant sitting in front of a chart and doing it by hand, but now, with more sophisticated and powerful software for system writing and testing, there is no excuse for people not to have properly back-tested systems.

WHY BACKTEST?

By backtesting you should get an idea of whether the system can work in the future. Don't fall into the trap of thinking you have a good system but never bothering to test it. If it didn't work on the backtested data, don't expect it to work in real time when you are risking money. By backtesting you give yourself a fighting chance with a system before putting your money at stake. If you find that your system is borderline or find that it doesn't work, throw it out before it costs you anything other than time.

Be careful because backtesting will not tell you how a system will perform in the future. Even a system that performs perfectly when backtested can fail miserably in real time. However, by thoroughly backtesting, you can become aware that it could have a 10-trade losing streak or a drawdown that lasts for 2 months and costs you $10,000. If that happened in the past, there is no reason to expect it to act differently in the future. Knowing the worst that could happen may prevent you from using a costly system altogether or from bailing on a good one after a few bad trades because you are frustrated with it. It is normal for systems to have losing streaks, and so it's important to know how big they can be.

COMMON MISTAKES TRADERS MAKE WHEN BACKTESTING

Before I get further into backtesting, I want to spend some time on common mistakes and things that should be avoided when one is backtesting. Sometimes it is easier to learn what to do by learning what not to do. By not doing the wrong things you have no choice but to do the right ones. For example, my cat Sophie doesn't really know she is supposed to scratch only her scratching post, but she has learned she is not supposed to scratch the couch, drapes, carpet, furniture, or my leg. Her options have been narrowed to only the proper ones. Now I just need to figure out how to get her to stop thinking 5 a.m. is the proper time to lick my face good morning and she'll be fine. After I go through the don'ts, I'll explain the proper things to do as well, but for now let's get the bad habits out of the way.

Not Knowing How to Evaluate Backtesting Results

The most basic mistake someone can make after backtesting a system is not knowing how to evaluate the results. Unless one can properly do this, it is impossible to tell how a system stacks up. Some traders look for the highest net return or for a high winning percentage when they backtest, but these things may not mean much if the system also has large drawdowns. You have to factor in a few other things when evaluating systems, including number of trades, profit per trade, consecutive losers, biggest loser, biggest winner, average trade, and distribution of returns. It is a combination of all these things that eventually will tell a trader if a system is good and how it compares to other systems.

Curve Fitting and Overoptimization

An important thing to look for in evaluating a system is whether the results were real or curve-fitted. Curve fitting in a nutshell is matching a system to the data. This is a problem of both system writing and backtesting. If you have a strongly trending chart and you write a system to buy and hold, you've curve-fitted the system to the data. Sometimes traders focus on the area of a chart that confirms their opinions and skip over places where the trades may not have worked as well. They then come up with a system that works well, but only on that portion of the data; if they don't test it on other data, the system shouldn't be used. Overoptimization is another problem for system writers. Those who keep fudging a system's parameters until it works perfectly are guilty of this. These people will try every combination of moving averages until they find the ones that work the best. This doesn't make for a good system but for one that will work on the data on which you tested it. When you backtest a system, you must take this into account. You need to realize that the more you have played around with a system's parameters so that it gives you better results, the less likely it is that it will work in the future.

Not Questioning the System

Not questioning the results is also a mistake traders make. They see decent results and are happy with them. Instead, they should try to find ways to break the system, to find the faults, abnormalities, or curve fitting that may make it seem better than it really is. Maybe the system showed great profitability because of one or two large trades. Will this system perform well if the same condition is not present in the future? Were you realistic about slippage? Were there enough trades to test it properly? If you don't question a system's results and deficiencies, you may be in for a surprise when actually using it. This is also true about a system that does not seem to work. Dig into it to see why it doesn't work and try to find out how you can make it better. You can learn a lot about trading by discovering what doesn't work. Maybe you have a theory that is no good and can abandon it, but you can do that only by questioning it thoroughly first.

Not Testing on Enough Data or Market Environments

Another common mistake in testing a system is not having enough data. The minimum number of trades one should have to make a test statistically acceptable is 30, but the more the better. If you do not have sufficient data you will not know if the results are valid or occur by chance. If you write a system and get only six signals when testing it and five of the signals work, you can't make a judgment about it. This may have been a winning streak that could soon be followed by a larger losing streak. With 30 samples it is fair to say that your system is valid and that the results were not just a matter of luck. You also need enough data to cover all types of market environments, not just the ones you like best. You need to know if your system works in uptrends, downtrends, choppy markets, volatile markets, flat markets, and so forth. Test your system on many markets. If it is good, it should work across the board in every market.

When you are testing on intraday data, don't test just a few months; instead, try to get a few years' worth of data. A year of data is a start, but it is not enough to base a system on. Many systems do great for a year yet act horribly over a 3-year span. Getting intraday data can be expensive and time-consuming when you are testing on futures, as each contract has to be tested individually, but trading is not cheap or easy; putting in the time and money will get the best results.

Not Having an Out Sample

One problem of not having enough data to test on is that it leaves you with little data to use as an out sample. When you are testing a system, it should be done on a portion of data that has not been used to write or optimize the system. After you think you have a good system and it is ready for the final test, it should be done on fresh, never before seen data. Some systems get optimized to fit the data and seem great, but they are never tested on fresh data to see how they would do. Although testing on data that was used to optimize the system will produce good results, the trick is to get the same results on clean data. This is where the out sample comes into play. Testing on fresh data is the closest you will get to trading in real time without having to risk money.

Ignoring Commissions and Slippage

Many traders ignore slippage and commissions when testing their systems. They may end up thinking they have great systems, but in reality they don't because they forgot to add or underestimated trading costs. Be realistic about how much it will cost you to trade or you will be in for a surprise when it comes to real trading. Every trade will cost you money in commissions and slippage, and so you must consider these costs when testing a system. A lot of the time traders don't allow enough for slippage. They think they will get filled wherever the signal was given, but I can't tell you how many times I put in a market order for a stock and got 30 cents to a dollar worse than I had hoped to get. If you remember my unexpected rate cut disaster, I had slippage close to $5 per share on several stocks. Trades that on paper may look fantastic in reality turn out to be small winners or losers, and systems that seem profitable can easily be losing ones when you consider commissions and slippage. Don't ignore them or your results will not be accurate.

GETTING STARTED WITH BACKTESTING

Curve Fitting

I'll start with curve fitting and then move on to optimization. Earlier, I described curve fitting as matching a system to the data. Curve-fitting a system makes it look great for a given period of time and for specific data. If you eyeball a chart and see that it is choppy, you can write a system that works well over that period. You also could write a filter that lets you be short just before a market collapses. It would have great results but this is deceiving. Will you really catch the next major collapse with the same signal? You probably could keep tweaking the system until it fit the data perfectly, but the problem with this is that the system is made for that data and probably will not work as well over any other data. You probably could come up with a winning system with a 2000 percent return over the data sample for any chart you look at if you tried hard enough, but this is useless if the market behaves differently in the future. As a trader you want to be concerned about how it will work on new data, not about how it worked in the past. This is why after you are happy with the system it is critical to test it on a fresh piece of data called the out sample, as I'll describe soon. The only true test of a system comes when it works on data on which it wasn't written or optimized. Systems that have been curve-fitted look great when backtested over the data they were created on but may give disappointing results in real time. In general, the more complicated and detailed a system is and the better the results are, the more likely it is that it has been curve-fitted.

Optimizing

Optimization is what happens when a system writer keeps searching for the best parameters and indicators for a system over a specific time period. If he is using moving averages, he will keep trying different period ones until he gets the ones that show the best results. If he is happy with a set of moving averages, he may then look to find the best parameters for a filter on his breakout level that will make the system perform even better. A person can go on forever playing around with parameters and indicators, always trying to come up with something better. With TradeStation this is real easy to do as the software does all the optimizations for you. In seconds it spits out the best parameters for any indicator you want. Though this may seem like a great feature, it can mislead you into believing a system is better than it is.

In optimizing, the goal is to increase the profitability of the system, but be careful not to overdo it. As long as the basic concepts of a system are sound, it doesn't matter what values are used for the parameters. What you hope to find when you optimize is a range of parameters that seem to work best. Maybe you are looking to see when the best breakouts of the highest highs occur. By optimizing you may find that as you use a longer lookback period, the system gets more profitable, but that once you get above 20 bars, the improvement is not much. Then you'll know that you want your lookback period to be about 20 bars instead of 5. Trying to pick the ideal one is useless because it will keep changing with different data.

When optimizing, I like to look for a range of parameters that work best and have similar results, and then I'll take the average. If I find that the 12-, 14-, and 17-period moving averages work best compared with all the others, I most likely will stick to the 14- or 15-period one. If I find the 12-, 14-, and 17-period ones worked well but that the 15- and 16-period averages did not have good results, there is something wrong with the system. A system should work whether the moving average is 5, 7, 10, or 15 periods. I don't care that the 14-period average worked best for this data set. I need to know that the overall concept worked, not that one period was a little better than all the rest. If only one or two parameters worked well, the system is not very good and has probably been curve-fitted to the data.

What I find optimizing to be good for is to see if the system works over different parameters or if it was mere luck that it worked on a specific set of parameters. Did the randomness of the market make something work in the past that may not work again? Was a buffer zone used on a breakout system to avoid one trade that was caused by random noise? Should this trade be taken to reflect reality? Some people will look at a chart and then pick the filter that corresponds perfectly to that chart. Try different parameters on the filter to determine if it was a fluke occurrence. Test it over different periods of data to see if it responds the same; you can even test it over different time frames of the same data to get a different perspective. When you are happy, go to your out sample and test the system there. The results should be similar.

The Out Sample

Probably the most important part of backtesting is having an out sample on which to test your results. Before going live with a system, make sure you test it on fresh data that was not used in making and optimizing the system. One common mistake made by beginning traders is that they write, test and optimize their system by using all the data they have available. If they have 3 years of data, they use all of it to find the best parameters without understanding the concept of having an out sample. So for those who don't know, if you have 3 years of data, use only 2 of them when working on the system. Don't look at the last year of data, not even a chart of it; this will be your out sample, and you don't want it to influence your thinking in the least. After you are happy with the system and it has been optimized and tested, and then reoptimized and tested again until you are even happier with the results, then and only then go to the data you have ignored. Now take this data (the out sample), which should be about one-third of all your data, and test the system on it. At the very least make sure the out sample is big enough to give the 30 trades necessary to make it statistically valid. If the system is good, it should work on the out sample;

if it doesn't, you need to go back to the drawing board to make adjustments or throw it out. Use the out sample to see what went wrong but never try to optimize on the out sample or you will defeat the purpose of having it. I like to look at the chart of the out sample to make sure the system acted as it was supposed to. However, be careful not to take the out sample into consideration if you decide to tweak the system some more.

By using an out sample you are allowing the system to see fresh data, reducing the chance that your results were due to overoptimizing. Since the optimized parameters never saw the new data, if the data works on the system, it is not because the system is curve-fitted to the data but because you may just have a good system on your hands.

How to Use Data

First of all make sure you have enough data. Testing a system over 6 months is meaningless, as anything could happen in that short a time period to skew the results. Also, keep in mind that 30 is the minimum number of trades you need in order to get statistically sound results. The fewer trades one has, the less reliable the results are. When you don't have enough trades, one or two extreme moves can throw the numbers out of whack, making a system that seems great only mediocre as more trades are taken into consideration. You also want to see how the system would have done in several different market environments, so make sure you have all the data you need.

The best way to use data is to start by writing your system using the first third of the data. Once you are happy with the basic system, go to the second third of the data to fine-tune it, optimize it a bit, and make the final adjustments. After you are done with that, test it on the last third. Another option could be to write and optimize the system on the middle two-thirds of the data and then use the beginning and ending sixths as the out sample. Whichever method you choose, what you hope to accomplish is to have percentage results in the out sample that are similar to those in the writing stage. This will tell you that the system works consistently over time.

Make sure that the different sets of data aren't all from the same type of trading environment. You also can test on different markets, stocks, and time frames as part of the out sample. If I have a system I wrote using IBM as my data, I will test it on Cisco, Merrill Lynch, Intel, Wal-Mart, the Dow, and the S&P 500 Index. If it works well, it should work on every stock, not just one. Try to make sure you are mixing up the markets and market conditions. Don't test the same system on 10 stocks that have the same chart pattern. Find stocks that are going up, down, sideways, and anything in between, as this will give you a more realistic representation of what can really happen.

EVALUATING A SYSTEM

Now comes the nitty-gritty part of backtesting: how to read the results and determine if you have a good system with a positive expectancy. A positive expectancy is needed to determine if a trader has an edge; without an edge one should not be trading. Charts 13–1 and 13–2 are typical printouts from TradeStation that evaluate two different canned systems in TradeStation. Though both are profitable, the second one, MACD, is much better not just because it made more money but because, as I'll explain, it met many other, more desirable criteria. I've purposely not included slippage and commissions in these results. I'll demonstrate later how big an impact they can have.

CHART 13–1

Test Results for Stochastic Crossover (System 1)

System Report: Performance Summary			
Stochastic Crossover SP_01U.ASC-30 min 06/01/2001 - 08/31/2001			
Performance Summary: All Trades			
Total net profit	$ 7025.00	Open position P/L	$ 625.00
Gross profit	$ 111600.00	Gross loss	$-104575.00
Total # of trades	182	Percent profitable	41%
Number winning trades	74	Number losing trades	108
Largest winning trade	$ 7000.00	Largest losing trade	$ -3500.00
Average winning trade	$ 1508.11	Average losing trade	$ -968.29
Ratio avg win/avg loss	1.56	Avg trade(win & loss)	$ 38.60
Max consec. winners	6	Max consec. losers	8
Avg # bars in winners	8	Avg # bars in losers	3
Max intraday drawdown	$ -18525.00		
Profit factor	1.07	Max # contracts held	1
Account size required	$ 18525.00	Return on account	38%

Created with TradeStation by Omega Research © 1997

CHART 13-2

Test Results for System MACD (System 2)

System Report: Performance Summary				
MACD SP_01U.ASC-30 min	06/01/2001 - 08/31/2001			
	Performance Summary: All Trades			
Total net profit	$ 32750.00	Open position P/L	$ 1750.00	
Gross profit	$ 84075.00	Gross loss	$ -51325.00	
Total # of trades	58	Percent profitable	43%	
Number winning trades	25	Number losing trades	33	
Largest winning trade	$ 9575.00	Largest losing trade	$ -3375.00	
Average winning trade	$ 3363.00	Average losing trade	$ -1555.30	
Ratio avg win/avg loss	2.16	Avg trade(win & loss)	$ 564.66	
Max consec. winners	3	Max consec. losers	6	
Avg # bars in winners	23	Avg # bars in losers	8	
Max intraday drawdown	$ -18275.00			
Profit factor	1.64	Max # contracts held	1	
Account size required	$ 18275.00	Return on account	179%	

Created with TradeStation by Omega Research © 1997

Profitability (Total Net Profit)

Total net profit is the overall bottom line of a system: Does it make money? These two examples are profitable, showing net profits of $7025 and $32,750. If these results had been negative, it would be back to the drawing board, as you couldn't expect to make money by using the system. Total net profit is something all people will look at when evaluating a system, but by itself it is not that great of an indication. Yes, you want a system that has a net profit and not a loss, but you also need to know how many trades it made, how big the swings were, how large a drawdown there was, what the average trade made, and so on. A trader may be tempted to jump into a system that shows a $50,000 return rather than one that shows only a $10,000 return, but the second may be a better system. Maybe the first one made 1000 trades in a year with a drawdown of $35,000; maybe some months had large losses and others had large wins. Meanwhile the second system made only 50 trades with a drawdown of only $3000 and showed a small profit every month. In that case the second system is a better, safer system even though it returned less. You need to decide what is more important: large potential profits or safe, steady returns. A smart trader will always choose the latter.

It's easy to be misled if one used only total net profit as a criterion for choosing a system. In Chart 13–1 the stochastics system seems okay at first glance, making over $7000 in this 3-month period, but when one digs deeper, it really is not a good system.

Total Number of Trades

In choosing between two systems that have similar results, stick to the one that has a lower number of trades in the same time period. This will reduce the damage done by slippage and commissions, which can be substantial. A system that trades less may be boring for some people, but if you can get the same results, always take the one with fewer trades. Not only does System 1 have a lower net profit, it makes 3 times as many trades as System 2. This means you are working harder to get worse results. Though making fewer trades is desirable, make sure your test has at least 30 trades in it or there is a decent chance that your results were due to chance. If you don't have 30 trades, you will need to get more data to test it properly.

Percent Profitable

This number means so little, yet people take so much notice of it. The best traders make money only 50 percent of the time, yet in real life people see 50 percent as failure. Any test one took in school required 65 percent for passing. If people see a system with a 40 percent win/loss ratio, they instinctively think it is a loser because they are conditioned to think of it that way. Instead, think of it like a good hitter in baseball; a .400 average is not too shabby. I don't pay much heed to percent profitability, but some traders may not feel comfortable using a system with only a 40 percent win/loss ratio. It doesn't matter if a system is right 30 percent, 40 percent, or 60 percent of the time. What is important is how big the average loser is compared to the average winner. If one has good risk management skills, even a system with a 30 percent win/loss ratio can be quite robust. Both of the systems here have percent profitability numbers in the low 40s, and this is what I typically shoot for.

Largest Winner Versus Largest Loser

This is something that I look for to see how valid a system is. First, I look to see if the total profit of the system was due to just one or two trades. In System 1, the total profit was $7025 and the largest winner was $7000. Take away this one trade and the system is profitable by $25 over 182 trades, which is not very good. If a system doesn't perform well after you take one or two of the largest trades away, it is not very reliable. The other thing to look for is that the largest losers are not bigger than the winners. The key to trading is to keep your losers smaller than your winners; the opposite situation can lead to disaster. If the largest losers are too big, you need to work on your exits and stops some more. I look for at least a 2:1 or 3:1 ratio between the largest winner and the largest loser but will settle for a 1.5:1 ratio before I'll consider trading a system. The same ratios hold for average winning trade versus average losing trade; unless the average winning trade is bigger than the average losing trade, I won't use the system. I also look to hold my losers shorter than my winners, so I like to look at the average number of bars in winners versus those in losers to make sure the system fits my trading methodology.

Consecutive Losers

How many losers in a row were there? Many traders can't handle 10 bad trades in a row and will abandon a system before it has a chance to work. By knowing how many losers in a row this system has had, you can decide not to trade the system because it may be more than you can stomach. Or if you are trading it and are going through a losing streak, you may stick with it because you know that it is common to have a six-trade losing streak. If you don't know what the largest consecutive losing streak was, you may abandon a system after four straight losses even though this is considered normal for the system.

BE PREPARED FOR THE WORST

I once spent months writing a system with which to day trade the S&Ps. I backtested and edited until it was, I thought, the perfect system. Its only drawback was that it had a high number of consecutive losing trades, but I didn't think I had to worry about that at the beginning. The winning trades were much bigger than the losers, and so the system was very profitable. I was confident it would make money from the start so that when the losers came, it wouldn't hurt. As you probably have guessed, the losing streak started immediately: I think the first eight trades were losers, and they put me and my partner about $12,000 in the hole, which we were not prepared for. We had to abandon the system and slow down our trading for a while, and as luck would have it, the very next trade was a huge winner. Over the next few trades the system would have made back all its losses and then some. The moral here is to know the system's drawdown and make sure you can afford it.

Average Trade

This is one of the more important numbers to look at as it can compare two systems to each other or one system to itself when changes are made. The average trade measures how the system does on a per-trade basis. This is the number that tells you how much on average you will make or lose every time you trade with the system. System 1 has an average trade of $38.60 (and this is before commissions), while System 2 has an average trade of $564.66. It doesn't take a genius to realize that it is more profitable on average to take a trade on the second system. If the average trade is negative, don't trade with the system; that's easy enough to figure out. What's harder is determining when the average trade is positive but too small to be worth using a system. Each trader must find an average trade he is comfortable having and then not trade systems with a lower amount.

Drawdown

Probably the most important factor in a system is the drawdown. The drawdown will tell you how much money you will need to start trading with this system in a particular market and give you a basis from which to measure risk. It tells you how much it would have cost you at its worst to use this system. This number will give you an estimate of how much starting capital is needed for each stock or market traded. You may think you have something good, but when you test it over extensive data, you may find that it would have lost $25,000 during its worst period. Don't think it won't happen again; the worst losing streak is always just around the corner. If you can't afford to go through a losing streak twice as long as the biggest drawdown, you shouldn't trade with the system.

Risk-averse traders are more likely to look at the drawdown than at any other statistic. If they can't stomach the drawdown they'll abandon the system or make changes to limit the losses. Money management plays a huge role in trading and should be considered in every aspect of trading. If two systems have similar results and one has a smaller drawdown than the other, it is probably less risky. If a system is too risky, one should avoid it.

Profit Factor

The profit factor is total gains divided by total losses. It tells you the amount that will be made for every dollar that is lost. If the profit factor is 1, you are breaking even. To be on the safe side, the profit factor should be at least 1.5. If you have a profit factor of more than 2, you have a very good system. In System 1 the profit factor is barely 1, and so this is a system that should be avoided. The profit factor of 1.64 in System 2 is considered decent, and so one could feel comfortable trading with it.

Distribution of Returns

Finally, one needs to see how volatile a system is. How did the system make money? Was it a steady flow of good returns, or were there wild swings in the system's equity over time? If you have enough data, look for steady monthly performance; if you are testing an intraday system, see how it does on a daily basis. A system with a steady positive return day after day with little variance from the mean is better than one that makes more but has wild swings. If the standard deviation is too wide, this may not be a good system to use, as the drawdowns could be large. If too many trades, days, or months fall more than 2 standard deviations outside the mean on the losing side, I'd be cautious about using the system. Stick to systems that have smaller equity swings, as they are more reliable. TradeStation will give you a month-by-month or trade-by-trade breakdown, and so you can see if the performance was steady. You also can use Excel or another statistical program to get these results. It's not a simple task, but it's one that a serious trader wants to do to make sure his system does not have wild swings.

COMMISSIONS AND SLIPPAGE

No one likes to talk about commissions and slippage, but these two items can really make the difference between a winning and a losing system and a winning and a losing trader. One thing to consider when developing a trading style is that every trade that's made—win, lose, or break even—will cost a trader some money. These are costs a trader can't do anything about, and they need to be considered in his system design or his systems will be unrealistic. First, one needs to include every trader's favorite thing, *commissions*. The second cost, *slippage*, is something some traders tend to (or would like to) forget about when considering their trading decisions. Basically, slippage is the cost associated with paying more for or selling for less than what a trader intended. It may be caused by the market moving away or may be due to the difference in the spread between the bid and ask prices. Ideally, a trader would like to buy on the bid and sell on the offer. Unfortunately, he tends to do the opposite, putting himself into a losing position from the start. On a per trade basis, commissions and slippage are trivial, but when added up over the course of time, they can be astronomical and can have a huge impact on a trader's profit and loss (P&L) statement. They can easily turn seemingly profitable trades into losing ones.

When designing a system a trader needs to make sure it will cover his trading costs or else it will become a losing system. If I go back to my original two systems and add modest commissions of $15 per round turn and slippage of $100 a trade (again, this is very modest for the S&Ps), you can see the dramatic change in the two systems (Charts 13–3 and 13–4). System 1 ends losing close to $14,000 instead of making $7025, while System 2 drops from over $32,000 to $26,515. System 2 is still a good system and has kept most of its desirable parameters, while System 1 should be avoided at all costs. The large number of trades in that system makes it hard for it to be profitable.

BECOMING A BETTER TRADER

To become a better trader you must backtest your trading ideas and systems properly before you trade them. If you do not do this, you will never know if you are trading with a sound system until you

CHART 13-3

System 1 Results with Trading Costs Added

System Report: Performance Summary				
Stochastic Crossover SP_01U.ASC-30 min 06/01/2001 - 08/31/2001				

Performance Summary: All Trades

Total net profit	$ -13905.00	Open position P/L	$ 625.00
Gross profit	$ 103520.00	Gross loss	$ -117425.00
Total # of trades	182	Percent profitable	37%
Number winning trades	67	Number losing trades	115
Largest winning trade	$ 6885.00	Largest losing trade	$ -3615.00
Average winning trade	$ 1545.07	Average losing trade	$ -1021.09
Ratio avg win/avg loss	1.51	Avg trade(win & loss)	$ -76.40
Max consec. winners	6	Max consec. losers	8
Avg # bars in winners	8	Avg # bars in losers	3
Max intraday drawdown	$ -29215.00		
Profit factor	0.88	Max # contracts held	1
Account size required	$ 29215.00	Return on account	-48%

Created with TradeStation by Omega Research © 1997

CHART 13-4

System 2 Results with Trading Costs Added

System Report: Performance Summary				
MACD SP_01U.ASC-30 min 06/01/2001 - 08/31/2001				

Performance Summary: All Trades

Total net profit	$ 26515.00	Open position P/L	$ 1750.00
Gross profit	$ 81387.50	Gross loss	$ -54872.50
Total # of trades	58	Percent profitable	43%
Number winning trades	25	Number losing trades	33
Largest winning trade	$ 9467.50	Largest losing trade	$ -3482.50
Average winning trade	$ 3255.50	Average losing trade	$ -1662.80
Ratio avg win/avg loss	1.96	Avg trade(win & loss)	$ 457.16
Max consec. winners	3	Max consec. losers	6
Avg # bars in winners	23	Avg # bars in losers	8
Max intraday drawdown	$ -20102.50		
Profit factor	1.48	Max # contracts held	1
Account size required	$ 20102.50	Return on account	132%

Created with TradeStation by Omega Research © 1997

are risking real money. If your system is not profitable, you don't want to find out by losing money. You are better off learning this by spending the time to backtest it. To backtest a system properly you will need to have enough data to give you 30 sample trades and cover all the different market conditions. You don't want to test a system just on a trending market, not knowing how it will react in a choppy market. If you don't test over different conditions, you are not backtesting properly and may end up with a system that was curve-fitted to work in a trending market.

You should use different data when writing a system and when optimizing your parameters. This will lessen the chance of curve fitting around the data. When you are ready for a final test, make sure you do this on an out sample of completely new data, preferably covering different market conditions and long enough to be statistically valid (30 trades). One of the worst mistakes a trader can make is writing, optimizing, and testing the system on the same data. If it's been optimized for a set of data, of course it will work great, but you will never know how it will work in the future. One thing to keep in mind is that no matter how great a system did when it was backtested, it can never predict the future, as markets change. After you are happy with the results you may want to go over a chart visually and see where trades would have been made to get a good feel for how the system worked. You also want to check that your results weren't due to one or two strong wins. You want to trade with a system that is more predictable and steady over time. These are the kinds of systems that end up doing best; ones with wild swings can be unpredictable and dangerous.

The last thing you need to do is to understand the backtesting results and know how to compare different systems. Overall profit and win/loss ratio are not as important as the average win and the profit factor. Look at the drawdown: Can you afford to trade the system? Don't assume that the drawdown won't happen right away, because it might. Make sure to account for commissions and slippage when you are figuring out total profits, as they will make a big difference in the results.

Take your time when backtesting. Don't ignore it or get lazy about doing it, as it is a crucial part of making you a better trader. And never trade a system without backtesting it thoroughly first.

Common Backtesting Mistakes

1. Not backtesting
2. Not knowing if your system will make money
3. Trading before you have backtested your system or trading methodology
4. Not knowing how to evaluate backtesting results
5. Not questioning the system and results
6. Getting hung up on the win/loss ratio
7. Putting too much emphasis on total profit
8. Ignoring drawdowns
9. Curve fitting the system to the data
10. Overoptimizing until it is perfect (for the data you optimized on)
11. Not testing on enough data or market environments
12. Not having a proper out sample
13. Not testing on enough markets
14. Ignoring commissions and slippage

Getting the Most Out of Backtesting

1. Use software that will do the testing for you.
2. Never trade with a losing strategy again.
3. If you are not happy with the results, don't trade the system.
4. Make sure you have enough data.
5. Have a sample of at least 30 trades.
6. Do final test on an out sample of fresh data.
7. Save at least one-third of the data for your out sample.
8. Test over different market environments.
9. Test the same system in different time frames.
10. Test the same system in different markets.
11. Don't overoptimize or curve-fit.
12. Know how to evaluate backtesting results.
13. Learn to compare different systems.
14. Don't underestimate commissions and slippage.
15. Make sure you can afford 2 times the largest drawdown.

16. Avoid volatile systems.
17. Make sure all the profits didn't come from one or two trades.

Helpful Questions to Ask Yourself

Did I backtest my system or ideas properly ?
Did I overoptimize my system?
Is the system curve-fitted?
Did I test on an out sample?
Does the system have a positive expectancy?
What does the average trade make?
Was I realistic about commissions and slippage?

CHAPTER 14

Employing a Money Management Plan

THE GAMBLER

I often compare good traders with professional gamblers because both have a lot in common and are consistent winners. Besides knowing probabilities and odds, inside and out, professional gamblers adhere to solid money management rules. They don't take unnecessary risks or gambles. They know when the odds are in their favor and will bet more when the odds get better. If the odds aren't there, they won't risk nearly as much, if anything. They know how to protect their winnings, and they know how to call it a day when Lady Luck is blowing on some other guy's dice. Having this discipline lets them come back to the table the next day.

Some of the best traders are professional card and backgammon players who converted their gambling skills to the trading arena. When Richard Dennis was looking for his turtles to train, professional gamblers and backgammon and bridge players were high up on his list of candidates. Successful gamblers and good traders have one trait in common: They know how to assess risk and make bets accordingly.

By a gambler I don't mean someone who likes to gamble but a person who does it for a living. Most people who gamble will lose; that's a simple fact. Professional gamblers, however, are more disciplined than the average gambler and know the probabilities of every outcome in their games. They make smart bets and do it not for the excitement, but to make a living. They are all risk-averse and will not make bets that don't have a positive expectancy. A professional card player doesn't go for big wins but is happy with consistent results. He won't go for a pot just because it is big if the odds aren't there. Gamblers don't mind losing, big or small, when the odds are there. They know that losing is part of being successful, and as long as they do the right things, they are okay with losing; they won't try to make it all back on the next hand. They know that if they stick to their rules, they will make it back in the future by being consistent. If a blackjack player doubles down when he has an 11 or splits a pair of aces and then loses, he knows he has made the right bet and does not get discouraged. In the long run these bets will pay off since they have a positive expectancy.

Successful gamblers also know they don't have to be in every hand. A good poker player is disciplined enough to fold hand after hand until the right one comes along. He may get bored out of his mind, but he's the one who has the mountain of chips in front of him. Bad players bet every hand all the way through, just as a bad trader is always in the market even when the trades are marginal. For the most part it's the amateurs who try to bluff. Pros do not do it nearly as much; they would rather go for the sure hands and sit out the rest. A professional gambler has both a strict game plan and a money management plan. He knows what he will be doing in all situations and never has to think about it. As the odds increase, so does the size of his bets. He doesn't necessarily increase the size of his bets because he is on a good streak or has doubled his money. Very rarely does a pro make bigger bets because he has a hunch or feels invincible. He keeps his bets steady according to the odds. The average trader can learn a lot from a professional gambler.

Some Traits a Professional Card Player Has That a Trader Can Benefit From

He will not chase a hand.

He will increase bets on high-percentage hands.

He will always know the risk/reward ratio of every hand.

He knows when to sit out.

He bets with the odds in his favor.

He is not afraid to lose.

He knows how to lose.

He has discipline.

He has a game plan.

He knows how to manage his money.

But most important, he knows when to hold 'em, knows when to fold 'em, knows when to walk away, knows when to run. . . . That was the very first 45 I ever bought; I guess that says something about me.

GAMBLING IN THE CAFETERIA

I think I've seen some traders play more card and backgammon games on the trading floor and in the cafeteria then I've seen them actually trading. I can't even remember a day when I was working on the floor that I didn't play liar's poker for hours. Many traders have gambling in their blood; I guess it's the nature of the business that attracts them to it. The ones who are the best gamblers end up becoming the better traders. The people who gamble for the excitement usually don't make good traders; they are the ones who tend to overtrade and take on excessive risk. The ones who have mastered a game such as bridge or backgammon turn out to be great traders. A lot of those bridge games in the cafeteria aren't played by amateurs. Some of those guys are tournament-quality players, and they are able to convert their skills to trading, making them top traders.

THE IMPORTANCE OF HAVING A MONEY MANAGEMENT PLAN

When you get down to the heart of what the difference between being a winning trader and a losing trader is, it's money management. I don't care what type of trader you are—whether you use trend-following or reversal systems, are a scalper or long-term holder, use purely mechanical systems or discretionary systems—those who follow a strict money management plan will have a much better chance of coming out ahead of the game. Too many traders don't have a money management plan, and even if they have one, they don't really know what to do with it. If you do not know how to manage your capital, there is little chance that you can make money as a trader, even if you are one of the luckiest traders around.

Money management is another subject that is not given enough attention in most trading books. You can find book after book on technical analysis, options, and even trading psychology, but you hardly see any devoted to money management as it pertains to trading. However, it is one of the biggest reasons traders end up losers. You can have the greatest system in the world, but unless you know how to manage money, you can easily end up a loser. I used to have several good systems but failed to concentrate sufficiently on money management and risk. I was able to make money for a while, but then I would give it all back because I started risking too much. As soon as a little bad streak hit, my profits and then some would disappear quickly because I was trading more heavily than I should have been.

In contrast, you can have a mediocre system, but if you have good money management skills, you can still come out ahead. Almost any halfway decent trading strategy can work as long as a trader has solid money management skills. Even the simplest systems can produce great results when they are used with proper risk techniques. Without those techniques, it is extremely hard to make it as a trader. The rest of this chapter deals with the importance of having a money management plan; the next chapter discusses what goes into one.

I would compare the importance of a money management plan to the brakes on a car. Every 18-year-old with a fast car will talk about what he has under the hood. He may have the fastest car on the road, but unless he has good brakes, he can't drive it without eventually doing some damage. Meanwhile, my mom in her big old Pontiac, who drives about 40 miles per hour and is more concerned about her brakes than about anything else, steadily goes on her way without ever getting into a fender bender. Money management relates to this in that while a good trading system can impress you, it's the money management that actually makes you a winner and keeps you from wiping out.

MONEY MANAGEMENT: WHAT ALL WINNING TRADERS HAVE IN COMMON

Getting into a trade is only a little piece of the puzzle and figuring out how to exit it is another piece, but knowing how to manage risk is more important to a trader's bottom line than are finding and exiting trades. Yet learning money management and setting risk parameters always seem to come last in a trader's education. People spend too much time looking at charts and making systems but ignore money management until it's too late. Some never even include it in a system's development stage; they just concentrate on indicators and totally ignore trading size when putting together a system, and trading size is one thing that can make or break a trader. Learning how to manage your capital properly is a lot more difficult than learning how to read charts, put on trades, and set stop losses. After 11 years this is still one of my biggest weaknesses.

I believe money management is even more important than trade selection. If you read *Market Wizards* or hear any top trader speak, you will notice that each trader may have a different approach to the market. One looks for trends, one looks for reversals, one scalps, one holds for years, one trades options, and another just spreads, but what they all have in common is that *they employ a strict money management program* and agree that it is the secret to their success.

THE GOAL OF MONEY MANAGEMENT

The goal of money management is simple: It's to allow a trader to still be around after having a bad trade, a bad day, or a series of losses. Learning how to control risk will help preserve precious capital, which ensures that a trader will be around even if he has a normal losing streak. A trader with a good grasp of money management can have a series of 15 losers and then make it all back in two good trades. Without a money management plan, a trader may have a series of 15 winners and easily blow it all in two bad trades, as he has no idea what he should be risking. Without a solid money management plan a trader can fail because he will not know how much he can afford to lose and a few losers can easily escalate to the point of wiping him out.

I read Charles Dickens's *David Copperfield* about 15 years ago, and one thing that always stuck in my mind was the scene where Mr. Micawber gave young David some advice about managing money:

> "My other piece of advice, Copperfield," said Mr. Micawber, "you know. Annual income twenty pounds, annual expenditure nineteen

nineteen and six, result happiness. Annual income twenty pounds, annual expenditure twenty pounds ought and six, result misery. The blossom is blighted, the leaf is withered, the god of day goes down upon the dreary scene, and—and in short you are forever floored. As I am!"

Basically, he is saying, Make more than you spend (lose) and you will do fine, but if you spend (lose) more than you make, you are ruined. Apply this thinking to trading and you will be successful as well. By the way, if you have never read *David Copperfield*, it definitely is worth the time.

PRESERVING PRECIOUS CAPITAL

Learning to keep losers smaller than winners is crucial to success. For many traders, learning to take a loss properly can be hard, but eventually one learns that it is better to lose $300 than $1000 in a trade. One of the most critical things you can learn is that it's not how much you make but how little you lose that counts. If you remember from Chap. 1 how important it is to preserve precious capital, you'll be around longer than most. I used to write "PPC" on the top of my trading pads every day to remind me of it; now I have it etched into the plastic on my computer monitor. I need the constant reminder; it keeps me in check when I lose track of reality and start losing more than I should.

One thing I know for sure is that regardless of his trading decisions, everyone who has blown out has done so because of poor money management skills and because he did not preserve his precious capital. Sure, bad trading helped a lot, but it was due to not knowing how to manage money and risking too much that eventually did these traders in. You can't trade anymore when your money is gone, so make sure not to risk it all.

WHAT GOES INTO A MONEY MANAGEMENT PLAN

Money management is composed of many things. It includes knowing how much to risk in general, how much to risk per trade, when to risk more, how much capital should be at risk at any time, what total exposure should be, where to have a cutoff point, how to choose position size, and how to pyramid properly. Money management will be part of a good exit strategy as stops and position size will be determined by a mixture of what the market says you can lose and your personal risk levels that are based on your equity. Deciding how many contracts to trade is a crucial part of trading. Not all trades are equal, and so some should be made with less size while others can be more aggressive. Your capital will help determine how much you should risk. A trader with a $50,000 account can afford to lose $1000 on a trade, but a trader who has only $3000 to start with should not take the same risk no matter how good a trade looks.

RISK LEVELS

Along with a concrete money management plan, all good traders have low risk levels. The consistent traders are not the ones who make the most but the ones who lose the least. People who have a low tolerance for risk usually make the best traders because they never dig themselves into a deep hole. They may not make as much as some other traders, but they are steadier.

The traders at professional trading firms who are given more freedom and more buying power are not the ones who make the most money, but they are the ones who lose the least when they do lose. Management is more at ease letting someone who takes small losses and makes conservative trades have more trading freedom than they are a gunslinger who swings for the fences and has volatile capital swings even if he is doing well. These gunslingers can be dangerous, and some do a lot of damage when they are wrong.

I don't know if risk tolerance is something that a person can change. I've been trying to cut back on my risk taking over the years, and it is something I have always had difficulty doing. I've been able to improve, but I'll still take on more risk than others will at times. If you have a problem with taking on too much risk, you must acknowledge it and try to do something about it. When you make a money management plan, set out your risk levels and make sure you can stick to them. It does you no good to have risk parameters that you can't keep to, so be realistic about your goals.

KNOWING HOW MUCH TO RISK

Before making his first trade, a trader should set out to have a good risk plan in play. This means knowing how much you are willing to lose at any given time. You should have a maximum dollar amount that you are willing to risk on a trade regardless of the market. You need to figure out what percentage of your capital you are willing to risk. You also should know how much you are willing to risk on all aggregate positions at one time and what your cutoff point is. You should know that if you lose x amount in a day or week or whatever time period you use, you will get out of all your positions or at least the ones that are not working. When you hit your cutoff point, sometimes it's best to take a few hours or days off to regroup. Everybody should have a loss limit during the day where if he reaches it, he either calls it quits for the day or gets out of his positions and takes a walk around the block. I hit such a bad streak a few months ago where I lost money almost every day for 3 weeks that I called it quits for a week and went on vacation. When I came back, I was able to start again with a clear head.

You should also know when to adjust risk. Risk changes constantly as the market changes. You should be aware of this and modify your trading accordingly. Some trades have a better setup than others, and so you may want to risk more contracts on them. Sometimes you may be in a position and the market starts to get more volatile or there is a major report coming out in 6 minutes. Risk will start to increase, and the smart thing to do is to think about getting out or cutting back to reduce risk exposure. The risk is no longer the same, and so unless you cut back, you can get hurt a lot worse than you originally planned on.

DON'T BE INFLUENCED BY THE LAST TRADE

There are times when a trader gets in a rut and has a bad morning, day, or week. Sometimes things can get out of hand, and a trader freezes or doesn't care anymore and begins to ignore any money management rules he may have. A typical scenario is that he starts out by trading the maximum contract size he can afford according to his risk money management parameters. If two contracts is what he typically trades and it goes against him quickly, he may ignore his stops and money management plan because he doesn't want to take a loss. Soon he has a larger than expected loss on his hands that he wants to make back. What some bad traders will do next (and I have taken a beating doing this) is trade four contracts on the next trade so that it is easier to make back the loss and go home positive. Even worse, if he is still holding the position, he may add to it, thinking, "If I liked it at 1351.00, it's even better at 1334.50. Besides, how much more can it possibly go down today?"

If you never trade more than two contracts, do not trade more than two contracts just because you've lost big on a previous trade. Never trade more than the maximum contract size that your money management plan allows. If you find yourself doing this for any reason, *stop* and think about what you are doing. Don't ignore your money management plan and start trading more aggressively because you want to make back losses; this is a surefire way to get hurt badly.

Equally important is sticking to your money management plan during a good streak. Some of the worst losses come after a major winning streak because people get too cocky and ignore their risk parameters. If you have a good money management plan, stick to it in both good and bad times. Your last few trades should never influence how much you risk on the next trade.

HAVE ENOUGH MONEY TO TRADE WITH

Here is another aspect of money management, but it is concerned more with your personal money management than with trading: Make sure you can afford to trade. Before starting to trade, make sure you have enough capital to trade and live on without dipping into your trading account. Are you planning to support yourself with your trading account and make it grow at the same time? Once you start doing that, it gets very hard to have an account grow. A trader should not have to take money out of his trading account to pay his bills; he will never get ahead that way. The weight that was lifted off my shoulders when I no longer had to worry about taking money out of my trading account to pay my bills was incredible. When my financial burdens were lifted, I was able to relax a bit and not press so hard to make money. That had a direct effect on my trading, as it became easier to make money. It is hard enough just to make money; taking profits out of an account doesn't help. Even if you set aside money just for trading, is it enough to do it properly or are you just going to throw away a few thousand bucks because you don't have enough to do it right? A trader needs to make sure that he can sustain a losing streak, even a really bad losing streak, without having it affect his capital to the point where he can't trade anymore. That's why you should backtest your trading systems: That will give you a rough idea of how big of a drawdown you may be in store for. Trust me, those drawdowns and losing streaks will happen, so be prepared for them.

SMALL ACCOUNTS

One thing I've noticed is that small traders will risk much more than will large traders. It's the same with small gamblers. They have only a little to lose, and so if they lose it all, it is not a big deal. A trader with a small account has to be more careful and diligent about how much he risks, because he doesn't have the luxury of making mistakes. People with small accounts tend to ignore position size and think money management does not apply to them because there is nothing they can do about it. They risk 50 percent of their capital on trades because they have no other choice. They have all their eggs in one basket and can get hurt very quickly if that basket breaks. They know that if they had $100,000 they would spread their risk out or risk no more than 2 percent per trade because that's what they read in all the books. Yet they risk the same $2000 on a trade with a $5000 account that they would if they had $100,000. It's easy to see which scenario has the better chance of succeeding here. It takes only two or three losses to wipe out the smaller trader, while for the bigger trader those losses are meaningless drops in the bucket. If you have a small account and must trade, don't take money management lightly; make sure you can afford what you want to trade and keep your risks small relative to your account size.

MAKE SURE YOUR STRATEGY HAS A POSITIVE EXPECTANCY

One thing I've read over and over is that, unless you are trading with a system that has a positive expectancy to win, no money management technique or position sizing strategy will make it profitable. Casinos and lotteries have positive expectancies, and no matter what strategy gamblers use, a casino will always win in the long run. Sure, people will beat them here and there, but casinos don't care about individuals; they are concerned about the whole. By repeatedly taking bets, casinos will win simply because they have a positive expectancy and the odds are in their favor.

This applies to traders as well. If you have a system with a positive expectancy, you can make money in the long run. If it has a negative expectancy, don't bother trading, as it's a losing proposition. You can tell if something has a positive expectancy by backtesting it. If it didn't work in the past, don't expect it to work in the future. Having a positive expectancy doesn't mean finding trades that work more than 50 percent of the time; it means finding trades that, when they work, will outperform the losing trades. Don't worry about a low win/loss percentage. You can be right 30 percent of the time and still make money. The goal is for the percent of trades that are winners times the average win to be greater than the percent of trades that are losers times the average loss. For example if you have a system with a 30 percent win/loss ratio but make on average $800 per winning trade and lose on average $300 per loser, your expectancy on this would be (.30*$800) − (.70*$300) = $240 − $210 = $30 average profit per trade. This is barely enough to cover commissions but is the start of finding a profitable trading system. You want a slightly larger average profit per trade to make this worthwhile. That can be done by having larger winners, smaller losses, or a higher winning percentage. Until you find a strategy that has a big enough positive expectancy to cover slippage and commissions, don't trade; instead, work on finding a better strategy.

BECOMING A BETTER TRADER

Becoming a better trader means knowing how critical it is to have and properly use a money management plan so that you can preserve your precious capital. Money management is probably the most important thing in determining who will be a winning trader. Finding and putting on trades are merely a part of trading; unless a trader knows how to manage his capital, he will find it hard to succeed. This doesn't mean only knowing how to control losses after a trade is made; there is a lot of work involved before one begins trading. You should know in advance how much you could afford to risk at any given time or per trade. You should know how many contracts you can have at once. You should know how much you will lose in a day before admitting defeat or taking a short break. Having a money management plan is important because it will ensure that you don't get blown out, letting you be around to trade the next day. If you expect to succeed, you should

make sure your system has a positive expectancy of working out. Without this, it is impossible to make money in the long run no matter how good a money management program you have. Having a money management plan doesn't mean much if a trader can't follow it. To succeed you have to have the discipline to stick to your rules and parameters.

The better traders are the ones who know how to control risk the most. Sure, others may make more money at times, but the ones who control risk best will be more consistent over time. By always being aware of risk and adjusting your trading according to risk, you will have a good chance of not losing much. Remember, it's not how much you make that makes you a winning trader but how little you lose when you do lose. You probably will lose more often than not, and so controlling those losses is the key.

The Danger of Not Having or Misusing a Money Management Plan

1. Losing all your money
2. Not knowing how to much risk
3. Having no guidance
4. Not knowing when to call it quits
5. Trading a system with a negative expectancy
6. Risking more than you can afford
7. Not adjusting for risk when it is called for
8. Not having the discipline to keep to a plan
9. Ignoring risk parameters levels when losing or winning big
10. Not believing you will have large drawdowns

The Importance of a Money Management Plan

1. It is a common thread among all good traders.
2. It lets you preserve precious capital.
3. It lets you know what you can risk.
4. It lets you prepare for the worst.
5. It helps you keep losses small.
6. It lets you know how many contracts to trade.

7. It lets you make sure you have enough capital to trade with.

8. It keeps you from blowing out.

9. It helps you set reasonable goals.

10. It gives you concrete cutoff points.

11. It keeps you from gambling.

12. It lets you predetermine maximum losses.

Helpful Questions to Ask Yourself

Do I have a solid money management plan?

Do I know how much to risk?

Do I have enough capital to trade with?

Does my system have a positive expectancy?

Do I stick to my plan?

Do I take on too much risk?

CHAPTER 15

Setting Risk Parameters and Making a Money Management Plan

It's easy to tell someone he should make a money management plan; the hard part is getting him to make one. But if you take the time to do this important thing, becoming a winning trader will become much easier. A money management plan doesn't have to be elaborate, but you should have some kind of guideline to keep you financially on track. When you make a money management plan, you will establish your risk parameters, and will know how much you can afford to lose, how much to risk, how many contracts to trade, and when to increase trading volume. This chapter should help a trader learn what goes into and how to make a money management plan. It may repeat a few things from the last chapter, but you'll remember the material better that way.

MAKE SURE YOU ARE PROPERLY CAPITALIZED

First and foremost, make sure you have enough capital to trade with. Trading with insufficient funds makes it hard to succeed because it is impossible to set good risk parameters when you don't have money. It becomes the norm to put on positions that are too large when you are undercapitalized. Some small traders feel that if they have enough to make a trade, they are properly capitalized. They may be always using their capital to the max simply because they have no other choice. The fact that you have enough capital to put on a trade doesn't mean that you are capitalized enough to do it. Undercapitalized people end up risking much more than they should, and it takes only a few mistakes to get them in trouble.

TRADE WHAT YOU CAN AFFORD

This leads to the next topic—trading what you can afford. A trader with a $5000 account may be well capitalized to trade corn but undercapitalized to trade soybeans or coffee. Some markets are too volatile to trade and should be avoided because of the risks involved. Trading what you can afford doesn't mean just picking markets that fit in your dollar range; it also means limiting the number of contracts or shares you trade. Day trading 500 shares of a stock when you should be trading only 200 shares can end your trading career quickly. In the long run it's better to make less while keeping losses reasonable than to try to make too much and have losses that are too large.

DON'T THINK OF IT AS MONEY YOU CAN AFFORD TO LOSE

Everyone knows that trading should be done with money one can afford to lose, but try not to think of it that way. If you have the mindset that what's in your account is risk capital and it's money you can afford to lose, you may be less inclined to fight to keep what you have. I do this when I go to a casino. I go in thinking I'll take $1000 with me and I'll have fun; if I lose it, I lose it. And guess what, I usually lose it. But at least the cash machine always pays off. When you trade, every penny in your account should be considered precious and not there to be lost. If you treat your capital like extra money you have, it won't mean as much to you.

THINK DEFENSE

Coaches always say that defense wins games. Sure, offense is important, but if the other team can't score, you can't lose. In trading you should always try to think defense first and offense second. Before making a trade, assess the risk first. Once this is done you can begin to think about whether the trade is worth making and, if it is, how many contracts or shares you can put on. You should always think about how little you can lose before thinking about how much you can make. If you concentrate on risk first, money management will have priority over trading decisions and opinions. Don't take unnecessary risks when you don't have to or when you have no control of the situation. If a report or number is coming out, you can't control how much you can lose if the market gaps against you. Situations like this are not worth the extra risk of being wrong. If you are not sure what the risk is, don't make the trade, or you are asking for trouble.

SETTING RISK AND MONEY MANAGEMENT PARAMETERS

How Much to Risk

The first thing one should do when making money management parameters is determine how much one should risk. Most novice traders don't know how much to risk, and this ends up being one of their biggest problems. They don't know how many contracts to trade, what portion of their capital to risk at any one time, how many different positions they should have on, which markets are correlated, how risk changes when one is holding several positions, where to place stops, and when to move them. As a result too many traders end up taking excessive risks. If you are trading with only $5000, you don't want to risk $3000 on any trade. There is a proper amount one can trade with and not be overexposed that you can discover when you are setting risk parameters. A trader has to be careful about how much to risk and have a good understanding about what size loss is best suited to his risk profile.

At-Risk Capital Versus Total Capital

Whatever your total available capital is, that should not be how much you trade with. Instead, you should take your available trading capital and divide it in half or whatever percent you feel comfortable with. If it's one-half, this is what you will use to trade with; let's call it the at-risk capital. Keep the other half in an interest-bearing account and use it only as a safety net. This is money that you will not use to trade with, but it helps ensure that you are properly capitalized. If you never have more than 50 percent of your total trading capital at risk, you can never get wiped out. Even if you go through a losing streak and lose your at-risk capital, you still have the other half to trade with. Doing this lets you make mistakes and still be around to trade in the future. It automatically forces you to reduce your risk exposure because you won't have as much capital to risk at any given time.

Fixed-Fraction Money Management

When one is deciding how much to risk on a trade, probably the most common method is to risk no more than a fixed percentage of one's capital on each trade. This is known as fixed-fraction money management. The typically accepted amount one should risk per trade is 5 percent or less of one's total at-risk capital. Though 5 percent per trade is an acceptable amount to risk, professional traders knock this down to under 2 percent per trade. Unfortunately, the average trader can't do this even with an account of $50,000. Risking 5 percent ($2500) does not allow for much room in some markets even when one is trading only one contract. When you get down to 2 percent it gets hard to make trades with any size at all. Forget about the people trying to trade with only $3000 in an account; they end up risking over 20 percent of their capital on practically every trade. One losing streak and they are done. The reason you never want to risk more than 5 percent is that this lets you be wrong 20 times in a row before getting wiped out, making it much harder for that to happen. Even after a losing streak you will have a fighting chance if you were conservative during that streak. If you don't allocate risk properly, it's easy to blow out after a modest losing streak. Having five losers in a row is not uncommon, and if you are risking too much, it can mean the end of your trading. If you are properly capitalized, it means nothing.

By using fixed-fraction money management, one always knows how much to risk at any given time. As his account grows a trader will begin risking more, but with the same percentage as before. If with a $10,000 account he risked 5 percent per trade, or $500, with $15,000 he can risk $750. He can do this by taking trades that have wider stop levels or by trading more contracts per trade.

Some people are tempted to add to their trading size as they hit a losing streak. This occurs for two reasons. First, they need to recoup losses and think the best way to do that is to double up on size. Second, they feel they are due for a win since they have been on a losing streak and their luck has to turn soon. These are not the times to increase risk because in both cases the odds are stacked against the trader. When someone is trying to dig himself out of a hole and has less money than he had before, he usually ends up getting deeper in the hole. Pressing is not a way to recoup losses; these trades usually are made with a bad mental state and are never made within the confines of a money management plan. People who do this end up overtrading and risking too much. As you lose money, you need to adjust your risk levels accordingly. You can't risk the same with $10,000 that you can risk with $25,000. I'm also wary about increasing risk during a good streak because it is inevitable that as soon as a losing streak comes, it will be bigger than the early wins in the winning streak. In essence, one or two bad trades that are made with more size can wipe out weeks or months of good trades with less size.

Position Size

How Many Contracts to Trade

Position size is a very important part of trading and can hurt traders. Not knowing how much to trade is something that can really end up hurting traders. Even if someone is right 60 percent of the time but has more at risk when he loses, he will end up a loser. Knowing how much you can risk per trade is just the first step; you then need to decide how many shares or contracts you should have at any time. This should be done in two parts. First, come up with a maximum allowable number of contracts to trade per market; that's the easy part. The hard part is figuring out how much you should have on depending on either market risk or how high the probability of the trade working out is.

Many traders end up losing because they trade too big, therefore taking on too much risk. This is especially true of traders with small accounts. When they trade one contract, they are typically undercapitalized, but when they make a bit of money and start trading two contracts, they really get overextended.

Not nearly enough attention is paid to deciding how much to trade. Traders are too concerned with getting into positions first and then setting stop levels, and few consider how much to trade. They either trade too much all the time, always maxing out their capital, or trade too little when the situation calls for more. Most don't have real position sizing rules; they simply use the same amount all the time or make it up as they go along, especially after a winning or losing streak, when in reality they should not change their money management plan at all. One thing traders should think about is that every trade made should not reflect the previous one. Whether you've lost big or won big, don't change your risk parameters on the next trade unless your money management plan calls for it. You also may want to include a provision for cutting back on trading activity during a losing streak. Bad streaks are normal. Don't get discouraged by them; just cut back a little in the middle of one.

Maximum Allowable Number of Contracts

Once you know how much of your capital you can risk per trade, you can get an idea of how many contracts you can risk per market. Each market is different, and so there is no simple catchall formula. You can't expect to trade the same number of contracts in corn as you do in the S&Ps because the risk in the S&Ps can be 20 times greater. Each stock and commodity has its own unique risk features, and one needs to trade it accordingly. Markets should be judged by risk or average true range (ATR). If a market has a $2000 daily range while another market has a $500 daily range, one can trade 4 times as many contracts of the second while still risking the same amount. Markets change over time, and so you need to reevaluate them constantly.

If you have $25,000 of at-risk capital and decide that you can risk 5 percent of it per trade, you know that $1250 is the most you should risk. Some commodity traders divide this by the exchange margin requirement as a way to figure out the most they can trade. I prefer to use the average true range of the market. If I am day trading, I will take this $1250 amount and divide it by the dollar value of the ATR of the market. You also may take half the ATR but I like to be more conservative. If I am trading longer-term, I use a multiple of the ATR, or look at the ATR of a weekly chart to determine how much is at risk. If I am day trading a stock that has a $4 average range, I can feel free to trade 300 shares of it; if it has a $2 range, I can trade up to 600 shares of it.

There is a difference between stocks and commodities in that with commodities you have to put up only a small fraction of the value of a contract. To risk $1250 in commodities you may need to use up only $1,000 of capital; with stocks, to risk the same amount you may have to buy $10,000 worth of a stock. Thus, with the same account you can trade and risk a lot more when you are trading commodities. The difference is that with stocks you will use up a lot more capital per position and still be able to risk 5 percent on any trade. For example, if you buy 100 shares of IBM at $100 per share and risk $10, you are using up $10,000 but risking only $1000. With commodities you need only use $1000 for margin to risk $1000, so you can have more contracts and positions on than you would be able to with stocks. It is for these reasons that people tend to lose a lot more with commodities. When they are wrong, they end up losing most of what they put up on a trade.

Setting the Maximum Number of Contracts

I like to make a table that tells me what my maximum allowed number of contracts per market is; that way I can keep myself in check all the time and not fall into the trap of getting in over my head or ignoring my money management plan. In Table 15–1, I am assuming that I have $25,000 I'm willing to use to put at risk and trade with and that I'm willing to risk 5 percent ($1250) on any trade. I use the daily ATR of the last 14 bars to determine the most I'm willing to risk up to on a per-contract basis. When I'm actually trading, I risk much less than this, but this is my guideline. The table shows the maximum allowed number of contracts per market to trade; you typically should trade less unless the market calls for more. Trading 600 shares every time because that's what you can afford to lose is the wrong way to figure out how much you should have on; good traders aren't maxed out all the time. If the risk is greater than normal, I will not trade anywhere near the maximum allowed number of contracts I've established. However, if a trade has a smaller risk because of proper stops that can be placed closer and has a good setup, technically speaking, I am not opposed to risking more than the number of contracts I've allowed for.

Setting Position Size Based on the Probability of the Trade

Position size ultimately should be based on how good you think a trade is and the risk involved. A high probability trade should get your maximum position size, a medium probability trade should

TABLE 15—1

Maximum Allowed Number of Contracts Per Market

Total capital		$50,000
Total at-risk capital = 50% of capital		$25,000
Risk per trade = 5% of at-risk capital		$1,250
Commodity or Stock	**14-Day ATR**	**Max No. Contracts Allowed**
S&P 500	$4,800.00	0
Mini S&P	$1,000.00	1
NASDAQ 100	$3,500.00	0
Mini NASDAQ	$700.00	1
U.S. T-bonds	$1,100.00	1
Swiss francs	$500.00	2
Crude oil	$750.00	1
Heating oil	$800.00	1
Wheat	$250.00	5
Corn	$175.00	7
Soybeans	$350.00	4
Lean hogs	$350.00	4
Live cattle	$250.00	5
Coffee	$550.00	2
Cocoa	$200.00	6
Sugar	$250.00	5
Gold	$300.00	4
AMAT	$2.50	500
KLAC	$3.00	400
MSFT	$2.00	600
GS	$2.80	400
LEH	$2.50	500
SLB	$1.90	600
DELL	$1.50	800
IBM	$3.50	300

get a medium size, and so on. Sometimes you see a great-looking trade but the proper stop is too far away, and so you should trade less. You still may take the trade, but don't risk nearly as much as you normally would because you need to protect yourself in case you are wrong. Sometimes a trade has a great setup and a proper stop is so close that you can trade more than your maximum allowable number of contracts. If the situation is just right, don't be afraid to go for it, but overall you should not exceed your maximum guidelines.

A Few Things One Can Look at When Deciding How Much to Risk

Are you trading with trend?

How close is the market to its trendline or moving average?

Has the market moved too much already?

How far away is the stop?

How much can you lose?

How much can you make?

How do you usually do with this type of trade?

How confident do you feel?

If you think the risk is too great but feel you must make the trade, do it with fewer shares. If you are trading in the direction of the trend, trade a larger volume; trade less when the trades are counter to the main trend. I tend to trade worse in the morning, when the market is uncertain, and so I will trade one-third of my normal share size until I see a good opportunity or trend develop; then I'll start to be more aggressive with my size. If I'm trading at lunch, I also do it with lighter volume because I know that historically this is not a great time to trade. But when I see something I really like or I am making a trade that has worked well in the past, I will be more aggressive.

Setting position size is not always easy, but remember to set your risk limits first, know in advance how much you are prepared to lose per trade, then calculate where stops should be, and finally figure out how many contracts you can trade. If the risk on a trade is too much, you don't have to take it. Zero is an acceptable choice as the number of contracts to trade. High-risk trades are worth skipping as you wait for the next solid opportunity.

Multiple Positions

After you have an idea how much to risk on any one trade and how many contracts to trade, the next task is to figure out how many positions and how much total risk you can have at once. Some people will trade only one market or stock at a time, but since most traders look at many markets, they have to know how much to risk at once. This varies with the person but I like to have no more than half my at-risk capital at risk at any given time. If I can lower that to under 30 percent, that's even better. If I were trading with $25,000 of at-risk capital, I'd want to have only about $8000 to $12,500 of risk on at any given time in uncorrelated markets. One thing people have to keep in mind is that having positions in two similar markets is almost the same as having one larger position. If you risk 5 percent of your capital in crude oil and 5 percent in heating oil, you are basically risking 10 percent on the same trade. To keep to your 5 percent rule you need to trade less in each. If you are trading different stocks or commodities in the same sector or group, you can give yourself a little leeway in terms of how much you can risk. Instead of 5 percent maximum risk, maybe you could risk 7.5 percent of your capital in that sector at any one time. If you normally risk 2 percent, you can let yourself risk 3 percent in correlated markets.

CAN'T GET ANY MORE UNLUCKY

I once had positions in about 15 different commodities at once. I figured that I was safe because I was well diversified. But by the end of the day every single one was a losing position. I was trading way beyond my means, and that one day cost me about $6000. This doesn't sound like much to me now, but then I had only $5000 in my account. I never expected to get hurt so badly in one day, but that's what happens when you overtrade and don't follow a money management plan.

In trading multiple positions it's important to pick stocks or commodities that have little correlation and don't move together. For example, corn, crude, sugar, copper, and Swiss francs is a good mix of commodities that will all move independently of each other. With stocks, if you trade a few semis, a few banks, a few drug companies, and a couple of oil drillers, you are well diversified. If you have 10 semiconductors long, for the most part you are trading one large position. You can do this if you want to, but know what the risks are and trade less in each one accordingly. Personally, if I like a sector, I prefer to trade a basket of stocks in it rather than just one or two of them. That way I am less at risk of something happening to one specific stock, such as a chief financial officer quitting. If I normally trade about 5000 shares in any given sector, instead of trading 2500 shares in two stocks, I'll divide it up among 10 stocks and trade 500 shares of each.

I also recommend having positions both long and short at the same time as a way to reduce risk. If the market looks like it is going up, always try to find some stocks that are not doing well and short them. That way if we do turn around, the weak stocks may get weaker and help cut my losses. As part of your money management plan you may include that you will not have a net position in the market of more than 5000 shares; if you are long 8000 shares of stock, you would want to short at least 3000 to stay at your risk level.

Increasing Trading Size

Knowing when to increase your risk levels and position size is another thing that should be in a money management plan. It takes more than saying, "If I have $5000, I'll trade one contract, and if I have $10,000, I'll trade two contracts." The first goal should be to lower the overall risk per trade to under 2 percent. Until that is accomplished your contract size per trade should stay the same. Afterward the maximum allowable share size should be adjusted on a regular basis. You may want to have a plan to review it every time your capital changes by a set amount or on a weekly or monthly basis. You can't just increase your size willy-nilly; it has to be done within the boundaries of a good risk parameter plan.

Many people make the mistake of increasing their position size unproportionately to the growth of their account. They start making money and will keep adding contracts until the ratio gets out of hand. They may begin to pyramid a position without knowing how to do it properly and soon end up risking way too much on one position. They go from trading one contract with $10,000 to trading five contracts with $15,000 as they get carried away with their success, when in reality they should still be trading one contract.

When you decide that the time has come to step up your trading, do it slowly. Don't make the jump all at once; instead, stick to what you were trading before until a good opportunity comes along and then try going bigger. You need to be careful when you increase your trading size because it takes a lot less to lose more when you are doing it with more volume. I don't recommend ever doubling your size, but this is tough to do for small traders who are only trading one contract or 100 shares. For them the next logical step is to go up to two contracts, but then they fall into the trap of being able to lose everything twice as fast. It is safer to increase size when you are going from three contracts to four or from ten to twelve, as a loss won't hurt you twice as badly. But small traders are always at a disadvantage, and so they have to be more conservative.

Finally, don't increase your size because you have been winning or losing; this is not the proper time to increase your trading size. This is not smart money management; emotions are making you do it, so avoid it. The only time I think it's okay to add to your normal trading size is when the market presents a great opportunity and there is little risk, but even then you should be conservative.

How to Pyramid Properly

Many traders do not know how to pyramid properly and end up doing it backward. Pyramiding occurs when you add to an existing position to take advantage of a sustained move in the market. The wrong way is to start with one contract and then add a second contract as it goes in your favor, then add two more contracts, then add three, and so on. The problem with this is that the trade becomes top-heavy as most of the contracts are done at higher prices. If the market does a quick turnaround, it can be costly. When a position is top-heavy, the market only has to retrace a portion of what it has moved to erase all the profits made in the initial move.

The proper way to pyramid is to have the most contracts at the bottom and then, as the trade begins to work, to add fewer and fewer. Thus, if you had started with ten contracts, you'd add seven, and later four, two, and one. This way, when the market turns, you don't risk nearly as much and can keep most of the early gains. When you do it this way you are building a geometric pyramid with a solid base like the ones they have in Egypt. Image if they had built them the other way around, with the point in the sand. Not only would it have been hard to get to the top, but I don't think the pyramids would have lasted 4600 years without toppling over. The same is true for trading. If you pyramid upside down, it doesn't take much to bring it crumbling down, so make sure you have your base at the bottom.

NICE WHILE IT LASTED

I had a friend who was trading wheat futures and started with $2000 in his account. He bought two contracts near the start of a major upswing in wheat; a couple of days later he had a nice profit in it and was able to cover the margin for another two contracts. As the market went up, he soon was able to buy two more, and this kept going on for weeks. He would add to his position every few days as he made more and could afford to cover the margin on new positions. As time went on he was adding faster and faster because with all the contracts he had, smaller moves would be sufficient to cover the margin requirement on new contracts. After 2 months, his $2000 in this wheat position was worth over $50,000 and he had over thirty contracts on. Eventually the market reversed and did so pretty hard. He started losing money, much faster than he had made it. On the way up he had his smallest amounts of shares for the whole ride and the largest amount only for the last bit of the move. On the way down, though, he had the most contracts at the start of the drop, and so his losses were multiplied compared to the gains. It took only a week to wipe out all his profits. This occurred because he got too aggressive, did not know how to pyramid, and had no real plan to increase his trading size.

THINGS TO INCLUDE IN A MONEY MANAGEMENT PLAN

When you are making a money management plan, you may want to include some of following provisions.

Know How Much to Lose

Not only should traders know how much to risk on any trade, they should have a maximum daily loss limit and maybe even a weekly or monthly loss maximum. They also should have a level where if they reach it, they will stop trading and reevaluate their trading plan, which includes their trading strategy and risk plan.

The daily cutoff point is an amount that if it is reached, one stops trading for the day. Sure, there will be days when you are down big and turn it around, but overall bad days tend to get worse. This daily loss limit should be a reasonable one. Don't have one that is too big, where there is no chance of hitting it or it will wipe you out if it is hit, and don't have one that is too easy to hit. Don't make the cutoff too close; you want to give yourself room to turn a losing day around. But have a place where you know from experience that once you reach it, you normally end up pressing and having a worse day. I'd say anywhere from 2 to 5 percent of your at-risk equity is a big amount to lose in a day. By setting a cutoff point at these levels, you will prevent yourself from having a ruinous day. I've seen people blow out in one day; if they had had a collar on, this wouldn't have happened. You don't have to stop trading for the day entirely; instead, you could have a provision that you will exit all losing positions, or cut back on shares if you do hit x amount.

Using the same thought process, figure out a point that if you reach it, you will cut down on your trading for the week or month or take time to reevaluate. These amounts vary by trader, but they should be thought out beforehand. For a complete cutoff point I would say that if you've lost more than 30 to 50 percent of your at-risk capital, you are doing something wrong and it's time to look at what you are doing. Take a break from trading and try to figure what is wrong. If you've lost this much, it is probably not by chance, so don't keep trading.

Don't Average Down

Have a provision in your money management plan that says, "Don't average down." Averaging down means adding to a losing position, and you shouldn't do it. This is one of the cardinal sins of trading. If you are losing, there is a good reason for it: The trade is no good. If it were any good, you'd be making money on it, not losing. There is no surer way of getting hurt badly than to start adding to a bad position. Some of my worst days ever were those when I wasn't convinced I was wrong and kept hoping for a turnaround that never materialized. Instead of taking my loss, I kept buying more and more as the market got worse and worse. When this happens, the losses can get out of hand.

GETTING REWARDED FOR BAD BEHAVIOR

Sometimes you get bailed out and rewarded for averaging down, but it really is a bad trading practice. Getting rewarded for bad behavior is detrimental because if it happens once, a trader will feel he can get paid for doing it again in the future. On paper it may look like a good trade, and of course you are happier with a winner than with a loser, but this is a bad trade. Where a trader should be bailing he is adding, and in the long run he will get hurt by making low probability trades like this.

Monitor Risk Levels

Make some kind of provision to monitor and review your risk levels. This includes not only going over and updating your money management plan and risk parameters but also monitoring positions once they are on. Keeping risk levels intact involves more than just doing your homework before entering a trade. Once a trade is on, you need to keep abreast of it to see if the reasons the trade was made have changed, to see if it is time to exit, to check if the market's volatility has increased, and so forth. You should know how often you will adjust risk on open positions and how often you will review your overall risk exposure plan. These things don't take care of themselves; a trader has to stay up to date on them.

Exit the Losers First

One of the rules that should be in your money management plan is to get out of the losing positions first and hold the best trades. Too many people do the opposite. When they have a bunch of trades on at once, they are tempted to take the ones with the biggest profits first. They don't want to give back their profits and believe that the losers are just about due to turn around, and so they hold them. This is bad trading. Keep the good positions; they are working, and you have momentum with them. The unsuccessful ones are not working because they are crap, so why hold on to them? This is true not just for losing positions but for laggards as well. If you are up 5 ticks in one trade and 40 in another, the latter is a better trade; if you want to lighten up, get out of the one that is barely working first.

Make Only Trades with an Acceptable Risk/Reward Ratio

When a trade is made, you should have some idea what you want the market to do. You should know where you will get out if you

are wrong and should have a rough idea of a target or profit goal
you think the market could reach. Only when you can get a good
ratio of potential profit to loss should you consider taking a trade.
Losers are always easier to define, as it is easy to say, "I'll risk no
more than $500 on any loss or I'll get out if it breaks the trendline."
If you are disciplined, it's easy to carry out the loss side of the equation. What is hard, though, is saying, I'll make $750 on this trade.
Actually its easy to say it; doing it, however, is as hard as catching
an oily watermelon in a pool. It just is not easy to guarantee that
what you'll make is what you were hoping to make. Sometimes
you are aiming at a $750 profit but end up making maybe only $400
or $89. One has to be realistic about how big one expects the win-
ners to be. By having a big win goal you may be disappointed often
and stay in positions longer than you should, as you will wait for it
to get met. When you do this, many times a winner ends up turning
into a loser. Though you have to be realistic about your profit goals,
you still have to make sure that you have a reasonable win/loss
ratio. It could be 2:1, 3:1, or whatever ratio you like, but if it is less
then 1:1 don't expect to make money trading. If you are making a
trade that has a $500 risk and you are looking to make only $100 on
the trade, you have too ask yourself, "What am I doing?" Even if you
did make money on the trade, it was a low probability money management scenario and one not worth making. Stick to trades that
have a high win/loss ratio and you will fare much better.

Other Uses of Funds

I like to set a little capital aside for long shots or option trades. If
you plan on doing this, make a provision for it in your money management plan. It's not too hard to do. Just note that you will allocate x percent of at-risk capital to other trades. You can even use
this extra risk capital to get more aggressive on a trade or two. But
once you lose it, don't go dipping into the rest of your capital to use
more money for this purpose. The use of other funds includes how
you will pay for trading costs, such as quotes, Pepto-Bismol tablets,
or whatever else you may need.

Staying Disciplined

The most important part of setting risk parameters is being disciplined in following them. It serves no purpose if you make a great

money management plan and then don't use it, especially during times when you are up or down big. Many people get a little greedy and starry-eyed when doing well, and ignore their money management plans. They hope to cash in on their success and start trading too many contracts and positions, not thinking that their biggest losses are just around the corner. Though it's easy to lose discipline when making money, it is easier and more costly to do so when losing. When they are losing, people can get an "I don't care anymore" attitude and throw out any sound plan they had. They give up hope, can't accept such a huge loss, or figure the only way to get their money back is to trade more aggressively. In any case they completely lose their discipline. If you've set risk parameters, do whatever you can to stick to them, as they will help you stay on track.

MAKING A MONEY MANAGEMENT PLAN

Here is a guideline one can use in making a money management plan. This is just to get you started. The plan can be much more elaborate and include some of your trading rules, such as not to average down. You also may want to include provisions for entering and exiting the market in stages. This could be something like the following: If you believe a trade calls for the maximum allowable number of shares, you will enter it with 50 percent of that amount, and if it is working after 30 minutes, you will add the remaining half. Different people will have different rules and ideas they may want to include, and so there is no one great money management plan.

MONEY MANAGEMENT PLAN IDEAS

1. Determine How Much Capital Will Be at Risk

I've got $30,000 to trade with, so I will only use $15,000 as at-risk capital; the other $15,000 I will keep in a money market account in case I go through the first $15,000.

2. Determine How Much to Risk on Any Given Trade

I will risk 5 percent of my $15,000 on any trade. This means that as long as my account stays about $15,000 I will not risk more than

$750 on any trade. My goal is to bring this down to 2 percent of total at-risk capital.

3. Determine How Much to Risk on All Open Positions

I will have no more than seven positions on at any time and/or will not have more than 20 percent of my capital at risk on open positions. If I have positions in correlated markets, I will not risk more than 7.5 percent total in those markets.

4. Determine Maximum Number of Shares Per Market

I will have a table of the maximum number of contracts or shares I will trade in each market. This table will be made by dividing the amount I can risk per trade by the average true range of the market. I don't need to trade this much, but if the trade looks like it has a high probability of working, I may consider trading up to this amount. On extremely good trades with low risk I may trade 1.5 times this amount.

5. Determine Position Based on Risk

After establishing how much I can risk per trade, I will determine stop levels by using technical analysis. By dividing my acceptable risk by the stop loss, I will be better able to determine how many shares I can trade. If the stop loss is less than my acceptable risk, I will make a trade. If it is not, I will pass on it.

6. Determine Acceptable Risk/Reward Ratio

I will only make trades that have a risk/reward ratio of 3:1 or higher. No matter how beautiful a setup may be, if I can lose more than I can make if I am wrong, I will not make the trade.

7. Determine Cutoff Point for a Day

If I am down more than $1500 (10 percent of my capital) at any given time, I will stop trading for the day. At $1000 I will begin to exit my worst positions first and take a short break before adding new trades.

8. Determine When to Adjust Risk Parameters

I will stick to the same risk parameters until I feel that I can comfortably lower my risk to 2 percent per trade, and then I will increase my dollar risk per trade every time my account increases by 20 percent. If I lose more than 20 percent of my capital, I will lower my risk accordingly.

9. Determine Cutoff Point before Questioning Trading Plan

If I'm down 35 percent of my capital since I started, I will stop trading until I review my system, risk parameters, and trading plan to determine why I am losing.

BECOMING A BETTER TRADER

Becoming a better trader means making a money management plan and setting up risk parameters. Don't take this lightly. By having a reasonable risk plan, you increase your chances of making money as a trader. You need to start by making sure you can afford to trade what you want to and are able to handle a losing streak. The only way to do this properly is to know the risks involved in trading and how much you are willing to lose before you start. One way to ensure that you will survive a losing streak is to risk only half your trading capital and save the other half for a rainy day. You also should know in advance that you will risk no more than a small percentage (2 to 5 percent) of your capital on any trade. When you set your risk parameters, you should determine what is the most of any market or market group you will trade at once. Don't make the mistake of trading the same number of contracts in every market. Each market has different risks, so take the time to learn how much each one could hurt you. You can do this by finding the true range of the market in a longer time frame; this also will help you set stops that are technically correct. Once you know the most of a contract you can trade, make a list so that you can reference it easily. You also should have an amount that you will risk in all your positions. I don't recommend having more than 30 percent of your at-risk capital on the line at any given time, especially when trading futures. With stocks you can use all your capital and still risk only a small portion of it; with commodities you have to be more careful, as it is easier to lose a higher percentage of what you use. Don't always risk the most you can; do this only when a trade merits it. There are times when you may feel that you should trade only two contracts even though you normally trade ten, and there will be times when you feel you should trade five or ten contracts and, on a few occasions, even more. Remember to trade what the trade merits.

When you make a money management plan, include any little rules that could help you hold on to your money. Make provisions for scaling and pyramiding into and out of the market. You want to spend time coming up with a realistic win/loss ratio. First make sure that your winners are bigger than your losers and that the risk/reward ratio of a trade makes the trade worthwhile. There are many things that can go into your money management plan, but the most important thing is that you make one. The second most important thing is that you stick to it. If you have a provision that you will not lose more than $5 per share in a stock, you need to exit that trade when the provision is met or your plan is useless. Without discipline, no trader will succeed, so always focus on staying disciplined to follow your plan.

Problems with Not Having a Proper Money Management Plan

1. Having no basis for setting reasonable goals
2. Competing with top traders who do have them
3. Risking too much all the time
4. Never knowing how many shares to trade
5. Letting losses get too big
6. Having horrendous days
7. Not knowing where to set stop levels
8. Averaging down
9. Risking the same amount on every trade
10. Not knowing how to pyramid or scale properly

Things to Consider When Setting Risk Parameters and Making a Money Management Plan

1. Trade what you can afford.
2. Think defense first, offense second.
3. Remember to keep losses small and let profits ride.
4. Never use all your money for trading; keep half for a rainy day.
5. Never risk more than 5 percent of your capital on any trade (2 percent is preferable).
6. Be careful with correlated positions.
7. Have a maximum allowable risk for all open positions.
8. Make a maximum allowable position size table.
9. Combine it with technical analysis to figure out how many shares to trade.
10. Don't always risk the most you can.
11. Zero is an acceptable number of contracts to trade.
12. Make only trades with an acceptable risk/reward ratio.
13. Have a cutoff point.
14. Cut back on trading when you hit a losing streak.
15. Know which markets are more volatile.
16. When pyramiding, start big and add smaller and smaller amounts.
17. Have a plan for increasing trading size.
18. Make your plan reasonable and easy to stick to.
19. Don't get aggressive or crazy because you are winning or losing.

Helpful Questions to Ask Yourself

Do I have real risk parameters?
Do I know how many contracts to trade in each market?
Do I take on too much risk?
What's the most I will lose in a day?
Have I lost too much?
Do I need to reevaluate my trading?

PART V
Self-Control

CHAPTER 16

Discipline: The Key to Success

Once a trading plan with solid entry and exit strategies and risk parameters is put together, the steps toward becoming a winning trader are almost all in place. What remains is the discipline to follow the rules that have been laid out. This is where the majority of traders fail. Many people know what to do or what they should do but still trade poorly because they don't have the discipline to do the right thing. No matter how many times they say they won't do it, they keep chasing the market, risk too much, or let losers go past stop levels. They may try hard to improve their trading skills, knowledge of the market, and technical analysis know-how, but unless they concentrate on their discipline, their results will not improve.

SUCCESS TAKES DISCIPLINE

To become a great trader one has to learn many skills, but aside from knowing what to do, a trader needs to have the discipline to do the right things. There are countless ways a trader can make or lose money. All traders know they have to cut losses, trade less, have a risk management plan, and do their homework, but without discipline it is impossible to put together all these tools and become a successful trader. Discipline is what ensures that all those things are carried out, and it is probably the single most important tool a trader needs. Discipline is needed in every aspect of trading and should be high on the list of what traders have to work on. Everything one does will be done better if one has discipline.

One of the things all the best traders have in common is that they have discipline. One of the reasons professional gamblers make money is that they are very disciplined individuals. A person who is undisciplined and reckless will find trading much harder than will a person who has very good discipline skills. Without discipline, traders will not be selective in their trading; instead, they will tend to overtrade, be sloppy, and let losses get out of control. A trader can have a great trading system but will lose money unless he has the discipline to stay within his money management and risk parameters. The traders who end up doing best are the ones who are most disciplined to follow their own rules. The rest of this chapter will discuss some areas where discipline is crucial and then help you work on being more disciplined.

HAVING THE DISCIPLINE TO WAIT FOR THE RIGHT TIME

I'm sure you've heard that patience is a virtue; how true that is when it comes to trading. Patience means waiting for an indicator to give you a signal or for a trendline to get touched before jumping in, in anticipation of it. It means waiting for a market to retrace after a breakout before getting in. It means not chasing every move because you are scared of missing something. It also means not trading out of boredom or for the excitement. One needs to be able to sit back and do nothing while waiting for the right opportunities to come along, even if that means not making a trade all day. Very few people I know can do this because they are "traders," not "watchers." They feel that if they don't trade, they are not living up to their title. It's hard for some people to sit around waiting for an opportunity without feeling compelled to do something. Traders want to trade and will get antsy waiting for the right opportunity, and so they jump into anything just to trade. Traders who seem to rush into trades as opposed to waiting for the higher probability setups have less discipline and do worse than they should. A good trader has the discipline to wait for a market to set itself up, as he knows it's better not to trade than to trade badly. Those who have the patience to sit out the market can wait on their 3 and 0 fastball down the middle and take advantage of it. For me one aspect of discipline was not to fight the urge to trade the little counterwaves of the main trend. I'd look at the stochastics or a channel line and think that the market was due for a bit of a retracement. Now I know these are low probability trades and so I try not to make them. It is hard sitting out and watching a market move in the direction you think it will, while waiting for a trend to continue, but a disciplined trader will be able to do that. Instead of jumping in, a disciplined trader will wait until the main trend resumes, because that is where the real payoff is. A trader who learns to wait for the high probability trades to come along before getting involved will improve his chances of coming out on top.

IT MAY BE BORING, BUT IT WORKS FOR HIM

One of the guys I trade with has the ability to do nothing for days on end. He can just sit there watching the market and reading the news until it feels just right. He has developed the discipline not to trade until he gets the setup he wants. We all tease him for not trading, but overall he does better than most of us do. I watch him every day and have no idea how he can resist the urge to trade when everyone else in the room is putting on trades and calling out stocks, but he manages to restrain himself. He wasn't always that disciplined, having dug himself into a tremendous hole by overtrading earlier in his trading career. But after taking time off from trading to find himself, he came back with discipline and is trading much better.

HAVING THE DISCIPLINE NOT TO OVERTRADE

A trader who is always in the market and/or always has too many positions on is not very disciplined. There can't always be a reason to be involved; there are times when it is best to sit out of the market or cut back on the number of positions and shares. This has always been one of my biggest problems. I always needed to be involved, no matter what the market conditions were. If I wasn't long, I believed I should be short; if I could afford to trade 5000 shares, I always wanted to trade the max. Finding the discipline to fight this urge has been one of my biggest hurdles. A trader is much better off making fewer trades and holding fewer positions while concentrating on timing instead. I truly believe that the best traders concentrate on just one or two markets and become experts on them. Once a person has too many positions on, it begins to affect his trading because he can't manage them. Yet some people use all their available capital all the time, even though the market may not merit it. The traders who are disciplined enough to sit back, trade lightly, and keep a manageable number of positions do better in the long run. They may not have the huge days an aggressive trader has, but they have more consistently winning days and fewer huge losing days. A lot of small winning days is better than a few big winning days and a lot of even bigger losing days.

HAVING THE DISCIPLINE TO DEVELOP, BACKTEST, AND FOLLOW A TRADING SYSTEM

Though trading can be enjoyable, it takes a lot of hard work. One of those areas where countless hours have to be spent is developing and backtesting a trading strategy. Some folks think they have a good system but don't put in the work to backtest it properly. They may test it on only a few months of data and think that it's fine when in reality they should test it on 3 years of data. Some don't bother to test it at all, but go into trading blindly, and this is not a bright idea. If you want to succeed, you need the discipline to work on your trading strategies and test them properly. This can take weeks and months of hard work, so don't get lazy about doing it or think that what you have is good enough. If you don't take the time to do this before you risk money, you are in my opinion a fool who soon will be parted from his money.

The next place where discipline comes into play is in following a proven backtested strategy. When I follow my trading systems and rules, I tend to do okay, but sometimes I lose my discipline, override my signals, or trade off the cuff because I have nothing better to do. If you have something you honestly believe works, don't second-guess it; just follow it, especially on the exits. It's one thing to miss a trade completely by not getting in, but if you are already in and ignore a stop, you are asking for trouble. If part of your strategy is to exit when the market breaks a trendline, you have to do that every time, not just when it catches your fancy.

HAVING THE DISCIPLINE TO MAKE AND FOLLOW TRADING RULES

Top traders have rules they trade by and have them written down in front of them all the times. These rules are a usually a culmination of everything they've read or heard that is supposed to work, such as "cut losers short." I have mine taped between two of my computer monitors, about 8 inches from my nose. It's one thing having them in front of me; the hard part is having the discipline to stay true to them. I know that when I'm losing, I tend to ignore my rules, and this is the time I should be looking at them more closely. I then have to acknowledge this and get myself back on track. One way I do this is that when I find myself getting into a rut, I stop, take a walk, and grab a soft drink. When I come back, I read my rules and get out of any positions that violate any of them, which usually leaves me with no positions. If I'm having a really, really bad day, I may ignore this step and of course end up having an even worse day. It's a hard thing to always follow your rules, but if you have a good set of trading rules, they won't do you any good unless you have the discipline to follow them.

Here is a copy, as is, of the rules I have on my desk.

FOLLOW THESE RULES AND I WILL DO BETTER

PPC

Trade less and **be more selective** per trade.

Trade light in the morning until I get a feel for the market's trend.

Don't need to be maxed out.

Exit losers 30 minutes after the open.

Have a reason for every trade.

Look for **better entry levels**; look at a chart first.

Don't trade the news.

Don't buy if stochastics are near the top.

Wait for the **pullback**.

Buy dips.

Dump the losers first.

Try to **trade in the direction of a stock's trend.**

On big days trade only in the direction of market—don't get cute.

Take **smaller losses** and take them quicker.

Exit bad trades within 45 minutes.

Think like a pro.

Avoid big losses.

Look at the higher time frame.

Have predetermined **stops**.

When losing bad, **take a small break.**

It's okay to lose on a trade.

Scale in and out.

Stay away from stocks that hurt me.

Don't need to hold out for top dollar.

If trade is done, GET OUT.

Don't be a gambler.

Don't chase.

Don't make stupid trades.

As you can see, most of the rules relate to just a few of my weaknesses: overtrading, timing, and cutting losses. When I have the discipline to control these weaknesses, I do much better. One thing I've noticed is that on bad days I tend to trade 3 times as much as I do on good days. This is the case because I get tempted to make up losses, and so I scalp more than usual. I'll also put on more shares and have more positions on. It's a hard temptation to fight, but it has to be done. As I'll describe in the next chapter, it's not important to finish each day positive. Ignore a bad day; you can easily make it back in the future. There is no need to press to make it back all at once; all that does is increase the odds of turning a bad day into a very bad day. A very bad day is harder to make back than just a bad day, so be careful.

HAVING THE DISCIPLINE TO MAKE AND FOLLOW A TRADING PLAN AND A GAME PLAN

There's little to say here except to make sure you have a trading plan. It may take a while to get this down right, but without one you will be trading from behind the eight ball. Some people would rather trade than prepare to trade. They don't have the discipline to develop a long-term trading plan and a daily game plan. They figure they have a good idea of what they want to do, and so they don't need to waste time making a plan. But a trader who trades without a plan probably is trading without discipline. It took me about 5 years before I had the discipline not to trade until I had made a good plan, and the reason I did that was that I was trying to raise money to trade with. Once I had a solid trading plan, trading became a lot easier. Like all other plans you make, a trading plan is good only when you are disciplined enough to follow it.

HAVING THE DISCIPLINE TO DO YOUR HOMEWORK

Next comes the discipline to do your homework and review the markets every night. The trading day is not a 9:30-to-4 job or whatever hours it is that the markets you trade are open. Being a good trader means having the discipline to work before and after the market is open. It means working late reviewing the day, looking over current positions, evaluating them, and planning the next day. It also means starting early the next morning, looking at your plan for the day, reviewing charts, and looking at any news that may help you determine what to do. If you don't do all this already, start setting aside time every night to study the market, look at charts, and plan the next day's trading strategy. Before putting on a trade, know what the charts in different time frames look like. Write down the different support levels, trendlines, break points, stops, and so on. Doing this in multiple time frames takes time, but it will help you see the market more clearly and make you a better trader.

The guys I know who are the best traders also work the hardest; they stay the latest and come in the earliest. They have stable personal lives and believe trading is their business. They don't take it lightly and do everything possible to succeed. They read the *Wall Street Journal* and *Investors' Business Daily* every day as well as every book available. They are always trying to get any edge they can. They have disciplined themselves to be the best they can be and tend to get rewarded for it. Those who come in 3 minutes before the opening and have their jackets on and are ready to go as the closing bell rings pay for their laid-back attitude. Even if they make money, they probably could make more if they were more disciplined about being prepared.

HAVING THE DISCIPLINE TO STICK TO MONEY MANAGEMENT PARAMETERS

One of the problems I faced in the past was that I would start trading with a small account and make great money management rules to fit my account size. I would be really conservative, making only smart trades with low risk while keeping my position size small. Then I would start making some money, and all of a sudden my money management rules were out the window. I started putting on too many contracts in too many markets, and before I knew it, I was risking 5 times what I had been before, but with only twice as much money. At that point it did not take me long to blow the whole thing. I had lost the discipline to follow my money management parameters, and I paid for it.

A trader should always have the discipline to follow his rules whether he is making or losing money. Losing streaks are normal. Don't get discouraged by them; just stick to your plan and maybe cut back on trading until they blow over. Winning streaks should be met with the same discipline. Don't get overexcited and think you are better than the market; stick to your plan and try to maintain the same pace. If you took the time to make proper risk parameters, it will do you no good unless you are disciplined enough to follow them.

HAVING THE DISCIPLINE TO SET LOSS LIMITS

One has to learn to set loss limits when trading. This applies to individual trades, daily losses, and one's overall account. If a trader cannot do this, he may end up taking overwhelming losses and possibly blow up his account. It's easy to set these limits in your money management plan, but then you have to be disciplined and stop when those levels are reached. Setting limits is not a matter of just choosing an arbitrary number; you really have to sit down and determine how much capital you can afford to risk. You need to know that you cannot lose more than $1000 on a trade or $2000 for the day or that if you lose $20,000 you will stop trading altogether for a week. Small traders have to be the most disciplined, as they are the ones most likely to blow up. Many small traders figure their capital is too small for them to follow a real money management plan, and so they ignore it altogether. But money management is for all traders, no matter how big or small they are.

HAVING THE DISCIPLINE TO EXIT A TRADE

Having the discipline to get out of both winners and losers is critical to one's success. Don't just get out because you feel like it; have rules for getting out or you will have different reasons for exiting trades on a regular basis. This is no good because you will be making undisciplined exits. Set your targets or criteria for exiting before you get in and then be disciplined about following them. Once you exit a trade, don't look back and say "what if." Yes, the market can keep going, but that isn't important. The important thing is to have the discipline to exit when you should. What happens afterward is insignificant. Many times you may miss an exit by a tick or two and then end up holding the trade in hopes of making that extra tick. You can end up watching it run 20 ticks against you because you were not disciplined enough to get out when you were supposed to. When its time to get out, get out and don't be greedy. Other times one may have a target in mind, and then, when the market approaches that level, one changes the order for no good reason. Don't change your original order unless there really is a good reason to change it.

Placing and using stops also takes discipline. A trader should always have the discipline to have a stop-loss level on every trade. Whether it is mental or real, no trade should be made without having a worst-case scenario. Nobody likes to think about his losses, and so many people ignore the stop. However, they should get into the habit of knowing where they will get out if the market turns against them, and then of course they must be disciplined enough to do so if it hits that level. Traders need to be disciplined to take a loss. You have to keep reminding yourself that *it is okay to lose a little, you don't have to make money on every trade, and losses are part of the game.*

When it is time to get out of a losing trade, just do it. Don't come up with reasons to stay in. One way for an undisciplined trader to get over this hump of not being able to get out of a trade is to give his predetermined exit points to a broker to handle. This way he knows he will always stick to his exit plan.

HAVING THE DISCIPLINE TO STICK WITH A WINNING TRADE

A trader also should have the discipline to stick with winning trades. You have to fight the temptation to get out of winning trades too soon. Every trader wants to be able to capture a major move, but the only way to do this is to let trades develop. If you consistently get out prematurely you will find it tough to succeed in the long run. Even if you can't hold good trades for very long, at least make sure you are winning more on your winning trades than you are losing on your losing trades. Traders who do the opposite show a total lack of discipline and won't be around very long.

HAVING THE DISCIPLINE TO WORK ON MISTAKES

Everyone makes mistakes; it's part of the learning process. How a trader deals with his mistakes is the difference between a winning trader and a losing trader. A disciplined trader will try to learn from his mistakes all the time; he will not ignore them as many traders do. He will take the time to review his trades and trading performance and make the changes needed to get better. One way to do this is to keep a journal. This may be time-consuming, but those who have the discipline to do it have a better chance of succeeding in the long run because, hopefully, they will not repeat the same mistakes over and over. Unless you know your weaknesses, you can't really fix them.

HAVING THE DISCIPLINE TO CONTROL EMOTIONS

Successful traders know how to control their emotions. They have the discipline not to bang on a desk, shout out in anger, or gloat about their successes. They also blame only themselves for losses. Someone who has a short temper, gets moody, and is always at war with the market is directing his attention to the wrong place. It should be focused on trading and nothing else. I have no emotion when I trade, especially when I'm losing big. I just keep quiet about it and keep it to myself without anyone ever knowing how bad it is. I never slam a keyboard or curse at a market maker. For me it comes naturally, but others may have to work at it. You accomplish nothing by getting emotional except looking a little silly. If you are trading from home, no one will see you, but it's still not a trait you want to have. There are many other emotions a trader needs to be disciplined about controlling in order to be the best he can be. Some of these emotions are fear, greed, hope, revenge, and overconfidence, and I will deal with them in detail later in the book.

WORKING ON DISCIPLINE

A lack of discipline is one of the biggest obstacles in a trader's path to success and the hardest to overcome. I find it the single most difficult thing I have to do every day. I know exactly how to trade well, what to look for, and what to avoid. But if I relax and let my guard down, I can easily overtrade and hold losers too long. I have to work hard to keep to my parameters, and it's all about discipline. Staying disciplined is an ongoing job that a trader needs to work on, as discipline affects every aspect of trading.

Whatever your weaknesses are, it is not enough just to know them; you also have to be disciplined enough to work on them. The way to start getting on the right track in learning to be a disciplined trader is to make a list of your weaknesses. Then pick the one you can most easily correct and work on that first. Starting with the easiest is good because it will be relatively easy to overcome that weakness, and then you will be more confident about tackling a bigger problem. I had a weakness of letting losing day trades sit for way too long, and so I started putting a 45-minute time limit on trades that were not working. This is easy to do. My software tells me how long I've been in each trade, and I just have to pay attention to it. After 45 minutes, if I'm down in it, I get out. I still have to learn to get out of bad positions sooner, but that will come. This is only one small step in the direction of becoming a well-disciplined trader, but it's an important step.

Learning discipline is one of the hardest things a trader can do, but to succeed, one really needs to work on it. Discipline is a trait some people have and others lack, but if you are dedicated and work hard enough, you will be able to develop it. I don't think it's something that can be taught in a trading book, but at least you can become aware of it and then consciously work on improving it. There are some people who are disciplined by nature: athletes, musicians, good students, and professional gamblers, among others. These are people who work hard and spend the hours they need to spend to become good at what they do. If they can apply their skills to trading, they become good traders. Others must work hard at making and keeping to a trading plan and a game plan. Traders should keep a list of their trading rules in front of them so that they can constantly check themselves. Discipline is not a trading problem but a personal problem, and so an outside solution can be helpful. Some traders seek help from professionals such as hypnotists or psychologists to get them to be more disciplined. Whatever the case, you have to work on it, because without discipline you will not be able to trade well. I've only touched the surface of how discipline can affect a trader. It is needed everywhere one turns, so don't neglect it.

PLAYING POKER: HOW I LEARNED DISCIPLINE

One of the best things I did to help me trade less and develop discipline was to practice playing poker properly. I used to play a lot of poker, and I played the way I traded. I always stayed in every hand, hoping for the miracle cards, or tried to bluff everyone out. I played for excitement and the big win, and so I rarely folded. When I decided to work on my trading discipline, I sat down at a poker table in a casino and began to play to win, not for fun. This meant I would follow proper poker rules, which I knew but rarely used. I began folding my cards immediately if I didn't have a strong opening hand. I would bet and meet raises only if the probability of winning was greater than the ratio of the potential win to the bet. For example, if I had to bet $10 to win $80 and the chances of getting the card I needed to win were 11 to 1, this would be a bad bet. To make this bet, the payoff on $10 would have to be at least $110. I was bored out of my mind, folding on most hands, but I came home a winner. The hands I entered were high probability ones, and as I result I won a good percentage of them. I then realized that this discipline to wait for the high probability situations would work in trading, and so I began changing my trading style.

BECOMING A BETTER TRADER

Becoming a better trader means, above all, being disciplined enough to do what you are supposed to do. It is one thing knowing how to trade; it's another actually being able to carry out the steps that can make you successful. A good trader has discipline in all aspects of his trading; that means getting prepared to trade before the market is open, doing your homework, and knowing why you want to make every trade you do make. A disciplined trader will not make random trades and will be able to wait for the right trading opportunities to come along instead of rushing into trades. He will have made a trading plan, have backtested his trading ideas, have solid risk parameters, and have the ability to follow them. It's not always easy following a trading plan, but a good trader has to be able to do it. Discipline also plays a role in being able to get out of losing positions when they merit that, and being able to hold good trades for as long as they work. Many traders do the opposite: They have too much trouble taking a small loss, and are so excited about seeing a win that they take it before it amounts to anything. Having the discipline to control your emotions is an often overlooked aspect of trading that can have a huge effect on how you do. Emotions can get the better of a trader, so learn to tame them. As a trader, I think it is always good to have trading rules to live by. One way to stay disciplined enough to follow them is to always have them within sight. This way, if you feel yourself going off on a tangent, you can review your list quickly and try to get back on track. Working on discipline is hard to do, but if you do have a problem with it, you need to find a way, because without it trading is nearly impossible.

How a Lack of Discipline Hurts a Trader

1. Not being able to follow proper trading rules
2. Overtrading
3. Lacking focus
4. Having poor entry points
5. Chasing the market
6. Not waiting for higher probability trades
7. Trading in choppy markets
8. Trading against the trend

9. Trading without a game plan
10. Not being prepared for what the market has to offer
11. Not following risk parameters
12. Letting emotions run rampant
13. Not being able to cut losses
14. Not being able to hold winners
15. Being nonprofessional

How to Become a More Disciplined Trader

1. Treat trading as a business.
2. Get someone to keep you on track.
3. Review your trades.
4. Set reasonable trading goals.
5. Tackle the easy problems first.
6. Review your performance.
7. Make trading rules and keep them visible at all times.
8. Make a trading plan.
9. Make a game plan.
10. Have a trading strategy to follow.
11. Ask yourself before every trade, "Is this the right thing to do?"
12. Do your homework.
13. Work hard to improve.
14. Use hypnosis.
15. Just do it.

Helpful Questions to Ask Yourself

Am I a disciplined person?
Am I a disciplined trader?
Do I do the work that is necessary to succeed?
Do I keep to my rules and plans?
Do I chase the market?
Do I make the same mistakes over and over again?

CHAPTER 17

The Dangers of Overtrading

BE MORE SELECTIVE

Some people get the impression that the more they trade, the better their odds of success become. Eventually they will catch some big trades that will make it all worthwhile, but unless they are always in the market, they won't have that chance. Others may believe that by constantly getting in and out, taking small winners, they will chip away at success. These thoughts are far from the truth. Overtrading is one of the least productive things a trader can do. Traders need to understand that success takes discipline. One of the most important times discipline comes into play is when one is learning the ability to be more selective and not trade all the time. Without this discipline, trading becomes haphazard and uncontrolled. Many times during a day a trader may get the urge to put on a trade without studying it adequately or analyzing the risk/reward ratio. Overtraders seem to be compelled to trade on whims, out of boredom, because of a news event, to recoup losses, or because they hear other traders mention something. Some of these trades can be rewarding, but many turn out to be mediocre to downright awful simply because they stem from a lack of planning and have no predetermined exit points or risk considerations. From my own experience and from watching other traders, overtrading is unrewarding and detrimental. The best traders are the ones who are the most selective.

Traders who have a tendency to overtrade reduce their odds of success if they trade too often without a set plan. To come out on top traders must have the patience and discipline to sit back and wait for the right opportunity. Since 90 percent of all traders lose money in the long run, it stands to reason that the less they trade, the better off they will be. If they cut their total number of trades down to zero they would improve by at least breaking even, which is better than most traders end up doing. The second the average trader puts on his first trade, the odds of keeping his account at breakeven are reduced dramatically, and with each new trade the odds get worse.

TRADING IS NOT CHEAP

The best overall argument against overtrading is that it helps a trader become a losing trader more quickly simply because of the costs of trading. When trading, one needs to try to keep costs at a minimum. The costs involved with each trade made (slippage and commission) can really hurt a trader's profit and loss (P&L) statement. The more one trades, the more these costs pile up in one's account and cause it to dwindle. If you want to remain a trader for the long haul, work on cutting costs, and the easiest way to do that is to trade less.

Commissions and Slippage

For starters, it is important to remember that every trade that's made—win, lose, or break even—will cost a trader some money. No trader can avoid paying commissions and fees and most trades include some slippage, and so the more one trades, the deeper a breakeven trader gets himself into a hole. Though commissions are an unavoidable cost of doing business, one should not take them casually because a trader's account can easily dwindle from commissions alone. Say, for example, a trader opens a fully serviced futures account (where commissions can range from $35 to $100 per round turn [R/T]) with $5000 and pays a modest $50 per R/T. In 100 trades he will go through the value of the account on commissions alone, and this won't take very long. If the trader is good enough to break even (not including commissions) on his trades and makes two trades a day, trading one contract at a time, in less than 2 months the capital in his account will be depleted. Once he starts trading multiple contracts per trade, this will happen even faster. Unlike stocks, where commissions can be on a per-trade basis and the cost is the same whether doing 100 or 500 shares, commodity traders pay per contract and commissions pile up quickly when one is doing multiple contracts. If this trader starts doing five contracts per trade he will be paying $250 every time he trades and making his broker quite happy. If he starts trading spreads, either between markets or between different months, commissions will be generated on both sides of the trade, adding up even faster. Traders need to be careful not to let brokers talk them into trades that are commission generators, such as spreads. Although spreads help reduce risk, they involve paying two commissions, and this can make them a losing proposition from the start if one is paying high commissions.

Here's an example of how much commissions can affect a trader's bottom line. I knew a broker who charged his clients commissions of $69 plus fees per R/T. A client who started with a $10,000 account sticks out in my mind. Both the client and the broker were aggressive traders, and they started off on a hot streak. In 2 months the account had grown to over $30,000. This may seem like a nice 200 percent return, but what was incredible was that the account generated over $25000 in commissions in those 2 months. The customer saw only $20,000 in net profits while his account had grossed over $45,000. He didn't realize how much he had given up in brokerage costs; he was just happy to be ahead. Every trade they made was for three, five, six, or ten contracts. They constantly would make trades in several markets and were always reversing positions. The third month was different. The hot streak ended, and they started losing on quite a few trades. They lost $25,000 in 2 weeks because they were trading with a heavier position size than before. The equity in the account dropped from over $30,000 to under $5000 as the losses and commissions piled up. When all was said and done, the trader lost $5000 while generating over $35,000 in commissions. His trading was gross positive by over $30,000, yet the account showed a loss because of the costs of overtrading. This was a case of both overpaying and overtrading, which hurt the trader but not the broker. Had he been more conservative, he still might have lost the same amount, but at least the broker wouldn't have done that well.

An obvious way to reduce costs is for traders to use discount brokers. But even in trading through a discount broker, at $12 to $15 per round turn, a moderately active trader can go through a $5000 account in a month or two if he is not careful. Back in my days as a floor trader I paid only $1.50 plus small fees per R/T on the markets I was a member of and $12 per R/T on the other markets. Despite paying so little, there were days when I racked up over $1000 in commissions. With my account size being about $25,000 to $35,000, 3 or 4 percent a day in commissions was way too high. Overtrading and paying this much per day certainly put a big dent in my account.

What is working in traders' favor is that commissions are getting cheaper all the time, but no matter how cheap commissions get, they still need to be considered. Picking market direction is tough enough by itself; add the huge burden of commissions and fees and it's easy to see how so many traders lose money. No matter what commission rate you are paying, fight for a lower one. Whether using a full-service or discount broker, try to find a flat commission rate and avoid fees as much as possible. Brokers hate losing business and will lower your rate if they sense you may switch your account, unless of course you are a pest who does only one trade a month; then a broker will help you fill out the new account and transfer forms.

Slippage also plays a large role in a trader's total P&L both in the delay it takes to get an order in and in the spread a trader pays between the bid and ask of a market. A system that is positive without slippage considered can easily become negative once slippage is added to the equation. Unlike commissions, which are predetermined, slippage is a cost that varies all the time by the market and its volatility. You never can estimate how big it can be, and it must be taken seriously, as it can play an important role in a trader's bottom line.

When one combines commissions with slippage, it's simple to see that every trade that is made is somewhat costly. It doesn't take long for an average trader who is prone to overtrading to lose most of his account simply because of the sheer number of trades he does. A person trading crude who buys at the market and pays 33.28 when the fair price is 32.25 and is also paying $35 in commissions and fees needs the market to move about 10 points in order to break even, since if it's trading at 32.35, he may get out at 32.32. In this example, the market moves 10 points and the trader just covers his commission to break even. Winning or losing on this trade doesn't matter; that 10 cents will still affect his P&L in the long run. On winning trades these costs take away from profits, and on the losers they compound the losses. At the end of the year a trader would be very happy to have those 10 points he gave away on every trade. Once a trader understands how much money it can cost to trade, he needs to realize that by trading less, he can preserve more of his precious capital and stay in the game longer. Traders should focus not on making money but on avoiding losses. Success will come eventually, but one needs to be around when the opportunities arise. If a trader were to look over his trading statements, he might be shocked to see how much he has given up on commissions alone. Trading really isn't cheap, and so a trader needs to concentrate on cutting back on the total number of trades and being more selective.

THE FLOOR TRADER'S ADVANTAGE

Floor traders who trade for their own account, known as locals, have an incredible advantage over the general public. Unfortunately, part of this advantage comes at the average trader's expense. First, instead of paying up for the spread, locals get the bid and ask on most of their trades, thus in a sense creating negative slippage. While maintaining a liquid market, a local constantly assumes risk as he is willing to buy and sell at any time. As compensation, he makes traders pay up to enter and exit trades, giving him an edge on every transaction. The second advantage locals have is that they pay less than a dollar per trade in commissions. That's 10 times less than what average discount traders pay. A local can cut a loss immediately and not worry about covering commissions. He can trade for a tick at a time and make a net profit without the market even moving just by capturing the difference in the spread. The average trader needs at least a 7-tick move in the market before being able to show a profit. Locals also know who is doing what; they can see if large orders are coming in and whether the market is being moved by institutions, locals, or small players. They are always surrounded by other good traders and have a better sense of what the smart money is doing.

However, the privilege of trading on the floor is not cheap. Locals have large fixed costs. They have to buy a seat, which can cost over half a million dollars in the larger markets, or lease one for up to

$5000 to $8000 per month. On some of the smaller exchanges, such as the Cotton Exchange, seat prices are under $75,000, but the volume and opportunity aren't the same. Even though seat prices may be high, they can be worth it. Successful locals tend to trade a lot, because the more they trade, the lower their fixed costs become. An active local can easily do a few hundred trades a day and be very successful by making 1 or 2 ticks per trade. The average trader doesn't have the same advantages, and so he cannot scalp the same way. Instead, he has to be much more selective in his trades.

STAYING FOCUSED

Diversification has its merits and being in a few different markets can help reduce risk, but one should keep in mind that professional traders normally concentrate on only one market or a select group of markets or stocks. Though big institutional trading houses are well diversified and are involved in practically every market, they typically have different traders for each market. Someone who trades energy does not trade grains, and a cocoa trader does not know or care about what cotton is doing. Someone who trades semiconductor stocks doesn't trade drug stocks. Even within specific groups top traders may stick to one market. A crude trader, for example, may not trade heating oil; he spends all his time concentrating on crude. The same holds true for floor traders; even though their seats may entitle them to trade all the energies, they normally stay in one pit and don't jump back and forth. Along with institutional traders, they are focused and are experts in their markets. By keeping things simple they can focus their attention on every minute detail of a market. They know their market inside and out, and coincidentally, they happen to be the top echelon of traders.

While some overtraders constantly get in and out of positions, some overtrade by being in too many markets at once. They figure that each market has to do something and that there's money to be made if they can figure out what that is. These traders like to keep track of everything from cocoa to euro dollars. They look at quotes and charts for 20 markets and trade them all with little preference. A chart is a chart is a chart and a good pattern can work in any market, but overdoing it may have diminishing marginal returns. When one starts to spread oneself too thin by trading in multiple markets, it is hard to stay focused. Getting into them is easy enough; an overtrader can make anything seem like a good opportunity. But when one has to manage and exit too many positions, the results can suffer.

I was known to trade in and out of 15 markets a day, at times with open positions in all of them. When they worked, it was great, but more often than not it was hard keeping track of everything and I consistently lost money. With so much going on it became easy to let good trades turn bad and let losers get out of hand. When one is focusing on just one or two markets, bad trades can be cut short more quickly, before they do serious damage. With 15 positions you'd think that the risk would be spread out, but there were days when everything would go sour at once, and it was devastating. On these days it gets hard to take losses because combined they can be huge. Either I would do nothing and hope some positions turned around or I'd exit the ones that showed any profits or small losses first while watching the bad ones get worse. Either way I stopped following my money management rules and took big hits on those days. Days when everything works right don't happen nearly as often because traders are quick to take profits and won't allow great trades to develop.

Traders should try to keep things simple and not worry about how much money they can make by being in every market. Instead of looking at every market, they should take the time to become experts on the ones they trade best. If one focuses on a few select markets, it's easier to time entry and exit points, and so risk can be controlled better. Individual trades suffer when one is looking at too many markets, as traders cannot concentrate as easily on waiting for the higher probability trades.

In trading longer-term and using predetermined exit levels with stops, a trader with the proper capital can handle many positions. Commodity trading advisers and fund managers typically do this when following a systematic trading system. They get clear-cut entry and exit signals and may hold trades for weeks. With long hold times and good nightly homework it becomes less important to watch trades tick by tick.

REASONS PEOPLE OVERTRADE

After seeing how costly each trade that's made can be to a trader's total P&L, it is easy to understand why traders who overtrade are likely to lose money. With this in mind, it's important to see what leads people to overtrade and then look at ways to prevent it. There are several reasons why people overtrade, and they can be divided into two categories. The first is emotional decisions, which are motivated primarily by fear, excitement, and greed. One problem many overtraders have is that they trade too frequently merely for the sake of trading. This is very common when one is day trading. Some people have an uncontrollable urge to trade. They feel that if they don't have a position on, they will miss a move if one happens or won't be taking full advantage of all the market's opportunities. They are uncomfortable sitting on the sidelines and waiting for the right opportunity. Others need the excitement, while some people overtrade because they are trying to make up losses. The second force behind overtrading has less to do with the trader and more with a trader's environment. The ability to trade online, choppy markets, and pressure from a broker are all factors that can lead one to overtrade. Emotions still drive the trader's actions, but they are secondary to these underlying environmental factors. Even though there are many reasons why one may overtrade, they all stem from the same place: a lack of discipline and failure to follow a trading plan.

EMOTIONAL OVERTRADING

Trading for Excitement: The Action Junkie

Some traders feel the need to be in the market at every possible moment. They constantly have a position on or always look for new opportunities. If they have money available, they try to use it all, all the time. When they get out of a position, they tend to reverse the previous position instead of waiting for the next opportunity. I refer to these traders as action junkies because when they don't have a position on, they start getting jittery and behave like a drug addict looking for the next fix. They won't feel at ease until they make a trade, and then it's only temporary as they are always looking for more action. These people get more internal satisfaction from putting on a bad trade than from sitting on the sidelines. Sure, they want to make money, but trading also satisfies a basic need for excitement. Some people genuinely like excitement and get an adrenaline rush, win or lose, that they don't get when sitting on the sidelines or holding a good position. They feel that once they have put on a position, the hardest work on that trade is done and finding a new trade is the next big challenge. They have a need to keep identifying every market opportunity and can relax only when the market closes.

Through the years I've learned that the best trading decisions are made after market hours. Yes, one needs to be quick enough to take advantage of moves and situations when the market is open, but a trader should have done his homework the night before. He should have a game plan so that he can react in different scenarios. This way, if something happens, he'll be prepared for it and make only anticipated trades instead of trading for the excitement.

Truly an action junkie, I was always more eager to find new trades than I was to manage the ones I already had. I can't begin to count how many times I sat in front of my computer screens scanning all the markets trying to find a trade. I would start flipping through my charts and say, "Wow, soybeans are bottoming; let me buy them now." Before I knew it I was on the phone with the soybean pit, buying five contracts. I never bothered to study the trade, consider risk and reward, look at daily or 60-minute charts, consider which wave of an Elliott wave formation the market was in, and so on. I didn't want to miss it, had nothing going on, had extra capital available, or wasn't getting enough action out of my current positions. Then, as soon as I would put on that trade, I'd look at the other markets and maybe put on a Japanese yen trade for the same reasons. Before I knew it, I had 12 haphazard positions and was not able to concentrate on any of them. With too many positions on I would let losses get too far away simply because it was impossible to manage them all. Although I did study the markets at night, I would get too caught up in any move I saw during market hours and act on it.

Besides the true action junkies, there are people who are guilty of trading for the hell of it, but at a more moderate level. I had several customers who would call up every day and ask if anything looked good because they wanted to put on a trade. If I told them soybeans looked good, they would say, "Okay, buy them. Don't let me lose too much and get me out when you think it's best." They didn't follow the trade very closely but liked knowing that they were in something and had a chance. Others, I think, were bored and liked speaking to a broker a few times a day. They didn't need the money and liked having something to complain about when they were losing. These people trade for the excitement and are okay with losing. It also provides them with a good conversation piece on the golf course when they tell their buddies how they got slaughtered in soybeans or pork bellies, or were brave enough to hold a position $12,000 against them to fight back and break even on it. Sometimes the war stories and excitement are worth the losses for them.

One of the hardest things traders need to learn is to control the urge to trade while becoming more selective in their trades. When one is trading for the thrill of it, the odds are strongly against one ever being a good trader. Trades done to satisfy an itch tend to be rushed and made without studying them. These trades generally are not as good as the well thought out ones. One may get lucky on occasion, but this is not proper trading and has a strong probability of creating losses in the long run.

BEING A BUSINESSMAN

I gave an example in Chap. 2 of how a trader needs to consider trading a full-fledged business. A businessman should not rush into any decisions but instead should analyze his alternatives with a clear head. A trader needs to make decisions the same way, without rushing into trades. A trader is trading to make money, and that's the bottom line. All his actions should lead to that outcome; by taking too many unmerited risks, he is straying from his business plan. If a trader cannot separate trading as a business from trading for the thrill of the action, he becomes a gambler and not a professional. Unfortunately, some people get caught up in the excitement of trading rather than working to make themselves better traders. As a person starts treating his trading like a real business, he begins to be more objective and can turn a steady profit.

Fear of Missing the Move

There are different reasons people overtrade, and each individual has his own motivating factor. For me it was more the fear of missing something big than the excitement of being in a trade. God forbid coffee or live cattle had a big day and I missed it. I had no problem making a lot of bad trades because I knew that soon enough I'd catch the big one. Through experience and many losing trades, I learned that there are times when a market is just not worth trading and that waiting until certain trading parameters are met rather than forcing a trade for fear of missing something is the best strategy.

In time a trader learns that it's okay to miss a move. Of course there are times you'll look at the market in hindsight and wish you had been in it, but unless the trade is part of a plan, you should try to restrain yourself and wait for a pullback to get in. Knowing that a market is in a trend is not reason enough to trade in it. It is important to wait for the market to reach a good entry level. Not waiting for good entry points makes it too easy to overtrade, as traders get caught up trying to enter every tempting breakout they see. Having the patience to wait 20 minutes, an hour, or even 3 days until the market gives a stronger indication of a good trade is too difficult for many traders. They feel that if they don't act immediately they could miss a great trade. It's not always easy for an action junkie to walk away from a trade, but there will be many, many trading opportunities and if one is missed, *so what?* Just wait for the trades that have a high probability and a good risk/reward ratio and you'll improve your chances.

One thing that comes with experience is knowing how to figure out which market environments lend themselves best to trading. A choppy, flat market can lead to overtrading, while a trending market can be easier to trade. If a market is in a strong trend, you don't need to get in and out as often. A position pretty much can be held until the trend ends, and this helps you save on costs. Reasonable stop-loss points are easier to determine in a trending market, so one can set them at levels where they will not be hit needlessly. If a trade is missed and the market is trending, you can avoid chasing it by waiting for it to come back to the trendline before entering. By not waiting you can end up getting in too far away from a reasonable stop, worsening the risk/reward ratio, and having a good possibility of watching the market blow up in your face right away. You may be in a good position but get shaken out because as the market drifts back toward the support area, the pain may become too much, causing you to sell for a loss. Then, frustrated, you get back in at the next peak and the process starts all over again. If the market never pulls back close enough to the trendline and a good opportunity is missed, a trader shouldn't let it get to him. He should move on and wait for the next opportunity. At the least, this will force him to make higher probability trades. Chasing the market also results in higher slippage costs. When one is buying and the market is pulling in, it is easy to get filled on limit orders. When the market is running away, however, a trader has to go to the market and pay the offer, which can be moving higher quickly.

In a choppy market, overtrading becomes easier because support and resistance levels are not as easily visible, making good entry and exit points harder to determine. When the market looks like it is breaking, it may just be turning. When it does break through, there may be little follow-through and the moves could be quick. When it looks like it will start to drop off hard, it rallies strongly instead, only to drop right back 20 minutes later. Other times it fluctuates over a small range, making for very limited profit potential. In a choppy market it is hard to find a place for proper stops, causing a trader to get stopped too often or lose more than he should. These market conditions can lead to getting whipsawed, as overtraders tend to end up on the wrong side of every move. Chasing the market becomes very easy to do, as every false move looks convincing. This is why it is crucial to learn not to chase every move and to know the market environment.

Trading One's P&L

Some traders put themselves in a bad situation and try to work their way out of it by overtrading. Being down quite a bit on the day, on current positions, or for the month is never a good thing, but how a trader deals with it makes the difference between a good trader and a bad trader. The smart thing to do when you are taking a beating is to respect your money management limits and walk away, accepting the losses. Unfortunately, what often happens is that traders try to make back what they've lost by trying harder. The common reaction when one is down big on the day is to stop thinking rationally and get overanxious in an attempt to make it back. These are the times when people tend to trade the most and, of course, make the worst trading decisions. Trading one's P&L basically means that one is making trading decisions on the basis of how much money he has made or lost. Traders need to realize that it's okay to lose and have bad days, and that when they're off their game, it's better to slow down than to press. Instead of trading his P&L, a trader should trade the market and keep doing the proper things. Some traders panic and revenge trade when trying to make back losses, but this typically leads to worse losses. Others begin scalping aggressively, trying to have a bunch of small winners in hopes of making back their losses. People should stick to their trading plans and money management rules regardless of whether they are winning or losing.

Revenge Trading

One thing that can lead to overtrading is trying to make back losses from earlier in the day or from a previous day. Some people revenge trade in an effort to get back their losses. Revenge trading happens when a trader feels that the market owes him money and will do whatever it takes to make it back. He mistakenly believes the market has screwed him (traders do this to themselves). He keeps getting back into the market and, convinced that he's smarter than it, will teach the market a lesson for messing with him in the first place. We all should know that the market is always right and usually has the last laugh. A common thought when revenge trading is, "#*?^%$!@*$#!! I've just lost $400 in soybeans; I'll make it back by trading more contracts on the next trade."

I've seen too many people, myself included, have a bad morning and begin revenge trading, trying to make up what they've lost, only to end up trading too heavily and carelessly. What happens more often than not is that a bad day turns into a devastating one. Yes, there will be times when a bad day is turned around, but in the long run overtrading to make up losses is murderous. It takes only one horrendous day of doing this to blow out a trader.

Traders need to realize that trading is not just a 1-day event. At the end of the year, one bad trade, one bad day, or one bad week means nothing. The best traders have lots of them over the course of the year; even the very best traders lose on about half their trades. This is part of trading and must be accepted. There is no need to panic over a bad start to the trading day, week, or month. It's okay to walk away and start afresh the next day; it's okay if it takes a few days or weeks to make back a loss. But when you start pressing to make it back because you don't want to go home with a losing day and you start making trades that are based on how much you've lost so far, it's usually not good. Each new trade should be independent of all other trades. This doesn't apply just to day trading; people tend to make the same mistakes when position trading, except they take a little longer to bury themselves. A trader may have a profit goal of $500 per trade, but if he loses $500 on a trade, he may be tempted to make $1000 on the next one. He may trade more aggressively, taking larger risks, and instead of making $1000, he can easily lose it. This can quickly spiral, and before long a trader may increase his goals and trading size as he revenge trades. As losses or losing positions escalate, trades can go into "panic mode." They can't take a $1000 hit because percentage-wise it might be a huge chunk of their total capital, and so they hold and maybe even put on a third contract in desperation. They are then holding three contracts, and the market keeps going down. Soon they turn pale; they are down $1800, and panic starts setting in. They begin thinking that the market is never going to bounce and they should maybe go short. All of a sudden they are selling six contracts (three to cover the longs and another three to go short). Usually this is when the market has a quick a bounce, and the trader now doesn't know what to do. Deep down he believes that his first trade was correct and that the market has finally decided to prove him right, but he just went short. He quickly scrambles to get back in on the long side and starts buying like there is no tomorrow. The later in the day it gets, the harder he tries, and maybe he buys six or eight contracts. Unfortunately, the bounce was just a normal upwave in a down day, and the down-trend continues. At this point he may hold for a while or flip his position again.

This sounds a bit far-fetched, but it does happen. I had a customer who was a one-lot trader get so distraught on a day like this that his last trade of the day was for 20 contracts. I had to liquidate his positions for margin reasons, but not before he lost more than $11,000 of his $17,000 account—all because he didn't want to take an $800 hit on a trade. He generated over $1000 in commissions that day, which was more than he had done in the prior three months combined. It had taken three months to get his initial account from $10,000 to $17,000, and in 1 day it was cut by two-thirds. This trader ended up calling it quits about 2 weeks later as he lost even more and got totally discouraged.

This style of trading is an easy way to curtail a trading career. If you never trade more than one contract, do not trade more than one contract just because you've lost big on a previous trade. Keep to your money management plan all the time. You made it with a sound mind, and it is there for a purpose: to keep you from getting crazy. If you find yourself deviating from your risk parameters for any reason, *stop* because you are beginning to overtrade. It is okay to trade more aggressively on the right occasion; just keep in mind that it is not always the right occasion. If you like to add to your position as it gets better, you may want to start with smaller volume. If you feel comfortable trading five lots at a time, start trading two or three lots at first to test the waters. When the time is right, you may add to it or do five contracts on the next trade, but never when you are losing. If a trader doesn't increase his contract size when losing, it will keep him from getting into situations where he's lost too much and is trying to catch up by overtrading. His losses will be reasonable and easier to make back in the future.

I learned this lesson very early in my career. On a day that's etched in my memory, I started the morning off on a bad note and quickly lost about $1000 by buying into a falling market that I thought was about to turn. This was a big total for me back then, and I let it get to me and affect my thinking. On the next trade, instead of trading my usual one or two contracts, I shorted five contracts, hoping to make it all back fast. But as soon as I went short, a buy program ran the market straight up. Before I knew it, I was down another $2000. At that point I stopped praying for a pullback and decided to flip my position again and went long another five contracts. As fortune would have it, the market pulled back almost the second I went long. Once more I suffered a big loss. I was behind the eight ball all day, making irrational, rushed trading decisions with way too many contracts. By the time the dust settled, my overtrading had cost me over $7000 of my $20,000 account. I had panicked, overtraded, and revenge traded. If I had thought of my first loss as just another trade and stepped out for a few minutes to clear my head, I might have gotten into sync with the market and had a normal losing day or even made some money. Instead, it took me 3 months to recuperate from that loss both financially and psychologically. That's not to say it was the last time I made this grave trading mistake. It took years and much more money to realize how devastating it can be. Now, when I'm in a bad trade, I know my thinking can be influenced by the position I have on. I've learned that the best thing to do is to close out any bad positions, stop trading for a few minutes, and then reevaluate the market from scratch. Holding bad trades or adding to a losing position and hoping for a turnaround may work on occasion if you are lucky, but trading is not about luck. You need to do the right things consistently, and taking a loss and moving on is the right thing; overtrading is not.

Scalping Your Way Back

After taking a loss, some traders overtrade by taking a completely different approach. They still throw away their normal trading strategy, but instead of adding size to their positions, they start scalping, hoping to chip away at losses. They are scared to take another loss and start taking profits as soon as they see them, never letting a good trade develop. It may take them 10 trades to make back what they lost at this pace. They think they can make back a $1000 loss by making 10 quick $100 trades. This is not a good money management practice: You can't take small winners and big losses. If scalping is not how a trader normally trades, he shouldn't let his P&L cause him to change approaches. If he can make 10 trades like that, why doesn't he trade that way all the time?

If you start getting into good trades but are quick to exit them, you are hurting yourself. It's important to remember that in the long run one bad trade is not very important. There is no need to tack on 10 more, because exiting winners prematurely is a bad practice whether money was made or not. If you want to scalp and trade for small moves, do so, but do it all the time and make sure the losses are small and your commissions are low. Some scalpers are very successful. They take small profits and even smaller losses. They have no tolerance for losses and cut them immediately. They rarely take the kinds of losses that would make them change their trading style.

Ego Trading

Nobody wants to take a loss on a trade or for the day, but some people take losses as a blow to the ego. If a trader is losing money, he should not fight the losses but needs to admit defeat and move on. When a trader is fighting the market, he's usually fighting his ego. An ego is strong-willed and can make people do things they shouldn't, both in and outside of trading. As a result, a trader who cannot control his ego, may let it be a major influence on his trading. When the ego takes over, a trader is prone to making irrational, emotional decisions and may overtrade. Traders need to exit all bad positions and then forget everything that happened before. After both good and bad trades, each new trade should be started mentally from scratch. Forget about what the market did to you before and never take it personally. Always remember that losing trades are a part of trading and that there is no way around them. Get used to them but try to keep them reasonable. One trade should mean nothing; if a trader takes losses too personally, maybe trading isn't for him. Don't bang the desk or blame anything for your losses; just accept them as a cost of doing business and never let them influence future trades. If a trader cannot control his ego, it can certainly lead to overtrading. He may be prone to revenge trading and making decisions that are based on his P&L, as in the examples given earlier in this chapter.

Another example of ego/revenge trading is when a trader cannot make money trading in a particular market. If he makes money over and over in crude oil but always loses in pork bellies, he should stick to trading crude and abandon the bellies. Yet an ego can get in the way and make you trade pork bellies over and over because it wants to prove a point: It can beat the bellies. People can start overtrading these markets since they have to make more and more money in them to recoup the losses they have amassed. Not only do they overtrade these markets, they may start pressing in other markets as well if they feel the need to recover losses from the markets in which they can't make a dime. I realized a long time ago that I could not make money trading gold and silver. I never figured out why, but I'd say 80 percent of my trades in those markets were losing ones. Eventually I gave up, and I haven't traded them in years. I admitted that my trading strategies just didn't work in the precious metals; I humbly bowed to the metals and pronounced them winners. Now I hardly look at or think about them. I don't beat myself up if gold has a major move and I'm not in it. It's not what I trade, and so I don't care. The best part about it is that I never miss trading the metals at all. I've probably saved myself a ton of money and have been able to concentrate on the markets that I trade better.

Egos Can Get Inflated Too

A trader also needs to be careful not to start trading too much when he is on a winning streak. The two biggest emotions in trading are fear and greed. When one is losing, fear takes over, but when one is on a hot trading streak, greed can rear its ugly head.

Some traders can start out doing well on the first few trades of the day or for a few successive days and accumulate a nice profit, and then a little bit of cockiness sets in as the ego swells. The trader feels he's conquered the markets and can't do anything wrong. He starts to believe that since he has the Midas touch, he should trade more aggressively and put on more trades. The best thing to do when this feeling starts to hit is to get out of all one's positions and call it a day. However, most bad traders let good luck go to their heads and start increasing position size or putting on stupid trades in many different markets without any reason other than that they feel invincible. They stop doing their homework and start trading on whims. They may get a few more winners, but many times after a good hot streak traders will experience their worst losing trades and periods ever. This happens primarily because of overtrading associated with the greed of trying to cash in on a hot streak. It's important to remember that trading is a game of probabilities and that in the long run it's extremely hard to maintain a series of winners. As soon as the streak ends, the first loss or two can wipe out quite a few of the earlier gains if a trader is not careful about avoiding overtrading.

Stops That Are Too Close

While discussing emotions I should mention that another reason traders may overtrade is that they have stops that are too tight. This is partially a result of fear, as some traders are afraid to lose too much money on any single trade. As I mentioned in Chap. 9, placing stops that are too close and within the market's regular movements creates a good chance of getting stopped out. Often after getting stopped out, traders get frustrated because it happened near the low of the move and then the market starts to go back the way they thought it would. They are stopped out of the market, and then it starts doing what they had hoped it would, so they get back in because they don't want to miss the move. They may use another tight stop, and the process happens over and over again throughout the day. When placing stops, make sure you give the market room to breathe. If the stop is placed properly and a trader gets stopped out, he should question whether it is wise to get back in. If you are getting stopped out too often, you may need to trade less volatile markets that won't scare you as much.

ENVIRONMENTAL OVERTRADING

Overtrading is not caused entirely by personality and the emotional issues facing traders. There are some factors arising from the trading environment, that traders need to deal with as well. Though in the long run it's always a lack of discipline that causes overtrading, it's important to realize what situations can lead a trader down this wrong path and know when to fight the urge to overtrade.

Trading during Choppy Conditions and Low-Volume Periods

A trader needs to learn when to trade and when not to trade. As was mentioned earlier, trading during a choppy market is difficult. A choppy market is characterized by a narrow sideways range and usually has light volume. Lunchtime is a great example. Trading tends to slow down, and liquidity is greatly reduced compared with that at the beginning and closing parts of the day. Market moves can be aimless and choppy around this time. When trading slows down, many floor brokers take a break and grab lunch. This causes the pits to thin out, and with less competition on the floor, the remaining brokers can widen their spreads a bit. The same holds true for market makers and specialists in stocks. When the spreads widen, a small order can seem to move the market, since a trader has to pay even more to get executed. A market that normally has a 3- to 5-point spread may widen to a 5- to 8-point spread during thin times. That may not seem like much more, but when the market is in a small range and it costs more to trade it, it gets even harder to make money. Chart 17–1 illustrates why lunchtime trading can be hard. You can see that the activity between 11:30 a.m. and 1:30 p.m. (shaded in gray) is spotty and trendless. There is very little range in general and several 10- to 15- point moves, each of which may be caused by one or two orders. There are a couple of times when there are no trades for a few minutes, and most of the other times there is approximately 1 tick per minute. Compare this to the nonshaded areas and you see a big difference in trading activity and trend. During lunchtime the moves are almost random and may cause a trader to get whipsawed with the market fluctuations. An active and impatient trader may be shorting at 34.70 (Point A) when it looks like the market will start selling off, and then go long at 34.90 (Point B), when it starts breaking higher. If not careful, it's easy to make a series of bad trades during this time, as one is always trying to catch a breakout that during low-volume periods does not normally follow through.

Overtraders keep looking for new trades all day, and lunchtime is no exception. If there is any time they should restrain themselves, it's then. When the volume starts to dry up and the spreads become wider, the fills received on market orders tend to be awful. With the market fluctuating over a small range, traders are more likely to be buying tops and selling bottoms than they would be if it were trending. It's not uncommon to see a small "rally," get carried away, and rush into a trade in fear of missing a move only to see the market immediately turn a bit lower. Then, for the next half hour, it can keep drifting lower until the trader gives up and sells the position or even goes short near the bottom of the range, again probably getting poorly filled. I've seen this happen over and over during the middle part of the day. A trader making two or three trades like this will only contribute to his losses. There is normally not enough market action to sustain a move during lunchtime. The moves may seem real at first, but there is little

C H A R T   17 - 1

1-Minute Crude Oil: Choppy Market Trading

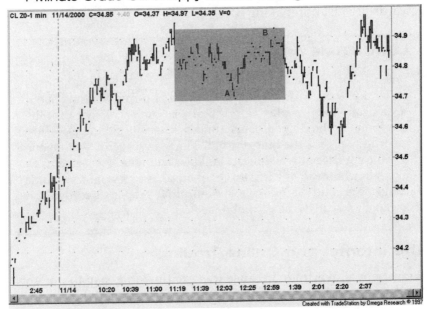

CL Z0-1 min 11/14/2000 C=34.85 +.40 O=34.37 H=34.97 L=34.35 V=0

Created with TradeStation by Omega Research © 1997

momentum behind them since many of the market participants are not involved. Many times you'll see the market reverse direction for the day around this time as traders close out their morning positions, igniting a bottom or a top in the market.

Traders shouldn't try to initiate new trades in a choppy, light-volume market environment. If you miss a move, don't worry; there will be other chances. There is no need to push the market for trades the whole day. Your job is not to catch every move the market makes, but to wait and take advantage of the best opportunities. This is not to say that if you are in a good trade you should get out, but try to avoid making unnecessary trades during this time. There may be occasional opportunities that seem great, but over the long haul lunchtime trading is not profitable. When volume dries up and half the pit is gone, take a cue from the pros—maybe they know something. If you control the urge, and wait for better trading opportunities, you will save some money.

There are also times when some markets are flat with light volume over a period of several days. There is little to be gained by trading them at this time. Bonds are notorious for this a couple of days before a Fed meeting or an unemployment report. If a market is flat-lining or fluctuating within a small range, it's wise not to trade it until it starts picking a direction. Any time the market is choppy or uneventful, save your money because the potential rewards are just not making it.

LUNCHTIME ACTIVITY

When I was on the floor, our lunchtime consisted of taking naps under a pile of coats, playing chess or liar's poker, boasting about sexual conquests, or playing practical jokes on each other (like the ever-popular holding a flame under someone's buttocks). My favorite story was the time one of the brokers wagered that no one could eat a slice of white bread in under a minute. We sent a clerk out at lunchtime to buy five loaves of bread as everyone thought he could do it, but I think maybe 2 out of 50 people succeeded. Go ahead and try it; it's nearly impossible.

The Internet and Online Trading

Some people overtrade because it is exciting and easy to do when trading online. It becomes too easy to enter trades all day long just by pressing a button, and if not careful, one can get carried away. If a trader is trading constantly, it may mean he is scalping and trying to take small profits on his trades the way a floor trader does. Taking small profits is okay as long as the losses are small as well, but an inexperienced trader can make 10 small winning trades in a row for 2 or 3 ticks and then hold losing trades until they go 15 points against him. Tack onto this commissions, however low, and it becomes tough to make a profit. Even when traders are good enough to cut losses quickly, excessive scalping (as can be done easily online) can lead to large costs. Knowing you can get out of a bad position quickly doesn't mean it's okay to make sloppy trades in hopes of catching a quick winner. The ability to trade online is not an open invitation to excessive trading. Traders still need to be selective in their trades and not trade for the excitement.

Contributing to overtrading are the online trading commercials on television. They are misleading and can make traders believe that they are on the same playing field with the professionals. Most of them emphasize that with an online account a trader at home has all the tools he needs to beat the market: quick execution, quotes, news, research, and so forth. They all seem to stress a quick "buy-sell, in-out" attitude. When you think about it, the only reason they are encouraging this is that they are brokerage houses whose revenues come from commissions. By getting traders to trade more, the brokerage houses earn more. They will do whatever it takes to emphasize making many quick trades regardless of whether it's best for a customer.

With the ability to trade online and not having to talk to a broker, a trader who is losing money may become even more inclined to overtrade. This is the case because a trader who is losing can be too embarrassed to speak to a broker. If he is able to trade all day without having to account for his actions to anyone but himself, he will make trades he might not have made if he had to call a broker. In situations where a trader may be apt to revenge trade, online access makes it much easier to do that. A lot of harm can be done when a trader, his damaged ego, and the power of the Internet get together without supervision. A good broker can at least try to talk some sense into a trader. I noticed this behavior in several clients who were digging themselves into deep holes by piling up heavy losses and overtrading. I eventually had to call them and suggest that they slow down, lighten up, or even take the rest of the day off.

They were trying too hard to recoup previous losses and were beginning to bury themselves. I'd call up clients and tell them to slow down a bit, forget about the losses, and start fresh tomorrow. They'd agree that that was probably the best thing to do, but 2 minutes after hanging up they were back at it and getting themselves deeper into hot water. I strongly believe that if they had to call me before entering a new trade, they would have thought twice first. No one wants to hear "I told you so" or be humbled by a patronizing broker who is a great trader in hindsight, and so these people would trade less.

Pressure from a Broker

Though online trading can lead to overtrading because of the ease of putting on trades by bypassing a broker, an aggressive broker also can cause overtrading as he tries to earn a living. A trader should always bear in mind that a broker's main goal is to generate commissions for himself and that he has his own best interest at heart. Yes, he wants his clients to make money so that they will be around for the long run, but he also wants them to trade actively and with size. Not all brokers are like this, but there are some who are out for themselves and have many tricks to make clients overtrade. They can suggest spreads or options to hedge against a position. They can encourage traders to trade smaller margined futures or cheaper stocks but to do more of them. Instead of trading one soybean contract, they may recommend three corn contracts. Don't let your broker call the shots for you. If you have a money management plan, stick to it. If you don't have one, work on one; it is essential to trading.

TRADING IS NOT A ZERO-SUM GAME

Futures trading is often described as a zero-sum game, meaning that for every dollar someone makes, someone else loses one. This is a myth, as in reality futures trading has a negative outcome once commissions are included. If Joe makes $200 on a 20-point move in crude and Sam loses $200 by being on the other side of the trade, there are two happy brokers taking their piece of the pie. Even though the trades add up to a zero-sum total, an extra $60 combined (assuming commissions of $30 per R/T per trader) comes out of that total. In this case the brokers pocket 30 percent of the traders' money. This is similar to playing poker at a casino. Players don't play against the casino but are pitted against other players. However, before the winner of a hand takes the pot, the casino takes a small amount out of the hand for itself. At the end of the night the combined total money all the players have is a lot less than what they had when they first sat down at the table. Play long enough and the casino ends up with most of the money. The reason games last all night is that players keep buying more chips. The same holds true in trading. The more you trade, the more the brokers keep of your money and the less you have to work with.

BECOMING A BETTER TRADER

Becoming a better trader means remembering that trading is not easy. Overtrading only makes it harder, not just because of the costs one can amass but also because of a lack of focus and the frenzied emotional decisions associated with it. If you notice yourself doing any of the things described in this chapter, you may need to trade less. Before you can fix the problem, you need to admit that there is one and determine why you overtrade and what factors motivate you to do so. Picture yourself in different situations to see if you fit a profile. If you overtrade and can figure out why, then comes the hardest thing: having the discipline to work on it. As I have stated over and over, to be a successful trader one needs to have good discipline. Losing traders tend to have little discipline.

Becoming a better trader also means avoiding emotional trading decisions. The best way to do this is by following your trading plan and knowing in advance what you should do relative to what the market does. Be prepared and don't let it surprise you. Don't trade any differently if you are winning or losing. How much you've made or lost before doesn't matter to the market, so just keep trading the same way. This is especially true when you are trading well and get too big for your britches. Part of having discipline is following a good trading plan, which you should have made before putting on a trade. One shouldn't trade without a solid backtested plan and money management guidelines. By sticking to a good plan that generates trading ideas, you will reduce the number of trades made because of emotional factors and those made off the cuff. Without the guidance of a trading plan, traders can too easily chase the market instead of waiting for the market to present a good opportunity. Learning to wait will certainly cut down on trading. This takes lots of discipline, especially for a restless trader. It's crucial to work hard on reducing the number of trades made while concentrating on making high-potential, low-risk trades. Whether you are a day trader or a position trader, wait for the market and be focused. Don't spread yourself too thin. You can do much better by concentrating on only a few markets than by entering positions everywhere. Also, think about expanding your time frame. Look at 30- and 60-minute charts instead of 1- and 5-minute charts to get your ideas. Consider holding trades for a few days instead of getting out at the close.

Trading should not be a means of entertainment; it should be considered a serious business. Therefore, avoid trades that are made out of boredom or because you are afraid of missing a move. Don't chase the markets; you will get bad fills, pay a lot more in slippage, and be a long way from support levels. Not chasing will cause you to miss many trades, but the ones you enter will be higher probability trades. Trading for excitement and entertainment will cause you to trade market situations that don't merit trading, such as lunchtime. You're better off hanging back and being more selective than trying to capture every move. Be careful of trading too freely if you are trading online and watch out for aggressive brokers; in either case make your trades count.

Finally, a major part of the loss in a P&L statement is created through commissions and slippage. These costs add up fast. There are three ways to lower them: (1) Find cheaper commission rates, (2) don't chase markets, and (3) trade less. Remember that if you do these things, more of your precious capital will be preserved, giving you the opportunity to stick around as you learn how to become a successful trader.

The Reasons People Overtrade

1. Excitement
2. Trading one's P&L
3. Revenge trading
4. Letting ego take over

5. Fear of missing the move
6. Bad use of stops
7. Broker's aggressiveness
8. Online abilities
9. Trading in a choppy market
10. Trading at lunchtime

Things to Help You Trade Less

1. Remember the costs of trading.
2. Cut down on slippage.
3. Discipline, discipline, discipline.
4. Do not trade without a plan.
5. Do not chase the market; let it come to you.
6. Look for high probability trades and cut out the low probability ones.
7. Accept losses as a part of doing business.
8. Do not revenge trade.
9. Do not increase size when losing.
10. When losing, take a break and clear your head.
11. Each trade should be made without any regard to previous trades.
12. Do not get cocky; hot streaks eventually end.
13. Expand time frames.
14. Focus on fewer markets.
15. Do not be an action junkie.
16. Don't trade out of boredom.
17. Avoid choppy markets; trending markets are easier to trade.
18. Avoid trading at lunchtime and other low-volume periods.
19. Do not be misled that online trading gives you an edge.
20 If your broker is pushy, fire him.
21. Place stops properly.

Helpful Questions to Ask Yourself

Did I overtrade today?

Am I an action junkie?

Am I sticking to my risk parameters?

Do I have too many positions on?

Are my commissions too high?

Do I stay focused?

Would I trade the same way if I weren't down so much?

The Inner Side of Trading: Keeping a Clear Mind

Rudyard Kipling's poem "If" was the first thing I thought about when I started to write this chapter. A lot of this poem can be applied to trading. If you've never read it, here it is, with some of the lines that relate to trading highlighted in italic. If you are familiar with it, it won't hurt to read it again. I've read this poem many times over the years and always find it enjoyable.

IF

If you can keep your head when all about you
Are losing theirs and blaming it on you;
If you can trust yourself when all men doubt you,
But make allowance for their doubting too;
If you can wait and not be tired by waiting,
Or, being lied about, don't deal in lies,
Or, being hated, don't give way to hating,
And yet don't look too good, nor talk too wise;

If you can dream—and not make dreams your master;
If you can think—and not make thoughts your aim;
If you can meet with triumph and disaster
And treat those two impostors just the same;
If you can bear to hear the truth you've spoken
Twisted by knaves to make a trap for fools,
Or watch the things you gave your life to broken,
And stoop and build 'em up with worn out tools;

If you can make one heap of all your winnings
And risk it on one turn of pitch-and-toss,
And lose, and start again at your beginnings
And never breathe a word about your loss;
If you can force your heart and nerve and sinew
To serve your turn long after they are gone,
And so hold on when there is nothing in you
Except the Will which says to them: "Hold on";

If you can talk with crowds and keep your virtue,
Or walk with kings—nor lose the common touch;
If neither foes nor loving friends can hurt you;
If all men count with you, but none too much;
If you can fill the unforgiving minute
With sixty seconds' worth of distance run—
Yours is the Earth and everything that's in it,
And—which is more—you'll be a Man my son!

KEEPING A CLEAR HEAD

Whenever I read the first lines, it reminds me that I need to keep my head and my cool and stay calm in times of panic. It helps me realize how important it is to trade with a clear mind and control my emotions. Yogi Berra once said, "Baseball is 90 percent mental; the other half is physical." Trading is no different: Without being mentally prepared you are going to have trouble succeeding. Trading is hard enough on its own, but when a trader starts to get distracted by things such as personal issues, stress, fighting a position, and having a losing streak, it becomes even harder. A trader has to have a clear mind when trading or he can get distracted and not be as professional. I know it is hard to do, but when too much is going on, one should find a way to get back on track or stop trading until one can resume with a clearer mind. Even something as simple as being tired can keep a trader's mind from operating at its peak level. Don't worry about past mistakes or losses whether they were a second ago or a few days ago. If you made a mistake, get out of it and clear your head. Think about your next move; the past is history, and a trader needs to move on.

It's important to achieve your peak performance when trading. It's hard for individuals to separate their personal lives from trading, but they should learn to do that. Someone who starts the day off by having a fight with his wife, is angered by being stuck in a traffic jam, or has any other concerns on his mind, such as how much money he recently lost, is at a disadvantage when he starts trading. It's hard to concentrate on the market properly when your emotions are focused somewhere else. When you are trading and have other issues lurking, it can lead to problems such as anger, anxiety, angst, and apathy, and none of these emotions helps a trader. It becomes easy to not care as much about losses or to get mad at the markets. All one's attention should be on the market, not elsewhere. When traders aren't able to concentrate fully on the market, they shouldn't be in it. It's okay to take time off when personal issues are overshadowing trading decisions.

I know there have been several times when I had too much going on in my personal life or had to make money to survive and ended up losing lots of money. One time I became depressed over a few things, including health issues, and my trading suffered because of it. Looking back, I should have taken time off during that period, yet I traded straight through it and lost a lot of money, depressing me even more. It wasn't until I fixed my personal problems that my trading turned around.

THE INNER CONFLICT

When I was starting to learn to play tennis, I read a few books, took lessons, and played 4 hours a day, but nothing helped me become a competitive player as much as a book called *The Inner Mind of Tennis*. This book has nothing to do with the physical aspects of how to play. Nowhere in it will you learn how to hit a backhand or a serve or the proper way to grip a racket, but it was more helpful than anything else was in getting me to play at a peak level. What the book does is explain how most people have an internal struggle going on in their minds when they play. Everybody who has ever played a sport has cursed out loud over a bad play he made. When you do this, you are only cursing at yourself, and in order for you to do that, there has to be more than one active part of your brain having this conversation. There is the subconscious mind, which is the one that really knows what to do, and then there is the conscious mind, which is too critical. To make this easier to relate to, think of the subconscious mind as always wanting to eat and the conscious mind as always telling you, "You need to lose weight." When you have an inner conflict like that, you cannot succeed; both of your minds have to work together. You eventually have to want subconsciously to lose weight and then you will stop eating as much; until then it will be a struggle.

With tennis I learned to let my subconscious mind take over. The goal was to stop worrying about playing great and let my body go on autopilot. After all, I knew how to play and my subconscious mind had seen the best players in the world play and therefore knew what to do and was nowhere near as critical about my playing. Besides self-hypnosis, one trick I would use was to imitate the body mannerisms of Jimmy Connors, my favorite player back then. I would drag my feet like he did, stand like he did, bend like he did, and sway like he did when waiting to return a serve. Doing this kept me focused on playing and kept me from criticizing myself. By transforming myself I would play more solidly and above my regular level as I took my conscious mind out of the equation. Another thing I learned was to have my conscious mind focus hard on reading the name and number on the ball and make believe I was actually riding on the ball. These things may sound silly, but they worked. I started to play as well in tournaments as I did in practice, and I stopped choking in important situations. It was always my mind that kept me from playing well in competitions; once I was able to get over that, my game improved by leaps and bounds.

I'm relating this story because one can do this in trading as well. If you can overcome your mental issues regarding trading, you will get better. Hypnotism is an option; so is making believe you are riding on the market, feeling every peak and valley. Don't slam the table when you are wrong and stop getting angry and cursing at yourself or the market. These things create inner conflict that you don't need. Traders who can control their emotions to the point where you can't tell if they are winning or losing tend to do quite well in the market. They never get upset or elated; instead, they keep on their steady pace from day to day, concerned only about the next trade. Try to think as if you were a top trader and do what he would do. Focus on trading like the best and you may start improving dramatically. I've had the luxury of having always been around good traders I could emulate. Eventually this sinks into your subconscious mind, and trading better becomes second nature. There are times I'll think to myself, "What would Joe do here?" and then act accordingly, knowing that Joe always makes money. Learn to think like a pro, and you will start heading in the right direction. Get your mind to start working for you and not against you, and you will become a better trader.

THE ELUSIVE "THEY"

Many people like to find fault elsewhere. When you are trading badly, it is your fault and no one else's. It's not the market maker's, a bad quote's, a broker's, a local's, or a computer problem's fault. There is no "they" that is out to get you. If you lost money or got a bad fill, it's your fault; don't blame anyone else. One has to accept responsibility for one's mistakes. If a broker misleads you, it's your fault for listening to him; at least the second time it is. Don't blame other people or other things for your bad trading. If you do, you will never get better because you won't be working on correcting your weaknesses, as you won't think you have any. If you want to be successful, you will accept the blame for losses and not pass it off to the market, a broker, or a bad fill.

TAKING A LITTLE BREAK

It doesn't seem like it should, but sitting in front of a terminal or two for 7 hours a day can be exhausting and drive you batty. Traders are wiped out after a day of trading. With all its emotional ups and downs, trading can drain the energy out of you as easily as doing hard physical labor can. When you trade, you need to be vibrant and focused, and this is one of the reasons many top traders take a break at midday. Volume slows down at midday not because traders need to take an hour for lunch, but because they need to take an hour off, as day trading can take a physical toll on them. Most of the traders I know take a break at lunchtime just to relax. It gives them a chance to clear their minds, rest their eyes from looking at the screens, and reevaluate the market. Lots of traders I know go to the gym at lunchtime for a workout or a swim; it revives them for the afternoon. Some take naps, and some like to play backgammon or video games. When I traded from Miami Beach, I took a daily lunchtime stroll on the beach to look at topless German tourists; it sure beat looking at the market. Whatever you do, trading straight through the day can be tough, so take a little break at some point to clear your head and get ready for the afternoon. If you trade a market, such as corn, that is open only for 3 hours and 45 minutes, you probably could make it straight through the day, but for markets with longer hours a break is helpful.

THE OUT-OF-BODY EXPERIENCE

Market perceptions can be distorted by emotional reactions and a person's positions. When you are long the market, you start to come up with reason after reason why the market will go up. It doesn't matter what the market actually is doing because you can't shake your perception of it. When this happens, you have to stop and try to get a clearer picture of the market. It's important to put a halt to irrational trading decisions and get back to using your plan. Bad traders will not admit that they are wrong or are not looking at the market clearly. They will hold on to positions way longer than they should because they are convinced they are right. I see it all the time. One guy is long and says, "The market looks strong, so I will hold on," while another guy, who is short, is saying, "Yes, but it is overdone and will be coming off any second now." Well, one of them has to be wrong, but both are thinking with their positions.

The thing I like to do, especially when losing, is to imagine that I am looking over my own shoulder to get a fresh perspective on the market. I try to imagine that I can leave my body and look at my positions and the market as if I were a nonbiased person. I ask myself, "If I didn't have these positions, how would I like the market?" There are times when you are long and clearly wrong, but mentally you can't get out. You know that if you had no position you'd be looking to get short, but as it is, you are staying long because you can't take a loss. You are thinking with your position, and that is not good, and so you should at least get out of what you have and start afresh with a clear mind.

THE BAD TRAITS

Many losing traders are not losers because they don't know how to read a chart or are lazy; they lose because they have mental issues that keep them from being successful. There are many bad traits and emotions that a trader has to overcome in order to succeed. Though I'm sure I will miss a lot of them, the rest of this chapter will discuss some of the ones I find the most dangerous when it comes to trading. These are the traits that distort your thinking and keep you from trading with a clear mind. If you have any of them, you should work on overcoming them.

Hope: A Sign of Trouble

When a trader is asked what he thinks the market will do and answers, "I hope it goes up," odds are he is long and the market is going down. Hope should never be a trading evaluation. It is normally an indication of not admitting a bad position or having unrealistically optimistic expectations about a trend continuing forever. Once hope sets in, traders need to reevaluate their position quickly because hoping just doesn't work. Just like a baseball player who wishes the deep fly ball down the line fair by waving his arms in the air, as Carlton Fisk did in the 1975 World Series, once it leaves the bat, there is nothing he can do anymore. All the wishing and hoping in the world won't make it go fair if it's curving foul. Everybody hopes he's right when putting on a position or picking market direction; that's normal behavior. Hope starts becoming detrimental when one is wrong, won't admit it or exit the market, ignores stop levels, and adds on to losing positions.

I remember having this conversation with a friend:

John: "What do you think hogs will do today?"
Me: "I'm hoping they go down."
John: "They've been pretty strong the last few days."
Me: "Yes, I know."
John: "Are you looking to buy them cheaper or do you want to get short?"
Me: " I am short already, I've been short for a week and have been getting killed. I shorted some more today, so now I really hope they go down soon."

Whenever the word *hope* is used in describing a position, a trader should know he is in trouble. He should know he is wrong and is stuck in a bad position that he refuses to get out of. When one starts hoping because one is on the wrong side of a trade, every little blip will look like a possible reversal. It doesn't matter what a chart looks like; people will become irrational when looking at it. As soon as a trader starts hoping the market will do something, his grasp of market direction may be lost. At this point it may be best to start looking to get out and reevaluate the market or stock with a clearer mind. This is not to say that if you are long and the market is drifting lower but has support or an indicator is oversold, you need to get out. However, when the market is trending strongly the other way or you have no idea of what it is doing, take the loss and move on. If the indicators don't turn the way you hoped they would, don't keep hoping it will happen. Accept that you were wrong and exit the trade. One of the nice things about being a purely systematic trader is that it takes hope out of the trading equation. One doesn't have to think as hard when a system is making all the decisions; all a trader has to do is follow the plan and hope it is a good system.

Hoping It Goes on Forever

Hope applies not only to losers but also to a person when trades are going his way and he is not being realistic about how much he could make on them. A trader may be hoping to get more out of a trade than a trade wants to give. You may hope it keeps going forever when the move actually may be coming to an end. You always have to trade the market, not your opinion of it. If you start thinking the market should do one thing and it doesn't and then start hoping the market does it because you want more, you are no longer trading the market, you are trading your opinion of it. By being alert to the market and having realistic views of it, you will be able to get out and keep more of your profits.

Stubbornness

Another unsuccessful trait is being stubborn, and stubbornness is the offspring of hope. A stubborn trader will refuse to admit he is wrong, staying in a position much too long, especially when it is not working. He will always think he is right and refuse to listen to anyone else's advice. There is not much I can say about this except that trading requires flexibility. A trader needs to be able to change his opinions as the market changes. Those who marry a position will find themselves getting hurt in the long run. If a trade is not working, let it go. If it is working, get out when it stops working. Don't get an idea stuck in your head forever; instead, go with the market.

Stubbornness also leads to revenge trading, which I discussed in the last chapter. Revenge trading happens when one is too stubborn to realize one can't win but has to prove that being right is more important than making money. When you are having trouble making money on a particular stock, day, or period of time, give up and move on. So what if you lost $5000 on IBM over the last week? That's history; you don't need to keep trading it over and over to prove you can make back your money. Instead, concentrate on the stocks on which you have done better with.

Greed

In the movie *Wall Street*, Michael Douglas's character, Gordon Gekko says, "Greed is good." It makes for a great line in a movie, but in reality greed is a thing that a trader wants to avoid. "Bears and bulls make money; pigs get slaughtered" is a common expression in trading that is very true. It is one thing to hold winners and another thing to get greedy. Trends don't last forever, and there comes a time to get out. Greed leads to overtrading, bad discipline, and poor money management. Greed can cause a trader to end up giving back much of what he has made as he tries to squeeze too much out of a trade overstaying his welcome. Greed can make a trader risk much more than he should in order to make more and more. Instead of trading two contracts, greed can make someone double or triple his position size in hopes of making more. Risking too much only leads to a quicker downfall.

A perfect example of this is when a trader needs to make money because he is behind on bills or wants to pay for his summer house in the Hamptons. He will start trading with dollar signs in his eyes. He no longer views the market as a place with trading opportunities but sees it as a source of cash. He will try to squeeze out more than it wants to give and will not exit a position until he makes his money. Meanwhile, a market can start reversing and a good trade can become a loser that will be held too long because the trader can't afford to take a loss. This trade may have been a good one if the trader was trading the market and not his P&L. He could have taken what the market was willing to give and done quite well, but greed got in the way.

As long as people want to make as much money as possible as quickly as possible, there will be greed. Greed is nothing new. Since the beginning of time greed has caused countless people to lose money on every possible endeavor one can think of. From the tulip craze in Holland in the 1600s to the NASDAQ run-up in the late 1990s, greed has caused people to stop thinking right as they looked only at how much money they could make.

THE DUTCH TULIP MANIA OF THE 1600s

I recommend that anyone who hasn't read Charles Mackay's *Extraordinary Popular Delusions and the Madness of Crowds* read it. Next to *Reminiscences of a Stock Operator,* it is the most highly recommended book for traders to read. It highlights several incidents throughout time when a fool and his money were parted because of greed. The most famous is the great tulip craze of the 1600s. People bought flowers simply because prices were going higher and they wanted to cash in. The market was flying higher every day with what seemed to be no end in sight, and people rushed to get in with price and realistic valuations not a concern because as long as the market rallied, there was money to be made. The speculative fire was fueled by people getting into debt just to get involved. Prices soared almost 6000 percent in just 3 years. Then, all of a sudden, *boom!* They collapsed, falling 90 percent in only 3 months, never to bounce back. The economy went into a tailspin as heavy debt caused bankruptcies to soar. Sounds familiar to many NASDAQ traders in 2000, but it's what took place in the 1630s as the frenzy for tulips took Holland by storm. It goes to show that times and people don't really change. Any time there is a chance of making a buck, greed will prevail.

Trends Do End

Greed comes into play when a trader has a nice profit in a trade and just won't take it. He wants more and sticks with his position way too long. A trader needs to learn when to let go of a position. He is not marrying a trade; it's more like a typical date: Find the trade, get in, get what you can out of it, and then get out without looking back. Sure, you'll promise to call the next day, but by then a different stock has caught your fancy.

Trends eventually come to an end no matter how good they are because when everybody in the world is long, who is left to buy? At times it may seem that a market can go only in one direction. The news is bullish, and the market rallies day after day to all-time highs as new traders are going long every day. But at some point there are no buyers left, and the smart money starts to sell as the market is flying up. These are the traders who bought before the market ran up and whose buying initiated the run-up. Once the general public joins in, they know it's time to sell. To trade successfully one must avoid the temptation to jump on the greed bandwagon.

It was greed that drove NASDAQ stocks up to overwhelming, overvalued prices in the late 1990s. People saw their friends and neighbors making crazy money and wanted to get in because it seemed so easy. Countless professionals left their careers to become day traders. Doctors, lawyers, dentists, musicians, waiters, housewives, and plumbers thought they had what it takes to be traders after taking a 3-hour course somewhere. They plunked down their hard-earned cash to join one of the many blossoming day trading firms that were springing up everywhere. Some stayed home and tried their hand at online trading. People kept buying more and more of stocks that were trading at 10 times what they should have been trading at. They all had dreams of retiring in 3 years with $2 million worth of Yahoo and Qualcomm. Greed made them not only hold on too long but keep buying more with every paycheck. Eventually this greed caught up to investors, and they all lost practically everything they had made, if not more. I took huge hits when the trend came to an end as I got a little bit too caught up in the buying frenzy. The reason I got hurt was that I had too much size as I got greedy. The reason I got greedy was that I had been having the best few months I had ever had just before buying S&P and NASDAQ futures. I began to think this was easy money and I should take advantage of it, and so I kept margining myself to the max. As soon as the market had its first really big down day, I lost most of what I had made in the previous few months.

I'll tell you from experience: Trade lightly and don't get caught up in the hoopla of the market. Trends will end and prices eventually will come back to normal, and when they do, it can be violent. The way to avoid getting hurt is to keep your head when all about you are losing theirs. Keep your positions small, expect the unexpected, and know where you will get out in advance.

Squeezing Water out of a Rock

One thing I am adamant about is not trying to capture every last tick of a trade. Yes, try to get as much out of a trade as possible, but don't get hung up on a number or area. One thing that traders do a lot is the following: If they are long and the market goes up to 36.75 and then dips a little, they start thinking this may be a good time to get out. But instead of getting out they think the market will make one more move and they will get new highs, and so they place a limit order to get out at 36.74, thinking the market will make new highs on its next wave and they will exit close to the top. The market then backs off a dime, and the trader sits and waits for it to go up so he can be filled. He hates to have to give up anything, and so he does nothing. Then the market may make a run at new highs, but not enough to fill him, before coming off again. Instead of taking his profit, he gets greedy, trying to capture those extra few ticks. Meanwhile, the market begins to sell off more as he watches. Now he won't get out because he would be giving up 30 cents of his potential profit. It keeps going lower and lower until all of a sudden he is down in the trade, all because he insisted on getting every last penny out of it. *When you know you want to get out and can't get your price, get out.* Don't worry about squeezing every possible point out of the trade; that's not as important as having the market turn around and losing a lot more than a few ticks. Once the move is over, you won't be the only one trying to get out, so do it as quickly as possible. The real money is not made by squeezing the last few ticks out of a trade; it is made by capturing a big part of the middle of the move. It is also made by cutting losses more quickly. The other problem in this category occurs when you have a good trade and have made $900 and want just a little more so that you can make it $1000. You are sure that there is just a little more oomph in the market that will take it there, and that's when you'll get out. If the market does get there, you start thinking you probably could make another few ticks, and so you hold even longer. Eventually it may come tumbling down, leaving you with nothing. You need to stop thinking that you will miss a little part of the move and be happy with a good profit if the market looks like it may stall.

If the market looks like it is going to stall soon, I throw out limit orders to get filled. This usually works if I'm trading with the trend and figure I can get more out of it when some unlucky trader comes late to the party with a market order. However, if I'm wrong and the market starts to turn, I use market orders to get out. I don't hesitate. If I have 10 stocks on, I go right down the list and get rid of them all. I don't want to be caught watching the market go against me when I have a big position. You give up a little with market orders, but it beats losing or doing even worse later on.

How Greed Can Lead to Getting Hurt

I've been affected by the greed bug throughout my career. I'd always want to make as much money as possible. If I was up $1000 on the day, I'd want to make $2000; if I was up $2000, I'd want to make $3000; and so on. To do this I would start adding more positions and contracts. Sometimes it worked great, but more times than not having too much on made it impossible to stay on top of things. After 12 years of trading I still find myself fighting the temptation of having too many positions when my trading is going well. There are times when, if I have a trade that is working, I'll add to it aggressively when in reality I should be starting to unload some of my position. Yet this little voice in my head says, "Buy more, load up, we can make a killing today."

Instead of trading 1 contract, traders will trade 3, 5, or 10 contracts because they get greedy and want to make more. Making a few hundred dollars a day is boring to them, and so they try to make a few thousand instead and end up overextending themselves. This also makes it much easier for a trader to blow out. Every time I blew out it was due to overtrading. Yes, I was wrong in my market opinion, but if I had been trading with smaller size, it would not have hurt me. The problem when you have too big of a position is that any loss is too big; nobody wants to take a big a loss, and so as a trader hopes it comes back, the loss gets larger and larger. When you start trading many positions you would think that the risk spreads out, but there are days when everything goes sour at once, and they can be devastating. With so much going on, it becomes easy to let good trades turn bad and let losers get out of hand. When you are focusing on just one or two markets, bad trades can be cut short more quickly, before they do serious damage. I find that traders who keep going for modest wins tend to do much better than do those who go for big wins every time. You get only a few big moves a year, and so most of the time you have to think smaller. What thinking smaller also does is let you get out of losers faster.

Fighting Greed

Fighting greed, like discipline, is not easy but has to be done. A trader will be more successful by not going for the big trades every time and just being consistent. The steps necessary to combat greed include having a money management plan and following it, setting predetermined realistic goals, having targets, and using stops. By having targets one avoids the temptation to let trades go on to infinity. The only problem with this is that when you get out and then watch a market keep going, you may start kicking yourself for having gotten out. I'm a strong believer in riding winners as long as possible, but I am also cautious to get out as soon as I see signs that a trade is over. When a market is breaking highs or lows, it's hard to figure out when it will stop. A market is never too high or too low and can always keep going. You have to be more cautious as it breaks into uncharted territory. When you are setting realistic goals, keep in mind the average true range of a market. Avoid trying to make $2 on a stock that has only a $2.15 range. A reasonable goal here would be to take 75 cents to $1.50 from the trade. If you are going for much more than that, you are getting greedy. Once a stock is nearing its average daily range, it's time to get out no matter what your profit is. Once again, don't worry about those few extra ticks; just go for the middle chunk of the trade.

Overconfidence

Overconfidence is a factor both before a trader starts trading and after he starts doing well. Before starting to trade everybody thinks he will do great and is not realistic about the possibilities. This overconfidence can lead a trader to be unprepared for what trading may have to offer. The bigger problem, though occurs when traders become overconfident and believe they are invincible. When a trader gets on a good winning streak and accumulates some profits and confidence, he starts to get cocky and his ego begins to swell. The trader feels he's conquered the markets and can't do anything wrong. He starts to believe he has the Midas touch and should start trading more aggressively. This is usually the beginning of his downfall. As a trader gets more confident, he begins making more mistakes and stops doing the things that got him on a good streak. He puts on marginal trades instead of waiting for good ones. He stops doing his homework and may ignore his trading plan. This is all due to greed and overconfidence as the trader tries to make too much too soon. The worst setbacks normally are suffered after good winning streaks, mostly as a result of the lack of discipline that comes with overconfidence. Remember, it takes only one or two losers at higher volume to wipe out a string of winners with less volume.

Most of my biggest hits came after a considerable run. In the summer of 1992 I was trading currencies, and they were moving in a perfect trend; as I made more and more, I kept adding to my position. I went from trading one Deutsche mark contract to having three Deutsche marks, three British pounds, five Swiss francs, and a few yen contracts. I had taken my account from $8000 to $20,000 in a few weeks, mostly by overtrading. I was riding high and started thinking about how I would spend some money. I was extremely overconfident and kept adding to my position as fast as I made money. Then, all of a sudden, everything came tumbling down. In 2 days my account dropped to $7000. I had to get out of a lot of my position because of margin requirements, but I was sure that I was right and held on to the rest. About a week later I had $2000 left in my account. Aside from overconfidence, my mistake was increasing my position tenfold while only doubling my account size. I had sworn I wouldn't do this, but as the going got good, I ignored my money management parameters as greed and overconfidence kicked in. If you are the kind of trader who gets a swelled ego after making a few good trades, keep yourself in check. Review your risk parameters carefully and make sure you are sticking to them. By keeping humble and having realistic goals, you will reduce the risk of getting hurt.

Fear

The two biggest emotions in trading are greed and fear, and neither is good. Like greed, fear can play a major role in a trader's demise. Though fear prevents a trader from taking large losses and keeps one on one's toes, it can cause traders to use stops that are too tight, take profits too soon, and not take trades because they are scared of losing. Some traders are too afraid to pull the trigger and just watch the market without ever getting involved. This is not good. If you are scared to trade, you shouldn't trade.

Scared to Pull the Trigger
Some traders are so scared of losing that they never pull the trigger. They repeatedly miss trade after trade, waiting for something

that never happens. Maybe trading isn't for these people. Some people may have a fear of succeeding and therefore keep bypassing every good trade that comes along. There is a difference between waiting for a good trade to come along and being scared to trade. Some traders sit and watch for the perfect setup, want to get in, but then just can't. Something doesn't feel right, and they hesitate. They are usually right in their original assessment of the market but are too afraid to act on it. I have someone like this in my trading room. He calls out great trading ideas, and most of the people in the room follow up on his ideas. Then they ask him how he did, and he says he never got involved, yet the rest of the room just made money from his call. He claims he is waiting for the market to get better to trade more aggressively, yet he keeps missing out on good opportunities because he can't pull the trigger. He took a bad beating in the market a few years ago and has been timid ever since. I don't think trading is right for someone with this mentality. If you are too afraid to trade, why do you want to trade? Find something more suitable to your risk level, such as accounting. Trading isn't for everyone; it takes someone with an iron set of balls to become a trader. Very few people have the mentality to start a career that they do not know they will make a living from. Most people don't like the uncertainty of not having a steady paycheck. Those who are too scared don't belong in the business.

Accepting Losses

Some traders have a problem with losing: They take it as a personal insult. But as I have said throughout this book, losses make up 50 percent of a good trader's trades. If one does not know how to take a loss or is scared to take a loss, one should not be trading. The best traders are the ones who know how to lose the best. First of all, you can't be scared to take a small loss. When scared to take a little loss, it can easily turn into a big loss later. If a trade goes against you, it's okay to get out of it. A trader doesn't have to be scared that someone will think less of him if he takes a losing trade. There is no need to sit in the trade hoping it moves back to positive so that you can exit with a profit. In the greater scheme of things a small loss or gain will not mean much in your total P&L.

What's even harder for some traders is taking a big loss. It's the large ones that can kill a trader. But small losses that are ignored can end up becoming large losses. When they get too big, some traders are afraid to get out of them because they can't fathom taking such a large hit. It is too scary to think about getting out of a position that will cost them that big a part of their equity. One of the hardest things to do is to admit when you are wrong and get out; there is no point watching a loss escalate to an even more devastating point. You can't be scared to get out. When you are wrong, you have to bite the bullet and get out, the sooner the better.

Stops That Are Too Tight
The other extreme is those who are so scared to lose any money that they use stops that are too tight. They follow the old advice about cutting losses too closely. Traders need to let trades breathe a little. If you have a fear of losing money, you will never be able to succeed because many trades that would have worked get stopped out before they have a chance to develop. Yes, a trader needs to be able to get out of trades as soon as possible when they are not working, but he also needs to find a balance that lets him stay in long enough for them to work.

Fear of Giving Back Profits
Then there are people who are scared of giving back any profits, and so they exit trades too soon when they have a profit. This is similar to getting out with a stop that is too tight. Trades need to develop, having a good trade on and exiting it too soon doesn't really help a trader. Big moves can make a difference, so let trades develop; it is okay to take small profits if that is your plan, but if you get into a trade looking for a major move, don't exit it too quickly. Keep in mind that the market will move in waves and decide beforehand whether the counterwaves are worth riding or getting out of. The thing you should never do is let a good winner become a loser. A small winner turning into a small loser is no big deal; don't let that bother you. It's watching a profit of $3 per share go negative that one has to be careful of; every time you do this, you are breaking a cardinal rule of trading.

Fear of Missing the Move
Probably the biggest fear of all is that of not being in a move when it happens; at least for me it is. I've always been motivated by the fear of missing something big; God forbid the market should move and I

miss it. I made bad trade after bad trade because I believed I had to be in it to catch the big one. I didn't want to miss any part of a move, either, and so I waited as long as possible to get out. That ended up being costly because I gave back more than I would have gained.

Some traders rush into every trade as if it were the greatest trading opportunity on earth. They get too anxious and chase markets, getting in at poor locations, or they jump the gun, anticipating a signal before one is given. This not only leads to poor timing but is a major cause of overtrading. One needs to realize that it's okay to miss a move or be a little late on it. If you miss one trade, there will be another one right behind it; if you miss the start of a move, that's okay as well because you can get in on the first pullback or look to capture a part of the trade and not the whole thing. Waiting for the market to settle after a move gives you a much higher probability trade than does chasing a trade after a breakout. Once you realize that it's okay to miss a move, you'll do much better. Of course there are times you'll look at the market in hindsight and wish you had been in the move. But unless the trade is part of a trading plan, you should try to refrain from making it and wait for the next opportunity to get in.

Anger

I've already touched on anger, so I'll restate my advice: Good traders do not get angry. They keep their cool and don't blame others or anything else for their losses. Anger is an unnecessary trait that keeps some people from trading at their peak. Sure, blowing off steam is good sometimes, but there are more productive ways of doing it than slamming your mouse or cursing nonstop at a specialist who can't even hear you. Try going to the gym to blow off steam; you'll get better results. In my opinion, getting angry is useless. You are just wasting energy on something that has already happened, and you can't do anything about it no matter how mad you get. If people could take the energy they use in getting mad and divert it toward a more productive outlet, they would improve not only as traders but in all aspects of their lives as well.

GETTING BACK ON TRACK

To wrap up, I'll talk about what a trader can do when he gets into a rut. Many times traders hit a losing streak and become distraught, as they have no idea what to do. Everything they do seems to be the wrong thing, and they keep on losing no matter how hard they try. The best thing to do at this point is to take a break from trading. Take a small vacation or do something other than trade for a few days, just as long as you forget about it for a while. You need to let the losses get out of your head somehow, and taking a break is a great way to do it. I've taken only a few voluntary breaks from trading over the years, but when I have, it has been helpful in getting me back on track. I took a monthlong break so that I could finish this book. My trading was beginning to suffer, as I didn't have the time to devote to it; now, when I get back to it, I hope to be on top of my game.

The other option that I use often is to go back to the basics. When I'm in a trading rut, I'll start trading with extremely light volume and start following the trading rules I may have ignored in the recent past until I get out of the rut. This is the time I'll review my systems, my risk parameters, and my trading plan, not so much to see if they are working but to see if I've been following them as I should. If they've worked in the past, I will stick to them, maybe making a few adjustments, but the problem usually lies within me, not in my trading plan.

BECOMING A BETTER TRADER

Becoming a better trader means being able to control your emotions, inner conflicts, and bad traits so that you can trade with a clearer mind. Trading with a clear mind is one of the most crucial things a trader can do. Trading takes a lot of energy and mental concentration, and when you start getting distracted by other things, your trading will suffer. It doesn't matter if you are stressed about your last loss or have personal problems that are weighing you down; you can't let it distract you. A good trader will not let it get to him, and if it does, he will stop trading until he can get back on track. If a trader can master the conflict within himself, he will get better. Instead of spending energy negatively, one should concentrate on thinking like a top trader. Keep asking yourself, "What would a top trader do in this situation?" Be honest with yourself and start doing the right things.

When you find yourself starting to get stubborn, hoping that a trade will work, or thinking with your position, try to imagine that you are looking at the market with a fresh point of view and give yourself an honest assessment of the market. If you do this and you are long but then realize you'd rather be short, *get out of your position*. All the hope in the world won't turn a market around.

Some of the things you need to watch out for are hope, greed, fear, stubbornness, laziness, and anger. All these things can cause a trader to lose in more ways than one and keep him from trading with a clear mind. Many would rather place the blame on other factors, thinking that someone is out to get them, but the truth is that you are responsible for your losses and nothing else is. Be an adult and take responsibility for your mistakes; then do something about the situation. By blaming others you will never get better.

If you are not trading up to par, take a break and try to figure out why. Is it because you are not following a good game plan properly, or is it because you don't have a good game plan? Whatever the case, there is no sense trading if you are in a big rut, so take a break or slow down dramatically until you can figure out why and are able to get your head clear.

Ways to Hurt Yourself Mentally

1. Having inner conflicts
2. Not trading with a clear mind
3. Thinking "they" are out to get you
4. Hoping the market will turn around
5. Hoping the market will go on forever
6. Being stubborn
7. Thinking with your position
8. Letting anger get to you
9. Trading for revenge
10. Being greedy
11. Trying to make too much
12. Being scared of missing the move
13. Being afraid of giving back profits
14. Being scared of losing too much
15. Being afraid of taking a loss
16. Not being able to pull the trigger

Ways to Clear Your Head

1. Take a break from trading.
2. Go for a walk.
3. Look at the market from a fresh prospective.
4. Take a loss and move on.
5. Make believe you are riding the market.
6. Get back to the basics.
7. Review your trading plan.
8. Make sure you have a money management plan.
9. Follow your plan.
10. Think like a pro.
11. Stop hoping and get real.
12. Set realistic goals.
13. Get professional help.
14. Try hypnotism.
15. Try yoga.
16. Go to the gym.

Helpful Questions to Ask Yourself

If I had no position on, what would I do?
Do I get angry too easily?
Do I let my emotions get the better of me?
Are personal problems affecting my trading?
How do I deal with a losing streak?

INDEX

Account size, 5–7, 13, 19, 20, 21, 26, 27, 29, 42, 43, 47, 54, 193, 292, 295, 300, 330
Amateurs (*See* Beginning traders)
Average Directional Index (ADX), 110–114, 119, 121, 140, 146, 148, 156, 157–159, 257, 258
  breakouts and, 156, 157–159
  exit strategies and, 111, 113–114, 156, 159
  high probability trading and, 111–114, 156, 157–159
  oscillators and, 140, 156, 157–159, 257
  timing trades and, 111, 112, 156–157
  trending markets and, 110–114, 157–159
Average True Range (ATR), 30–35, 37, 49, 189, 190, 191, 193–194, 196, 204, 234, 255–256, 376
Backtesting (*See also* Systems, evaluating), 3, 52–54 163, 172, 213, 233, 262, 264, 267–285, 294, 296
  common mistakes, 268–271, 273, 284
  evaluating test results, 268, 274, 275–281, 283, 284
  including slippage and commissions, 247, 271, 277, 281, 283, 284
  use of data, 267, 269, 270–275, 283, 284, 325
Beginning traders, 2–6, 9–10, 19–20, 24–25, 41–43, 48, 62, 202
Blowing out, 6, 7–9, 12–13, 20–21, 22, 25–26, 27, 37, 39, 41–42, 43–44, 241, 289, 291, 295, 301, 311, 329–330, 375
Breakout patterns, 149–150, 151–154, 174
Breakouts, 32, 35–35, 100–101, 116–117, 149–177, 196–197, 215–217, 252, 254, 272–273
  as continuation of trend, 149–150, 151, 152, 154, 161–162
  as reversals, 149–150, 151, 152, 154, 159–160, 163–164
  channels and, 35, 100, 150, 152, 158–159, 169, 196
  countertrends and, 161–162, 175
  due to news, 32, 151
  expected vs. unexpected, 172, 176
  false, 35–36, 100–101, 154–155, 161, 170–172, 175, 252–254

Breakouts (*Cont.*):
  filters, 156, 171–174, 176, 272–273
  high probability trading and, 100, 197, 156–163, 169, 170–172, 215–217
  measuring the move, 151–152, 169, 174, 176
  new highs/new lows and, 149–151, 156, 157–158, 160, 162–163, 172, 196–197, 216, 252–254
  range bound market and, 149, 151, 152–154, 157–159, 164, 215–217
  retesting the breakout area, 101, 156, 159, 161, 198
  trendlines and, 100–101, 107, 116–117, 149–150, 151–152, 158–160, 161, 163–164, 171, 176, 196
  volume and, 156, 160–161, 164, 168, 172, 174, 175, 176, 177
  why markets break, 32, 150–152, 153–154, 160–161, 164
Breakout strategies, 156–163, 172–174
Brokerage, 24–25, 48–51, 54, 337, 339
  commissions and, 24–25, 48–51, 54, 337
  discount, 24–25, 48–50, 54, 339
  online, 25, 48–51, 54
Brokers, 49, 51–55, 338–339, 357–358
Buffers, 115, 156, 171–174, 176, 191, 196, 202, 203, 208, 209, 210, 252–254, 259, 272–273
Capital, 3, 5–8, 9, 11–13, 19, 21–24, 27, 37, 38, 39, 41, 43, 47, 55, 81, 184, 279, 290–292, 294–295, 296, 299–304, 307–308, 311, 314–318
  at-risk, 300, 301–302, 304, 307–308, 311, 314–316, 317–318
  preserving, 3, 11–13, 21–22, 24, 27, 37, 43, 185, 208, 290, 291, 296, 300, 340
  starting, 5–6, 39, 43, 279, 294
  trading, 5–7, 9, 23, 38, 41, 47, 81, 294, 299–300
  working, 6–7, 13, 19, 20–22, 39
Capitalization, 55, 184, 342, 299–303, 317
Channels, 34–36, 88, 99–100, 103, 119, 152, 153, 158–159, 169, 196, 217
  breakout of, 100, 153, 158–159, 169
  high probability trading and, 88, 103, 158–159, 217

Channels (*Cont.*):
  price objectives and, 169, 217
  timing trades and, 34–36, 88, 100, 103
Chasing the market, 4, 8, 15–16, 36, 37, 44,
    62, 65, 65, 70, 83, 101–103, 111, 113, 116,
    118, 119, 120, 121, 126, 137–139,
    155–156, 158–159, 168, 175, 217, 227,
    346–347, 355, 360
Choppy markets, 107, 109, 111–114, 128,
    129, 140, 257–258, 346–347, 354–356
  identifying, 107, 111–114
  oscillators and, 128, 129
  trading strategies, 112–114, 128, 129,
    257–258
Commissions (*See* Costs)
Contrarian thinking, 96
Countertrends, 96–98, 101–102, 103–104,
    115, 117–118, 175
Countermoves, 97–98, 101–104, 119
  high probability trading and, 101–104
Curve fitting, 17, 18, 178–179, 184–185, 188,
    249, 269, 270, 271–274, 283, 284, 357
Cutting losses, 17, 18, 89, 164, 178, 179,
    184–185, 188, 249, 357
Data, 262, 267, 269, 270–275, 283, 284, 325
  correct use of, 270, 273–275, 283, 325
  having sufficient data, 262, 273–274, 284,
    325
Day traders, 33, 35, 56, 81, 94, 102, 373
Day trading, 32, 33, 48–51, 55, 81, 102, 108,
    164, 194, 195, 300, 367, 373
  made easier, 48–51, 55, 373
Discipline, 14, 163–164, 185, 199, 214, 226,
    239–241, 286–287, 292, 297, 314–315,
    318, 322–337, 354, 358–359
  controlling emotions and, 331–332, 364
  exiting losers and, 163, 164, 185, 199, 314,
    318, 330, 334, 335
  following the rules and, 323, 326–327,
    329, 334, 335
  importance of, 239
  making a trading plan and, 240, 327–328,
    333, 334, 335
  overtrading and, 324–325, 327, 354,
    358–359
  risk limits and, 292, 297, 314, 318, 329–330
  sticking with a winning trade and, 164,
    331
  stops and, 330
  waiting for a high probability situation
    and, 226, 287, 333, 334
  working hard and, 328, 329
  working on discipline, 14, 332

Disciplined trader, the, 199, 331, 334
Divergences, 131, 134, 136, 141–142, 146,
    147, 215, 217, 256
Diversification, 141–143, 341
Drawdowns, 163, 268, 276, 279–280, 295
Easy Language, 247, 251–260, 262, 263
Ego, 21, 118, 351–353, 358, 376–377
Emotions, 4, 12, 16, 32, 232–233, 331–332,
    358, 364, 368
  controlling, 4, 232–233, 331–332, 364
Entering the market, 35, 82, 92–95, 101–102,
    103, 108, 116, 118, 122–123, 137–139,
    144–146, 156, 162, 165, 170–171, 176
  limit order and, 116, 156
  scaling into a trade, 92–93, 95, 108, 118,
    176
  stops and, 116, 162, 165, 171, 174, 175, 252
  timing trades and, 35, 82–83, 94, 95,
    101–102, 103, 122–123, 137–139,
    144–146, 156
Entry signals, 108, 109, 166, 167, 172–174,
    178, 233
Exiting a trade, 4, 10, 16, 18, 30–36, 83, 88,
    94, 108, 110, 118–119, 122–123, 129–131,
    137–139, 159, 164, 169–170, 172–174,
    175, 178–187, 217, 258–264, 313,
    330–331, 342, 351, 370
  getting out when its time, 30–31, 33–36,
    110, 118–119, 169, 181, 182–183, 184,
    186, 330
  importance of, 164, 178–179, 258
  in stages, 108, 114, 125, 159, 175, 181–182,
    183, 209, 210, 315
  overstaying welcome, 10, 16, 18, 30–31,
    32–36, 42–43, 117–119, 169–170, 175,
    182–183
  predetermined exit strategies, 16,
    173–174, 181, 185, 207, 209, 210, 212,
    232–233, 238, 246, 313, 330–331
  prematurely, 4, 16, 94, 126, 179, 331, 379
  stops and, 163, 164, 169, 171, 172–173,
    178, 184, 187, 198, 258–259, 330
  taking losers, 182, 184, 313, 330, 370, 376
  taking winners, 113–114, 119, 125, 179,
    182, 200, 330
  timing exits, 35, 36, 83, 88, 94, 100,
    122–123, 137–139
  when entry reasons have changed, 72,
    181, 183–184, 186–187, 204, 209, 237,
    313, 370
Exit signals, 90–92, 108, 109, 113–114,
    129–131, 143, 163, 172–174, 233–234,
    257, 258–260, 263–264

Exit strategies, 138–139, 178, 181–185, 194–203, 233, 258–260, 263–264, 292

Fear, 110, 171, 179, 188, 345–347, 352–353, 355, 377–381

Fibonacci levels, 115–117, 119, 121, 169, 196, 220

Filters (*See* Buffers)

Floor traders (*See* Locals)

Focused, being, 222, 227, 232–233, 239, 341–342, 358–359

Fundamental analysis (*See also* News), 60–67, 69, 78, 244

Gambling, 40, 70, 154, 286–288, 295, 333, 345, 359
    compare to trading, 154, 212, 219, 222, 286–288, 295, 345, 359

Game plan, 185, 190, 230–231, 238–241, 327–329, 333, 344

Gaps, 153–154

Goals, 30–39, 42–43

Greed, 9, 12, 41–42, 118, 169, 174, 183, 209, 330, 352–353, 371–376

High probability trading, 16, 30–37, 62, 64–67, 70–72, 96–97, 100, 106, 110, 129–139, 141–148, 193, 211–227, 305, 342, 346, 356, 376, 380
    breakouts and, 100, 156–163, 169, 170–172, 174, 197
    definition of, 212
    oscillators and, 129–131, 132–134, 135–139, 141–146, 147–148
    patience and, 156, 169, 170, 172, 213, 215, 217, 219–220, 223, 226, 227, 380
    predetermined exit strategies and, 16, 233, 173–174, 212, 213, 214, 220
    reason for every trade and, 212, 213, 217–218
    reversals and, 166–168, 171
    risk/reward ratio and, 156, 158–159, 162, 174, 197–198, 212–213, 215–217, 220–221, 223, 226, 305, 346
    trending markets and, 96–97, 100, 106, 110, 112–114, 129–131, 137–139, 157–159, 174, 197–198, 213–217, 227, 346
    using different time frames and, 80, 90–92, 100, 144–147, 156, 157–159, 167, 170, 214–217, 222–223 226

Hold times, 17, 81, 86–90, 94, 120, 121, 144–146, 213, 235, 250

Inner conflict of trading, 363–383

Internet, the, 48–52, 55–56, 57, 247, 356–358
    as source of information, 48, 50–52, 57, 247

Journal, keeping a, 14–18, 22, 331

Learning years, the, 2–5, 11–13, 19–22, 25, 38–39, 42–43, 290

Learning from mistakes, 3–5, 7–10, 11–13, 25, 29, 36, 42–44, 237–238, 240, 268, 331, 367

Leveling the playing field, 8, 47–57

Locals, 20, 47–49, 54, 202, 340–341, 354–356

Losing traders, 8, 21, 41–42, 62, 72, 102, 119, 139, 189, 287, 354–356, 368

Losses:
    controlling, 163, 185, 194, 235, 291, 342, 350, 374
    keeping losses reasonable, 4, 11–12, 18, 29, 37, 104, 184–185, 208, 311, 350, 352, 370
    knowing loss potential, 208, 233, 301, 307, 313
    learning to take, 3, 10, 11, 18, 163, 164, 179, 184–185, 208, 291, 330, 352, 368
    letting losses get too big, 179, 180, 182–183, 194, 202, 203, 209
    money management and, 291, 308, 311–313
    versus winners, 179, 184–185, 291, 351

Low probability trading, 8, 10, 15–16, 31, 65, 70, 75, 84–87, 102, 103, 104, 114, 143–144, 155–156, 161, 168, 172, 183, 189, 223–225, 226, 312–313, 314, 342, 349, 355, 357

Measuring a move, 115–117, 169, 220

Marrying a position, 4, 71–73, 74, 75, 118

Money management, 12, 37, 185, 212, 234, 249, 280, 286, 288–298, 291, 317, 329
    capital considerations and, 192–193, 234, 292, 294–295, 298, 317, 329
    controlling losses, 12, 37, 185, 290, 293, 296, 297, 329–330

Money management plan, 3, 41, 230–231, 234, 240, 286–298, 299–319, 329–330, 347–349, 358, 377
    goal of, 290–291
    importance of, 249, 288–289, 297, 308
    making of, 315–317, 319
    position sizing and, 234, 240, 290, 292, 293, 296, 297, 299, 300, 302, 303–311, 316
    risk levels and, 234, 240, 290, 291–293, 296, 297, 301, 307, 309, 313, 315, 319
    setting capital requirements, 41–43, 234, 294–295, 299–300, 301–303, 314, 315, 317
    setting loss levels, 240, 293, 299, 311, 329–330

Moving Average Convergence/Divergence (MACD), 123, 134–137, 216–217
    calculating of, 137
    divergence and, 136
    high probability trading and, 135–137, 216–217
    interpreting, 134–135
    overbought/oversold territory, 135–137
Moving averages, 90–92, 105–111, 118–121, 135–137, 253, 254–256, 259–260, 272–273
    crossover of, 90–92, 110, 135–137, 255, 259
    exiting trades and, 90–92, 259–260
    high probability trading and, 90–92, 106, 110
    multiple moving averages, 108–110
    periods, 106–110, 118, 119, 120, 254, 272–273
    stops and, 191, 196, 198, 200, 259
    systems, 90–92, 108–109, 254–256
    timing trades and, 90–92
    trending markets and 106–111, 119
Multiple positions, 92–93, 308–310
Multiple time frames, 80–95, 100–103, 144–147, 157–159, 167–168, 170, 197–198, 222–223, 226, 227, 244, 252, 265, 284, 359
    getting the big picture, 82–88, 93–95, 102–103, 120, 121, 157, 167, 168, 172, 194, 214–217
    monitoring time frame, 86–89, 90, 94, 95, 121, 206, 252
    stop placement and, 88–89, 94, 191, 194, 196–198, 206, 210
    timing time frame, 80, 83, 88–89, 92, 94, 95, 170, 197–198
News, 3, 32, 52, 55, 60–75, 78, 150, 154, 187, 235
    bad news is good news, 60, 65–69, 70–71, 73
    buy the rumor and sell the fact, 65–66, 69, 74, 75, 154
    discounting of, 62, 65–69, 74, 78
    fading the news, 62–65, 70–71, 74, 75
    high probability trading of, 62, 64–67, 70
    market's reaction to, 62, 63–72, 74, 75, 150, 154, 187
    trading scheduled news releases, 66–67, 70–71
    unexpected vs. expected, 66, 68–69, 70–71, 74, 154
    you're always the last to know, 55, 62–65

Online brokerage (See Brokerage)
Online trading, 25, 48–51, 54, 56, 57, 356–358, 373
    bonuses of, 44, 50
    problems with, 50, 51, 356
Optimization, 107, 126, 270, 271–274, 284
    of indicators, 107, 126, 272–273
    out sample and, 270, 271, 274, 284
    TradeStation and, 272
Oscillators (See also specific topics), 34–35, 79, 112, 122–148, 256–258
    basics, 122–126
    combining indicators, 112, 122–123, 140, 143, 147, 257
    defined, 124–125
    divergence and, 131, 134, 136, 141–142, 146, 147, 215, 217, 256
    high probability trading and, 129–131, 132–134, 135–139, 141–146, 147–148
    in strong market, 122–123, 125, 129–131, 133, 137–139, 143–144, 214–215, 257
    interpreting, 123–124
    misusing, 122, 126–128, 139–140
    overbought/oversold, 124, 125, 126–133, 135–143, 146–148, 158–160, 164, 217, 225, 256–257
    range bound markets and, 131–134, 157–159, 215–217
    timing trades and, 34–35, 122–123, 137–139, 144–147
Oscillator based strategies, 129–131, 132–134, 135–139, 141–146, 256–257
Out sample data, 270, 271, 273–274, 284
Overextented market, 83, 88, 94, 95, 100, 102, 110, 119, 120, 121, 158–160, 164, 255, 256–257
Overbought/oversold, 34, 83, 88, 124, 125, 126–131, 132–133, 135–143, 146–148, 158–160, 164, 217, 225, 255
Overtrading, 4, 9, 11–14, 27–29, 35, 41–42, 51, 89–90, 94, 107, 109, 111, 173, 175, 189, 225, 233, 241, 303, 308, 324–325, 336–362
    broker's pressure and, 358–359
    chasing and, 355, 350
    choppy markets and, 35, 109, 354–356
    costs and, 35, 111, 337–340, 357, 359, 360
    ego trading and, 351–353
    fear of missing the move, 345–347, 355, 360, 379–380
    online trading and, 51, 356, 360
    P&L trading and, 347, 352, 360

Overtrading (*Cont.*):
  panic and, 348, 350
  problems of, 35
  reasons for, 342–360
  revenge trading and, 347–349, 352, 357
  scalping and, 341, 351, 357
  stops that are too close and, 111, 189, 353
  trading for the excitement and, 343–345, 356, 358, 360
Panic, 41–42, 62, 116, 348–350, 364
Paper trading, 4–5, 19, 22, 24
Patience, 86, 113, 120, 137–139, 156, 161, 168, 169, 170, 172, 174, 213, 215, 217, 219–220, 223, 226, 227, 252, 323–324, 333, 337, 342, 345, 356
Position size, 81, 166, 192–193, 208, 221–222, 290, 292, 293, 296, 297, 299, 300, 302, 303–311, 319, 324–325, 329, 333, 349, 377
  as determined by risk involved, 166, 193, 208, 210, 221, 293, 305–307, 316, 317
  based on probability of trade, 81, 221, 293, 305–307, 316
  determining maximum number of contracts, 193, 208, 210, 299, 304–310, 316
  increasing, 88, 108, 299, 309–311, 319
Positive expectancy, 232, 245, 249, 262, 275, 287, 295–296, 297
Preserving Precious Capital (PPC), 3, 11–13, 21–22, 24, 27, 37, 43, 185, 208, 290, 291, 296, 300, 340
Professional gamblers, 221, 286–288, 323
Professional traders vs. individuals, 14, 19–20, 24–25, 27–28, 43, 46–49, 51–52, 62, 203, 212, 244–245, 292, 303, 340–341, 357, 367
Profit and loss (P&L) trading, 339–340, 347
Profit goals, 16–17, 24–25, 28–29, 33–36, 42–43, 207–208, 314
Profit potential, 33, 216
Profit taking, 33, 35, 42–43, 113–114, 119, 125, 142, 179
Pyramiding, 292, 309–311
Range bound market, 79, 100, 107, 112–114, 132–134, 149, 151, 152–155, 157–159, 164, 215–217, 256
Real time information, 47–49, 51–53
Realistic goals, 6, 20, 21, 24–43, 292, 314, 370
Rectangles, 152, 169, 170–171
  breakout of, 152, 169, 170–171
  high probability trading and, 170–171
  measuring a move and, 152, 169

Reinforcing bad behavior, 9–10, 18, 312–313
Relative Strength Indicator (RSI), 123, 131–134, 141–142, 214–215
  calculating of, 131–134
  divergence and, 134
  high probability trading and, 132–134, 141–142, 214–215
  interpreting, 131–132
  overbought/oversold territory, 132–133
  range bound markets and, 132–134
  technical analysis patterns in, 133–134
  trending markets and, 133
Retracements, 35–36, 37, 83–84, 94, 100–102, 110, 111, 113–116, 119, 121, 125, 137–139, 145, 156, 157–159, 161–162, 172, 175, 176, 213, 227
  measuring, 115–116, 121
  using to enter trades, 83–84, 100, 102, 110, 111, 116, 119, 125, 137–139, 161–162, 172, 198
Reversal patterns: 164–165, 174, 175
  double tops and bottoms, 165
  key reversal days, 164–165
  M and W formations, 165
  reversal days, 164–165
  rounded tops and bottoms (saucer patterns), 165
  triple tops and bottoms, 165
Reversals, 30, 31, 33–35, 106, 113, 115–118, 123, 125, 129, 149–150, 151–152, 159–160, 163–169, 256
  measuring potential move, 115–118, 151–152, 169
Reversal strategies, 163–169
  high probability trading and, 166–168, 171
  risks of, 163
  stops and, 163, 164, 166–167, 171
Reversal systems, 164–165
Reviewing trades, 18, 22, 240, 313, 331
Reviewing trading performance, 18, 22, 230, 237, 240, 327, 331, 335
Risk, 4, 17, 27, 41, 51, 70, 100, 102, 116, 121, 156, 158–159, 162, 166, 169, 192–194, 230–233, 236, 286, 289–298, 299–319, 325, 329–330
  adjusting, 198, 200–201, 204, 239, 293, 297, 300, 313, 317, 318
  controlling, 51, 70, 83, 100, 110, 116, 121, 158–159, 162, 191, 193–194, 204, 232, 290, 291, 293, 296, 297, 309
  managing, 17, 43, 51, 185, 201, 289, 325

Risk (*Cont.*):
measuring, 17, 40, 100, 110, 116, 121, 158–159, 162, 166, 169, 191, 193–194, 204, 217, 220, 232, 279, 290, 292–293, 300–301, 307, 308, 316, 317
preference of trader and, 27, 42, 231, 292
setting risk parameters, 192–193, 234, 290, 292–293, 299, 301–317, 329–330
Risk aversion, 27, 42, 182, 189, 190, 206, 221, 280, 292
Risk vs. reward, 10, 28–29, 37, 104, 121, 130, 156, 158–159, 162, 169, 174, 175, 185, 190, 197, 208, 210, 212–213, 215–217, 220–221, 223, 226, 286, 313–314, 316, 319, 346
Scaling into trades, 92–93, 95, 108, 176, 193, 315
Scaling out of trades, 125, 181–183, 196–197, 200–201, 209, 210, 315, 341, 350
Scalping, 81, 87, 89, 107, 235, 347, 351, 357
Signals, 108, 129–131, 132–134, 135–137, 178, 204
entry, 166, 108, 178, 204
exit, 163, 108, 204
Slippage (*See also* Costs), 86–87, 90, 156, 187, 188, 271, 277, 281, 283, 284, 296, 339–340, 346
Small traders, 6, 21, 29, 41–42, 47–49, 50–52, 54–55, 295, 299, 303, 309–310
Specialist, 187–188, 339–340, 346
Spreads, 49, 156, 281, 339, 354–355
between bid and ask, 49, 156, 281, 339, 354–355
narrow, 49
slippage and, 156
Standard deviations, 193–194, 196, 204–207, 208, 210, 253, 255, 259–260, 263
accessing risk and, 205–206
formula for, 204–205
stops and, 189, 196, 204–207, 216, 259, 263
TradeStation code for, 206–207, 259, 263
Stochastics, 35, 84–86, 105, 123, 125, 126–131, 141–146, 156, 157–160, 164, 168, 215–217, 256–257, 263–264
calculating of, 127,
crossovers, 129–131, 256
divergence and, 131, 215, 217
extreme readings, 129–131, 164, 168, 259, 263–264
high probability trading and, 84–86, 129–131, 141–146, 156, 157–160, 215–217

Stochastics (*Cont.*):
interpreting, 126–128, 215, 217
Overbought/oversold territory, 84–86, 124, 125, 126–131, 164, 168
range bound markets and, 157–159, 215–217
timing trades and, 35, 138–139, 156
trending markets and, 125, 127–131, 159–160
Stop and reverse, 204, 258, 343
Stops, 10, 14, 17, 79, 88, 102, 111, 115, 129–131, 159, 161, 164, 166–167, 171–175, 178–179, 181, 183, 184–210, 212, 217, 220, 292, 234, 258–259, 263–265, 346
buffers and, 102, 115, 121, 173–174, 191, 196, 202, 203, 208–210, 259
controlling risk and, 185, 188, 200
disaster stops, 203
discipline and, 184, 185, 199, 225, 330
entering the market and, 162, 165, 171, 174, 175
entry signals and, 252
fixed dollar stops, 190, 195–196, 209
goal of, 185–186, 188
high probability trading and, 102
indicator based stops, 129–131, 183, 199
knowing before entering a trade, 17, 185, 187
mental stops, 202, 208–210, 212, 220
money management stops, 191–193
multiple time frames and, 88–89, 94, 197–198, 206, 210
percentage move stops, 193–194
placing proper stops, 79, 88, 94, 161, 166–167, 185, 188–192, 204, 209–210, 305–307, 316, 353
position size and, 166, 186–188, 191, 203, 208, 209, 305–307, 316
problems with, 186–188, 191, 203, 208, 209
standard deviation stops, 204–207, 210, 259, 263
stops that are too far, 159, 176, 185, 190, 208–210
stops that are too tight, 111, 185, 188–189, 191, 203, 208–210, 377
technical stops, 161, 163, 185, 188–192, 193, 195–201, 209, 210
time stops, 14, 17, 187, 194–195, 210, 235, 239
trailing stops, 181, 198, 199–201, 210, 217
volatility and, 204–207

Stress, 364, 381
Stubbornness, 4, 67, 72–73, 74, 75, 119,
  370–371, 381
Successful trader, the, 8, 11, 20, 43, 70, 80,
  94, 119, 138–139, 172, 174, 185, 208, 265,
  288, 331, 366–367
Support and resistance, 30–31, 80, 83, 86,
  89, 94, 100, 103, 107, 110, 114, 119, 121,
  133, 149, 151–154, 155, 156, 157–159,
  161, 162, 166, 172, 191, 196, 256, 347,
  358
Systems, 54, 111, 172–174, 204, 215–217,
  233–234, 243–266, 347, 358
  adapting to different market conditions,
    111, 233, 257, 260
  backtesting and, 54, 172, 233, 267–285, 325
  breakout systems, 172–174, 215–217,
    252–254, 263–264
  combining indicators, 257, 263–264
  oscillator based systems, 256–257,
    263–264
  suiting to a trader's style, 172, 243, 247,
    248, 250–252, 264
  trading costs and, 247, 271, 339
  trend following systems, 90–92, 108–109,
    254–256
Systems, evaluating, 54, 163, 233, 268, 274,
  275–281, 283, 284
  average trade, 268, 276
  comparing different systems, 268, 281,
    283, 284
  consecutive losers, 163, 268, 278–279
  distribution of returns, 268, 276, 280, 283
  drawdown, 163, 268, 276, 279–280
  largest loser, 268, 278
  largest winner, 268, 278
  percent profitability, 277
  profit factor, 268, 280
  profitability, 268, 276–277
  total number of trades, 268, 276, 277
System trading, 17, 108, 213, 243–266, 370
  definition of, 243
  systematic vs. discretionary, 243–245,
    260–261
  using different time frames, 90–92, 95,
    244, 252, 265, 284
  using discretion, 140, 244–245, 258,
    260–261, 264
System writing, 3, 52–53, 247, 251–260, 262,
  264, 267–285, 290
  backtesting and, 52–53, 233, 262, 264,
    267–285, 325

System writing (*Cont.*):
  common mistakes of, 249, 262, 265
    268–271, 273
  curve fitting and, 249, 269, 270, 271–274,
    283, 284
  entry signals, 109, 233, 252–260, 263, 265,
    172–174
  exit signals, 109, 172–174, 206–207,
    233–234, 246, 257, 258–260, 263–264,
    265
  keeping it simple, 105, 249
  optimizing and, 269, 270, 271–274
  rules and conditions, 252–260, 263–264
  stops and, 204, 206–207, 258–259, 263,
    264, 265
System writing software, 52–54, 57, 244,
  247, 247–248, 262, 267, 272
Technical analysis, 3, 60, 72, 74, 75, 78–79,
  192
  combing with fundamental analysis, 60,
    67, 72, 74, 75
  vs. fundamental analysis, 60, 78
Technology, 14, 32, 47–49, 50–54, 56
Time of day, 14–15, 222–223, 239, 307,
  354–356, 367
Time stops, 14, 17, 187, 194–195, 210, 235, 239
Timing, 35–36, 80, 83, 88–89, 94, 95, 101–102,
  114–115, 119, 122–123, 137–139, 144–147,
  170, 208, 216, 220, 226
TradeStation, 52–54, 244, 247–248, 251–260,
  262, 272, 275, 280
  as charting software, 52–54
  backtesting capabilities, 52–54
  EasyLanguage and, 247, 251–260, 263–264
  programming of, 272
Trading (*See also* High probability trading)
  capital, 5–7, 9, 23, 38, 41, 47, 81, 294,
    299–300
  compared to gambling, 286–288, 333, 345
  for the excitement, 4, 40, 116, 333
  in choppy markets, 109, 128, 129, 140
  in trending markets, 96–119, 129–131,
    143–144, 173, 175, 213–217, 227
  strategies, 129–131, 132–134, 135–139,
    141–146, 147–148
  style, 41, 78, 81, 87, 88, 105, 107, 123, 170,
    172, 230–231, 235, 247, 250–260, 281
Trading as a business, 39–41, 44, 328, 345, 359
Trading costs, 35, 41, 48, 49, 54–55, 56, 57,
  107, 111, 236, 237, 247, 270, 271, 277,
  281, 283, 284, 296, 314, 337–340, 346,
  349, 357, 359

Trading costs (*Cont.*):
  commissions and fees, 35, 49–50, 54–55, 56, 57, 81, 90, 107, 237, 242, 271, 277, 281, 296, 337–340, 349, 357
  slippage, 86–87, 90, 156, 237, 247, 271, 277, 281, 283, 284, 296, 339–340, 346
Trading methodology (*See* Trading strategy)
Trading plan, 4, 41, 44, 212–214, 230–242, 243, 327–329, 333, 334, 335, 348, 358–359
  fitting to trader's style, 230–231
  importance of, 230–231, 232–233, 358–359
  including the unexpected, 232
  ingredients in, 41, 232, 233–238
  money management plan and, 230–231, 232–233, 234
  trading methodology and, 230–231, 233–234, 243
  vs. game plan, 230–231, 238
Trading rules, 326–327, 329–334, 335
  breaking of, 327
  following of, 326–327, 329–334, 335
  writing down, 326–327
Trading strategies, 129–131, 132–134, 135–139, 141–146, 172, 214–217, 230–234, 252–260
Trading tools, 8, 47–49, 51–54, 82
Trading with a clear mind, 16–17, 18, 37–38, 350, 363–383
Trailing stops, 181, 198, 199–201, 210, 217
Trend following indicators, 105–114
  ADX, 79, 110–114, 119, 121, 156, 157–159
  channels, 99–100, 158–159, 169
  moving averages, 105–110, 111–118, 119–121
  trendlines, 98–99, 110–112, 119
Trend following strategies, 79, 108–109, 112, 129–131, 133, 200, 214–217, 254–256
Trend is your friend, 96, 97, 100, 102, 104, 119
Trending markets, 96–121, 129–131, 133, 137–139, 143–148, 158–162, 173–175, 213–217, 227, 346
  high probability trading and, 96–97, 100, 106, 110, 112–114, 129–131, 137–139, 157–159, 174, 197–198, 213–217, 227, 346
  identifying, 96–100, 105, 110–113, 144
  measuring a move, 115–117
  retracements and, 100–102, 110, 111, 113, 114–117, 119, 121, 143, 145, 157, 161–162, 200, 203, 213, 227

Trendlines, 34, 52, 86, 98–102, 105, 107, 110–112, 119–121, 143–144, 158–164, 191, 215, 217, 259
  breaking of, 86, 98, 100–101, 110, 116–117, 119, 149–150, 151–152, 159–162, 163–164, 166–167, 171, 173, 176
  drawing of, 52, 98, 152
  high probability trading and, 86, 100–102, 110, 143–144, 158–162, 166–167, 171, 174, 215, 217, 346
  stops and, 111, 115, 116, 162, 171, 191, 196, 198, 200, 203, 346
  testing of, 86, 98–101, 110, 112, 114, 158–159, 198, 215, 217, 346
  timing trades and, 34, 116, 119, 215, 217
  using to measure risk, 99–102, 110, 116, 121, 162, 217
Trends, 38, 72–74, 79–84, 95–121, 157–162, 175, 176
  breaking of, 98, 107, 121
  countertrends and, 92, 96–98, 101–102, 103–104, 115, 117–118, 153, 161–162, 175, 176
  defined, 96–97
  end of the trend, 38, 72–73, 88, 100, 107, 110–111, 113–114, 125, 143, 150, 151–152, 160, 164–168, 371–373
  fighting the trend, 72–73, 74, 86, 96, 99, 103–104, 108, 114–115, 120, 128, 163, 223–225, 258–259
  high probability trading and, 83–87, 90–92, 100, 106, 110, 116, 129–131, 133, 137–139, 143–146, 147–148, 213–217, 227
  identifying, 80, 95, 96–97, 98–100, 105, 110–114
  intraday, 100, 158–159
  long term, 82, 97–98, 100, 103–104, 120, 157–159, 161–162
  major, 83, 94, 97–98, 100, 101, 106, 107, 145, 157–159, 161–162, 176
  minor, 97–98
  oscillators and, 122–123, 125, 127–131, 133, 137–139, 143–146, 157–160
  reversals and, 101, 104, 118, 149–150
  short term, 82, 97–98, 120
Trend trading, 79, 96–121, 122–123, 125, 128, 163, 176, 254–258
Triangle patterns, 152, 153, 170–171
  breakout of, 152, 153, 170–171
  flags, 153
  high probability trading and, 170–171

Triangle patterns (*Cont.*):
  measuring a move and, 151
  pennants, 153
  triangles, 152, 153, 170–171
Tuition of trading, the, 2, 5–8, 9, 12–13,
    19–20, 20, 22, 38
Undercapitalization, 4, 7, 9, 13, 20–21, 22,
    29, 39, 43, 163, 262, 299–300, 303
Volatility, 105, 172, 190, 192, 204–207, 253,
    313
Volume, 79, 105, 118, 156, 160–161, 164, 168,
    172, 174, 176, 177, 253–254, 354–356,
    367
  importance of, 79, 160–161
Waves, 33–34, 44, 96–97, 114–118, 121, 128,
    129, 131, 137, 158–159, 164, 169, 176,
    379
  measuring, 33–35, 115–117, 169

Winning trader, the
  (*See* Successful trader, the)
Working on weaknesses, 14, 17, 18, 36
Win/loss ratio, 262, 277–278, 296, 314
Winners, 4, 33, 89, 94, 95, 164, 169–170, 174,
    178–181, 184–185, 199–201, 217, 314,
    331, 334, 342, 351, 379
  holding, 89, 94, 95, 164, 174, 217
  letting winners ride, 89, 17, 114, 178–181,
    184, 331, 334
  overstaying welcome, 10, 16, 30–34,
    42–43, 88, 118–120, 122, 169–170, 175,
    182–183, 314, 330, 372–375, 380
  protecting, 181, 199–200
  taking small winners, 33, 179
  taking prematurely, 4, 89, 94, 126, 209,
    331, 342, 351, 379
  versus losses, 179, 184–185, 291, 351

ABOUT THE AUTHOR

Marcel Link has been trading professionally since 1991. He is the founder of linkfutures.com and is a TradeStation consultant. Visit www.linkfutures.com for more information on trading system developing, seminars, or market information.

Mr. Link can be reached for questions or comments at marcel@linkfutures.com.